Near-Death Experiences

As Evidence for the Existence
Of God and Heaven

A Brief Introduction in Plain Language

J. Steve Miller

Dedication

*To bold researchers
who dare to explore new frontiers,
possessing an insatiable scientific curiosity
that drives them to push the boundaries of science
by questioning the prevailing paradigms*

Advance Praise

"…a masterful job…Although there have been large numbers of books and articles written in medical journals from prestigious institutions, for many the question remains . . . what might be next? Near-Death Experiences explores the science surrounding the question. This book is the first one I have read on this subject that doesn't try to convince the reader of what he or she must believe. Filled with authoritative references from a wide range of respected members of the medical and science research community, inquiring minds will have much to ponder. Although this book should be used as a college textbook it is written in such a way that even the casual reader will find it fascinating." - Ralph Lee Thomas, author and newspaper columnist

"For some time we've needed a well-researched, compelling introduction to this exciting field that focuses on the evidence. Miller delivers!" - Jeffrey Long, MD, author of the New York Times bestselling *Evidence of the Afterlife: The Science of Near-Death Experiences*

"…fascinating and very compelling…this book fills in a lot of the gaps in my own belief and inspires me to give more thought to my life, my purpose on earth and what to expect in the hereafter. I would recommend this book to anyone and everyone who has an interest in this sort of experience. - Dr. Robert E. McGinnis, author and educator

"Can we survive death? Is there a God or a heaven? Miller provides the discerning reader with ample reason to think that the answer to these all-important questions is 'yes'." - Dr. Peter Schaefer, Senior Research Psychologist, Department of Defense

Cover design by Carole Maugé-Lewis. The gate to the other side was inspired by a personal interview with an 11-year-old NDEr from Ukraine.

Publisher's Cataloging-in-Publication data

Miller, J. Steve, 1957-
Near-Death Experiences as Evidence for the Existence of God and Heaven: A Brief Introduction in Plain Language / by J. Steve Miller

p. cm.

Includes bibliographical references and index

LCCN 2012953057

ISBN-13: 978-0-9883048-5-7

1. Near-death experiences. 2. Future life. I. title

BF1045.N4M 2012
133.901'3 – dc22

For corrections, book orders, bulk discounts, author appearances, inquiries or interviews, contact publisher by email or regular mail at:

Wisdom Creek Press, LLC
5814 Sailboat Pointe NW
Acworth, Georgia 30101
www.wisdomcreekpress.com
jstevemiller@gmail.com

The table *Sources of Anecdotes Involving Apparently Nonphysical Veridical Perception*, in Appendix 8, is republished with permission of ABC-CLIO, LLC, and author, Janice Miner Holden, from *The Handbook of Near-Death Experiences*, edited by Janice Miner Holden, et al, 2009, permission conveyed through Copyright Clearance Center, Inc.

Foreword

by Jeffrey Long, MD

Although I've never had a near-death experience (NDE), they've significantly changed my life. Nothing in my medical training prepared me for my first exposure to an NDE, spontaneously shared by a good friend's wife over dinner. I was absolutely astonished! I recall thinking that these experiences could change my views about life, death, and God. I devised a plan to collect and study NDEs. This study changed my worldview and reorganized my priorities.

As a radiation oncologist (a medical specialty that treats cancer with radiation), I work daily with patients who know their earthly lives may soon end. My exposure to NDEs enables me to help them face their cancer with courage and confidence. For over 35 years, medical doctors and academics have published significant NDE research, scrutinizing the experience in both professional journals and books. I've personally studied over 3,000 NDEs that I collected at www.nderf.org. While further clinical studies are always encouraged, it seems to me that a major challenge today, for thinkers everywhere, is to sift through the mountains of data that's been collected and bring to light the implications.

Important questions today for both NDE researchers and people everywhere include: Do NDEs provide compelling evidence for the existence of God and the afterlife? What is the evidence? Is the evidence strong or weak? If some of these experiences are indeed encounters with the afterlife, how should this impact my life priorities?

While other books, such as my own, take up this challenge, I believe that Miller's book offers a valuable contribution to NDE literature. First, he offers a fresh voice by employing creative analogies and fresh angles to clarify salient points. Second, he avoids the insider academic jargon that may obscure more than enlighten. Third, he remarkably manages to consolidate recent research into a document that packs more of a punch for its brevity. By focusing on the evidential value of NDEs, Miller can explore the possible implications without burdening the reader with extraneous detail.

If this is your first exposure to the near-death experience, fasten your seatbelts! You've embarked upon an exhilarating ride that just might transport you to places you never imagined. - Jeffrey Long, MD, author of *Evidence of the Afterlife: The Science of Near-Death Experiences*

CONTENTS

Preface

What if you slept?
And what if, in your sleep, you dreamed?
And what if, in your dream, you went to heaven
And there plucked a strange and beautiful flower?
And what if, when you awoke, you had that flower in your hand?
Ah, what then?

- Samuel Taylor Coleridge

What then? Indeed.

This is essentially the promise that many near-death researchers claim to fulfill – a glimpse into eternity, verified with corroborating evidence. This book intends to discover if they've fulfilled their promise.

What's a Near-Death Experience with Corroborating Evidence?

A patient undergoes a risky brain surgery that requires lowering her body temperature to about 50 degrees Fahrenheit and draining all the blood from her head. By three primary tests – a silent EEG, an unresponsive brain stem, and no blood flow through the brain – she's clinically dead. Yet, after the surgery the patient reports that she was very much alive during the surgery, viewing the procedure from outside her body. She described in accurate detail a conversation that transpired during the surgery and the specialized instruments used by the surgeons. Even if her vivid, conscious, out-of-body experience took place prior to the draining of her blood, her eyes were taped shut, she was deeply anesthetized, and 100-decible clicks assaulted her ears over 10 times per second to monitor her brain stem activity. Except for the small surgical area on her head, her entire body was covered.(1)

But who reported this event? An anonymous person who submitted it to a collection of stories on a website? The patient? The surgeons? Could she have guessed the conversation, or seen the instruments prior to the surgery? If it really happened, what hypothesis best accounts for the event?

Later, I'll talk about this remarkable episode and many fascinating studies, which introduce evidence for the afterlife beyond mere anecdotes.

Why This Book?

Much has been written recently about near-death experiences, from people sharing their personal experiences, to doctors reporting their clinical studies in great detail. I felt that a brief, readable introduction to this fascinating field was in order, concentrating on the evidential value of the NDE. Here you'll find:

- Reports from those who claim to have visited heaven.
- How these reports are corroborated and what type of evidence they offer.
- Introductions to the primary researchers in the field.
- An emphasis upon the findings of clinical studies and scholarly, peer-reviewed literature.
- The results of my own NDE interviews, suggesting ways that anyone can get closer to the evidence by conducting their own interviews within their circles of trust.
- An examination of naturalistic hypotheses.
- Discussions of the impact of personal expectations of death and cultural differences.
- A comparison of the content of NDEs with traditional Christian teachings.
- Recommendations for further study.

My Personal God Quest

Some readers might be interested in my background and motivations for writing, to personalize your reading experience and to help you understand my approach to research and style.

Forty years ago, at the age of 16, I became obsessed with the importance of seeking God. I reasoned that since earthly life was but a brief moment compared with eternity, my first priority should be to determine if God existed and, if He did, to figure out what He wanted out of my life. The words of Jesus Christ at times inspired, at other times haunted me:

For what does it profit a man to gain the whole world, and forfeit his soul?

But I had a problem.

You see, I'm a skeptic. Always have been. Not in the narrow sense of someone who puts down religion, but in the general sense of one who always questions everything. My dictionary defines skeptic as "one who by nature doubts or questions what he hears, reads, etc." That's me. My picture should be in the dictionary beside that definition.

When someone tells me something outrageous that a political leader (regardless of political party) said or did, I ask,

- "Who reported it?"
- "In what publication?"
- "In what context?"
- "Could the reporter be biased by her political affiliation?"
- "Was it reported objectively, or with sensational spin?"

As you can imagine, my skeptical bent led me to continually question religious claims, repeatedly subjecting them to rigorous scrutiny. Although I committed my life to God as a sophomore in high school, I soon plunged into periods of doubt as I wrestled with questions concerning God and the truth claims of Christianity.

My Academic Quest

As a result, my academic career reads like a God search. I attended five institutes of higher learning – diverse colleges, universities, and graduate schools – primarily searching for spiritual truth. My course of study included many classes relevant to the study of God and religion - philosophy of religion, world religions, Bible, Greek, Hebrew, philosophy of science, deductive logic, history of philosophy, ethics, sociology, psychology, psychology of religion, theology, etc.

Whether my professors were agnostics, Christians or Buddhists, I questioned their beliefs and did independent research to separate fact from fantasy, personal taste from uncomfortable truths. In my spare time, I often read books arguing for and against religious beliefs, collecting quite a library along the way. This broader view of religious and philosophical studies helps me when I study a particular slice of evidence such as near-death experiences.

Naturally, I sought God not only academically, but also through prayer and trying to maintain a teachable, open heart.

How My Background Informs This Study

With this background, you'll better understand several aspects of my writing.

First, I read widely and document my sources obsessively, so that if you wish to do further research or check my interpretation of certain studies, you can find the original sources. Beyond documentation, my endnotes and appendixes, which make up a large portion of the book, contain expanded material that I feared might bog down less enthusiastic readers. So if an argument seems weak or incomplete, check the endnote to see if I pursue it further there. If I've overlooked important sources or misunderstood the ones I refer to, please alert me at jstevemiller@gmail.com.

Second, I seldom use words that speak with finality such as "prove" or "proven." This is partly because of my skeptical nature but also because of my desire for precision. Since "prove" indicates "100 percent certitude" in fields such as Math and Deductive Logic, I'll tend to use the more humble phrase, "sufficient evidence," which is more appropriate for subjects of a scientific or legal nature.

Example: For centuries, scientists thought that all swans were white, since they'd observed tens of thousands of white swans. On the basis of such strong evidence, many would have been tempted to declare with finality, "We've proven that all swans are white." But then someone visited Australia and saw a black swan. That one observation ended the "all swans are white" theory.

So please don't think I'm playing down the strength of an argument when I speak of "sufficient evidence." Our biggest decisions of life are made by weighing evidence rather than holding out for logical certitude. We convict murderers on the basis of sufficient evidence. Yet, one more piece of evidence could overturn our verdict. We choose our cars and houses and spouses and vocations on the basis of sufficient evidence. In my opinion, absolute, logical certitude is typically found, not in the real world, but in abstract worlds like math.

Third, I try to write as simply as possible. Sloppy argumentation often dresses up in technical vocabulary and literary profundity. Thus, while some NDE literature speaks of myocardial infarctions, I'll simply call them heart attacks.

Fourth, I want to approach this subject humbly, recognizing that I have so much more to learn. While I'm far from exhaustive in my research, I've tried to read the best resources representing various positions. Again, if you feel I've overlooked significant data, feel free to correspond.

Introduction
The Search for Shangri-La

Imagine that you've heard tales of an extraordinary lost civilization somewhere in the mountains of Tibet called Shangri-La. Your curiosity gets the best of you and you're itching to find out if it's real. But how could you gather evidence without launching your own costly expedition?

Your best bet would be to talk to scads of people who claim to have independently visited Shangri-La and compare their stories, while evaluating their intelligence, honesty, and sanity. And it wouldn't hurt if they produced corroborating evidence, like a souvenir that could have come only from Shangri-La.

Essentially, this is what many people claim about the afterlife. Since we're told that the most popular way to meet God face-to-face is to die, it's simply not practical to schedule a trip over Spring break. That leaves us with the option of interviewing levelheaded people who claim to have visited the other side.

But how could they ever prove that their experiences were more than vivid dreams? And what could they possibly bring back as corroborating evidence? Those questions kept me from taking near-death experiences seriously.

Until recently.

Chapter 1
A Four Year Old's Near-Death Experience

A relative read the popular book *Heaven is for Real* and wanted my opinion.[1] I wasn't interested, but read it as a favor. In the book, a father tells about his four year old child, Colton, who described his visit to heaven during a medical crisis.

Several things about the story intrigued me. First, the father was a respected, highly visible member of a rural community (a pastor, wrestling coach, and volunteer fireman who operates a garage door company). If he were making things up, people in the community would likely start poking around and asking questions. Eventually, his reputation would be ruined and neighbors would likely report the farce to the press and complain on reviews,

> "The father's weird; his wife's prone to hysteria, and Colton's delusional. My son goes to school with Colton. Last week the kid swore to his teacher that he owned a pet unicorn."

Had the family been low-profile residents of a large city like Los Angeles, it would be easier to fabricate a story, sell it as real, and get away with it.

Second, there was corroborating evidence. Colton shared insider knowledge that he probably couldn't have known from earthly sources. He claimed to meet his miscarried sister, whom he'd never been told about. He told details of a great-grandfather that he supposedly couldn't have known. He saw his father praying in a separate hospital room, which he claimed to have viewed from outside his body.

It was an interesting book, but to me wasn't very helpful as evidence for the afterlife. I needed more. To satisfy my skeptical mind, I needed:

- Reports from the doctors and nurses.
- Reports from people in the community about the family's integrity.
- Evidence that Colton couldn't have overheard talk about the supposed "corroborating evidence" at a time when family members didn't realize he was listening.
- Evidence that his experience wasn't an elaborate dream, the details of which were supplied by his religious upbringing.

Also, I thought it rather weird that Colton said nothing about the experience when he first woke up. After all, don't young kids typically report spectacular neighborhood events when they first burst in the front door?

The story seemed evidentially weak, but intriguing nevertheless. In the blurbs section, an author who studied near-death experiences commented that Colton's experience jived with the many NDEs he'd studied. If others were reporting similar experiences with better corroborating evidence, this line of inquiry just might provide evidence for the afterlife.

Chapter 2
Studies on Near-Death Experiences

So I looked for serious books on the subject – books by objective authors (not pastors or new age gurus who might be out to evangelize) who had the academic credentials to do solid research on multiple cases. I began by reading Dr. Raymond Moody's seminal 1975 study, *Life After Life*.[1] Moody studied medicine (Psychiatry), enabling him to evaluate scientific evidence for possible medical explanations of the phenomenon. Additionally, he held a Ph.D. in philosophy, which often helps researchers to more accurately evaluate hypotheses and to be more precise with their conclusions.

I started with Moody because he was one of the earliest researchers to seriously study and popularize NDEs. Thus, it was highly unlikely that his subjects had read about NDEs or seen them discussed on TV. This could likely rule out the psychological explanation that people have these experiences because they've heard about them and thus expect to have them.

Moody came from a nonreligious home, where his father, a surgeon, scoffed at religion as "institutionalized superstition." It's no wonder that Moody grew up thinking that death was the end of life.[2] But while studying philosophy at the University of Virginia, one of his professors mentioned Dr. George Ritchie, a respected psychiatrist in their medical school who had been declared dead and later regained consciousness, reporting a fantastic experience on the other side. Fascinated, Moody went to hear him speak to a group of students.

Dr. Ritchie reported dying of double pneumonia. (He passed around a copy of his death certificate for the students to examine.) While he was clinically dead, he left his body, making observations that he would later confirm by visiting the location.[3] He could walk through people and doors. The laws of space and time didn't seem to apply – he could think of a place and be there immediately.

He returned to the hospital room to find his body and a voice said "Stand up! You are in the presence of the Son of God!" A magnificent being appeared and showed him every detail of his life, from his birth to when he was pronounced dead, all within what seemed like a brief period of seconds. The being asked, "What have you done with your life?" He replied, "Well, I'm an Eagle Scout." The being responded, "Yes, that only glorified you."

Then the being sat next to him, allowing him a glimpse of the heavenly realm. Finally, Dr. Ritchie returned to his body.[4]

Moody became friends with Dr. Ritchie, eventually dedicating *Life After Life* to him and catching his passion for Psychiatry. Ritchie said that when he spoke of his experience, people would often come up afterward and report similar experiences. Moody became fascinated. Could it be that this experience was fairly common, but people were reluctant to report it out of fear that people would think they were crazy?[5]

When Moody began teaching philosophy at East Carolina University, a frustrated student approached him, suggesting that they should focus on important stuff, like life after death. The student described being in a car accident, where the doctors had pronounced him dead. Before he was resuscitated, he found himself fully conscious, outside his body. He travelled through a tunnel and met a person who let him see his entire life. It changed his life. To the student, that sounded more interesting and relevant than most philosophy.

So Moody began asking his students if they had experienced anything like this. Some would share their stories. When he entered medical school, he continued interviewing doctors, professors, and others who reported such experiences, recording them on a cassette player. These shared experiences, numbering about 150, became the substance of his book.[6] In it, Moody wrote snippets of his interviews, organizing them under 15 common characteristics, such as leaving the body, hanging out with deceased relatives, passing through a tunnel, meeting a being of light, and reviewing their lives.

The accounts were astoundingly similar, yet personalized and detailed, often containing corroborating evidence. Finally, he evaluated and ruled out possible naturalistic explanations, such as oxygen deprivation, psychological explanations, or drugs administered during medical crises.[7]

Life After Life was enlightening, but left me wanting more. Decades had passed since Moody's study and I wanted someone to pull together the subsequent research. Also, Moody's subjects lived in America. Although his subjects claimed to have diverse beliefs, could the pervasive Christian worldview at least partially explain the similar experiences? Had further research of more culturally diverse subjects confirmed or refined or overturned Moody's conclusions?

Enter Dr. Pim van Lommel, a world-renowned Dutch cardiologist, who wrote *Consciousness Beyond Life: The Science of the Near-Death Experience*. Working in a hospital cardiac wing where clinically dead patients were often resuscitated, he began to rethink his naturalistic assumptions. According to van Lommel,

> "I grew up in an academic environment where I was taught that there is a reductionist and materialist explanation for everything. And up until that point, I had always accepted this as indisputably true."[8]

What changed his mind?

Many of his resuscitated patients reported trips to the other side, in vivid detail, that occurred when they were clinically dead. While their lifeless bodies lay on hospital beds, with their hearts flat lined and their brains should have been incapable of producing consciousness, they reported experiencing something that was vivid, astounding and life changing. After resuscitation they spoke of being very much alive somewhere else. As one patient said,

"Dead turned out to be not dead."[9] Corroborating evidence (things his patients saw and learned while clinically dead) indicated that the experiences were real.

Van Lommel's scientific inquisitiveness lit a fire under him and he embarked on a 20-year study of near-death experiences. He interviewed patients soon after their experiences and re-interviewed them years later to see if their memories and life changes remained true to their original reports. His research was so well done that it was published in the prestigious medical journal, *The Lancet*.[10]

One reason van Lommel's research intrigued me was his location. He interviewed patients in Holland, where most people don't believe in life after death.[11] If people who didn't believe in heaven had vivid heavenly experiences, you could hardly attribute the experience to their rather boring expectations of after death nothingness. But remarkably, the experiences reported in Holland paralleled Moody's findings in America.

Van Lommel went beyond his own research and Moody's to compare many independent studies on NDEs after Moody. Finally, for those who can't get enough of a good thing, he took several chapters to theorize about the mind/brain phenomenon and possible explanations based upon quantum physics. It's well documented and shows a thorough command of the relevant literature.

Van Lommel's conclusion?

Near-death experiences don't fit into a naturalistic worldview. There *is* life after death. His patients experienced, not vivid dreams, but very real journeys to the other side, the most significant part of which was an encounter with a personal being of light.[12]

After reading van Lommel, I slowly worked my way through the other primary researchers in the field. Each study left me with additional questions that were typically addressed in other studies. (If you're interested in going deeper, see Appendix 9 – Guide to Further Research. With hundreds of NDE books available, you'll likely want to concentrate on serious studies of multiple cases.)

Beyond books, NDEs are no stranger to scholarly, peer-reviewed literature. Over 900 articles on NDEs were published in scholarly literature prior to 2005, gracing the pages of such varied journals as *Psychiatry*, *The Lancet*, *Critical Care Quarterly*, *The Journal for Near-Death Studies*, *American Journal of Psychiatry*, *British Journal of Psychology*, *Resuscitation* and *Neurology*.[13] In the 30 year period after Moody published *Life after Life*, 55 researchers or teams published at least 65 studies of over 3500 NDEs.[14]

It's important to note that most of these researchers don't come across as heralding their pet theological or philosophical positions. Most that I read began their research doubting that NDEs involved anything spiritual but became convinced by the weight of the evidence. They write like objective, scientifically-minded people who became fascinated with a perplexing phenomenon that had the potential to teach us not only about the afterlife, but the very purpose of our existence.

I also conducted my own informal interviews with friends, relatives, and those they trust. Even after reading scads of scholarly studies, the skeptic in me kept saying, "If these experiences are as prevalent as they say, why haven't I heard of even one NDE within my own trusted circles?" So I began to ask friends and relatives and was astounded to hear people I had every reason to trust, with no apparent ulterior motives, telling me about their experiences on the other side. In Appendix #3, I suggest how anyone can study NDEs by interviewing their circles of trust.

Chapter 3
A Collage of Near-Death Experiences

NDEs aren't rare. Studies found four percent of the populations of Germany and the USA reporting that they had experienced one. That's over one out of 25 people, or over nine million Americans.[1] But if you don't hear about them from friends and family, don't be surprised. People tend to keep these experiences to themselves, fearing that people will think they're crazy.[2] This helps explain Colton not immediately sharing his NDE with his family. (Alternatively, perhaps Colton delayed because he was still ill immediately following his NDE. Additionally, since a four-year-old might not realize the unusual nature of his experience, it's understandable that he might not bring it up until a relevant conversation prompted him.)

Researchers share the fascinating details of thousands of NDEs. I'd recommend reading many experiences in their entirety to get the full impact. I also recommend interviewing some NDErs face to face. There's something very compelling about hearing a person you trust share his or her experience.

At this point, I should lay out in a bit more detail what I mean by a near-death experience. Rather than tell full stories, which are readily available in many other works, I'll put together the exact statements of many NDE reports, drawn from NDE researchers and my own interviews, to form an abbreviated, coherent story. Note that most people experience some of these elements, but not all. For example, some might leave their bodies, view the medical team trying to revive them, talk to a few deceased relatives, then return to their bodies, without experiencing a tunnel trip to a being of light. Note also that most of them struggled to put their experiences into words. It seems that no earthly experiences provide close enough analogies.

So here are some first-hand reports from the other side.[3]

> I'd never heard of a near-death experience, and I'd never had any interest in paranormal phenomena or anything of that nature.

> I suddenly became aware of hovering over the foot of the operating table and watching the activity down below around the body of a human being. Soon it dawned on me that this was my own body. I also heard the doctor say that he thought I was dead. (Later he confirmed saying this, and he was astonished to learn that I'd heard it. I also told them that they should mind their language during surgery.)

> I was there. I was on the other side. It's simply too much for human words. Our words, which are so limited, can't describe it.

> It was real – as real as me sitting across from you and talking to you now. Nothing could ever convince me otherwise.

> I didn't have to think, I knew everything. I passed through everything. At once I realized: there's no time or space here.

> I saw the most dazzling colors, which was all the more surprising because I'm color-blind.

> All the pain vanished and I began to experience the most wonderful feelings. I couldn't feel a thing in the world except peace, comfort, ease. I felt that all my troubles were gone. I've never felt so relaxed. I've never felt this happy before. It was so emotional that I can't possibly describe it.

> I was overcome with a feeling of peace that I'd never known on earth…. An overwhelming feeling of love came over me, not the earthly feeling I was quite familiar with, but something I can't describe.

What I saw was too beautiful for words. I was looking at a magnificent landscape full of flowers and plants that I couldn't actually name. It all looked hundreds of miles away. And yet I could see everything in detail. It was both far away and close. It was completely three-dimensional and about a thousand times more beautiful than my favorite holiday destination in spring.

I was always surrounded by loving spiritual beings of light.

I had the impression that this was a different dimension altogether. And if anything was missing it was our earthly conception of time!

Everything was suffused with an indescribable love.

The knowledge and messages going through me were so clear and pure.

I talked with Mr. Van der G., the father of my parents' best friend. When I told my parents after waking up, they said to me that Mr. Van der G. had died and been buried during my coma. I couldn't have known that he was dead.

I saw both my dead grandmother and a man who looked at me lovingly but whom I didn't know. Over ten years later my mother confided on her deathbed that I'd been born from an extramarital affair…. My mother showed me a photograph. [It was] the unfamiliar man I'd seen more than ten years earlier.

I went through this dark, black vacuum at super speed. You could compare it to a tunnel, I guess. The darkness was so deep and impenetrable that I could see absolutely nothing; but this was the most wonderful, worry-free experience you can imagine.

I saw a bright light, and on my way there I heard beautiful music and I saw colors I'd never seen before. The light…was of a kind that I'd never seen before and that differs from any other kind such as sunlight. It was white and extremely bright, and yet you could easily look at it. It's the pinnacle of everything there is. Of energy, of love especially, of warmth, of beauty. I was immersed in a feeling of total love.

...from the moment the light spoke to me, I felt really good – secure and loved. The love which came from it is just unimaginable, indescribable. It was a fun person to be with! And it had a sense of humor, too – definitely! I *never* wanted to leave the presence of this being.

My whole life so far appeared to be placed before me in a kind of panoramic, three-dimensional review, and each event seemed to be accompanied by an awareness of good and evil or by an insight into its cause and effect. Throughout, I not only saw everything from my own point of view, but also I knew the thoughts of everybody who'd been involved in these events, as if their thoughts were lodged inside me. It meant that I saw not only what I had done or thought but even how this had affected others, as if I was seeing with all-knowing eyes. And throughout, the review stressed the importance of love. I can't say how long this life review and insight into life lasted; it may have been quite long because it covered every single subject, but at the same time it felt like a split second because I saw everything at once. It seemed as if time and distance didn't exist.

It was clear to me why I'd had cancer. Why I had come into this world in the first place. What role each of my family members played in my life, where we all were within the grand scheme of things, and in general what life is all about. The clarity and insight I had in that state are simply indescribable.

I had wanted to stay there...and yet I came back. Back to the pain and to the doctor's deafening screams and slaps. I'm furious, incredibly furious! From that moment it was a real struggle to live my life inside my body, with all the limitations I experienced at the time.... But later I realized that this experience was in fact a blessing, for now I know that the mind and body are separate and that there's life after death. My worldview underwent a radical transformation.

As people examine their NDEs from every angle, they reject suggestions that their experiences were visions or vivid dreams or hallucinations. They believe they actually experienced the other side. That's why they hesitate to share it with their doctors or even friends and family. It would be easy to say, "Hey, I had the most fascinating, realistic dream during surgery! Want to hear it?"

But they can't say that.

They believe it was *real, more* than a dream, putting them in the uncomfortable situation of having a life-changing experience that they fear nobody will believe. Not knowing how common these experiences are, they keep it to themselves or share it privately with a trusted soul-mate.[4]

When van Lommel re-interviewed patients at two years and eight years after their NDEs, they reported life changes that differ significantly from his control group of people who had heart attacks with no NDE. For example, they have no more fear of death, see the vast importance of love, gravitate toward helping professions, and show greater empathy and compassion. They're also less materialistic and often a bit uncomfortable living in a material world where so few understand enhanced spiritual values.[5]

Chapter 4
Naturalistic Explanations

People suggest many possible explanations for NDEs, and we should welcome their thoughts and analyses. Science progresses as researchers dream up every conceivable explanation (or hypothesis) and evaluate which explanation makes the most sense in light of the available data.

Of course, one explanation is that NDEs are real experiences with life after death. I'll consider the arguments for that position later. But first, let's consider some objections to this position. Moody[1], Sabom[2], van Lommel[3], Sartori[4], and the other primary NDE researchers seriously consider naturalistic explanations, but ultimately find them inadequate.

Since this book is introductory rather than exhaustive, I'll briefly discuss some of the *primary* naturalistic suggestions, while noting other sources (see extended discussions in my endnotes and appendices) for those who wish to explore further. For a more in depth discussion, I'd recommend *Science and the Near-Death Experience*, by Chris Carter. The entire book (almost 300 pages) is dedicated to evaluating naturalistic hypotheses in a thoughtful, well-researched, well-reasoned manner.

I'll divide these explanations into five general categories: materialistic, theoretical, methodological, psychological, and physiological. If it becomes boring and tedious (some early readers had a low tolerance for detail) feel free to hit the main points, get the gist, and move to the next section rather than give up and miss the positive evidence altogether.

Explanations from a Materialist Worldview

Objection #1: The mind doesn't exist separate from the brain. Thus, the mind can't survive the death of the brain. NDEs must therefore be produced solely by the brain.[5]

According to this objection, what we call "mind" is typically viewed as a higher function of the brain, the mind being totally dependent upon the brain to function properly. Proof: As we age, our minds tend to work less efficiently. An elder may say, "My mind's not what it used to be." But if the mind were separate from the deteriorating brain, why wouldn't our minds be just as sharp at 100 years as they were at 25? And what about mind-altering diseases like Alzheimer's, which impact such mind functions as personality and decision making? If the mind were *independent* of the brain, why would it appear to be totally *dependent* upon the brain for its function?

In light of these observations, many argue that what we call "mind" must be purely a function of the brain. As such, the mind couldn't exist apart from the brain and near-death experiences must be explained solely in terms of brain function.

> **Reply #1: Decrease in mental functions could just as easily be explained by the brain functioning as a receiver.** Imagine that you've never seen a radio. You turn it on and hear music. But where does the music come from? Is the music contained completely in the radio, much like the music in a CD player is contained in a CD within the player?

> Several observations would support the "everything's in the machine" hypothesis of the radio. First, if you drop the radio, the speakers may thereafter produce an annoying buzz. Second, if you twist the tuner too hard, it becomes difficult to change to different music. It would be easy to conclude from these observations that the music is totally dependent upon the radio and contained solely in the radio. "Since damage to the

radio results in damage to the sound," you might reason, "the music must be solely contained in and produced by the radio. If the radio were destroyed, the music would be destroyed with it."

But in the case of the radio, your observations would have led you astray. The radio doesn't *produce* the music; it's merely a *receiver* that allows you to *hear* the music. Granted, the condition of the radio impacts the quality of the music that you hear through it. But the invisible waves that carry the music to the radio are still carrying the music whether your radio is in a condition to receive it or not. If the radio dies, the waves that carry the music don't die.

Similarly, van Lommel, Carter, and many others surmise that the brain functions as a receiver for the mind. The mind connects with the brain while we are in our body, but isn't dependent upon the brain for its existence. Damage to the brain impacts our ability to *access* our minds, much as damage to a radio impacts our ability to access radio signals. This hypothesis would seem to be just as compatible with our observations (mental decline during Alzheimer's, aging, etc.) as the hypothesis that the mind is merely a function of the brain.[6]

Reply #2: NDEs provide strong evidence that the mind is very much alive and well while the brain is dead. Corroborating evidence details the mind's activity outside of the body (e.g., hovering over the body observing the details of surgery, returning with details learned from deceased relatives, etc.). We'll expand upon this point in Chapter 5.

Objection #2: I'm a very scientific person; I believe what I can see and touch. A brain I can see. But disembodied minds remind me of ghosts and goblins and fairies, which lie beyond the reach of science, since I can neither see nor touch them.[7]

Reply: Science now recognizes that the tiny building blocks of matter aren't solids that we can see and touch. They're more like invisible waves – more mind-like than particle-like. Granted, the entire concept of disembodied minds appears rather foolish to some scientifically minded people – but perhaps only to those who slept through the scientific breakthroughs of the 1900s, or failed to fully break from the older scientific paradigms. Early physicists tended to view solid atoms as the smallest bits of solid matter. They felt matter could be fully explained with mathematical descriptions of how those atoms moved around, bounced off one another, and combined to form new things.

But now we know that atoms aren't solid. In fact, they're 99.999 percent empty space.[8] And even the parts of the atom wandering around in all that empty space aren't really "solid." We've never "seen" electrons with our eyes, even after our most powerful visual microscopes magnify them. We see their *effects*, so that we know they exist, but we have difficulty figuring out precisely what they *are*. We know they're *there*, but we can't know their exact location when we're not observing them. In fact, scientists have strong evidence that electrons don't actually *have* a location until they're observed. In their essence, they seem to be more like invisible waves than observable particles, yet their activities affect what we call physical things.

If this seems strange to you, welcome to the wacky world of quantum physics! As bizarre as they are, these qualities of subatomic particles have been confirmed over and over by numerous experiments and are taught today as standard scientific knowledge.

My point? Scientists work with invisible, nonmaterial stuff (like electrons) every day. This nonmaterial stuff interacts with and provides the building blocks for what we call physical stuff. Just because you can't see it or feel it or fully comprehend it doesn't mean it doesn't exist. We know electrons exist, not because we can see them, but because we observe their effects.

So it seems to me rather unscientific to dismiss the possibility of independently functioning minds outright, just because we can't see them. If we find sufficient evidence of their effects, we'd do well to believe in them even though we don't fully understand them.

As astronomer V.A. Firsoff wrote,

> "To assert there is *only matter* and no mind is the most illogical of propositions, quite apart from the findings of modern physics, which show that there is no matter in the traditional meaning of the term."[9]

Groundbreaking physicist Werner Heisenberg put it this way,

> "Atoms are not *things*. The electrons which form an atom's shells are no longer things in the sense of classical physics, things which could be unambiguously described by concepts like location, velocity, energy, size. When we get down to the atomic level, the objective world in space and time no longer exists, and the mathematical symbols of theoretical physics refer merely to possibilities, not to facts."[10]

The revered Cambridge and Princeton mathematician and physicist James Jeans wrote:

> "The stream of knowledge is heading toward a non-mechanical reality; the universe begins to look more like a great thought than like a machine. Mind no longer appears to be an accidental intruder into the realm of matter; we ought rather hail it as the governor of the realm of matter."[11]

Theoretical Objections

Objection #3: If everyone has a soul, shouldn't everyone who suffers cardiac arrest have an NDE?[12]

Reply #1: Perhaps all have the experience, but not everyone remembers it. For example, people with frightening near-death experiences sometimes mention the experience immediately after being resuscitated, but then immediately forget the experience, perhaps due to repressing it.[13]

Reply #2: Perhaps the trigger for NDEs isn't a cardiac arrest, but another physical activity that sometimes, but not always, accompanies cardiac arrests. As research shows, many who have NDEs don't experience a cardiac arrest. This suggests that a physical trigger, if one exists, may be other than the cardiac arrest itself.

Reply #3: Perhaps the trigger isn't physical at all. Remember, it's not their final death, just a *brush with* death. If there is indeed a God, He knows the NDE is a parenthesis in earthly life, not a final entrance into the afterlife. Perhaps He allows only those who need a glimpse of the other side (e.g., for personal assurance or a challenge to life change) to get a glimpse of eternity.[14]

Objection #4: Sometimes what people see on the other side doesn't jive with reality, like encountering people who aren't yet dead, mythological creatures, or making predictions that don't come true.[15]

Reply #1: These may be pretty rare, because these specifics haven't been described in any of the reports from large-scale studies I've read. For example, concerning predictions (true or false), Moody notes that they occur in "an extremely small percentage of NDEs".[16] I did my own study of 100 complete NDEs on Dr. Long's NDERF site. None of these contained any of these elements, indicating to me that they must be extremely rare.

Reply #2: We'd expect a few quirky stories to be mixed in with the mainstream.

We expect anomalies to surface from time to time, since during an extended trauma people might have multiple experiences that get confused. Surely, in such a state, we'd expect the occasional report that confuses hallucinations and vivid dreams with their NDEs as they come in and out of consciousness, sometimes numerous times. Surely, with massive trauma to the brain, someone may experience not only a legitimate NDE, but later hallucinate Barney and Big Bird, later confusing the two memories. If such experiences were *typical* of an

NDE, we'd have reason to question the totality of the experience. But they're apparently not typical.

Reply #3: A subset of people who report these experiences may be a bit loony, or prone to lie or to use their experience for their own purposes. A corrupt radio preacher may report that, in his NDE, God told him that the world would end by the end in 2015. But if the world doesn't end, that hardly calls into question all reports from the other side.

Objection #5: But you can't be 100 percent sure that there's no natural explanation. Science may one day completely explain NDEs as a result of purely naturalistic, material causes.[17]

Reply: True. And if that day comes, I should reweigh the evidence and humbly conclude, "Wow! Was I wrong about NDEs!" But unfortunately, I can't transport evidence from the future and weigh it to make up my mind today.

Future scientific evidence may disprove the big bang theory and quantum mechanics and relativity and many of the other scientific theories that currently make the most sense in the light of our current observations and experiments. Yet, scientists believe these theories because *today's* evidence clearly weighs in their favor. Future evidence is an unknown that can't be accounted for.

Methodological Objections

Objection #6: Many NDEs are reported years after the experience. Thus, as with all stories we tell and retell, we tend to embellish them until they only faintly resemble the original experience.[18]

Reply #1: Some researchers interviewed their subjects as soon as possible after the event, often while they were still in the hospital.[19]

Reply #2: When these same subjects were re-interviewed many years later, researchers found the stories to remain remarkably

unchanged. They were not embellished.[20] These follow-up studies give us reason to trust the accuracy of stories reported to other researchers years after the experiences. As a person I interviewed said of her NDE, which occurred 38 years ago, "I remember it like it was yesterday."

Objection #7 - Researchers probably bias their observations because they're typically people who already believe in the afterlife.[21]

Reply: Of the researchers I read, almost all of them indicated that they dismissed the validity of NDEs before they studied them. Van Lommel specifically stated that prior to his research, he was a thoroughgoing materialist and reductionist, meaning that he didn't believe in God, heaven, or valid religious experience. As he stated, "That death is the end used to be my own belief."[22] Prior to Dr. Rawlings' (*Beyond Death's Door*) encounter with an NDE, he "had always thought of death as painless extinction." To him, religion was "all hocus-pocus."[23] Dr. Sabom studied NDEs to refute them, to prove that they could be explained naturalistically. It was not until he'd researched for a year that he began to believe people truly left their bodies.[24] Later, Sabom would conclude, **"I have searched for such an explanation [naturalistic] over the past five years and have not yet found one that is adequate."[25]** Sartori dismissed the first NDE she encountered as "wishful thinking."[26] None of the researchers I read appeared in any way to have started out as paranormal advocates who set out to study NDEs to prove their worldviews.

According to Dr. Bruce Greyson, professor of Psychiatry & Neurobehavioral Sciences at the University of Virginia and one of the most respected researchers in the field, "Most near-death researchers did not go into their investigations with a belief in mind-body separation, but came to that hypothesis based on what their research found."[27]

Psychological Explanations

Objection #8: The descriptions of hospital rooms and doctors doing CPR could be explained by everyone's familiarity with television hospital scenes.[28]

Reply #1: This might explain some reports. But when researchers speak of corroborating events, they don't consider such general reports as "I saw nurses dressed in white and a doctor beating on my chest." Stories used for corroboration include *unexpected* details that someone couldn't have guessed. For instance, during open heart surgery, one patient observed, from outside his body, his cardiac surgeon "flapping his arms as if trying to fly." He reported his NDE and the quirky movement to his cardiologist, who showed great surprise that he could have known that. The explanation? This surgeon had a peculiar habit. If he had not yet scrubbed in and wanted to avoid touching anything with his hands, he would hold his hands against his chest and guide his assistants by pointing with his elbows. The researcher confirmed this event with the cardiologist, Dr. Anthony LaSala.[29]

Reply #2: Dr. Sabom set up a control group of cardiac patients who did not report NDEs. When he asked what they thought happened during resuscitation from cardiac arrest, they made significant errors, as opposed to the accurate descriptions by NDErs.[30]

Objection #9: It's only natural that they should dream of the afterlife, since they're psychologically primed by the common belief in an afterlife.[31]

Reply #1: A visit to the afterlife was NOT expected by those who didn't believe in the afterlife, which was a large percentage of van Lommel's subjects in Holland.

Reply #2: Much of what they experienced was totally unexpected, even by people who believed in an afterlife. First of all, many, if not most, didn't think they were dying. For the great majority, their experiences didn't come toward the end of long-term illnesses like cancer, where people know they're about to die and thus psychologically prepare for death. Rather, many have a chest pain and suddenly flat line, so that there's no chance to think, "I'm dying." In van Lommel's study,

> "Most patients experienced no fear of death preceding their cardiac arrest; its onset was so sudden that they failed to notice it."[32]

Even for those who have indicators that they're in danger of death, remember that the first psychological reaction people experience when confronted with possible death is often denial, not acceptance.[33]

So expectations of death wouldn't seem to impact an event before which most weren't expecting death. Consistent with this observation, in many NDEs, when a person hovers above his body, it takes a moment for him to figure out that he's dead. Obviously, he wasn't expecting to die.

It's also relevant how many report being *astounded* at various points in their experience. They were astonished that they could see their bodies from above. They were astonished that nobody in the room could see them and they could go right through people. I could go on and on. Why would they have been so astounded if this were precisely what they were expecting? Of the hundreds of experiences that I read, I found no person reporting, "It's exactly the experience I expected to have when I died." The reports were quite the opposite. As researchers have discovered, "Experiences often run sharply counter to the individual's specific religious or personal beliefs and expectations about death."[34]

Reply #3: Even for those raised in church-going families, the typical NDE experience isn't at all what they'd expect.

If I believed I was close to death, I'd be expecting my *final* death rather than a death I'd return from. Thus, drawing from my childhood exposure to Christianity, my mental picture of death consists of me standing in line, waiting to see a God with a visible body who sits on His throne.

I certainly don't have an expectation of first meeting loved ones in a place void of space and time where I hover over my hospital bed, communicate wordlessly to deceased relatives, travel through a tunnel, etc. In fact, I wouldn't expect any of the elements listed by Moody, at least not in the manner that people report experiencing them, even though I believe in an afterlife.

Again, if I thought I was dying, I'd expect what I picture for a *final* death, not an intermediary experience from which I'll return.

Reply #4: Although today many people have heard or read about NDEs, thus giving a subset of today's population some idea of what to expect, this certainly wouldn't explain the cases when Moody did his interviews in the 1970's, before this was widely reported.

Objection #10: Some experiences conform to cultural expectations.[35]

Reply #1: Often the differences mentioned weren't differences in the experiences themselves, but in their *interpretation* of the experience. For example, a Jew may report that he saw Jehovah; a Christian reports that she saw Jesus; a Muslim reports that he saw Allah. But upon further questioning, they may have each seen and spoken with a great bright light, which they *assumed* was to be identified with the God of their spiritual heritage.[36]

Reply #2: If these experiences are directed by God, it makes sense that He might personalize the experience to make it meaningful and comforting for each subject. Example: When children have NDEs, they often see their deceased pets rather than dead relatives (of which a five year old may not know any).

Reply #3: Once again, the really astounding thing about these experiences is the remarkable similarity of experiences, regardless of sex, race, ethnicity, socioeconomic status, education, or religious (or irreligious) preference. This has been demonstrated in well over a dozen studies.[37]

Physiological Objections

Objection #11: Parts of NDEs have been induced by electrically stimulating the brain or being disoriented as a pilot. Pilots on long, boring flights have been known to see themselves from outside the plane, looking in on themselves. During electronic stimulation of the brain, some people have seen certain body parts from a position outside the body.

Response #1: These experiences seem vastly different from the ones experienced in NDEs. A visual of your body in the distance (memories we could easily pull from our brains, since we typically imagine ourselves from a bird's eye view, for example, imagining ourselves walking along a beach) is far different from a visually stunning, interactive, direct communication with deceased friends and relatives and a personal life review discussed with a being of light.

Response #2: The much-heralded reports of electrical stimulation, magnetic stimulation, and epileptic seizures causing NDE-like experiences have been investigated and found unconvincing. They show no "striking similarity" to NDEs.[39] Temporal lobe seizures produce "random disorganized experiences."[40] Ernst Rodin, Medical Director of the Epilepsy Center of Michigan and Professor of Neurology at Wayne State University, stated: "In spite of having seen hundreds of patients with temporal lobe seizures during three decades of professional life, I have never come across that symptomatology [classic components of NDEs] as part of a seizure."[41]

Objection #12: Fighter pilots, during rapid acceleration, sometimes experience tunnel vision, pass out, and dream of friends.[42]

Reply: These experiences have been studied extensively and are very unlike NDEs. The dreams are reported as dream-like, not experienced with the extremely vivid, life-changing force of an NDE. The pilots see *living* friends and relatives in their dreamlets, not *dead* people. The so-called tunnel vision experienced by pilots is the absence of peripheral vision, not the perception of a tunnel or the experience of moving through a tunnel. (It's caused by the reduction of blood pressure in the eyeballs, preceding a temporary loss of vision.) There's no life review. It doesn't end with a decision to return. The dreams aren't consistent at all – one will dream about being at home with his family, another in a grocery store, another floating in the ocean on his back.[43]

Objection #13: Oxygen deprivation can lead to certain elements of an NDE.[44]

Reply #1: In many NDEs, the subject wasn't deprived of oxygen. In some cases NDEs occurred before any physiological stress[45], like an imminent traffic accident[46], or in a hospital where the oxygen levels in the blood were being carefully monitored.[47]

Reply #2: Researchers who are cardiologists are intimately familiar with the impact of oxygen deprivation in their patients, yet reject the depleted oxygen hypothesis. It's relevant that van Lommel, Sabom, and Rawlings are not only practicing physicians, but cardiologists – and not just your average cardiologists next door. Dr. Rawlings taught other physicians as part of the National Teaching Faculty of the American Heart Association.[48] Dr. van Lommel is a world-renowned cardiologist. Dr. Sabom was assistance professor of medicine, division of cardiology, at Emory University Medical School. It's an essential part of their daily medical practice to understand and monitor the impact of anoxia (no oxygen) and hypoxia (reduced oxygen) on their patients, particularly during a cardiac arrest, where anoxia can cause brain damage in as little as three to five minutes.

Reply #3: Many experiments have been done with oxygen reduction, so that the impact is well known. Reduced oxygen produces mental laziness, irritability, difficulty concentrating, difficulty remembering. As the oxygen supply dwindles further, the person becomes more disoriented and confused until he passes out. When the oxygen is cut off entirely, the brain ceases to function. This is precisely the opposite of the experience reported by those with NDEs, who speak of extremely vivid experiences, heightened clarity of thought, and extreme peace. In the thousands of cases where researchers have progressively reduced the oxygen supply to their subjects, not one has reported an NDE.[49]

Reply #4: We can often pinpoint the time of the NDE, ruling out the NDE occurring just before blacking out or immediately prior to resuscitation. Reports from outside the body as to what was happening in the hospital room seem to rule out the NDE occurring just before blacking out or immediately prior to resuscitation.

Reply #5: An NDE is very different from experiences caused by lack of oxygen. A British Royal Air Force pilot experienced high altitude anoxia, then years later experienced an NDE. He reported that the two experiences were completely different.[50]

Reply #6: Let's imagine, for the sake of argument, that if you deprive your brain of enough oxygen, it will produce a full-blown NDE. Would this actually prove anything? After all, the more you deprive your brain of oxygen, the nearer you come to death. Thus, are you really saying nothing more than "taking a person close to death tends to produce a NDE?" But we already knew that. Drain a person of a certain amount of his blood and he may experience an NDE. Collide head on with a transfer truck at 70 mph and you may experience an NDE. Cut off your oxygen long enough and you might experience an NDE.[51]

Reply #7: Finding the trigger may not explain the experience.
Imagine that I say to a ten-year-old, as we both stare at my computer, "It's beyond me how I can type a few words into the search box on my browser and a video trailer for 'The Hobbit' plays for me." The child might reply incredulously, "It's this button, silly old man – pressing the 'on' button makes it all happen!"

Well, of course pressing that button starts the computer. But discovering the computer's "trigger" doesn't get us any closer to explaining the inner workings of a computer.

So theoretically, even if scientists one day shock a part of my brain that triggers a high definition, fully interactive near-death experience, they've done nothing more than found a trigger that makes it happen. The deeper questions would remain unanswered:

- "What's actually happening?"
- "Is the experience I triggered coming solely from the brain, or did I merely find a trigger in the brain that opens a gate to the other side?"
- "Why is it happening?"

If an NDE were purely naturalistic – a vivid visual experience that's somehow hard-coded into a large number of brains, awaiting someone to push the go button (via oxygen deprivation, an electrode to the brain, etc.) - why is it that *this* very predictable experience, rather than an infinite number of other possible experiences, is hard coded there? And what worldview would best explain its presence in the brain – an atheistic or theistic worldview?

If the NDE experience were not an out-of-body experience, but were merely a high definition, interactive dream experience hard-coded in the brain, then from the atheist worldview it would seem that NDEs should produce some kind of significant survival benefit, otherwise classic Darwinism would imply that the experience would have never evolved and survived. But what possible survival benefit might that be? Rather than causing those who experience NDEs to yearn for a longer earthly life and expend their resources to make that happen, NDEs instead cause people to view their earthly lives as less desirable and focus more on the well-being of others rather than their own survival.

More useful than the current NDE, from a naturalistic standpoint, might be an experience whereby the being of light reviews, with great displeasure, instances where the subject consumed Big Macs and Twinkies while avoiding vegetables and exercise.

I'll let three of the most respected authorities in NDEs – Dr. Bruce Greyson, Dr. Emily Williams Kelly, and Dr. Edward F. Kelly, sum up the current state of research on physiological explanations.

"…theories proposed thus far consist largely of unsupported speculations about what might be happening during an NDE. *None* of the proposed neurophysiological mechanisms have been shown to occur in NDEs. A naturally occurring ketamine-like substance, for example, has not been identified in humans (Strassman 1997, 31). Moreover, some of these proposals, such as the role of expectation or the presence and effects of anoxia, are *inconsistent* with what few data we do have."[52]

Reflections on Naturalistic Explanations

We could talk about many other explanations, which have also been considered and found inadequate over the past 35 years of NDE study:

- Natural chemicals released by the body during trauma can have a euphoric effect. (While these might explain a feeling of peace, they hardly explain the appearance of all the specific elements of NDEs.)[53]
- The impact of drugs administered during cardiac arrest. (But what about NDEs in the absence of these drugs?)[54]
- Perhaps those who experience NDEs are prone to delusions. (Subjects are typically screened for this. Studies have found them psychologically

healthy, not differing from those who don't experience NDEs regarding "age, gender, race, religion, religiosity, intelligence, neuroticism, extroversion, anxiety, or Rorschach measures."[55]

- Perhaps patients are making things up. (But why the consistency of their stories? And what are their motives, since most NDErs are extremely reluctant to tell their stories, for fear of being ridiculed?)[56]

- Perhaps NDEs are a deception by Satan. (So why do the experiences motivate people to seek God, love people, and practice godly virtues?)

- Perhaps not one, but multiple physiological and psychological factors converge to produce the experience. (See my appendices on two such attempts: Susan Blackmore's 'Dying Brain Hypothesis,' and Dr. Kevin Nelson's book, *The Spiritual Doorway in the Brain*.)

Summary of Naturalistic Explanations

None of the naturalistic hypotheses I studied came anywhere near explaining this experience. As one thorough review of the studies on NDEs (up to 2005) concluded,

- "...research has not yet revealed a characteristic that either guarantees or prohibits the occurrence, incidence, nature, or aftereffects of an NDE."[57]

- "...very little evidence exists that supports any of these hypotheses."[58]

Other literature reviews concluded similarly.[59]

If this is indeed the current state of research, what is to be made of occasional articles with sensational titles that boast that naturalistic explanations have been found? For example, in 2011, *Scientific American* published the article "Peace of Mind: Near-Death Experiences Now Found to Have Scientific Explanations – Seeing your life pass before you and the light at the end of the tunnel, can be explained by new research on abnormal functioning of dopamine and oxygen flow."

Articles of this nature that I've read fail to show an even basic familiarity with the wealth of NDE research over the past 35 years. Instead, they just repeat the same worn-out hypotheses that have been shown inadequate time after time during decades of research.[60] For a review of this popular *Scientific American* article, see Appendix #2.

The present state of research finds naturalistic explanations inadequate. But this doesn't mean that we must instead accept a hypothesis that invokes the supernatural. One could always argue that better naturalistic explanations may present themselves in the future. Yet, the evidence presented in the next section makes doubtful the potential of any hypothesis to explain NDEs as purely naturalistic phenomena.

Chapter 5
Do NDEs Provide Compelling Evidence That God and Heaven Exist?

As I said in the preface, when making decisions, we typically seek sufficient evidence rather than the absolute proof that can be obtained only in predefined fields such as math. I can prove absolutely that $1 + 1 = 2$, but only because we agree to a definition of each of those symbols and because my little equation currently refers to nothing in the real world.

But what if my wife says, "Check the house before we go to bed. How many people are here?" I might peek in every room and report, "I count only two of us." (Applying my math, Cherie plus me equals two.) But upon reflection, once I introduced real objects into the equation, I also introduced doubt. After all, did I really check *every* closet *and* the attic? And even if I checked the house thoroughly, how could I know with absolute certitude that one of our stealthy teens didn't climb in through a window immediately *after* I checked his room?

My point? There will always be evidence pro and con for any decision we face and multiple hypotheses can be set forth to explain any phenomena. So in the same way that we make most of life's important decisions, whether they be in our personal lives ("Should I marry her?"), in a scientific field ("Is relativity correct?"), or in a courtroom ("Is he guilty?"), *we're weighing the evidence to decide which hypothesis best fits the data we've observed.* Some call it *inferring to the best explanation.*

While many arguments have been forwarded to try to explain NDEs naturalistically, don't let the number of proposed explanations cloud the issue. We could spin new hypotheses all day long.[1] But at the end of the day, our task is to decide which explanation best explains the data.

To simplify matters, we have only two broad explanations before us:

Explanation #1 - *The spiritual explanation* - In a near-death experience, the person is truly alive, with a fully functioning mind, in a nonmaterial, spiritual world outside the body.

Explanation #2 - *The naturalistic explanation* - The NDE experience can be explained solely in terms of brain function. It may be caused by lack of oxygen, psychological expectations, or a host of other naturalistic causes. If it can be satisfactorily explained in naturalistic terms, there's no need to postulate an independently functioning mind and heavenly realms.

Above, we examined the main explanations put forth to defend a naturalistic explanation. Now we'll look at the evidence for the spiritual explanation. As you read, ask yourself the question, "Which of these two explanations (hypotheses) best accounts for the known facts?"

Exhibit 1 - Reports (from outside the body) of the hospital room or accident location provide corroborating evidence.

According to Moody, "Several doctors have told me…that they are utterly baffled about how patients with no medical knowledge could describe in such detail and so correctly the procedure used in resuscitation attempts, even though these events took place while the doctors knew the patients involved to be 'dead.'"[2]

Here's an example:

A comatose man was found in a park and given heart massage by passers-by. Upon arrival at the coronary unit, while he was still comatose, a nurse removed the man's dentures and put them in a crash cart. After about ninety minutes, his blood pressure and heart rhythm stabilized, but he remained comatose and was transferred to intensive care. Over a week later, he came out of his coma and was transferred back to the coronary care unit, where he spotted the nurse and said, "…you know where my dentures are." He described the crash cart, with bottles on top of it, and the sliding drawer underneath, where his dentures had been placed.

He said that he watched the entire scene from above, outside his body. Further, he accurately described the room and those who were present, noting that he was very concerned that they might stop trying to resuscitate him. The nurse confirmed everything, including the fact that during their attempts at resuscitations, they were "extremely negative about the patient's prognosis."[2]

This isn't an isolated example.[3] The books and studies I read presented an abundance of cases with specific, corroborating evidence.[4] Evidence of accurate perception while outside the body might involve finding objects that were lost, accurately reporting specific conversations they heard while under deep anesthesia, identifying unexpected or unusual objects, seeing people in another room doing an activity like praying, giving vivid detailed descriptions of the operating procedure, seeing someone on the other side who they didn't know had died, meeting someone on the other side who they'd never met and/or knew existed (like a still-born sibling or their real father - who could be later identified with pictures), etc.[5]

Cases claiming corroboration are scattered throughout the professional literature.[6] Fortunately, Professor Janice Holden, Chair of the Department of Counseling and Higher Education at the University of North Texas, identified over 100 such cases, noting the publication and page numbers. Many more corroborated cases exist, but she chose to exclude, for example, autobiographical books, books that didn't report a systematic study of NDEs, and "single case studies described outside the peer-reviewed literature." She included only incidents where people were actually near death. (Those who want to read a large number of cases with corroboration can use Holden's collection in Appendix #8 as a starting point.)

If I were an atheist, this evidence would make me squirm. Attempts to explain this naturalistically appear to fall woefully short. If these are merely good guesses, as some suggest,[7] naturalists should put forth a reasonable hypothesis as to why people guess so extraordinarily well during NDEs. (Or perhaps great guessers, for some naturalistic reason, tend to have NDEs. Let them compete on Jeopardy.) As the evidence stands today, good guessing falls short as an explanation, once you read the cases in detail.[8]

Dr. Sartori, in her five-year prospective study of NDEs in the United Kingdom, tested the "good guesses hypothesis." She asked cardiac patients who didn't report seeing their bodies to try to guess what happened during their resuscitation. According to Sartori:

> "Twenty-eight of these patients were unable to even guess as to what procedures had been performed. Three reported scenario based on things they had seen in popular hospital dramas on TV and two guessed about the scenario. All had errors and misconceptions of the equipment used and incorrect procedures were described. Many guessed that the defibrillator had been used when, in fact, it had not. ...This contrasted significantly with the surprisingly accurate accounts made by patients who claimed to be out of their bodies and observing the emergency situation."[9]

Cardiologist Michael Sabom did an exceptional job of questioning his NDErs about their operating procedures. Skeptical from the start about the reality of their claims to out-of-body experiences, he slowly came around after he saw how detailed and accurate they could be in their descriptions. Sabom notes that each resuscitation can differ in significant ways, making it very unlikely they could guess which procedures, in what order, were used in their cases. Concerning one patient, Sabom reports,

> "When I asked him to tell me what exactly he saw, he described the resuscitation with such detail and accuracy that I could have later used the tape to teach physicians."[10]

Imagine you've been chosen for jury duty, deciding a case where a doctor has ordered his patient to enter a psychiatric ward because, after her cardiac arrest, she claimed to have visited heaven and spoken to angels. The defense argues that she is perfectly sane and actually visited heaven. The prosecution argues that such events are impossible and all who claim them are delusional. During eight hours of testimony, the defense lines up 100 NDErs to testify that they too made the trip to the other side. Accompanying each NDEr are doctors, nurses, and family members who verify things seen and heard while outside their bodies. Would this evidence be compelling to an unbiased jury?

Exhibit 2 - NDErs report enhanced mental functions while their brains are severely compromised.

NDEs can't be explained by brain processes if the brain isn't functioning well enough to produce vivid consciousness. This is what initially baffled van Lommel concerning his early patients who experienced NDEs. The experiences occurred when their brains were apparently not functioning.[11] To expand upon this for his readers, he wrote entire chapters on "What Happens in the Brain When the Heart Suddenly Stops?" and "What Do We Know About Brain Function?"[12]

Atypical cases of consciousness while under anesthesia or during cardiac arrest do exist. An extremely small percentage of people (.18 percent, or less than two out of 1,000)[13] have reported brief episodes of consciousness under general anesthesia. For those who do experience consciousness (sometimes due to improper administering of anesthesia), it's not pleasant.[14] There have been cases of people experiencing brief consciousness during CPR[15], before the heart establishes a rhythm of its own. But the reason such cases are written up in the literature is that they're so rare.

By far the typical experience reported by those undergoing anesthesia or experiencing cardiac arrest is no memory of anything. In such circumstances, the brain is unable to either maintain consciousness or form memories.[16] Yet, during this time, NDErs consistently report, not vague, confused consciousness, but vivid, "realer than real" consciousness. It's like their brains are on hyper drive, some reliving their entire lives within a brief span of time.

And their memories, as we have seen, far from being cloudy and fleeting (as we'd expect from a compromised brain) are retained so efficiently that decades later they report remembering each detail as if it happened yesterday.

Corroborating evidence from studies of patients observed in the hospital room during their out-of-body experiences confirms that many NDE's couldn't have been vivid dreams that occurred immediately prior to unconsciousness or during the early stages of resuscitation. Other medical data argues against patients piecing together information they picked up while still conscious. During the brief moments when the brain is losing or regaining consciousness, due to loss of blood flow to the brain (e.g., in cardiac arrest) or anesthesia, brain function is disorganized and confused. Memory is also severely impacted.[17]

Here's an example (which we summarized in the preface):

Pamela Reynolds, a thirty-five-year-old mother, underwent a complex surgery to repair a giant aneurysm in a cerebral artery. As reported by cardiologist Michael Sabom and Neurosurgeon Robert Spetzler, in preparation for the surgery they lowered her body temperature to about 50 degrees Fahrenheit and drained all the blood from her head, so that her brain was had ceased functioning by all three clinical tests - "her electroencephalogram was silent, her brain-stem response was absent, and no blood flowed through her brain...." Additionally, her eyes were taped shut, she was put under deep anesthesia, brain stem activity was monitored with "100-decible clicks emitted by small molded speakers inserted into her ears" and her entire body, except for the small area of the head they were cutting on, was covered completely.

During this time, Reynolds experienced a vivid NDE where she watched part of the surgery and reported back to the doctors what she saw - describing in minute detail the specialized instruments they used for the surgery. For example, she described the saw as looking "a lot more like a drill than a saw. It even had little bits that were kept in this case that looked like the case that my father stored his socket wrenches in when I was a child.... And I distinctly remember a female voice saying: 'We have a problem. Her arteries are too small.' And then a male voice: 'Try the other side.'"

The instruments were covered prior to her surgery, so there's no way she could have seen the instruments beforehand. She went on to describe passing through a tunnel, talking to deceased relatives who looked like they were in the prime of life, and being sent back to her body to wake up at resuscitation. Note: Reynolds describes her NDE as a continuous, uninterrupted narrative, from the onset of her surgery till she was sent back from the other side and regained consciousness.

Doctors Sabom and Spetzler (director of the Barrow Neurological Institute) confirmed the accuracy of what she both heard and saw in the operating room. Even if portions of her near death experience took place during general anesthesia rather than after the blood was drained, this vivid, accurate experience occurred while she was heavily sedated, with her brain monitored in three ways to ensure that she was deeply anesthetized. Before the draining of the blood, her eyes were taped shut. A loud clicking at a rate of 11 to 33 clicks per second continually assaulted her ears. The volume of the clicks, between 90 to 100 decibels, has been likened to the sound of a subway train, a whistling teakettle, or a lawn mower. Even if the sedation failed, the clicking would prevent her from hearing and the tape would keep her from seeing. How could she have known these things unless she was observing them outside of her body?[18]

If mental functions present themselves as remarkably clear, lucid, and even enhanced,[20] while the brain is severely compromised, the afterlife hypothesis (the mind can exist independently from the brain) would seem to fit the data better than a naturalistic hypothesis (mental functions are produced solely by the brain).

Exhibit 3 - The presence of remarkably consistent, yet unexpected elements, are not what we'd predict from a psychologically induced dream state.

Remarkable Consistency

Dreams differ wildly from individual to individual. So why the remarkable consistency of NDEs, if they're simply dream states?

Reflect upon the random nature of dreams. If 20 people go to sleep agitated, some may indeed have dreams that reflect agitation, but each dream would likely be completely different. One dreams of hanging out with an obnoxious person. Another dreams of camping out in poison ivy.

We'd be shocked and mystified if we interviewed hundreds of people who fell asleep agitated and find that 95 percent of them reported a uniform dream – like living in a large city inhabited by zombies. We'd be even more mystified if they reported uniform zombie characteristics that differed from typical zombie movies, such as "all zombies in my dream communicated via tapping Morse code on each other's shoulders." With no expectations of such strange behavior, the uniform experience would likely defy explanation.[20]

That's why there's something very odd about what Moody refers to as the "striking similarity"[21] of NDE reports. What people experience on the other side forms a pretty consistent picture of life in another dimension. Why such consistency, if it's nothing more than a dream state? While the reports are personalized (for example, the content of their conversations and the familiar relatives they see) they are remarkably consistent regarding the specific, often unexpected nature of this otherworldly life.

As Dr. Rawlings writes:

> "The remarkable repetitive sequence of events and parallel experiences in completely unrelated cases seem to exclude the possibility of any coincidence or connecting circumstances during this out-of-the-body existence."[22]

Unexpected Details

If NDEs were merely vivid dreams that resulted from people's expectations concerning death, I'd expect a close correspondence between people's expectations and what they actually report.

Yet, most of what they report was totally unexpected. Who would expect the typical experience of communicating directly mind-to-mind rather than using the medium of language? Who expects to encounter a dimension where both time and space seem to vanish, where they can see both up close and far away with equal clarity, and view an entire lifetime in an instant? A bright light might be expected by some, but who expects the common experience of not having to squint while looking at the extreme brightness?

If such consistent elements were due to people's expectations, those reporting NDEs should typically report that they experienced precisely what they were expecting. But they don't. Who would possibly be expecting such odd things, unless they've studied NDE literature and believed the reports?

Yet among Van Lommel's subjects, 43 percent hadn't even *heard* of NDEs, much less believed in them.[23] Those who are aware of NDEs, believe in their reality, and expect one to occur would seem to comprise an extremely small percentage of the population, especially in a land like Holland, where more than half of the population "is relatively confident that death is the end of everything."[24] Thus, the average Dutch patient would have the expectation of seeing absolutely nothing after death.

And remember, NDEs weren't widely reported prior to Moody's study, so that it's very unlikely that any of his subjects had heard of NDEs. Moody actually coined the phrase, "near-death experience."

Moody (later confirmed by other researchers) noted 15 specific, common elements that people reported with remarkable consistency. (The 11 elements I mention below actually take place *during* the NDE.) As I reflect upon the list, I find that all of these elements have qualities that differ significantly from what I'm expecting when I die. I'd suggest that I'm fairly typical of mainstream religious Americans here, representative of many of those studied by Moody.

Again, please note that my expectations, as well as almost anyone who comes near death, would be of a *final* death rather than a *near-death* experience. Surely nobody comes to the brink of death thinking, "I'm about to die and come back to life!"

So here are the common elements of an NDE as observed by Moody, contrasted with my differing expectations.

- **Ineffability** - Before studying NDEs, I assumed that if I had such an experience, I could pretty easily describe it to others.
- **Hearing a doctor or someone saying I am dead -** I don't expect to hear this.
- **Feelings of peace and quiet -** After death and before some sort of judgment, I'd expect some combination of incredible excitement and a severe case of the jitters, certainly not the complete state of peace reported in NDEs.
- **Hearing a noise** - A buzz or ringing. No expectation of this.
- **The dark tunnel -** Heard of it, but not expecting it.
- **Out of the body -** Yes, I expect to be out of my earthly body, but not in my hospital room, near those who are still living, looking down at my body from the ceiling.
- **Meeting others -** Yes, I expect to meet people who've died before me, but after some kind of meeting with God. I have no expectation of communicating with beings directly from mind to mind. I picture speaking and hearing in English, since that's my native language.
- **The being of light -** I expect to meet God, but picture Him as having bodily features (face, arms, hands) rather than just light.
- **The life review -** I expect some sort of reward for deeds done while on earth, but not the type of life review that people are reporting – with no sense of time, almost reliving it rather than just watching in a detached way, experiencing all the feelings of those I impacted when I see myself

doing things. I also expect this to come *after* a word from God about Jesus' atonement. (Were my sins truly forgiven?)

- **A border or limit -** I don't expect to come to a place where I feel that if I go beyond, I'll have to stay.
- **Coming back -** I don't expect to return to my body after I die. I'm expecting a final exam, not a midterm.

So when people say, "An NDE is no more than a vivid dream caused by people's expectations of the hereafter," I couldn't disagree more. It's not at all what I would expect; neither does it seem to be what the vast majority of others expect. Moody concurs:

> "…what is most generally reported is manifestly not what is commonly imagined, in our cultural milieu, to happen to the dead."[25]

And since many of the people didn't even know they were dying, how can those be deemed psychologically induced?[26]

People hold widely diverse beliefs about what will happen immediately following death. Several studies have found that that beliefs prior to the NDE didn't impact whether people had an NDE or not – neither prior knowledge of NDEs, their religious beliefs, nor their standard of education.[27] Many who had NDEs didn't have a prior believe in life after death at all. According to van Lommel,

> "Any kind of religious belief, or its absence in nonbelievers and atheists, was irrelevant…."[28]

It's typical for people to report repeatedly how astounded they were at what they experienced, underscoring how totally unexpected many of their experiences were.[29]

- Van Lommel speaks of the "utter amazement" people report concerning such elements as being in the hospital room, out of their bodies, without people being able to hear or see them.[30]

- One subject reported, "Now, this whole thing had just astounded me, took me completely by surprise."[31]

The combination of astounding consistency with unexpected details seems much more consistent with actually visiting the other side (the spiritual hypothesis), rather than a vivid dream brought about by expectations (a naturalistic hypothesis).

Exhibit 4 - NDEs aren't abruptly interrupted, distinguishing them from dreams and hallucinations.

This is related to Exhibit #3, but perhaps deserves special treatment. For a week or so, reflect upon your dreams immediately upon awakening. Did your dreams typically end with closure, like the end of a movie, or were they interrupted mid story upon awakening?

Analyzing my own dreams over a period of months, I found that all of them stopped mid-stream, often in the middle of a sentence. There was no closure. A story would be developing, a conversation would be taking place, but then it would cut off abruptly when I woke up. And if you think about it, that's precisely what we would expect of dreams and hallucinations. They should end when we wake or return to reality, regardless of where they are in the story line, *because dreams aren't timed to end when we wake.*

If NDEs were either dreams or hallucinations, wouldn't we expect them to end abruptly, when sedation is discontinued or when the heartbeat is restored?

Yet, NDEs bear more resemblance to movie endings than dream endings. Meg Ryan finds the perfect guy. They fall in love and move into their dream home. The end. We'd be shocked if the film cut off abruptly, mid plot, mid sentence. Why? Because movie story lines aren't random – they're planned, scripted, designed to end with closure.

Moody identified "coming back" as one of the common elements of NDEs.[32] In Long's study, most of his NDErs reported being involved in their decision to return to their bodies.[33] As Sabom reported, "In the majority of cases, this 'return' was either influenced or directed by another spiritual being."[34]

This seemed significant to me. Yet, I wondered, what of the reports where there was no discussion about coming back? Did they cut off mid sentence and find themselves abruptly back in their bodies? Although I'd never run across a case like that, perhaps they were common but researchers never reported them. I decided to research it myself.

I studied 50 consecutive NDEs (from the most recently submitted working back consecutively) plus over 50 nonwestern NDEs as submitted to Dr. Long's website.[35] I fully expected that at least some would report an abrupt ending, since most scientific studies seem to find anomalies and outliers. Yet, *not one of these NDErs reported a disruptive ending.* Indeed, the majority spoke of a conversation ending in a decision to return, or just knowing that it was time to return. But even in cases that didn't include a conscious decision to return, I saw no NDE that was cut off abruptly, like mid-sentence.

For an example of closure, here's the conclusion of an NDE from someone who almost drowned:

> I heard a voice say, "It is not yet your time. You'll be alright." I couldn't tell if it was a male or female voice. Next thing I knew, my brother grabbed the back of my coat and pulled me out of the water.[36]

Since I've not heard this issue discussed among researchers, I'd like to leave it rather tentative. Perhaps it's very significant. On the other hand, perhaps further NDE research will yield alternate explanations. In personal correspondence with NDE researcher Bruce Greyson, he suggested, "We don't know whether the account of making that decision or being sent back is a retroactive distortion of how the NDE really ended."

I'd like to see more research on this. Are there parallels to this experience in dream research, such as the brain retroactively inventing a story line to go with a certain feeling or pain or intuition? If so, is it likely that the closure story could be triggered by the brain to retroactively coincide with the feeling of regaining consciousness?

But even if some decisions to return could be explained in this manner, it still doesn't explain why so extremely few, if any, NDEs are interrupted mid sentence, as we typically find in dreams and hallucinations. They seem more like movie scripts – planned, directed, and designed to end with closure. This data seems to fit better with NDEs being a real experience with the other side, rather than a naturally occurring dream state or hallucination.

Exhibit 5 - Children's NDEs provide unique evidence.[37]

Seven-year-old Katie was found floating face down in a YMCA swimming pool. Pediatrician and medical researcher Melvin Morse resuscitated her in the emergency room, but she remained profoundly comatose – massive swelling of the brain, no gag reflex – with an artificial lung breathing for her. He gave her a ten percent chance of surviving.

Astonishingly, she made a full recovery within three days.

When she returned for a follow-up appointment, Katie recognized Morse and told her mom, "That's the one with the beard. First there was this tall doctor who didn't have a beard, and then he came in. First I was in a big room, and then they moved me to a smaller room where they did X-rays on me."

She mentioned other details, like putting a tube down her nose – all accurate, but "seen" while her eyes were shut and her brain was deeply comatose.

Morse asked her what she remembered about her near drowning. After all, if it resulted from a seizure, she might have another one.

She responded, "Do you mean when I visited the Heavenly Father?" That sounded pretty interesting, so Morse responded, "That's a good place to start. Tell me about meeting the Heavenly Father."

"I met Jesus and the Heavenly Father," she said. Perhaps it was his shocked expression. Perhaps her natural shyness kicked in. Whatever the reason, that's all she'd say for that appointment.

Next week, Katie was more talkative. She remembered nothing of the drowning, but recalled an initial darkness, then a tunnel through which Elizabeth came. She described her as "tall and nice," with bright, golden hair. Elizabeth accompanied Katie through the tunnel, where she met several people, including her late grandfather, two young boys named Mark and Andy, and others.

Katie also reported visiting her earthly home, where she saw her brothers pushing a GI Joe in a jeep, while her mom cooked roast chicken and rice. She even knew what they were wearing. Her parents were shocked at the detailed accuracy.

Finally, Elizabeth took Katie to meet the Heavenly Father and Jesus. The Father asked if she wanted to go home. She wanted to stay. Jesus asked if she wanted to see her mother. She said, "Yes" and then woke up.

It took about an hour for Katie to tell the story, but that hour changed Dr. Morse's life. He interviewed the intensive care nurses, who said that Katie's first words were, "Where are Mark and Andy?" She asked for them repeatedly. Morse reflected on Katie and her manner of telling the story. Although extremely shy, she spoke of the experience in a "powerful and compelling way."

Morse spent hours talking to the parents about anything from Katie's background that could help explain such an experience. They were Mormons and hadn't talked to her about tunnels, guardian angels and such. When Katie's grandfather died, her mom had told her that death was like sending someone on a boat ride, while the friends and family have to stay on the shore.[38]

Morse published the case in the *American Journal of Diseases of Children*[39] and considered further research. He had a grant to do cancer research, but the grant director, Janet Lunceford, supported his wish to instead study children with NDEs through Seattle Children's Hospital. He assembled a team of eight researchers, each of whom had relevant expertise. For example, Dr. Don Tyler was an expert on anesthetics and their effects upon the brain. Dr. Jerrold Milstein, director of the Department of Child Neurology at the University of Washington, studied the brain stem and hippocampal function.[40]

Morse concluded from his three-year study:

> We are taught in medical school to find the simplest explanation for medical problems. After looking at all the other explanations for near-death experiences, I think the simplest explanation is that NDEs are actually glimpses into the world beyond. Why not? I've read all the convoluted psychological and physiological explanations for NDEs, and none of them seem very satisfying.[41]

He published the results of his study in a medical journal and wrote a book to give further detail.[42]

When children have NDEs, they experience the same elements as adults.[43] Yet, it's extremely doubtful that they've heard of NDEs or have expectations similar to adults. Their childlike spontaneity in describing events totally outside their previous learning or experience provides a unique and powerful line of evidence. This is part of the appeal of little Colton's NDE in *Heaven is for Real*. His reports were spontaneous and childlike, describing from his point of view things that adults could more fully understand.[44]

If childhood experiences were tailored to what they wanted to see in a time of extreme illness, surely they'd dream of their parents. Instead, they often see deceased grandparents or pets. And like adults who experience NDEs, their lives are impacted for the long haul. They become more empathetic than their peers, sensing the emotions behind spoken words. They want to help others and gravitate toward the helping professions – nursing, medicine, and social work.[45]

Here's another child's experience. A five-year-old contracted meningitis, fell into a coma, and awoke reporting that he'd met a little girl on the other side who claimed to be his sister. She said to him,

> "I'm your sister. I died a month after I was born. I was named after your grandmother. Our parents called me Rietje for short."

When he awoke and told his parents, they were shocked and left the room for a moment, then returned to tell him that he indeed had an older sister named Rietje who'd died of poisoning a year before he was born. They had decided not to tell him until later in life.[46]

The childhood NDE seems to clearly fit better with the spiritual hypothesis than naturalistic hypotheses that lean on expectations or wish fulfillment, especially when corroborating details are present.

Exhibit 6 - Deathbed visions provide corroboration.[47]

The first known attempt to pull together accounts of people's deathbed visions was by Sir William Barrett, professor of experimental physics at Ireland's Royal College of Science. His study was prompted by his wife (who was a physician), who rushed home to tell Sir William about a remarkable vision seen by Doris, a lady who was about to die after giving birth to her child. Doris spoke with great delight about seeing her deceased father. Then, with a rather puzzled expression, she said, "He has Vida with him." Doris turned toward her and repeated, "Vida is with him." She soon died.

Doris' sister Vida had died three weeks before, but nobody had told Doris, due to her state of health.[48]

Three large-scale studies of deathbed visions were done in the second half of the twentieth century. The first study collected and analyzed the reports of nurses and doctors concerning over 35,000 patients. A second gathered about 50,000 reports. These were both American studies. Later, a third study compared 255 reports of deathbed visions in India. Amazingly, "the results from the Indian survey were in agreement with results from the earlier surveys on almost all points."[49]

Some points of evidential interest from these studies:

1 - Those who said that the deceased relatives or angelic beings had come for the purpose of taking them away, tended to die sooner than the ones who merely spoke of seeing beings on the other side.[50]

2 - Sometimes the visions were reported by people who were not expected to die, thus ruling out expectations as the cause. A college-educated Indian man, still in his 20s, was doing very well after a hospitalization. He was to be discharged that day and both the doctor and the patient fully expected a recovery. Suddenly the patient shouted, "Someone is standing here dressed in white clothes. I will not go with you!" He died within ten minutes.[51]

If these visions were caused by culturally influenced expectations, you'd expect them to differ vastly from person to person and culture to culture. Their high degree of convergence would seem to fit better with a spiritual explanation (there is an afterlife) than a purely naturalistic explanation (there is no afterlife).[52]

Exhibit 7 - "Shared NDEs" provide multiple eye witnesses.[53]

Often, those who are near (relationally and/or physically) the dying share the NDE. These reports are evidentially valuable in that several people may independently report and corroborate the experience. Additionally, these reports can't likely be explained by naturalistic explanations such as the dying brain hypothesis, since those sharing the experience were not in the process of dying. Neither were they suffering from oxygen deprivation, hypercarbia, fear of personal death, or other symptoms that may influence the brain at death.

Here's an example experience, corroborated by all who were present:

Five members of the Anderson family in metro Atlanta were at their mother's bedside as she was dying. Since this was the end of an extended illness, none were especially psychologically distraught at the time. As one of the daughters reported, "Suddenly, a bright light appeared in the room." The appearance of the light was unlike "any kind of light on this earth. I nudged my sister to see if she saw it too, and when I looked at her, her eyes were as big as saucers. …I saw my brother literally gasp. Everyone saw it together and for a little while we were frightened."

They next saw lights that shaped themselves into an entranceway. Her mother left her body and departed through the passage, ushering in a feeling of ecstatic joy. They all agreed that the entranceway resembled the Natural Bridge in the Shenandoah Valley.[54]

Other shared experiences may include portions of the deceased's life review, so that they see and experience friends of the deceased that they never knew. One experiencer subsequently looked in a year book and recognized people first seen in the life review.

Since these experiences come unexpected, researchers can't attribute them to wish fulfillment. And even if some fervently wish to see someone's soul depart, it's unlikely that they'd share such unexpected elements as distortions in the room, which were reported in many unrelated cases.[55]

When I read Moody's recent book on shared experiences, I assumed that such experiences were pretty rare. Only Moody, I reasoned, could come up with a large collection of shared experiences, since he's interviewed thousands of people with NDEs over his lifetime.

Thus I was surprised that in interviewing my own close contacts, I found one of my relatives, a retired history teacher who holds a masters degree, telling me of his own shared death experience. Bucky woke at 3:00 AM feeling an extreme heaviness on his chest, much like people report in a heart attack. He saw a light in the distance, then came out of his body and looked down at his body from the viewpoint of the ceiling and observed some celestial beings. (From this vantage point, the light was now behind him.) He experienced the extreme peace reported by so many in NDEs. He came to in his bed, in a serious sweat, and immediately the phone rang. His father, who lived 90 miles away and had not been ill, had suddenly died of a heart attack.[56]

Reports of the shared death experience seem to take the evidence to a new level, since more than one person can often testify to experiencing the same paranormal phenomena. And again, since friends and family weren't experiencing the psychological and physiological symptoms of dying, you can hardly attribute it to anoxia or another characteristic of dying brains. Moody shares scores of these accounts, many of them containing corroborating evidence, in his 2010 book, *Glimpses of Eternity: Sharing a Loved One's Passage from This Life to the Next*.

Exhibit 8 - Face-to-face interviews have a strong impact on researchers.

Dr. Moody says that before his interviews, he would have dismissed such tales out of hand. The interviews changed his mind.[57] Dr. van Lommel was a convinced materialist, but never forgot that extremely emotional patient who came back from a cardiac arrest speaking of "a tunnel, colors, a light, a beautiful landscape, and music."[58] Dr. Rawlings originally regarded most of the NDE stories he heard as "fantasy or conjecture or imagination," until one of his patients repeatedly died and resuscitated, each time reporting with great emotion what he was experiencing on the other side. The genuineness of the patient compelled him to take the experience seriously.[59]

One of the men I interviewed was a successful, intelligent, respected, self-confident man of about 60 years. I started the interview with friendly chitchat, then asked him about his experience. He choked up. I don't mean I saw a hint of a tear in his eye as he talked. I mean he couldn't speak at all until he reined in his emotions. He apologized and took a few more moments to regain his composure.

To me, from the perspective of the interviewer, I had no doubt that he was profoundly sincere – absolutely certain he'd left his body, entered another dimension, and spoken to three beings about whether or not to return to earth. He said it was "absolutely distinct from a dream." What he experienced was real, powerful, unforgettable, and life-changing.

While this may at first seem like a rather subjective point, remember that in a court of law the apparent sincerity of the witness can legitimately count as evidence. If a woman appears to be genuinely scared of her husband, the judge may issue a restraining order. Of course, she may be a great liar and actress, and with NDE reports, each case should be screened for attention seekers.

On the one hand, little Colton (*Heaven is for Real*) seemed to be innocently childlike in his reports. On the other hand, my skeptical side tells me that children like attention, and Colton's descriptions of heaven provided plenty of it! That doesn't necessarily invalidate his testimony, but we'd be unwise to ignore this potential motivation. In the case of certain ministers, a YouTube interview dramatizing their NDEs might be just the thing to rejuvenate their book sales.

But in the case of most NDE reports, there's scant motivation for lying. As we've seen, the typical hospital patient is extremely reluctant to share her experience, as is borne out by many studies. They don't stand to get a cash reward or a respectability badge for claiming to have been to heaven and back. In fact, they have very strong motives for *not* reporting the event or for lying by claiming "it was only a vivid dream."

If you're interested in this line of evidence, look for several intelligent, level-headed people who've experienced NDEs. I found a dozen by simply asking friends and family members if they knew people who'd had NDEs. I personally interviewed some of them. Seeing NDErs' sincerity – their utterly convincing inflections and expressions – led many interviewers to conclude, "They're totally convinced that they visited the other side. Had I had their experience, I'd likely believe just as strongly that I'd been to the other side. So why should I wait for my own experience in order to believe?"[60]

Moody, reflecting on the many people he interviewed, notes,

"No one has seen fit to proselytize, to try to convince others of the realities he experienced. Indeed, I have found that the difficulty is quite the reverse: People are naturally very reticent to tell others about what happened to them."[61]

"…many have remarked that they realized from the very beginning that others would think they were mentally unstable if they were to relate their experiences."[62]

Exhibit 9 - The deaf "hear."

Listen to the account of a boy who was born deaf, describing his near-death experience:

> "I was born profoundly deaf. All my relatives can hear, and they always communicate with me through sign language. Now I had direct communication with about twenty ancestors via some kind of telepathy. An overwhelming experience…."[63]

"Overwhelming" indeed. He's neither heard nor understood verbal communication. Yet he finds himself communicating effortlessly, not through sign language, but directly mind to mind, without learning a new form of communication. This in no way fits what we know of the workings of the brain.

Exhibit 10 - The color-blind see colors.

I'm color-blind. Actually, I can see some colors, enough to understand the concept of differentiating colors. But it's serious enough that the last time I took a color-blind test, the nurse laughed at me: "Come on! Surely you can see *something* there!"

Thus, if I ever have a near-death experience, I'll likely be astounded at the range of colors. Although those who aren't color-blind also mention seeing new colors, the range seems particularly astounding to the color-blind.

Consider this NDE:

"I can distinguish the primary colors, but pastels all look the same to me. But suddenly I could see them, all kinds of different shades. Don't ask me to name them because I lack the necessary experience for that."[64]

Reflecting upon this phenomenon, although I understand the concept of colors, I can't even conceive of the colors I can't see. Thus, if I were to encounter a life-threatening situation, I have neither a visual expectation of certain colors (psychological preparation), nor memories of the elusive colors for my brain to pull from (to be revealed in stimulation of the brain). Predictably, I don't see new colors in my dreams.

Once again, naturalistic hypotheses seem inadequate to account for this experience.

Exhibit 11 - The blind see.[65]

People born blind don't dream in visual images. Even those who lose their sight during their first five years tend to not have visual imagery later in life.

Yet, when researchers studied 31 blind people (nearly half of them blind from birth) who reported NDEs, they found:

- "...blind persons, including those blind from birth, do report classic NDEs of the kind common to sighted persons; that the great preponderance of blind persons claim to see during NDEs and OBEs [out of body experiences]; and that occasionally claims of visually-based knowledge that could not have been obtained by normal means can be independently corroborated."[66]

- "...inspection reveals no obvious differences among sight subgroups with respect to the frequency of NDE elements. Thus, whether one is blind from birth, loses one's sight in later life, or suffers from severe visual impairment, the type of NDE reported appears to be much the same and is not structurally different from those described by sighted persons."

- "Like sighted experiencers, our blind respondents described to us both perceptions of this world and otherworldly scenes, often in fulsome, fine-grained detail, and sometimes with a sense of extremely sharp, even subjectively perfect, acuity."[67]

Take the case of Vicki, who was born blind and at the age of twenty-two fell into a coma after a car wreck. According to Vicki,

"I've never seen anything, no light, no shadows, no nothing.... And in my dreams I don't see any visual impressions. It's just taste, touch, sound, and smell. But no visual impressions of anything."

After the wreck, she found herself viewing, with perfect clarity, a scene in an emergency room where a medical team was frantically working to revive a person. She recognized her wedding ring (which she knew by touch) and began to realize that the body was hers and that she must have died. She went up through the ceiling and saw trees, birds, and people for the first time. "...it was incredible, really beautiful, and I was overwhelmed by that experience because I couldn't really imagine what light was like." Before coming back, she went on to meet some people who had preceded her in death.[68]

Dr. van Lommel reflects upon Vicki's experience:

"This is impossible according to current medical knowledge.... Vicki's reported observations could not have been the product of sensory perception or of a functioning (visual) cerebral cortex, nor could they have been a figment of the imagination given their verifiable aspects."[69]

Regarding evidence of life after death, these experiences are quite compelling in several respects. If these reports are legitimate (and the authors give sound reasons for trusting these sources), then all of the naturalistic hypotheses, whether they be psychological, physiological, or whatever, fall woefully short. Psychologically, those born blind are in no way primed for a visual experience of this nature, since they have no understanding of even light and dark, much less colors, shades of colors, textures, visual distance, etc. Physiologically, they have no visual memories to pull from. Electric stimulation to parts of the brain might bring up memories of tastes and sounds, but not visual memories.

If the blind can see in a near-death experience, they're not seeing through their physical eyes, which lie closed and useless on a hospital bed or beside a wrecked car. They're apparently seeing through the upgraded "eyes" of a spiritual body that no longer suffer the limitations of the damaged set of goods that they left behind.

Naturalists should consider the near-death experiences of the blind as a serious challenge to their worldview.

Exhibit 12 - It's extremely convincing to the one who experiences it, completely unlike a dream.

Compiling the results of five independent studies on people with near-death experiences, only 27 percent of the subjects believed in life after death before their NDE. But even twenty plus years after the NDE, after they've had plenty of time to analyze the event from every angle and attempt to explain it away, 90 percent of them reported believing in life after death. It seems that the more years they have to reflect, the more they believe in an afterlife.[70] In one study, while only 38 percent believed in life after death before their NDE, 100 percent believed after the NDE. Needless to say, this is a huge shift in a fundamental belief to be caused by a single life event.[71]

It Was Real

One of the men I interviewed was emphatic. He looked me in the eyes and said:

> "It was real – as real as me sitting across from you and talking to you now. Nothing could ever convince me otherwise."

It was such a strong, emotionally charged statement that I brought it up two more times. He knew, beyond any shadow of a doubt, that it wasn't a dream or hallucination. This intelligent, rational man was totally convinced that he'd visited the other side.

As you can imagine, people who've had NDEs have analyzed their experiences relentlessly. But they consistently rule out vivid dreams or hallucinations.

"I couldn't understand it. But it was real…. My mind wasn't at that point where I wanted to make things happen or make up anything. My mind wasn't manufacturing ideas. I just wasn't in that state of mind."[72]

"It was nothing like a hallucination. I have had hallucinations before, when I was given codeine in the hospital. But that had happened long before the accident that really killed me. And this experience was nothing like the hallucinations, nothing like them at all."[73]

Some report it as *more* real than what we experience in daily life.

- "More real than what we call reality…."[74]
- "It was so vivid and real – more so than ordinary experience."[75]

Moody notes that the experience is "incredibly vivid and real"[76] and summarizes – "It must be emphasized that a person who has been through an experience of this type has no doubt whatsoever as to its reality and its importance."[77]

As researchers note, their subjects go beyond *verbally* insisting on its reality; they make long-term life changes consistent with such an experience.

As creatures of habit, we resist change. Yet their attitudes and actions changed for the long haul. Van Lommel followed up with his NDE patients after two years and eight years and found them profoundly different from the control group that had experienced a cardiac arrest, but had no NDE.[78]

Their conviction that they truly visited the other side is also reflected in their reluctance to tell people about their experiences. It would be so easy to tell the doctor, "Wow, did I have a vivid dream while I was asleep!" But they can't say that. They feel very strongly that it was real. Naturally, they're reluctant to say, "While I was dead, I was very much alive in another realm." They're smart enough to know that their nurses and friends would likely pat them on the head and deflect the uncomfortable topic – "Well, you've been through a lot in the last few days."

The Evidential Value of "Incredibly Vivid and Real"

At first glance, I assumed that this "feeling of real" had no evidential value, except perhaps for the person who had the experience. "So they had a dream that seemed much more real than a normal dream," I reflected. "That proves nothing. If I had an extremely vivid dream, I'd be objective and skeptical enough to describe it for what it was – an extremely vivid dream. "

But the more I thought about it, the more I felt I was missing something.

First of all, my reaction shows that I assume I'm smarter and more objective than the people who had the NDEs. Yet many studies show that we, particularly men, tend to think we're smarter than average.[79] The fact is, most of us are, well, average. NDE researchers describe their subjects as intelligent and psychologically sound. I think I can therefore assume that most of them are evaluating their astounding experience in the same ways I'd be evaluating it.

This naturally leads me to believe that if I were to switch places with the people I interviewed, I'd be the one swearing that I'd seen the other side. No matter what I think now, if I were to have this experience, after it I'd likely be saying,

> "It was real - as real as me sitting across from you and talking to you now. Nothing could ever convince me otherwise."

How Do I Distinguish Reality from Dreams?

"But being *convinced* it's real doesn't mean it's real," someone may object. "Perhaps this person merely had a vivid dream."

But reflect a bit more deeply. How do you know that what you're experiencing *now* is real?

You might say, "When I'm awake, I can feel and see things in such a vivid way that when I wake up from a dream I can say, 'That was a dream and this is reality.'" Ok, but did you hear what you just said? It's the *vividness* of your conscious experience that proves to you that you're *really* reading this book instead of *dreaming* that you're reading this book.

But that's precisely what these people are saying about their out-of-body experience – it was qualitatively different from a dream. It was as real as their normal experience with reality. In fact, they often report that the NDE was "more" real than their normal experience with reality.[80]

Someone might respond, "Granted, if I ever have this experience, I'll probably believe as well. But until I experience it, I don't have enough evidence to make a decision." Please indulge me a short story to respond.[81]

A Skeptical Fellowship Examines NDEs

Let's imagine that I'm a thoroughgoing materialist (believing that immaterial things like God, souls, and minds don't exist) and enjoy nothing more than meeting once a month at a local grill with nine of my materialist friends. We're all equally skeptical of all things religious.

Early one morning Mike calls me from the hospital, having suffered a cardiac arrest. I meet him there and discover that, to his utter amazement, he experienced an NDE. Then he looks me intensely and says, with great assurance and emotion -

> "And it was *real*. I've thought long and hard about all the possible naturalistic explanations, and none of them explain away my experience. Steve, it was real – just as real as me sitting here talking to you – even MORE real. And I saw specific things happened in that operating room while I was unconscious that the doctors confirmed afterwards. I'm afraid I'm no longer a materialist."

So what would I make of that?

Being a skeptic, I'd sift through the evidence and try to follow Mike's line of argument. But of course I didn't have the "realer than real" experience. It's quite possible that in my next meeting, I'd talk it over with my buddies and conclude, "Well, obviously ole Pete wasn't as strong a materialist as we thought he was. If I'd been the one with the NDE, I'd have woken up saying, "Wow, what an experience! And it seemed so real! But I'm scientific enough to know that just because it *seemed* real doesn't mean it *was* real."

But over the ensuing years, imagine that two more of my buddies have NDEs, one during a traffic accident and another during surgery. So I tell my remaining materialists, "It's hard to believe that Mike, Pete, and Jed now believe in the afterlife! Do you suppose that if each of us had NDEs, we'd believe as well?"

"But why should we wait for our own experience?" reflects Austin. "They all thought just like we did. They were materialists. We're not likely smarter or more informed than they are. Just like us, they didn't buy into all this mind/soul/heaven stuff. Just like us, they weren't psychologically primed for an NDE; they were expecting utter nothingness after death. I think we can safely assume that if we shared their experiences, we'd all believe in the afterlife as well. So why should we hold out for our own NDE? We can predict, with the evidence already set before us, that if we had NDEs, we'd most likely believe just like our friends. So shouldn't we believe on the basis of their testimonies that they've indeed seen the other side?"

"But that approach violates everything we stand for," I might object. "We don't believe things because other people believe them. We believe them because we have adequate evidence."

"But we're not mindlessly believing simply because they believe it," replies Austin. "We're accepting their testimony, which we deem reliable, about an experience that we may never have. Since I'll likely never go to the moon, I trust the experiences of those who've been there. Apparently, many bright, trustworthy, skeptical people have been granted, prior to their final deaths, a taste of eternity. Since we may never experience an NDE, shouldn't we believe on the basis of evidence provided by multiple testimonies that we deem trustworthy?"

Back to Shangri-La

And so we return full circle to the beginning of this book, where we were investigating the existence of Shangri-La. We decided that we needed reliable testimony from people who'd been there, hopefully with some corroborating evidence in hand. That's precisely what we've found regarding the afterlife – a growing multitude of witnesses with 12 lines of corroborating evidence proclaiming consistently that life endures after death.

Summary of the Evidence

In the mid 1900s physicians obsessed on keeping dying people alive, leaving family, friends, and ministers to deal with the apparently unscientific questions regarding life after death. When NDEs occurred, patients seldom told their doctors for fear of ridicule or referral to a psychiatrist.

When Raymond Moody published his interviews and analyses in 1975, the public became fascinated and medical professionals responded with guarded disbelief.[82] How could such a significant experience be happening to their patients without their knowledge? And if it was indeed happening, surely it could be easily explained by psychological or physiological processes.

So far, such explanations have failed.

Each naturalistic explanation – anoxia, hypercarbia, expectations, wishful thinking, etc. - fell woefully short when compared with the data collected during subsequent scientific investigations.

But lack of a naturalistic explanation doesn't necessitate resorting to spiritual explanations. Instead, we can examine the data as it stands after 35 years of scientific investigation and judge which hypothesis provides the best fit for the data.

Such an examination reveals a perplexing phenomenon, the characteristics of which we'd have never predicted from naturalistic worldview. These are not characteristics that one can skim halfheartedly; rather, they demand deep reflection over time, much as the researchers contemplated their data over years of study.

- **If NDEs are caused by expectations of heaven or wishful thinking**, then why are both the religious and irreligious surprised by how the experience fails to conform to their expectations? Especially in the early studies, before NDEs were popularized, nobody was expecting an experience of leaving the body, observing resuscitation efforts, meeting deceased relatives, reviewing their lives, and discussing whether or not to return. Why don't people's NDEs differ significantly according to their differing worldviews and expectations? And why do they occur in people who weren't expecting to die?

- **If the experience happens totally within the brain**, then how can we explain corroborating evidence showing that the mind was active apart from the body – the scores of detailed descriptions of surgeries, meetings with deceased relatives that they were unaware had died, etc.? How could the brain produce a vivid (reported as more clear than normal reality) conscious experience when the brain is often, from our present scientific understanding, incapable of rational thought and memories? And how can the inner workings of the dying person's brain explain the shared NDE of others in the room, or even those unaware of the person's physical state, at a distance?

- **If NDErs are making things up or embellishing**, then what are their motives? All studies show NDErs overwhelmingly reluctant to share their experiences for fear of ridicule. What do they have to gain by telling such a tall tale to their doctors? And why are their "made-up" stories so similar, since most subjects were unaware of NDEs and there's no evidence of mass collaboration or conspiracies? Why do longitudinal studies find that years after the event, their stories remain the same in all details? And if patients are fabricating NDEs, why do such stories produce long-term life changes?

- **If the researchers are fudging their data to seek fame**, then how do they get away with publishing hundreds of articles in respected peer-reviewed journals, knowing that their methods and results are subject to intense scrutiny by skeptical peers? Each published study risks rival researchers replicating the study and showing the earlier study to be a sham. These highly successful doctors and professors put their teaching positions and reputations at risk if they publish nonsense. And how do the studies get through the peer reviewed publication process in the first place if their methods are questionable?

- **If NDEs are dreams or hallucinations,** then why are they so consistent among the thousands of NDErs who've been surveyed and studied? Dreams and hallucinations are extremely random from person to person. If NDEs were such, we'd expect a colorful array of almost infinitely varied reports, such as talking to a fish named Wanda who claims to be God, herding cattle which feed on sea scallops, etc. And why the cohesive story line rather than unrelated segments? And why would stories end with closure ("It's not your time; you must go back now.") as if the dream or vision knew ahead of time exactly when it needed to end?

- **If NDEs are purely naturalistic**, then why do the deaf report hearing, the colorblind report seeing colors, and the blind report seeing, when this goes against everything we know about the dream states and physical limitations of those born with these disabilities?

While each of the lines of evidence has weight on its own, taken together they weigh in powerfully – twelve lines of evidence that build a strong case for life after death and the existence of higher spiritual beings. A close study of NDEs has led many researchers to reject naturalism and embrace the idea that we're more than our physical bodies, with death being merely a transition to another realm. We seem to have found a "black swan" that for many overturns naturalism.

As prominent Dutch Psychiatrist Frederik van Eeden once stated,

> "All science is empirical science, all theory is subordinate to perception; a single fact can overturn an entire system."

Chapter 6
What We Learn from NDEs

"You are not a human being having a spiritual experience.
You are a spiritual being having a human experience."
- Pierre Teilhard de Chardin - French philosopher, geologist, paleontologist,
and priest who also taught physics and chemistry.

They Are Not Consistent with Every Worldview

Some may assume that while NDEs seem incompatible with naturalism,
beyond that they don't really support any one religion or worldview. "Since
they're consistent with most any form of spirituality," we may surmise, "they
have no evidential value for choosing a specific religious faith."

But if you agree that the main elements of NDEs paint a reasonably accurate
picture of life on the other side, they seem to throw doubt on several
worldviews and religious opinions. For example:

> **a. Philosophical materialists** believe all that exists can ultimately be
> explained in terms of the interactions of purely material things. NDEs
> reveal a dimension where thinking, communication, and transportation
> aren't apparently dependent on material objects.

> **b. Determinists**, whether religious or secular, believe there is no free
> will. Yet NDEs report celestial beings discussing a person's future and
> changing plans based upon a person's prayers or expressed will. The
> being of light may urge a person to "go back and do better this time,"
> which implies the ability to make conscious life choices.

c. Pantheists and Deists tend to believe in an impersonal God who created (or continues to create) the physical universe, but doesn't get involved in people's lives. Yet, NDEs reveal a personal God who both knows and cares about each of us.

What NDEs *Don't* Teach Us

We've noted that a small portion of NDEs appear to contain a mixture of fantasy and reality, which is understandable for some who've endured serious trauma and long recoveries. Thus it would seem unwise to take everyone's reported experience in minute detail and try to paint an accurate picture of the afterlife. If someone reports seeing Big Bird, I don't take this as a revelation that Big Bird exists and is waiting for me on the other side. (I am aware this may disappoint some Big Bird fans.)

For this reason, I think it's safer to focus on the NDE elements that are most commonly reported – those included in what researchers call a "remarkable convergence," which may indeed give insight to the other side.

If NDEs were all the evidence we had to go on, it would be going too far to conclude with finality that one certain religion is the true religion. After all, NDEs don't absolutely prove that there's only one God. Perhaps different people travel through different tunnels to meet different lights. Maybe the light's name is Jehovah; but then again its name could be Allah, or even Fred. Or perhaps the Light is just a way to connect with the Cosmic Mind spoken of in New Age circles.

While it appears that those who meet the being of light during an NDE are all meeting the same being (the descriptions of his personality and abilities and effects are remarkably similar), it would be going too far to say that NDEs *absolutely prove* that God is one. Rather, I'd say that they *suggest* there is one God.

What NDEs May Teach Us

Although they don't tell me all I want to know about God and the afterlife, they at least provide strong evidence that there's more to life than meets the materialist's eye. And for those who believe they provide a peek into eternity, they may yield even more insights.

While many of the NDE researchers I read don't appear to be particularly Christian, their primary findings (as I detail them below) seem remarkably consistent (though perhaps not exclusively so) with Christianity. And since van Lommel's patients in particular contained many diverse beliefs, you can hardly take the below similarities to be due to their Christian expectations.

Since Jesus Christ claimed to have come from heaven, claiming to bring his own corroborating evidence in the form of miracles, it would be relevant to know if the Bible's teachings either corroborate or contradict what people report from their NDEs.

Furthermore, those who believe that these are real brushes with eternity might aspire to live *as if they'd experienced an NDE,* since NDErs typically claim that their lives are fuller and richer as a result. Many of those who study NDEs report that their lives change as a result of their research. I believe this study has impacted my own life.[1]

Here are my comparisons. Each point begins with an observation by an NDEr or researcher, followed by a related passage from the Bible.

About The Being of Light

Questions regarding the existence and character of God have occupied not only philosophers and religious scholars for millennia, but also average folks who wonder and fret about eternal matters. What are NDErs telling us about God?

a. God exists.

According to van Lommel, "During an NDE, the encounter with 'the light' is felt to be the most intense and most essential part of the experience."[2]

Moody calls it "the most incredible common element" of the experience, "which has the most profound effect upon the individual." No matter what the person's religious (or nonreligious) background, "not one person has expressed any doubt whatsoever that it was a being, a being of light."[3]

While it's theoretically possible that each person is seeing a *different* being of light, they seem to describe the same personality and attributes, leading us to believe there's *one* being at the end of the tunnel rather than a pantheon of competing gods. Nobody that I read claimed to meet multiple gods.

"In the beginning, God...." (Genesis 1:1)

b. God is love.

"This encounter [with the light] is always accompanied by an overwhelming sense of unconditional love and acceptance."[4]

"God is love." (I John 4:8)

c. God knows us intimately.

"It is often obvious that the being can see the individual's whole life...."[5]

"Indeed, the very hairs of your head are all numbered." (Luke 12:7)

d. God is personal.

"…it is a personal being. It has a very definite personality."[6]

"The LORD, the LORD God, compassionate and gracious, slow to anger, and abounding in lovingkindness and truth…." (Exodus 34:6)

e. There's an attractiveness to God.

"The love and the warmth which emanate from this being to the dying person are utterly beyond words, and he feels completely surrounded by it and taken up in it, completely at ease and accepted in the presence of this being. He senses an irresistible magnetic attraction to this light. He is ineluctably drawn to it." This description is "utterly invariable."[7]

"Whom have I in heaven but Thee? And besides Thee I desire nothing on earth. My flesh and my heart may fail; but God is the strength of my heart and my portion forever." (Psalm 73:25,26)

f. God is just.

It's instructive that nobody I read of comes back to life saying, "I got so infuriated at God - He was so *wrong* in his evaluations of things!" Rather, they seem convinced that He's right in His ways.

"It was clear to me why I'd had cancer. Why I had come into this world in the first place. What role each of my family members played in my life, where we all were within the grand scheme of things, and in general what life is all about."[8]

This reminds me of C.S. Lewis' statement that he believed one of his first exclamations, upon meeting God in heaven, would be "Of course!" Because at that time he'd presumably understand the answers to all the questions he had on earth.

"...all his ways are just...." (Daniel 4:37)

g. God is associated with light.

"The light...was of a kind that I'd never seen before and that differs from any other kind such as sunlight."[9]

"There will be no more night. They will not need the light of a lamp or the light of the sun, for the Lord God will give them light." (Revelation 22:5)

About What Really Matters

According to atheist Susan Blackmore, there is no ultimate purpose in life. And if life is pointless, we're pointless as well; as Blackmore puts it, we're "eminently dispensable."[10] But what if Blackmore is wrong? What if we were put here for a purpose? Wouldn't we want to discover that purpose?

I want to know what's important in life – what counts in the final analysis. What if being kind to my younger brother is more important than winning a book award? What if helping struggling students is sometimes more important than achieving all A's? What if being kind to a waitress is more important than developing six-pack abs? Here's what NDErs report about what really matters in life.

h. Your life choices matter to God.

"...[during the panoramic life review] people understand how they lived their life and how this affected others. They realize that every single thought, word, or action has a lasting effect on themselves and others."[11]

"...so that each one may be recompensed for his deeds in the body, according to what he has done, whether good or bad." (II Corinthians 5:10)

i. Material things are temporary and not worth obsessing over.

"…some aspects of life become important while others become completely irrelevant. After an NDE, people only want to spend time and energy on things of lasting value. Almost all ephemeral and material things, such as a lot of money, a big house, or an expensive car, become less important."[12]

"Do not lay up for yourselves treasures upon earth, where moth and rust destroy, and where thieves break in and steal…." (Matthew 6:24)

j. It's important, in fact a huge part of why we're here, to love people.

"As they witness the display [life review], the being seems to stress the importance of two things in life: Learning to love other people and acquiring knowledge."[13]

"And if I…do not have love, I am nothing." (I Corinthians 13:2)

k. It's important to love God.

"Lovest thou me?" (Question from the light during an NDE)[14]

"You shall love the LORD your God…." (Matthew 22:37)

l. Prioritize those closest to you – family and neighbors.

"…other differences [outcomes] pertained to a greater involvement with family."[15]

Pastor Steve Sjogren (*The Day I Died*) returned from the other side with the strong impression that although he had accomplished a lot of ministry outside his family, he had done some of it at the expense of those closest to him - his family and neighbors and friends. "Right there in the ICU ward, I realized that I didn't know the names of any of my children's friends!"[16]

"Husbands, love your wives...." (Ephesians 5:25)

"You shall love your neighbor as yourself. " (Matthew 22:39)

m. Seeking knowledge is very important.

"...many others have emphasized the importance of seeking knowledge."[17]

"She [wisdom/knowledge] is more precious than jewels; and nothing you desire compares with her." (Proverbs 3:15)

n. Requests, desires and prayers seem to be taken into account.

When people ask a celestial being for permission to return to earthly life to complete a worthy task, the being may grant the request, as if the person's desires and asking are taken into account. Other times the prayers of those still on earth seem to be taken into account. The response is consistent with both free will and the efficacy of prayer.[18]

"The prayer of a righteous person is powerful and effective." (James 5:16)

o. Don't lust for power.

"...their interest in possessions and power had decreased."[19]

"The greatest among you will be your servant. For those who exalt themselves will be humbled, and those who humble themselves will be exalted." (Matthew 23:11,12)

p. Be a decent person. Forgive. Tell the truth. Don't be aggressive. Give to charities.

After experiencing NDEs, people become "more forgiving, more tolerant, and less critical of others…more compassionate and caring." They are "more likely to donate to charities or to dedicate themselves to a social cause." They have a "greater sense of justice" and are motivated to "tell the truth…."[20]

"Command them to do good, to be rich in good deeds, and to be generous and willing to share." (I Timothy 6:18)

"Forgive, and you will be forgiven." (Luke 6:37)

"…speak truthfully to your neighbor…." (Ephesians 4:25)

q. Don't be consumed with cultural norms.

Those with NDEs were less likely to focus on social norms such as "keeping up appearances."[21]

"And do not be conformed to this world…." (Romans 12:2)

r. Appreciate ordinary things.

Eight years following an NDE, 84 percent of van Lommel's subjects report being more appreciative of ordinary things.[22]

"And be thankful." (Colossians 3:15)

About Aspects of the Afterlife

The longer I live, the shorter my earthly life appears. My youngest children are seniors in high school. Wasn't it just yesterday when we carried those tiny twins around in backpacks? Truly, life is merely a vapor when compared to eternity. Although a *near* death experience may not be in all ways equal to a *final* death experience, it seems reasonable that the NDE tells us something about what to expect after our final deaths. After all, the deceased relatives and friends encountered on the other side have often been there for years.

s. Death isn't the end of life.

"...dead turned out to be not dead."[23]

"...he will receive...in the age to come, eternal life." (Mark 10:30)

t. Time is different.

"And if anything was missing it was our earthly conception of time!"[24]

"...with the Lord one day is like a thousand years, and a thousand years like one day." (II Peter 3:8)

u. We will have spiritual bodies, which are different from and superior to our physical bodies.

"So, to adopt a term for it [the new form in which they find themselves] which will sum up its properties fairly well...I shall henceforth call it the 'spiritual body.'" – Raymond Moody.[25]

"...it is sown a natural body, it is raised a spiritual body." (I Corinthians 15:44)

v. The mind can exist apart from the body. It's the mind that's truly us, that's eternal. The earthly body is merely an earth suit.

> "I suddenly became aware of hovering over the foot of the operating table and watching the activity down below around the body of a human being. Soon it dawned on me that this was my own body."[26]

> "…prefer rather to be absent from the body and to be at home with the Lord." (II Corinthians 5:8)

w. We know and understand things much more clearly on the other side.

> "The knowledge and messages going through me were so clear and pure."[27]

> "For now we see in a mirror dimly, but then face to face; now I know in part, but then I shall know fully just as I also have been fully known." (I Corinthians 13:12)

x. There are intermediaries between God and people.

> People I interviewed reported talking to angelic or celestial beings. This is pretty common. Somehow they're identified as distinct from deceased people.

> "Are not all angels ministering spirits sent to serve those who will inherit salvation?" (Hebrews 1:14)

y. The other side isn't rosy for everyone.

> Moody[28], van Lommel[29], and subsequent researchers[30] note briefly that some near-death experiences are hellish or distressing. Just remember, this is halftime, not the end of the

fourth quarter, so NDEs may not take place in a person's final resting place. Perhaps it's a warning. Some consider distressing NDEs more of a vivid dream than reality, since there may not be as much consistency between hellish experiences as there are with positive experiences. Yet, they do seem to have the vividness and convincing nature of an NDE.[31]

"Outside the city [the holy city, the New Jerusalem established after Armageddon and the judgment] are the evil people...." (Revelation 22:15, NCB)

z. Heaven is a place you want to go.

Van Lommel introduces his book with an account of the cardiac arrest of a patient during his first year of cardiac training where he served as attendant physician. An alarm sounded on the cardiac wing. The patient flat lined. The medical team exploded into action with CPR, a defibrillator shock to the chest, IV drip, and a second shock. When the patient finally resuscitated, everyone in the room felt happy and relieved...with the exception of one.

The patient.

He was extremely disappointed to find himself back in his second rate body, having just experienced the music and beauty and pain-free existence on the other side.[32]

The heavenly experience is so wonderful that it's beyond words, reminding me of the heavenly vision of Revelation 21:4, where God "shall wipe away every tear from their eyes; and there shall no longer be any death; there shall no longer be any mourning, or crying, or pain; the first things have passed away." (Rev. 21:4)

And as little Colton concluded, there's strong evidence to believe that it's more than a fantasy; it's "for real."

Conclusion

For Dr. van Lommel, Dr. Rawlings, Dr. Moody, Dr. Sabom, and a host of others, a close examination of NDEs compelled them to believe that death isn't the end of life. With the state of research today, even if NDEs were my only evidence, I'd choose theism over atheism, survival over extinction. This fascinating field provides remarkable evidence for both life after death and the existence of a loving, brilliant Being who knows us intimately. To me, NDEs are remarkably consistent with a theistic worldview, woefully inconsistent with an atheistic worldview. (For a more thorough discussion of some of the most important points, read my appendixes.)

Unless future research overturns the results of the present research, we have strong evidence to support both life after death and the existence of a personal God.[33]

But there's more evidence for the supernatural beyond near-death experiences. Fifteen further lines of evidence converge to convince me that God exists and that He's worth serving. I'll discuss those further lines of evidence in a future book.

Pause to Reflect

Respected educator Howard Hendricks once said that some people need to read less and reflect more. We often lose the impact of a book when we begin the next one without reflecting adequately upon the last one.

I recommend taking a few moments to ponder what you believe about NDEs. These questions may help:

1. Do you think NDEs provide compelling evidence for life after death?

2. What are the strongest arguments pro and con?

3. If someone told you that NDEs could be adequately explained as purely natural events, how would you respond?

4. What would you like to study further about NDEs? (See Appendix #9, "Guide to Further Research.")

5. If someone asks you tomorrow what you believe about NDEs, how would you respond in a two-minute "elevator speech"?

6. If you had an NDE, in what ways might your priorities change?

7. Knowing what others claimed to experience on the other side, in what ways could this impact your priorities?

Appendix 1
Do NDEs Differ Across Cultures?

The Pattern

I'm following the Sci-Fi series "Fringe" with my kids. In the opening episode, a passenger jet lands with every passenger dead. As the FBI investigates, they find that this isn't an isolated, anomalous event. Related events have been reported around the globe, referred to by other investigators as "The Pattern." This pattern indicated a common cause – perhaps natural but more likely by design.

One of the most intriguing, unexpected attributes of NDEs is their pattern – the remarkable consistency of elements, where no such consistency would be expected. Studying philosophy at the University of Virginia, young Raymond Moody read Plato's *Republic*, which contained Socrates' story of the soldier Er, who apparently died on the battlefield, but a few days later sat up and described a remarkable visit to a heavenly realm.[1]

Later, Moody heard Psychiatrist George Ritchie's similar report of the other side after being pronounced dead. To Moody, Ritchie was a modern-day Er.

> "As far as I knew, George Ritchie was the only living person to have gone through such an experience. I didn't make the inference that there must be more people like Ritchie...."[2]

But a few years later, as Moody began teaching philosophy and collecting such stories, he noticed that "a pattern was beginning to emerge...."[3]

Ah, "The Pattern."

The Pattern in the Western World

Moody found common elements – leaving the body, meeting dead relatives, tunnels, a light, beauty, love, etc. Why the common elements if they were random hallucinations of a dying brain?

Now it's important to note that "pattern" in this context doesn't mean "carbon copy," even when we look at NDEs solely within American culture. Each NDE comes wrapped in an individualized package. Some report only a brief separation from their bodies. Some have a tunnel experience; others don't.

The sides of the tunnel may be the deepest black or textured or various colors. Deceased relatives may be old, young, or in their prime. Celestial beings may appear as bright lights, as clothed bodies with lights for faces, or as relatively normal people. They may speak the language of the experiencer, or communicate wordlessly – mind to mind.

Why the differences, even within the same culture? Surely it's relevant that the world described by NDErs is consistently nonphysical. Outside of their bodies, people seem to consist of something more akin to energy than cells. This could explain why, when one NDEr expressed surprise that her deceased relative looked so old, the relative explained that she could appear however she wanted and immediately changed to a younger look.[4]

Thus, *perhaps there is no tunnel* – at least as a physical entity – merely the *appearance* of a tunnel to communicate to the NDEr that she's travelling to another dimension. Another NDEr may experience a rapid ascent through space seeing stars retreating in the distance, but no tunnel. Another may experience an escalator, giving the same visual effect of moving to another world.

What would we expect to see people wearing on the other side – a place where clothes may serve no practical purpose for a spiritual body? (Will we need a winter wardrobe in heaven?) Perhaps a visual experience including clothes is more for the observer than the "wearer." With this insight, would you imagine that Socrates' Er more likely saw celestial people dressed in a) ancient Greek attire, b) pure light/energy c) 21st century South Korean business/casual or d) whatever was popular in heaven at the time? I'd respond, whichever would have been more meaningful to Er – probably a) or b).

If I'm on track here, then the pattern we'd expect from NDEs would differ from the pattern we'd expect from Shangri-La. If Shangri-La visitors reported a bridge over a large canyon as the only entrance to Shangri-La, we'd expect every visitor to describe the same bridge. It was either metal or wood, an arch bridge or suspension bridge, painted a certain color or left unpainted. But the pattern we'd expect from a visit to a nonphysical world might consistently include an entryway, although it might be described in a variety of ways.

Thus, I'd recommend, before studying nonwestern NDEs, to read scores of entire *Western* NDEs (such as on the NDERF site), in order to see both the pattern and the diversity within the pattern.

Moody was amazed that NDErs consistently reported leaving their bodies, meeting deceased relatives, going through tunnels, following a light, reviewing their lives, being sent back, etc. The pattern held, regardless of expectations, prior religious beliefs, age, or type of medical event. Yet all his subjects lived in America. Would the pattern be found in other cultures as well?

Van Lommel found the same pattern in Holland, which differed from American culture in many respects, not the least of which was that the majority didn't believe in life after death. But although Dutch culture differs from American culture, it's still Western culture, significantly influenced by Christianity. Would the pattern hold in nonwestern cultures, with vastly different traditions, religions, and cultural symbols deeply embedded in their psyches?

The Pattern in Nonwestern Cultures

Since many of the aspects of the pattern (type of clothes, type of tunnel, etc.) may vary to accommodate different people within a culture, then we'd expect certain aspects to differ between cultures as well, since individuals interpret data through their own cultural grids. This is indeed what some researchers have found.

A great article summarizing NDE studies in various cultures is Chapter 7 of *The Handbook of Near-Death Experiences*. Here are some NDE distinctives reported from nonwestern cultures.[5]

- In a study of 45 NDEs in India, not one reported a tunnel. Tunnels were also rarely, if ever, reported in Thailand.
- Again in India, life reviews tend to consist of a person reading the review to them, rather than experiencing it as a visual experience.
- In Thailand, the review tends to consist of one particular incident in life, rather than covering the entire life.
- An NDEr may refer to the light by the name of the ultimate God as known in their culture.
- The other realm may have characteristics of the buildings and landscapes they're familiar with.

Studies such as this, which attempt to lay out only the differences, rather than laying out each NDE in its entirety, often left me with the impression that nonwestern NDEs may differ significantly from American NDEs. I wanted to read full accounts and compare. When viewing full western NDEs side-by-side with full nonwestern NDEs, would the basic pattern still hold?

I needed to dig deeper.

[Note: Much more NDE study needs to be done in nonwestern cultures. Many of the nonwestern studies are so small that it's difficult to draw conclusions. (E.g., only four cases were published in Guam.) Also, if the interviewer fails to ask certain questions, the NDErs may not think that an element is important to report. I saw indications of this in my reading of global NDEs from the NDERF site. In the initial description of the event, an NDEr may not mention a tunnel. But when asked about a tunnel, he may mention it. This tendency could have skewed the results of earlier studies.]

Method: I examined nonwestern NDEs from Dr. Long's NDERF site, since people from many countries answered the same set of extensive questions. For the purposes of this study, I excluded all NDEs from countries dominated by Western European and American influence, especially those with an overwhelming Christian influence. If a person lived in a predominantly non-Christian country, I still excluded their report if they indicated being a Christian. I was looking for nonwestern, non-Christian reports of NDEs. Perusing over 3,000 NDEs, I found 58 meeting my criteria.

Distribution: Twelve different countries, with India having 26 NDEs, by far the largest number. Saudi Arabia had six, Egypt five, Turkey three, with the rest of the countries having two or one – Iran, Russia, Korea, Tunisia, Libya, Uzbekistan, Iraq, Singapore, China.)

Comparing the above suggested cultural differences with my findings:

- Although an earlier study found no tunnels in the Indian experience, 11 out of 26 (42 percent) of the Indian experiences I read included tunnels, which interestingly is a *higher* percentage than the 34 percent Dr. Long reported for his global (including western and nonwestern) sampling.[6] Again, perhaps the earlier study didn't ask specifically if they experienced a tunnel and NDErs didn't consider it important.

- In my nonwestern sample, I saw no significant difference in life reviews compared to western life reviews. All that I read were visual, one being described as a "movie of myself and of my entire life," another as a "panoramic review of my life," another "like a powerpoint" presentation.

- An Indian reported a person with a beard, looking through books to see if the NDEr was to remain or to be sent back. This was consistent with religious Indian traditions, so that it was meaningful to the NDEr. I'd not seen this in Western NDEs, but it wasn't inconsistent with (contradictory to) the variety of ways people were sent back in the West. The bulk of my nonwestern sample (including others from India) was sent back in the way most westerners report being sent back – a relative or celestial light indicate that it's not their time – or they remember that their family on earth still needs them.[8]

But even if future research confirms the earlier nonwestern studies rather than mine, the differences they're seeing don't appear to me to be at all disruptive to the pattern. A difference in the type of life review or the type of entrance to the other side (tunnel vs. no tunnel) would seem to leave the pattern intact, especially when we consider the apparent nonmaterial nature of the other side.

So, does the pattern break down across cultures?

Not in my opinion. As in western NDEs, some experienced only a few of the elements, while others reported a much deeper experience. But I found all the common western elements in the nonwestern experience: leaving the body, heightened senses, positive emotions, stating that it was definitely real, a tunnel experience, seeing a light, meeting deceased relatives, talking to celestial beings, altered time and space, life review, a beautiful heavenly realm, special knowledge, coming to a barrier, returning to the body, changed lives, and the overwhelming priority of love.

The Priority of Love

Let's reflect upon that last characteristic of the pattern – the encounter with life-changing love. I was amazed that even those who experienced only a brief NDE were typically motivated to change their lives – specifically to love, serve, and help people.

But why this consistency?

Individuals, families, and cultures exhibit a widely diverse view of life priorities. Many children grow up with daily exhortations to do better at school – academic success consumes their lives and report cards judge how they're doing in life. Others live to get ahead and make something (materially and socially) of their lives. Others are taught, by example and word, that we must often run over others to get ahead. After all, it's just survival of the fittest. Right?

Love is not consistently pushed as THE main thing in life in every family and every culture. So if NDEs were merely hallucinations of dying brains, informed by our own very diverse values, why doesn't the hedonist come back saying, "I've got only one brief life to live. I need to start my bucket list of exciting things to do before I die!" Why doesn't the high achiever come back saying, "I learned that I should take school more seriously, bringing my B's up to A's." Aren't those the values that many instill in their children, both by their example and their words? When we drop our kids off at school, aren't we more likely to say "Work hard at bringing that math grade up!" rather than "Be empathetic to hurting students and overworked teachers; they may need some encouragement today."?

If NDEs merely preach back to us our own values, why do so many NDErs indicate that this experience with love represented a *change* in life direction for them? Apparently, compassionate attention to family and acquaintances wasn't a former priority.

Why then the consistent, overwhelming pattern of love as being what really matters, whether the NDEr is a child or adult, a defensive tackle or a mother of small children, a pastor or a Marxist, a connoisseur of recreational drugs or an academic high achiever?

To me, this consistent pattern of "compassionate service is what it's all about" is more consistent with NDEs being very real encounters with spiritual reality than a naturalistic creation of dying brains. As a formerly agnostic physician from India put it, "…I was skeptical of religion or anything that could not be called strictly scientific." Yet, he reflected that his NDE couldn't "be explained in normal objective terms. I underwent a positive personality change. All my arrogance vanished."[9]

The Pattern of Love

Here's how some NDErs around the world put the outcome of their experience in their own words (note – I quote them exactly, although for most of them English is a second language).

Chen from China

Background: "I believed in Marxism. I joined the Chinese Communist Party when I was in university and I had a great ambition when I was employed. I deeply believe[d] in materialism and I strongly rejected anything that relate to idealism. Neither did I believe in God. However I experienced an NDE and it has changed me completely."[10]

Impact: "After the NDE... I started to concern about the suffering in the world. I comfort others who is in despair ... I filled my life with love and I loved to help others. I don't care about money or fame anymore."

Victor from Russia

Background: No religious background. Formerly plagued with depression, particularly about difficulties completing college. "I simply didn't see the point of my own existence."

NDE: "The light was extraordinary. In it were love and peace. I was completely enveloped by love and I felt totally secure."

Impact: "Some invisible force had opened up new paths along which I must travel, something to strive for, that my life was not in vain, and that I should have goals that fill the needs of those around me as well as my own, and that every day should be filled with good and meaningful activities."[11]

Hazeliene from Singapore

The NDE: "Someone spoken to me for a while, I heard and that voice came from that light. You know what I felt when I saw that light? When I saw that bright light, I felt that someone loves me very much (but no idea who it was) I was very overwhelmed with that bright light. And while I was there, I felt the love and that love I never felt before. That light welcoming me very warmly and loves me very much. My words to the light before I woke up was this: I wanted to stay here, but I love my two kids."

"Reason why I felt very overwhelmed? I felt that only that light ever love me and no one does. All people knows only to beat me, hurt me, criticized me, offended me, and many more. Nobody love me like that kind of love before."

Impact: "As a single mother/parent I have to love my children unconditionally. My mission is to raise them up in a proper manner and help poor people."[12]

Suresh from India

Impact: "I realized that god was love, light and motion and to be able to receive him in the heart one had to cleanse it and mind by apologizing to all people I was associated with and with whom I had differences, arguments or quarrels or all those whom I might have knowingly or unknowingly caused pain. The kind of love that I experienced there cannot be expressed in words."

Gülden from Turkey

Impact: "I meet people with more joy. I hardly get angry. My daily life is full of love and peaceful. I feel pleasure by helping to strangers."[13]

Muhammad from Egypt

Impact: "I felt that love is the one thing that all humans must feel towards each other, only then we would be happy."[14]

Conclusion

There *is* a pattern – a distinct pattern that permeates NDEs around the world. While it may come in a culturally meaningful package, no matter what their former religious beliefs, priorities in life, level of education, personalities, or family backgrounds, they report leaving their bodies and travelling to another dimension where time and space somehow vanish. Once separated from the body, their minds experience consciousness on steroids – communicating directly and effortlessly – their sight unencumbered by the limitations of eyes, their hearing unencumbered by the limitations of ears. They talk to deceased relatives, experience strong emotions, and commune with a loving being of light. They review their lives and decide that compassion to their fellow life travelers is what really matters.

And they swear it wasn't a dream. It was real.

Thus the pattern holds. The source of this pattern may point to the very meaning of life and the purpose of our existence.

Appendix 2
Two Recent Articles Proclaim That
Science Has Explained NDEs' Paranormal Features

A recent article in *Scientific American* announced dramatically, in its subtitle: *Near-Death Experiences Now Found to Have Scientific Explanations.*[1] It's based almost entirely upon a more scholarly *Trends in Cognitive Sciences* article titled: "There is nothing paranormal about near-death experiences," by Dean Mobbs and Caroline Watt.[2]

These articles claim that since elements of NDEs can be produced in ways other than coming near death, that there's no need to suggest that God and heaven have anything to do with them. Although I deal with naturalistic arguments in Chapter 4, I felt that a more specific response to these articles was warranted since they received widespread popular coverage by outlets including NPR, BBC, Discovery, and Discovery News, as well as significant international coverage.[3]

I'll concentrate on the *Trends in Cognitive Sciences* article, since it's the source of the other article and includes the scholarly documentation.

Evaluation

1. It unfairly implies that NDE researchers ignore discussions of naturalistic arguments. "This [Moody's *Life after Life*] and other bestseller books have largely omitted discussion of any physiological basis for these experiences, and instead appear to prefer paranormal explanations over and above scientific enlightenment." That may be true of certain popular books, but all the respected NDE researchers I've read are well aware of these arguments and have dealt with them extensively.

Moody actually devoted a significant section of *Life after Life* to examining and ruling out many of the same explanations that keep getting published as if they're new, including pharmacological, physiological, neurological, and psychological explanations – some of the very same explanations forwarded in this article.[4] These explanations have been extensively tested and discussed, with summary articles and literature reviews pulling together the results of decades of research. Chris Carter devotes 66 pages to examining research on naturalistic arguments,[5] van Lommel 30 pages,[6] Penny Sartori 63 pages.[7] Greyson, Kelly, and Kelly wrote a 21 page literature review of these explanations.[8] It's significant that all of these reviews of the research concluded that naturalistic explanations were inadequate.

2. It fails to take into account relevant data from peer-reviewed NDE studies. If an article in a scholarly journal isn't presenting its own fresh research, we assume that it's tying together the relevant research from past studies. Thus, if Mobbs and Watt want to stand for "scientific enlightenment," why did they ignore the large body of scientific research that contradicts their thesis? Why did they fail to mention even one of the many review chapters and articles that sum up the current state of research?

In an interview, co-author Watt gave this explanation:

> There's a category of articles in that journal called Forum: Science & Society. These articles are deliberately designed to be provoking of debate. The whole idea of this group of articles…is not to claim that you're making some comprehensive review. It's not to produce any new evidence for testing a theory, for example. It's a bit like an opinion piece, like an editorial in a newspaper, where you make an argument that is intended to stimulate discussion or provoke debate.[9]

Unfortunately, the article itself never states this. Thus, readers worldwide read it as a serious attempt to sum up the scientific research on the subject, not an opinion piece to provoke controversy.[10]

2. It states, "a handful of scientific studies of near-death experiences do exist." Actually, over the past few decades, over 55 researchers or teams have published over 65 studies of over 3500 NDEs.[11]

3. It misquotes van Lommel's study, attributing to him a case that indicated the NDE was happening during REM sleep. Van Lommel never described such an event. In fact, van Lommel states that his research indicated that REM sleep "could not account for their life reviews," since their brains were not functional enough to produce consciousness.[12]

4. The title of the *Scientific American* article sensationally claims to provide significant new information: "Near-Death Experiences Now Found to Have Scientific Explanations." Yet, it presents primarily the same worn-out hypotheses that have been tested repeatedly (and found wanting). Watt's view of the original article? "The content of the article itself is not saying anything new."[13]

(Since I responded to naturalistic hypotheses in Chapter 4, I'll forego responding to each explanation offered by Mobbs and Watt.)[14]

5. The article states, "*A priori* expectations, where the individual makes sense of the situation by believing they will experience the archetypal near-death experience package, may also play a crucial role," citing only Blackmore's book, *Dying to Live*, but no specific pages. I don't recall Blackmore ever arguing this. In fact, in *Dying to Live* she approvingly quotes a review of NDE literature that concludes that a person's "religious background did not influence the chances of having an NDE."[15]

Concerning the *kind* of NDE a person has, Blackmore states, "Once again, demographic variables appear not to be particularly important…Other irrelevant variables seem to be strength of religious beliefs, *previous knowledge of NDEs* [emphasis mine]…."[16] Besides, how could prior expectations have accounted for the NDEs Moody studied, before virtually anyone was aware of the common elements of NDEs?

6. It ignores the positive evidence we've forwarded in Chapter 5. Although the article claimed to prove that "*There is nothing paranormal about near-death experiences,*" the elements it attempted to explain don't include the deaf hearing, the blind seeing, corroborated veridical perception, etc. Mobbs and Watt don't even acknowledge this data. Until those aspects can be explained naturalistically, the argument fails to disprove paranormal activity.[17]

As Dr. Bruce Greyson, professor of Psychiatry & Neurobehavioral Sciences at the University of Virginia observed:

"If you ignore everything paranormal about NDEs, then it's easy to conclude, there's nothing paranormal about them."[18]

So why the misleading title? Co-author Watt explains, "…the editor requested that we change the title to something which is much more bold and deliberately making a statement that would provoke a reaction. … However, I believe it's an over-statement."[19]

And the overstatement worked. It apparently went worldwide, assuring people that science had finally explained NDEs as a completely natural phenomenon. Yet, it never even dealt with the most relevant data.

I'll conclude by reflecting upon one of the article's sensational statements. Here's the original:

> "This and other bestseller books have largely omitted discussion of any physiological basis for these experiences, and instead appear to prefer paranormal explanations over and above scientific enlightenment."

Having immersed myself for some time in the scholarly NDE literature, I think the statement could be reworded to reflect my thoughts on the Mobbs and Watt article:

> "This article omits any significant discussion of the large body of scientific literature on near-death experiences, and instead appears to prefer highly speculative and often disproven naturalistic explanations over and above scientific enlightenment."[20]

Appendix 3
Interviewing Circles of Trust
Tips and Observations from My Original Research

I shared the results of my original research in the body and endnotes. But perhaps my most important takeaway was that fellow skeptics can often get closer to the evidence by conducting their own interviews. NDE accounts lurk everywhere – in our neighborhoods, at work, within our circles of trusted friends and relatives. Anyone who's gained the trust of a significant group of people should be able to study many reports first-hand. Below, under Strategy #1, I give suggestions for conducting such personal interviews.

Strategy #2 is useful for filling in details that we don't find in other research. Since thousands of people have contributed their NDEs to Dr. Long's site, we can tabulate, for example, what percentage of NDErs report colors in their tunnels.

Strategy #3 is valuable for exploring death-bed visions and shared death experiences, since hospice workers deal with the dying and their families on a daily basis.

Strategy 1: Interviewing Circles of Trust

As we will discuss in Appendix #4, personal testimonies differ in their evidential value according to several factors, one being our degree of trust. Revisiting our imaginary investigation of Shangri-La, we should be more inclined to believe reports of a faraway land from trusted relatives and friends than the reports of strangers.

No wonder Dr. Sabom remarked, upon first hearing about Moody's interviews, "I don't believe it." After all, Sabom didn't know Moody personally. Neither did he know the NDErs Moody interviewed. Besides, none of Sabom's patients had ever told him of such an astounding experience. But when Sabom took the challenge to interview his own patients, he was shocked to find that many had experienced NDEs. Personally interviewing his own patients over a period of time made a believer out of him.

But why should I trust Sabom? Granted, he worked with a team of professionals in respected hospitals and published in peer-reviewed journals; so there's some accountability there. Further, I can be reasonably sure that he didn't cherry pick the experiences that fit Moody's descriptions. After all, he denied doing this, and if he did cherry pick, his medical peers could always try to replicate his findings. It's risky to fudge research in peer-reviewed journals, especially if you teach at a well-respected institution such as Emory Medical School.

But still, I don't know Sabom or his patients personally. The evidential value of testimonies increases to the degree that I trust the testifier. Thus, it seems to me that the problem of remoteness can be solved by interviewing our own set of trusted NDErs. Here's how I went about finding them, and how others with trusting relationships can do the same.

Finding NDErs You Can Trust

First, tell your friends and relatives (those with sound minds and trustworthy character) that you're studying paranormal experiences and are looking for trustworthy accounts. Ask if they've had any experiences such as visions or hearing from God or knowing about a friend's death before you got official word or leaving their bodies during a medical crisis. Casting a wide net for any paranormal experience guards you from cherry picking only experiences that conform to Moody's elements.

Second, ask if they know friends or relatives (their trusted circles) who've had such experiences.

Most of the people I asked either had such an experience or knew of one experienced by someone they trusted.

Conducting Interviews

Interview the people personally, explaining to them up front that you won't publish their names. This makes them more likely to open up about an experience they may be reluctant to share. Also, it keeps attention-seekers from making stuff up in order to get famous.

First, let them share the experience in full without interrupting, since you don't want to influence the story in any way. After they finish this initial telling, there's probably much more to be harvested. As we've seen, people typically have vivid memories of their NDEs and can reflect back to fill in interesting details.

Here are some follow-up questions:

- Were your alertness and consciousness about normal, less than normal, or better than normal? Can you describe it?
- Were your vision and hearing worse than normal, better than normal, or about normal? Can you describe it?
- Describe your emotions during the experience.
- Did you experience a tunnel or light?
- Did time speed up or slow down?
- Did it cut off in the middle of something, or have closure?
- Is your memory of the event normal or better than your normal memory?
- Did it change your life in any way?
- Have you had other similar experiences?
- Do you believe it was real, or just a vivid dream?

Conclusions

1. My personal interviews verified that the experiences reported by researchers have the same elements as those reported in my circles of trust.

2. Personal interviews can be compelling. Attention to facial expressions and inflections of voice underscore their authenticity. The ones I interviewed truly believe they've visited the other side.

3. The experience is indeed widespread. Most of my friends and relatives either had such an experience or knew someone they trusted who'd had one. I easily found a dozen NDEs and deathbed visions by asking about 15 of my friends and relatives. Since I have a wide circle of friends and acquaintances that trust me, this approach may be more fruitful approach for me than a person who has few close relationships.

4. More than one person that I interviewed shared corroborating evidence, such as Bucky's shared NDE in the middle of the night, at the precise time that his father died hundreds of miles away. This report requires trust on the part of you the reader, since you probably don't know me or my relatives or me personally; but for me, knowing Bucky and others who can corroborate the timing, this provides unique evidence that NDEs are truly brushes with a reality outside our brains. This underscores the evidential value of interviewing within your circles of trust.

Strategy 2: Utilizing Dr. Long's NDERF Site

Thousands of NDErs share their experiences on this site. I discussed earlier the strengths and weaknesses of this approach, but it does give anyone free access to a large number of complete reports to use for research.

First, I wanted to examine NDEs to see if they consistently exhibit closure rather than being cut off abruptly. To study this, I started with the most recent report and worked my way consecutively backwards (to avoid cherry picking reports that supported my hypothesis) through 50 reports. [Case #3089 (7/21/12) through Case #3139 (9/9/12). I threw out one report, although it wasn't inconsistent with my hypothesis, because it mentioned the title of a book she'd written. This gave her an ulterior motive for possible embellishment. Otherwise, since the reports don't include full names, attention seekers would find little satisfaction in writing fictional experiences and answering the long list of questions.]

The results:

- I found no NDEs reporting abrupt endings.
- Twenty-seven ended with definite closure, typically either following a discussion about their need to return, or the people somehow knew that they should return instead of passing a barrier.
- Twenty-three simply returned at the end of the experience. Nothing was interrupted, but neither was there a decision to return.

Second, I wanted to see if a pattern held for both western and nonwestern NDEs. To accomplish this, I consulted the summaries of over 3,000 NDEs and copied each NDE in its entirety if it came from nonwestern culture and wasn't strongly influenced by Christianity. I found 56 of them from 12 different countries. I collected them in a file and studied them, concluding that the pattern did indeed hold, as I discussed more thoroughly in Appendix #1.

Third, I wanted to see if reports cited by Keith Augustine of mythological creatures and people who were still alive on earth represented a significant percentage. I found no such reports in the 100+ cases (50 global and 56 nonwestern) I examined. Thus, I attribute such reports to such possibilities as a) hallucinations that mimic certain characteristics of NDEs b) hallucinations that become confused with NDEs through subjects coming in and out of consciousness multiple times c) errors or fabrications in reporting or d) delusional individuals.

Strategy 3: Interview Long-Term Hospice Nurses

After reading Moody's book on shared NDEs and finding one in my own circles of trust, I wanted to see if I could find more shared death experiences, since they offer enhanced evidence by including multiple eye-witnesses. I haven't completed this survey but will update the manuscript after conducting it and compiling the data, if I find anything of significance. Do you know some hospice nurses? Perhaps you could pursue this!

Appendix 4
But is the Evidence Scientific?

Moody's NDE studies convinced him that NDErs leave their bodies and experience life in another dimension. Thus, I'm puzzled when he occasionally deprecates the scientific nature of the evidence:

> "There is one problem with NDEs: As it now stands, they are just anecdotal evidence. It has not been possible to scientifically duplicate them or study them on a closer level than what we could call 'word of mouth.' Until the NDE phenomenon can be duplicated, science can't accept these stories as proof of anything but the existence of something that happens to people who almost die."[1]

Typically, the scientists doing original NDE research have been extremely cautious and tentative in their conclusions – wisely seeking to keep discussions on a scientific, rather than hysterical, level. Thus, rather than conclude in a professional journal article, "Obviously, the mind can therefore exist apart from the brain!" they'll instead conclude, more humbly, "These findings seem to have implications for discussions of mind/body issues." Moody has been especially humble in this regard.[2]

Yet, for those seeking evidence of the existence of God and heaven, it's critical to clarify the type and quality of the evidence that NDEs offer. Questions such as the following aren't often clarified in NDE research:

- In what way is the evidence scientific?
- Is scientific evidence the only legitimate evidence?
- Can reports from patients serve as evidence, or should they be dismissed as "mere anecdotes"?

In part, neglect of these foundational questions may be explained by the fact that so much of the research is done by physicians. Trained to view evidence through the specialized lens of medical science, they tend to define "scientific evidence" in relation to large-scale, double blind clinical trials – a very specific and limited application of the scientific method. Perhaps viewing NDEs through the lenses of other branches of science, and through the lens of legal evidence, could clarify the nature and significance of NDE evidence.

1. Must Events Be Repeatable to Be Scientific?

Repeatability can be important in medical science. If Mary takes 1000 mg. of Vitamin C and claims that it cured her cold, scientists will rightfully insist that, to establish this claim, the same effect must be replicated in a large group of patients under controlled conditions.[3]

Yet, duplication isn't possible in many branches of science, such as cosmology. Just try to repeat "The Big Bang" in your laboratory. Besides being extremely difficult, most would consider it more than a bit dangerous. Yet, although the Big Bang is not repeatable, we can gather data (e.g. observing an expanding universe and noting radiation that appears to have come from the Big Bang) and infer to the best explanation (also called abduction). And yes, scientists consider this scientific, even though we can't repeat the Big Bang.[4]

Indulge me an illustration. I believe strongly that my wife and I were married in a ceremony in Illinois on June 2, 2001. Admittedly, I have no scientific evidence of this event, in the narrow definition of "scientific" that requires repeatability. Even if we were to repeat the ceremony in a laboratory, the repetition would do nothing to prove that a similar event took place in 2001.

Yet, I believe I was married because of very strong *historical* evidence. Although photos can be tampered with and false testimony can be obtained with bribes, 1) I have a strong memory of the event, and 2) I can corroborate that testimony with my wife and other trusted attendees. Additionally, 3) my life changed dramatically as a result of the experience and those changes remain to this day.

Now take away my wedding pictures and wedding certificate. The remaining evidence that I'm married is very close to the evidence we have for a *shared* near-death experience. Several reliable people were there and testify to sharing the experience (accompanying the person through a tunnel, etc.). Plus, the experiencers report being transformed over time. In this case, the historical evidence can be quite compelling.

My point? Repeatability isn't a requirement for sufficient proof. While repeatability may not prove that I'm married, I can assure you, I'm married. If you don't believe me, ask my wife.

In another sense, NDEs are in fact repeatable. Unlike the Big Bang, NDEs keep happening under predictable circumstances. Thus, past NDE studies can be replicated with a fresh set of patients to check the findings of earlier studies. While it's not practical (not to mention moral) to study NDEs by causing cardiac arrests, isn't it sufficiently scientific to study, for example, the 20 percent of cardiac arrest patients who report NDEs and infer from the resulting data to the best explanation? After all, in prospective NDE studies, many of the subjects are on operating tables, being monitored carefully and observed by medical professionals during their NDEs.

Since naturally occurring NDEs occur on a regular basis, they're available for our observation and study on a prospective basis. In this sense they are indeed repeatable.

2. Is the Evidence Purely Anecdotal?

Defining "Anecdotal"

Although people use the word "anecdotal" many different ways, in this context they typically mean "evidence that's deemed substandard because of a reliance on personal accounts that amount to little more than hearsay."[5]

Some seem to imply that science, by its very nature, deals with facts and research, as opposed to personal accounts, as if personal accounts have no place regarding scientific evidence. That this is a gross overstatement is made clear when we note that studies of the effects of prescription drugs (such as pain killers) are often heavily reliant upon patient accounts of what they experienced after taking the drug.

On Science and Personal Reports

NDE researchers explore many facets of the phenomenon, using many scientific approaches, such as:

- Research into the present state of scientific knowledge concerning what happens in the brain during cardiac arrest or anesthesia.
- Screening of patients for possible psychiatric issues.
- Monitoring consciousness via blood pressure, EEG, etc.
- Testing naturalistic hypotheses with blood tests to detect hypercarbia or anoxia.
- Surveying diverse people groups to test the possible impact of culture and expectations.
- Asking standard questions to a set of patients to determine if prior beliefs about the afterlife, levels of education, etc. might impact the occurrence or content of an NDE.

Some of these approaches indeed involve asking patients to describe their experiences; but if done according to scientific standards, this is far from hearsay. In fact, patient reports are one of the primary tools used by doctors to accurately diagnose illnesses.

Much of what many consider scientific evidence can be deemed *less* reliable than testimonial evidence. Take a specific case in forensic science. You're investigating a murder. You find a glove and a hair in the victim's car. You run a DNA test on the hair and find that it matches the DNA of the accused. So did you scientifically *prove* who murdered the victim? No. If two respectable eye-witnesses (upstanding citizens, no apparent ulterior motives) testify that they saw the real murderer plant the hair on the glove, the eye-witness testimony may overturn the evidence from the "more scientific" DNA test.

So personal testimony can provide strong evidence – convicting criminals, educating us about the side effects of drugs, and helping doctors diagnose illnesses. Thus, when studying NDEs, testimonies of experiencers shouldn't be dismissed *a priori*, but rather examined to distinguish weak from strong testimony, hearsay from persuasive reports.

Moody's Study

In *Life After Life*, Moody collected stories from 150 NDErs, delineating and describing different elements of NDEs that kept turning up (tunnels, meeting deceased loved ones, encountering a barrier, etc.). Although his study wasn't, by his own admission, scientifically rigorous, his background in philosophy and medicine allowed him to reflect on possible explanations for the phenomenon. His informal interviews and distinguishing of common elements performed a valuable service in motivating other scientists to study NDEs in a more controlled and rigorous way.

Skeptics could rightly ask of *Life After Life*:

- Since he didn't present complete interviews, did he cherry-pick from interviews the parts that intrigued him and fit snugly into his NDE characteristics?
- Did he find interviewees by looking for those who had a similar experience to the ones he wanted to explore, thus not hearing from those who had vastly different experiences?
- When people mentioned seeing things while they were unconscious, were these claims corroborated?
- Were people interviewed so long after the experience that they'd begun to forget or embellish?

In sum, although Moody performed an invaluable service by exposing millions of people to a fascinating phenomenon, his casual methods and reporting left many saying, "Not very scientific. Mostly anecdotal."

Sabom's Study

Sabom tended to disbelieve Moody's claims and tested them by doing his own prospective study. The evidential value of the reports he collected was enhanced in several ways.

- He interviewed them as soon as possible after the event often in the hospital.
- He checked patient records and personally interviewed patients to rule out psychiatric problems.
- He verified claims of veridical perception with a control group (Can patients likely guess the specifics of their resuscitations?), medical records, family, and attending doctors and nurses.
- He considered possible ulterior motives for sharing their experiences. Are they a bit too eager to share? Are they searching for attention?

Van Lommel's Study

Van Lommel conducted his interviews similarly to Sabom, but additionally re-interviewed at two and eight years to see if their reports changed (through embellishment or faulty memories). They didn't. This helped to establish that NDE memories remain fixed. This finding was replicated in other studies.[6]

Is it likely that NDErs are making things up? Many researchers note that NDErs make serious life changes, differing from control groups that have a cardiac arrest but with no accompanying NDE.[7] Why would their lives change as a result of an experience that they fabricated?

Furthermore, researchers found NDErs very reluctant to share their stories for fear of being considered mentally ill.[8] There seems to be little upside and a strong downside for sharing their stories, especially if researchers are providing no cash or publicity incentives.

Jeffrey Long's Study

Dr. Jeffrey Long obtained his interviews anonymously, over his website. This approach takes away from the evidential value in certain ways:

- When NDErs claim they had veridical perception, such as seeing events in the hospital that others can supposedly verify, we must take them at their word, since I don't see indications that Dr. Long tried to corroborate these testimonies.
- Some might report fabricated NDEs as a joke.

Yet, anonymous surveys also have evidential benefits.

- Much larger groups can be surveyed, which can make for more meaningful statistics.
- Asking redundant questions (similarly worded questions with the same meaning) can help weed out false reports.
- People who would never report an NDE face to face might report one anonymously on a site.
- It's easier to survey people from across the globe, gaining a more culturally diverse sampling.
- Since they all answer the same questions, the interviewer is less likely to lead people (consciously or unconsciously) to answer a certain way.

Anyone can read the questions to judge whether or not they were clearly and fairly worded.

- Being anonymous, there's no incentive to get attention (e.g., a first step toward a magazine article or talk show interview.)

Those unfamiliar with earlier research may deem Dr. Long's study to be worthless, since all the statistics are based on largely uncorroborated stories. But those familiar with past prospective studies have reason to trust such reports, since they've come to see NDEs as a legitimate experience, reported by people who are typically reluctant to share, whose testimonies don't change over time, and have little incentive to lie.

Factors in Weighing the Evidential Value of Personal Testimony

In a court of law, personal testimony can be dismissed as hearsay or deemed compelling enough to sway a jury. What makes the difference, and how can these factors apply to evaluating NDEs? Here are some factors to consider:

1. Recent memories typically trump distant memories.

2. Those with something to lose by sharing trump those with something to gain.

3. Eye-witness testimony trumps second-hand testimony (hearsay).

4. Memories of difficult-to-forget events trump memories that quickly fade or change over time. (Don't ask me what someone wore to a party. I typically have no clue.)

5. Reports from trustworthy (deemed sane and reliable) sources trump those from questionable sources.

6. More witnesses trump fewer witnesses.

7. Corroborated testimony trumps uncorroborated.

8. Consistent interview methods trump random interviews.

9. Accountable research and reporting trumps isolated incidents. (For example, Dr. Sabom teamed with Psychiatrist Dr. Kreutziger and interviewed in well-known hospitals among other professionals. Dr. van Lommel did his study in respected hospitals with a team of people. Dr. Penny Sartori

researched under the oversight two respected academics, with the assistance of doctors and nurses in an intensive care unit. The results of all of these were reported in peer-reviewed journals.)

Summary on Anecdotal Evidence

Personal interviews are used extensively in science. Yet, as with all data, we must be careful to distinguish scientifically evaluated interviews from those that amount to little more than hearsay (anecdotal). NDE researchers should be evaluated on a case-by-case basis as to the evidential value of their interviews and accompanying data.

I do think that the dominance of medical specialists doing NDE research may lead to weaknesses in evaluating the evidential value of the research. I'd suggest that scholars in other fields could add value by reviewing NDE research through the lenses of their specialties. I'd especially like to see input from experts in legal evidence and philosophy of science.

3. Isn't Invoking Spiritual Realities Such as God and Heaven Just Another Case of "God of the Gaps?"

Throughout the history of science, people have observed processes or events that defied scientific explanation and concluded, "God must have caused them." If science later explained the process, to the embarrassment of the theorizing theists, the mistake was chalked up to "god of the gaps" – the assumption that gaps in our scientific knowledge must be filled with God.

Example: Last summer I visited a cave and saw a spiraling stalactite that currently defies scientific explanation. Since gravity consistently pulls drops of water toward the center of the earth, the minerals deposited by the drop should produce stalactites that point straight down rather than spiraling. Had I suggested to the guide that God must have created it, she could rightly reprimand me for invoking "god of the gaps."

But the case of NDEs differs from the spiraling stalactite. NDE researchers aren't typically invoking the existence of God as a *cause* for something that defies scientific explanation. In fact, researchers tend to remain bewildered as to what triggers the event. Research indicates that the closer a patient gets to death, the more likely he is to experience an NDE.[9] Yet, as to whether it's triggered by a physical event (e.g., an event in the brain that typically occurs near death, that may open up a "door" to the other side) or triggered by something (or Someone) from the other side, researchers can only hazard guesses at this point.

Rather than arbitrarily invoking the existence of God as a *cause* for NDEs, reports of meeting God are found as a common part of the experience to be explained. So our scientific study of NDEs necessarily leads us to ask the question, are the places and beings described by NDErs illusory or reality?

NDE reports lead us to consider all the relevant scientifically gathered data and use it to infer to the best explanation. One explanation is that the experience is generated entirely by their brains. Another is that NDErs experience consciousness outside their bodies. That's precisely what we evaluated in this book, which is far different from a god of the gaps argument from ignorance.[10]

4. Are NDE Researchers Using the Scientific Method?

Here's an over-simplification of Sabom's first prospective study, organized around the typical steps of the scientific method.

a. Ask a Question (Do NDErs sometimes observe their resuscitations from outside their bodies?)

b. Do Background Research (What research has already been done in this area?)

c. Construct a Hypothesis (NDErs reconstruct their resuscitation stories from what they've seen on TV and heard in the hospital.)

d. Test Your Hypothesis by Doing an Experiment (Interview patients with cardiac arrests and NDEs to record accurately what they report, in a clinical setting. Compare their out-of-body perceptions of medical procedures with a control group of cardiac patients who didn't report NDEs.)

e. Analyze Your Data and Draw a Conclusion (NDE patients accurately reported, in minute detail, their resuscitations. The control group consistently guessed wrong. Thus, NDE patients apparently saw their resuscitations from outside their bodies.)

f. Communicate Your Results (Publish results in peer-reviewed journals so that other scientists can freely comment and try to replicate the findings.)

I think the last step is significant. Rather than publishing in niche new age magazines or sensationalist newspapers, they published in the appropriate professional journals. As I said in the body,

> Over 900 articles on NDEs had been written in scholarly literature up until 2005, gracing the pages of such respected journals as *Psychiatry*, *The Lancet*, *Critical Care Quarterly*, *The Journal for Near-Death Studies*, *American Journal of Psychiatry*, *British Journal of Psychology*, *Resuscitation*, and *Neurology*. In the 30 year period after Moody published *Life after Life*, 55 researchers or teams published at least 65 studies of over 3500 NDEs.[11]

Publication in appropriate journals gives scientific accountability in at least two ways. First, professional journals have peer review teams who screen articles for adherence to scientific methods. The reputation of the journal is on the line if they publish scientifically substandard work.

Secondly, peers in each respective field may comment on the study in later issues, or refer back to the study in later studies. Both the author of the study and the journal editors have their reputations on the line if the study shows bias or if later studies fail to replicate the results.

5. Does the Evidence Point Beyond our Final Death?

Since "death" is typically defined as the final, irreversible cessation of life in our earthly bodies, those resuscitated from "clinical death" (i.e., cessation of heartbeat and breathing) were never truly dead. Thus, some argue that NDEs tell us nothing about what happens after a person's *final* death.[12]

It's certainly arguable (as I have argued) that they didn't visit their final destination. But while they were on the other side (perhaps we could call it heaven's front porch) many claimed to find evidence that there was more to come after their final deaths.

- Many met friends and relatives who had experienced their deaths many years before. These stayed dead (not merely clinically dead), from the earthly standpoint, but had apparently been experiencing an otherworldly life for years of earth time.
- Many reached a barrier, which they understood to be a point of no return. They believe that they peered to the other side, which would have been their first steps into the after-death existence.

- Some were shown a glimpse of heaven, such as Dr. Richie, the first person to tell Dr. Moody his NDE.
- Death-bed visions are reported by people who are entering their final death. They seem very consistent with NDEs.

As far as NDErs are concerned, what they experienced on the other side provided overwhelmingly sufficient evidence that life will continue after their final deaths. This explains why so many of them no longer fear death.

Conclusion on the Scientific Nature of NDE Research

NDE researchers typically use scientific methods. Whether or not they apply scientific methods rigorously should be determined on a case-by-case basis rather than dismissing the entire field as based upon anecdotes.

Yet if I'm on target, why then would Moody, well-trained in medical science, deprecate the scientific evidence? I'd suggest that Moody was speaking more as a philosopher than a scientist. As an admirer of Socrates, who could dismantle dogmatic opinions with a few probing questions, Moody shunned concrete statements, preferring the role of the ever-questioning skeptic. According to Moody,

> "My goal in this research was to remain a true skeptic in the ancient Greek sense – one who neither believes nor disbelieves but who keeps searching for truth."[13]

Yet, by the time he wrote his 2012 biography, he admitted that he'd finally become "brazen" about voicing his conviction that God and an afterlife exist. Why the change?

> "After more than four decades of studying death and the possibility of an afterlife, I have come to realize that my opinion is buttressed by thousands of hours of research and deep logical thought of the type that few have devoted to this important topic."[14]

Appendix 5
Dr. Susan Blackmore's "Dying Brain Hypothesis"

Dr. Blackmore and Her Book, *Dying to Live*

Since Blackmore has presented one of the most comprehensive naturalistic hypotheses concerning NDEs, her hypothesis deserves special consideration in an evaluation of the evidential value of NDEs. She's no stranger to the relevant fields of study, having an academic background in psychology and physiology (Oxford University) and a Ph.D. in parapsychology (University of Surrey). She documents her sources and shows familiarity with much of the NDE research. I also appreciate that she often expresses her conclusions with appropriate tentativeness when they're built more upon educated guesses than facts. When she can't find an answer, she may go the extra mile by corresponding with a researcher or conducting her own survey. She writes clear prose and organizes her thoughts within workable divisions that flow logically. For these reasons, although I disagree with many of her conclusions, I consider *Dying to Live* to be a good book that I benefited from reading – the best attempt I've seen to defend a thoroughly naturalistic position.

The Two Competing Hypotheses

Blackmore clearly defines our two fundamental choices:

- The 'Afterlife Hypothesis' "suggests that the NDE is a glimpse into life after death."
- Her 'Dying Brain Hypothesis' holds that "all the phenomena of the NDE are…products of the dying brain…that will ultimately stop when the brain's activity stops."[1]

Points of Agreement with the 'Afterlife Hypothesis'

Blackmore agrees with the 'Afterlife Hypothesis' on many important points, including:

- People have these experiences (they aren't fabricating them) and are typically convinced they represent a trip to the other side.
- They are generally sane, intelligent people and can't be brushed off as delusional.
- The experience is generally consistent from culture to culture, no matter what NDErs believed previously about the afterlife.[2]
- Many of the typical explanations – psychological expectations, oxygen deprivation, etc. – fail to fully explain the phenomenon.[3]
- NDEs significantly change people's lives.[4]

Blackmore's Argument

I'll attempt to sum up Blackmore's argument, as presented in *Dying to Live*, as follows:

1. If NDEs can be explained naturalistically, there's no reason to invent other worlds, minds and souls (the 'afterlife hypothesis') to explain them.

2. Since each of the elements of the NDE can be produced by other means than coming near death (e.g., drugs, dreams, oxygen deficiency, etc.), we have reason to believe that the entire NDE (made up of those elements) may also be explained naturalistically.

3. The 'Dying Brain Hypothesis' suggests ways that each element of an NDE might occur naturalistically during a near death event. For example, the feeling of peace and joy may be produced by natural opiates released by the body during extreme stress. The life review may be produced by "random activation and seizures" in the part of the brain that organizes memories. Although none of this has been proven, it makes sense that it might happen this way.

4. This hypothesis makes better predictions for each of the NDE elements than the spiritual hypothesis. For example, the 'afterlife hypothesis' gives no reason why people should pass through a tunnel, rather than through a door or an elevator or a row of hedges. The dying brain hypothesis predicts that there should be a tunnel. Hypotheses that make predictions trump hypotheses that don't.

5. If the physically unconscious (e.g., their brains are incapable of consciousness) could be shown to be fully conscious in some other realm (e.g., if they could verifiably see events in the operating room) this would overturn the dying brain hypothesis and confirm the spiritual hypothesis. Yet, the evidence for such events are never compelling.[5]

6. Therefore, the best hypothesis we have is a naturalistic one, i.e., the 'Dying Brain Hypothesis'.

In its favor, this hypothesis takes into account many near death studies and other relevant scientific studies. The book is well documented and makes some accurate predictions.

Weaknesses in the Hypothesis

Although Blackmore's attempt is admirable, in my opinion it falls short in several significant ways.

1. The hypothesis is based largely upon "What ifs" rather than proven facts. She admits this when she writes,

> "What happens to the brain when a person approaches death? A first approximation to an answer is simply to say that we do not know."[6]

Yet, she can reason from known facts and propose explanations of how the dying brain *might* produce a NDE, so she proceeds to speculate. To confirm her hypothesis, her speculations would need to be tested, but she admits that many of her explanations hadn't been tested at the time of writing.[7]

Over the past 35 years of near-death studies, many of her explanations (e.g., for the tunnel and the light) have been researched and found wanting, so that by 2009 a summary article of the peer-reviewed research by leading NDE researchers could conclude:

"Theoreticians over the past 30 years have proposed various models to explain NDEs. From our review of the characteristics of Western NDErs, we found little evidence to support previously proposed biological, psychological, or sociological explanations as the sole cause(s) of NDEs."[8]

Note my earlier discussion of naturalistic explanations for a fuller discussion.

2. Her assumption that each of the NDE elements can be reproduced by natural means needs to be demonstrated rather than assumed.

Typically, the similarities break down upon closer inspection.[9]

3. Some of her predictions were disconfirmed by later research.

- **Her hypothesis suggests that the dying brain should consistently produce a tunnel vision experience.[10]** Yet, in Jeffrey Long's survey of over 613 NDErs, only one third reported going through a tunnel.[11] The 11-year-old boy I interviewed passed through a gate rather than a tunnel.

  Further, the tunnels reported are often very different from the tunnel vision experience. One of my interviewees reported the light as shining from behind him as he watched his body from above. Yet, according to Blackmore, the light should be in the middle of the line of site. Some NDErs report tunnels with vibrant colors, rather than black, which again wouldn't be predicted by Blackmore's hypothesis.[12]

- **Her hypothesis predicts that people who "dream in a bird's-eye view" should be more likely to have out-of-body experiences.[13]** Sabom tested this prediction in his Atlanta Study. "No difference was found…between the dreaming modes of near-death experiencers with (21 persons) and without (19 persons) an autoscopic near-death experience."[14]

4. She fails to argue adequately for the nonexistence of the self and the world, which is central to her hypothesis.[15]

In Chapter 7, Blackmore challenges the argument that NDEs must be real glimpses of the afterlife, since they seem "realer than real." I fully expected her to argue that just because something *seems* real doesn't mean that it *is* real. After all, our brains can fool us. But she took a philosophical turn that shocked me.

Blackmore argued that our brains build constructs to interpret the input from our senses; but since these constructs often fail, they can't be trusted to give us an accurate view of what's outside of ourselves. In fact, since there's no proof that a real world exists outside of our selves, she dismisses perceived reality as an illusion, including the "I" that's supposedly perceiving it. Thus, she speaks of "the illusion that there is a real world out there.... This way there is nothing to find and no self to find it."[16]

What are the implications of this view to understanding NDEs?

- If life as we perceive it – the rocks and trees and people – are merely illusions constructed by our brains, then obviously any afterlife outside of this world is illusory as well.[17]

- As the brain dies, it can no longer maintain the illusory construct of the self. This explains NDErs reporting a sense of timelessness. "...time and self are all part of the same mental construction."[18]

- Decisions are illusory. There's no self to make decisions. Things happen because they happen, not because of our choices.[19]

- NDErs' lives change because they experienced for a moment the breakdown of "the self-model, which was the root of all our greed, confusion and suffering."[20]

I don't want to argue extensively against this worldview, since the burden of proof would seem to be on Blackmore to argue that we don't exist. After all, most of us take our existence and the existence of an outside world to be self-evident. But I will mention two seeming inconsistencies relevant to the present discussion.

a. It seems to make no sense to argue for our nonexistence in a book that's written for the purpose of convincing "others" of something. If these "others" are simply collections of nonexistent individuals, why try to convince "them" of things?

In fairness to Blackmore, she's a smart, well-educated person. I'm sure she's thought through all these obvious objections to her view on existence and if we were to sit down and discuss it, I could better understand her line of reasoning. Yet, since she gives no extensive argument for this position, many readers will surely wonder about these apparent inconsistencies.

b. The reports from NDErs don't seem to describe in any way this dissolution of self. Quite the opposite, they consistently report a strong sense of self.

- The *self* is amazed to find it*self* disconnected from its body.
- Deceased relatives greet the NDEr, her*self*.
- The *self* experiences its mind on hyperdrive – thinking, communicating, making observations, laying down memories.
- The *self* reflects on the decisions it made during life, realizing the importance of both *self*ish and compassionate choices.
- The *self* is often involved in the decision of whether or not to return.
- The *self* interacts with other selves, without losing its own sense of self.
- Once back, *the self*, rather than concluding that it doesn't exist, determines that it exists for a reason and purposes to make better, more compassionate life choices.

Much research indicates that NDErs report a stronger sense of self, not weaker, and attribute life changes to a sense of purpose and importance. Blackmore suggests that when people regain consciousness, their brains reconstruct the illusion of self and interpret their NDEs in the light of this. Yet, since the primary data we're dealing with is NDErs' reports, if their reports aren't accurate, how can we formulate any meaningful hypothesis of the experience?[21]

Since we form theories by considering all the data and inferring to the most reasonable explanation, the afterlife hypothesis seems to fit the data much better than one that denies the existence of the self and the world.

Which is the more extravagant hypothesis?

If inventing other worlds to explain NDEs seems a bit extravagant to Blackmore, I'd suggest that explaining NDEs by denying our present world, to the point of denying our own existence, is at least as extravagant. After all, if we deny our selves and the perceived world, what do we have left to reason about? If the constructs built by my brain are ultimately flawed and there's no way to improve upon my construct, then haven't we destroyed the scientific method, since it's a construct as well? If the world doesn't exist, what then is left for science to study?[22]

Granted, if her argument holds up, then she truly destroyed the argument that NDEs are real because they seem so real. Yet in doing so, she destroys any notion that anything whatsoever is real, destroying the reality of science, us, and the present world along the way.[23]

5. She fails to adequately explain away the corroborating evidence. Blackmore admits that verified veridical perception would disprove her hypothesis. Concerning the claim that people leave their bodies during NDEs, Blackmore states, "If these claims are valid then the theory I am developing is wrong...."[24]

I appreciate that Blackmore devoted an entire chapter to claims of corroboration, dealing especially with Sabom's research. In essence, she suggests that Sabom's patients, although deemed unconscious, could possibly hear and feel more than Sabom thought, thus enabling them to construct visuals of their resuscitations.

I'd argue that a close examination of Sabom's work would yield Blackmore's explanation unlikely; but she suggests that survivalists need to find NDEs where there's stronger proof that the patients couldn't have constructed visuals from data gathered from other senses. She traced down a few reports of the congenitally blind reporting seeing during NDEs, but concluded they were all dead ends. Yet, six years after Blackmore published her book, Ring and Cooper published their report of the congenitally blind reporting veridical perception. If these reports hold up to scrutiny, they provide strong evidence against Blackmore's hypothesis.[25]

6. She accuses the afterlife hypothesis of making no significant predictions, making her hypothesis the preferred one due to making actual predictions that could be tested.

Yet, it seems to me that the afterlife hypothesis makes significant predictions, many of which have proven accurate by 35 years of near-death studies. Here are some examples:

Prediction 1 - People born deaf might report hearing, since an out-of-body auditory experience wouldn't be dependent upon physical ears.

Prediction 2 - People born blind might report seeing, since an out-of-body visual experience wouldn't be dependent upon physical eyes.

Prediction 3 - If people claim to be very much alive outside their bodies while clinically dead, we'd expect to occasionally find confirmation of events they witnessed (details of the operating room, etc.)

Prediction 4 - If God were involved in these events, we'd expect the experience to exhibit some purpose, which should be evidenced by subsequent life changes.

Prediction 5 - We would expect vivid experiences even when the brain is verifiably not capable of producing consciousness, although the memory of these experiences might be dependent upon variables such as what drugs the doctors administered.

Prediction 6 - We would expect elements of the event to possibly include relevant, meaningful (as opposed to random dreamlets with no meaning) subjects such as, a) whether or not to return, b) how you lived your life, c) whether or not you need a mid-life tweaking.

Prediction 7 - We would be more likely to encounter people who had died rather than currently alive. We might even see some people we weren't aware were deceased.

Prediction 8 - The experience should make sense as a unified whole rather than consisting of random memories or random hallucinations. It would likely have closure, rather than an abrupt, mid-sentence ending.

Prediction 9 - The experience would likely feel real, since it would indeed be real.

All of these predictions are borne out by NDE studies.

Appendix 6
Dr. Kevin Nelson's *Spiritual Doorway in the Brain*

Dr. Nelson teaches neurology at the University of Kentucky. While the book encompasses spiritual experience beyond NDEs, they are central to his thesis and at the forefront of his discussions. Why does the book warrant treatment in an appendix?

- It's a recent book (2011), which has received coverage in the popular press.
- It's one of few book-length attempts to explain NDEs naturalistically.
- He claims to offer fresh insights from his specialty of neurological science.
- From beginning to end, Nelson takes bold, brash, patronizing shots at other researchers:

"I watched with wry amusement and professional concern as cardiologists, radiologists, and cancer specialists speculated wildly about brain activity during near-death experiences. I was dismayed when their misuse of science led to what I knew were misunderstandings and myths: people returning from brain death miraculously intact, or near-death experiences that *proved* God exists and we are all headed for an afterlife."[1]

"Under the guise of science, researchers have claimed that near-death and out-of-body experiences 'prove' that mind exists separate from the physical brain. Such a claim is the most extraordinary in all of science, surpassing even the dramatic assertion that other intelligent life exists in the Milky Way, our galaxy."[2]

Strengths

- Nelson writes with clear and lively prose, making relevant neurology accessible to the rest of us. I loved his descriptions of the marvelous workings of the brain.

- I appreciated his humility to admit that we're far from a complete understanding of how the brain works.

  > "…neurologists inhabit domains isolated by their insights into the anatomy, chemistry, and physiology of an organ whose depths may be as unfathomable as the astronomer's void above."[3]

- Nelson brought relevant research to bear on spiritual experiences that's not typically considered in NDE discussions, such as insights by respected intellectual William James, author of *The Varieties of Religious Experience*.

- Nelson defends his own unique hypothesis that NDEs occur when "part of the dreaming brain erupts in a brain already awake. And blending REM with waking consciousness creates experiences that are realistic and memorable."[4]

Weaknesses

Caught in a Paradigm?

Nelson appears to have begun his study with his naturalistic conclusion pretty well set. As a neurological intern, he encountered his first NDE in one of his patients:

> "I knew that the brain that fuses Monet's strokes of color to perceive a water lily was also responsible for the hyper-realistic image Joe saw when he was close to death."[5]

So, how did Nelson *know* this so assuredly before even studying NDEs? He seemed to never seriously consider that the patient might have experienced something outside his body. Rather than purposing to objectively weigh the evidence for the out-of-body experience, he purposes to deconstruct the natural brain processes that he assumes are responsible for the experience.[6]

While researchers such as Moody, Sabom, and van Lommel also began their studies with a naturalistic bias, their exposure to NDEs caused them to question that paradigm. The tone and content of Nelson's book indicate that he never seriously considered that the experiences might have been true encounters with God and heaven.

Now it may sound fanciful for me to consider that a trained neurologist's scientific objectivity could be swayed by his own paradigm. But Thomas Kuhn's influential *The Structure of Scientific Revolutions* revealed a strong tendency among scientists to resist evidence supporting rival theories. Many can't objectively evaluate competing theories, even when the evidence mounts to the point that it should be compelling.

My evidence for suggesting that Nelson is unduly influenced by his naturalistic paradigm? Besides the description of his first encounter with NDEs, and his dismissive and demeaning attitude toward NDE researchers who disagree with him, note the following weaknesses in his research.

1. His fresh study of NDEs seems sensationalized and flawed.

In his prologue, Nelson claims that he and his team of neuropsychologists "collected one of the largest numbers of research subjects with near-death experiences ever compiled and compared their sleep experiences to the experiences of other people matched by gender and age. What we found intrigued the scientific community and sparked international media attention."[7] Compare this description with his actual study:

- **He studied 55 subjects that he contacted through Dr. Long's NDERF site.**[8] So why is he trumpeting his study as so large, especially for a retrospective study? In comparison, Dr. Long has collected over 3,000 NDE experiences, doing an extensive analysis of 613 of them. Dr. Fenwick studied 300 NDEs, Dr. Moody 150, and Dr. Ring 102. What's so groundbreakingly huge about interviewing 55 people who were already collected by Dr. Long?

- **His survey questions failed to distinguish experiences before and after their NDEs.** Research has found that after having NDEs, many claim to have ongoing paranormal experiences that they didn't have prior to their NDEs.[9] Thus, we'd expect to find many more NDErs claiming to, for example, have experiences where they see or hear things that others can't see or hear. To ascertain whether certain people are predisposed to NDEs by their tendency toward such "paranormal" experiences, Nelson would need to ask if they had these experiences *prior to* their NDEs. He doesn't indicate in his book that he made that distinction, thus invalidating his conclusions.[10]

2. He fails to reveal contrary evidence.

Example: Nelson explains the NDE tunnel experience by referring to the tunnel vision experienced by pilots.[11] Is he aware of the extensive criticisms that have been leveled at this explanation over the past 35 years?[12] If so, shouldn't an objective scholar at least mention why serious NDE researchers typically reject this as a sufficient explanation?[13]

3. His reporting of research can be sensational.

Example: Nelson sees "enormous" implications from a study by Dr. Thomas Lempert that compared the symptoms of fainting to the elements of NDEs. This intrigued me, as it appeared to represent a new line of evidence.

Nelson reports:

> "Lempert's team compared the experience of their subjects to Moody's descriptions of the near-death experience. Surprisingly, they found "*no real difference* [emphasis his] between the two types of experience."[14]

This is quite a claim. From Nelson's description, Lempert has practically reproduced NDEs with induced fainting.

Yet, a perusal of Lempert's study shows significant differences in almost every respect. Review Moody's elements. Compare Lempert's study. None of Lempert's subjects reported experiencing such common NDE elements as a life review, meeting a being of light, talking with deceased relatives, an impression of "realer than real," distortions in time and space, approaching a border, a decision to return, ineffability, changed lives, etc.

Even the characteristics deemed similar were, upon closer inspection, vastly different:

- Lempert noted that 17 percent of his fainting subjects reported "appearance of light," compared to 14 percent of NDErs. That sounds pretty similar, until you realize that the "appearance of light" in the fainting subjects consisted of seeing "gray haze, colored patches, or bright lights." This is wildly different from the unearthly, exceedingly bright point of light that NDErs are drawn to, can observe without squinting, and are convinced is a personal entity.

- Sixty percent of the fainters heard "audible noise or voices," which "ranged from rushing and roaring noises to screaming or talking human voices, but never contained intelligible speech."[15] Hearing unintelligible speech is worlds apart from NDE reports of clear, effortless, easily-recalled communication with deceased relatives and celestial beings.

- Fainters reported "visual perceptions," which appear much like dreams. Yet the quality and content of these perceptions appear radically different from NDEs.

How could someone possibly conclude from this study that "they found *no real difference* between the two types of experience"? This claim is akin to saying, "I sometimes throw utensils in the kitchen and professional quarterbacks throw balls on a football field. Therefore, the two experiences are strikingly similar – no real difference at all."

Lempert's study did find some fainters reporting feelings of being out of body and a tunnel experience, but he describes neither of these in detail. Often in studies of this nature, once we have more detail, we find more dissimilarity than similarity. A feeling of being outside the body can refer to everything from a vague sense of disconnectedness to dreaming of an experience with a bird's eye view, both very different from the out-of-body experience of an NDEr.[16]

4. When he occasionally mentions opposing research, it's often misrepresented.

- He castigates van Lommel for claiming that his cardiac arrest patients had been "clinically dead," claiming, "The brain is nowhere near physically dead during near-death experiences. It is *alive* and *conscious*."[17] He goes on to argue that brain death occurs when a cell ruptures and "there is no putting it together again."

Yet, Nelson here blurs the common distinctions between "brain death" and "clinical death." "Clinical death" is typically defined (for example, in the authoritative Oxford Dictionary of English) as the cessation of heartbeat and respiration, which is precisely how van Lommel used the term.

- Next, Nelson attacks the Pam Reynolds case. First, he has "no doubt" that Pam "awoke during surgery," although he admits that this happens in only 0.18 percent (almost two in a thousand) of patients.[18] Yet, he fails to mention that her state of consciousness was being constantly monitored via EEG and brain stem response – with much greater safeguards in place than a more typical surgery.

Second, he argues that she overheard conversations while they thought she was unconscious. But how could she possibly hear with the loud clicking in her ears? Again, he failed to mention that. His explanation makes one wonder if he ever read the original report as detailed by Sabom.[19]

5. He fails to grapple seriously with the positive evidence.

After finishing the book, I had a déjà vu from when I finished the last episode of the TV series LOST. There were too many loose ends. If NDEs can be naturalistically explained as special dream states, then:

- Why do they differ so dramatically from dreams?

- Why do they consistently exhibit closure?

- Why do people who are born deaf report hearing and those who were born blind report seeing?

- Why are there such consistent elements in a story line that makes so much sense and has such meaning to the experiencer?

- How do you explain the 100+ corroborated out-of-body experiences reported in professional studies?

- How do you explain shared experiences, where people who are neither depleted of oxygen nor in fear of their own death, experience the same NDE simultaneously?

Nelson blithely ignores this relevant data. These oversights are quite astounding, especially in the light of his demeaning attitude toward other researchers.

Nelson appears to assume that by suggesting naturalistic explanations of certain elements of the experience, that he's explained away all supernatural elements. If so, his argument runs something like this:

> Since we know that natural processes, from dreaming to fainting to taking LSD, can cause elements similar to those in NDEs, the experience requires no explanation beyond the brain.

But suggesting naturalistic hypotheses in no way disproves all the positive evidence. Allow me to illustrate.

Imagine that Dr. Nelson recently extracted a tumor from my brain and he's visiting me several days later in my hospital room. I tell him, "I'm feeling so much better! In fact, I escaped from the hospital this morning and sipped a latte at the Starbucks next door."

Dr. Nelson replies, "Mr. Miller, please understand that after a surgery of this nature, people often slip in and out of REM sleep in such a way that they experience vivid hallucinations. Since we know that the brain can produce dreams of this nature, there's no reason for me to believe that you shuffled over to Starbucks in your hospital gown."

"But Dr. Nelson," I object, "here's my Starbucks cup and my receipt, dated at 8:30 AM. Why don't you call Starbucks and ask the baristas if they just served a patient in a hospital gown?"

Therein, to me, is the central weakness of the book. Nelson assumes that if he can show that the brain can produce an experience resembling an NDE, that he would thereby prove that NDErs never leave their bodies. He needs to go further and deal seriously with the positive evidence that researchers offer to corroborate the stories.

Example: Nelson tells of his friend Jake, who woke suddenly at 3:00 A.M., "felt a breath on his face, smelled his mother, and strongly sensed her presence. At that apparent moment she died a continent away."[20]

Nelson explains this experience naturalistically in two ways. First, we know that stimulating a specific region of the brain can cause a person to sense a presence, although none is there. Thus, perhaps Jake was dreaming of his mother and woke suddenly out of REM sleep, experiencing her presence because his "temporoparietal region was still turned off from REM."[21] So let's grant that the brain can produce a sense of someone's presence.

But what of the remarkable timing? Nelson suggests that perhaps it was merely *close* to the time of her death, but not exactly.[22]

At this point, it would seem that Nelson shows a deplorable lack of scientific curiosity. In his first mention of the incident, he says that Jake woke at the "apparent moment" that his mom died. Well, you referred to Jake as your friend. Why not ask him some relevant questions to get to the bottom of this? Did he look at his clock when he woke to make sure it was 3:00 AM? Is there confirmation (death certificate, report from the family or hospital) that his mom died at precisely 3:00 AM? Does he often wake up sensing his mother's presence, thereby increasing the odds that this would happen on the morning of her death?

If Jake has never before woken up abruptly, sensing his mother's presence, then why, during the week of her illness, out of 56 possible sleeping hours, did he wake and dramatically sense her presence at the precise hour (or even precise minute, if this could be verified) that she died?

And how does this compare with the many other reports of people sensing a friend or relative's death? I mentioned my cousin Bucky waking in the middle of the night with a shared death experience at the precise time of his father's passing, then immediately receiving the phone call that his dad had died. In Bucky's case, he hadn't been worrying about his father's health. The heart attack was sudden and unexpected. He'd not been ill.

Granted, the brain can produce many varied experiences. But the remarkable timing suggests to me that something outside of Jake's and Bucky's brains prompted their experiences.[23]

Dueling Neurologists

Since Nelson emphasizes repeatedly that trained neurologists are uniquely qualified to understand the nature of NDEs, those who read Nelson should also read Dr. Eben Alexander's *Proof of Heaven*. Alexander is an academic neurosurgeon who taught for 15 years at Harvard Medical School and published over 150 articles and chapters in professional medical literature. After experiencing a deep NDE of his own, he examined his experience in the light of neurological science. Alexander concluded that he truly experienced life and God in another dimension, separate from his body.[24]

Appendix 7
Reflections on NDEs and Christian Teachings

NDE researchers run the religious spectrum from traditional to New Age, from fundamentalist to atheist. Christians often want to know how NDEs mesh with Christian teachings. It's interesting in this regard that Dr. Ritchie, the psychiatrist at the University of Virginia who profoundly influenced Moody, reported that the being he encountered was "the son of God."[1] When Moody asked Dr. Ritchie if he could dedicate *Life after Life* to Him, Richie replied, "I appreciate that, but I would rather you dedicate it to Jesus Christ because he is the one who gave me this experience."

But Moody wanted to "stay neutral on the question of religion," so he dedicated it "to George Ritchie, MD, and through him to the One whom he suggested."[2] It's interesting that as Ritchie spoke to groups about his experience, people began sharing their experiences with him and writing him letters. Not having the time to respond, his wife threw them away. Had he put them in a book, the beginning of NDE research might have had a more distinctively Christian flare.

Yet, it's questionable whether the scientific community would have responded at all, since it would have been considered a "religious" book. Perhaps it's providential that Moody presented NDEs to the world in a nonreligious context, making no claims about religious implications. In this way, doctors and other scientists felt comfortable studying them objectively, as a scientific rather than religious enterprise.

Here are a few thoughts that Christians should consider.

1. The dominant experience appears to be consistent with biblical teachings. I laid out some of those consistencies in Chapter 6.

2. Elements that occur infrequently – that aren't considered part of the core experience – should be regarded with more skepticism. After all, in a medical crisis, a person might have both a legitimate NDE and a vivid hallucination, failing to distinguish the two. Reports of prophecies, memories from past lives, etc., should especially be looked upon with a skeptical eye, since they aren't reported in the typical experience.[3]

3. Jesus, angels, and other specifically biblical beings and imagery are often reported in NDEs. Yet it's often difficult to determine if the experiencers merely *assumed* that the being they saw was an angel (or Jesus), or if the being actually identified itself in some way. In other words, a celestial messenger may be reported by a Christian as an angel (transliterated "angel" from the Greek word meaning "messenger") or identified by a Hindu as a Yamadoot (also a messenger). Perhaps both saw the same being – a celestial messenger – but named that messenger according to their traditions. (It's interesting that in Dr. Ritchie's NDE, the being wasn't *assumed* to be the Son of God; He was *introduced* in the NDE as the Son of God.)

4. Discern the difference between the experience (which may be legitimate) and the interpretation (which may be influenced by a person's worldview). One person may insist that her experience proves that we're not individuals at all, but a part of a universal consciousness. But was this conclusion drawn solely from the experience itself, or did she interpret it in the light of her worldview?

5. Maintain a healthy skepticism. Solomon warns us that "The naïve believes everything…." So don't be naïve. If someone claims that, in her NDE, God told her to start a new church and that you should join, should you believe her?

"Don't believe every spirit," the apostle John warns us, "but test the spirits, whether they are of God, because many false prophets have gone out into the world." (I Jn. 4:1) Just as false prophets in Old Testament times said "Thus saith the LORD" when God hadn't spoken (Ezekiel 13:6, Jeremiah 23:16), so today's self-proclaimed prophets should be tested as well. The ancient Hebrews tested prophets in several ways. Had 100 percent of their previous prophecies come true? (Deuteronomy 18:21,22) Were their prophecies consistent with what God had previously revealed? (Deuteronomy 13:1-3) Do they have potential ulterior motives for sharing their stories (e.g., speaker fees, book sales, etc.)?

Christians have various views on NDEs. Christian apologist Gary Habermas argues that, while veridical perception provides a good argument for the separation of mind and body, there's no evidence to verify that people's experience with God and other celestial beings is accurate, since we have nothing to corroborate that part of the experience. He holds that NDEs provide strong evidence for life after death, but no evidence for the distinctive truth claims of any one religion.[4]

6. Be wary of seeking the experience. It's tempting to assume that since NDEs are such life-changing experiences, we should seek elements of the experience, such as training ourselves to astral project or trying to communicate with deceased relatives. While the scriptures speak of people having visions and even on occasion communicating with the dead (Matthew 17:1-3), we're never encouraged to seek such experiences.

Scriptures teach that just as there are good and evil people on earth, so are there good and evil beings in the spiritual dimension. Malevolent beings are often reported in distressing near-death experiences. Since the evil one "masquerades as an angel of light" (II Corinthians 11:14), how can we be certain that everything we (and others) might experience on the other side is benevolent and represents the truth?

Thus, the Scriptures consistently forbid consulting mediums. "Do not turn to mediums or seek out spiritists..." (Leviticus 19:31). Again, even if mediums truly contact beings in a spiritual dimension, how can we know that the beings are benevolent and speaking the truth?[5]

7. Determine your primary source of spiritual knowledge. Christians typically believe that their Scriptures are authoritative in matters of teaching. Thus, they should be wary of any experiences that teach anything contrary to the Scriptures, or that claim to add new revelation, even if it appears to be spoken by an angel from heaven (Galatians 1:8,9; Deuteronomy 4:2,12:32; Revelation 22:18,19).

In this regard, it seems wise to regard NDEs as natural revelation (e.g., learning about God from His creation) rather than special revelation (learning about God from Scriptures and His actions in history). By observing the created world, many philosophers and theologians deduce that a wise and powerful God exists. But magnifying atoms and observing galaxies tells us little about how to secure heaven after death. Those who hope to learn this from NDEs may be expecting too much.

8. The lack of "sharing the gospel" by celestial beings may bewilder some people. If salvation is through Jesus, then shouldn't NDErs typically report Jesus urging them to accept Him as their savior? Yet, this would seem to violate the general thrust of Scriptures – that God has left the sharing of the gospel story in the hands of believers. We never see a vision in the Bible that includes a presentation of the gospel. When Saul had his vision, Jesus directed him to enter the nearby city, where Ananias spoke to him. (Acts 9:1-18)

9. Why do some NDE studies report experiencers moving away from traditional Christianity (like leaving church) and adopting a more non-traditional spirituality (like New Age)? Actually, research is divided on this point. Van Lommel reported a tendency for NDErs to leave the traditional church, but also noted that this may have been due to a general movement away from the church in Holland, rather than being caused by the experience itself.[6] Sabom researched this issue in his second NDE study, concluding that NDErs became *more* committed to their local congregations, not less.[7] He concluded that "A belief in reincarnation and in Eastern, universalist religion is *not* a direct aftereffect of the near-death experience."[8] In Sartori's study, "All patients reported an increased tendency to pray, go to church, and read the Bible."[9] Of course, NDErs typically crave more information about their experiences. If they find satisfactory explanations offered by a certain religion, they may gravitate toward that religion.

10. Don't confuse near-death experiences with final death or Revelation's New Jerusalem. Christians often picture life after death as identical with the "new heaven and new earth" of Revelation 21, complete with a "new Jerusalem" and streets of gold. But according to Scripture, this is established *after* the final judgment and *after* the earth as we know it has "passed away." Perhaps the near-death experience is closer to what the apostle Paul experienced when he spoke of being "caught up to the third heaven" and "caught up into Paradise, and heard inexpressible words..." (2 Corinthians 12:1-7). "Inexpressible" – we've certainly heard that from many NDErs!

Since the Bible never purports to tell us everything about the afterlife, shouldn't Christians remain humbly open concerning how creatures or "geographical" sections of the afterlife should appear? Perhaps life on the other side offers virtually endless visual feasts, with an extraordinary variety of breathtaking flora, fauna, and vistas. Perhaps its inhabitants can travel endlessly through diverse lands and cultures. In light of the possibilities, let's be careful not to put God and heaven into a tidy, but unnecessarily limiting box.

Conclusion

NDEs seem, as a whole, to be consistent with a biblical worldview and have much to offer Christians. While historical and philosophical arguments for religious claims appeal to some, many others find such arguments dry and tedious. Yet, NDEs seem inherently fascinating and compelling.

And it's not just those who *experience* NDEs whose lives change – those who *study* NDEs are impacted as well. A survey of those studying NDEs on the university level found the students reporting increased compassion, increased self-worth, a stronger conviction of life after death, a strengthened view of God, a stronger spiritual orientation, and a stronger conviction of the purposefulness of life.[10]

I suggest that we need more engagement with these and related issues from theologians, philosophers, and pastors. Sartori noted a puzzling dearth of literature by theologians examining NDEs.[11] People who experience NDEs spend significant time trying to understand their experiences. New Age writers have done an excellent job of describing the experience within the context of their worldview. Regrettably, the literature from Christians has so far been scant. An experience of such importance to the experiencer, and of such interest to the general public, deserves a more thorough examination by theologians specifically and Christian thinkers in general.

Appendix 8
NDEs with Corroboration

(This chart was originally compiled by Janice Miner Holden and republished with permission from ABC-CLIO, LLC, originally Table 9.1, p. 194, in *The Handbook of Near-Death Experiences*, edited by Janice Miner Holden, et al., 2009, permission conveyed through Copyright Clearance Center, Inc.)

Sources of Anecdotes Involving Apparently Nonphysical Veridical Perception

Source (See full documentation in endnotes)	# of Cases	Page Numbers
Atwater, P.M.H. 1999 **(1)**	1	96-102
Bonenfant, R.J. 2001 **(2)**	1	89
Brumblay, R.J. 2003 **(3)**	1	214
Clark, K. 1984 **(4)**	1	243
Cobbe, F.P. 1882 **(5)**	1	297
Cook, E.K., Greyson, B., and Stevenson, I. 1998 **(6)**	10	384,385,387-388,389-90,391,391-92,393-94,395-98,398,399
Crookall, R. 1972 **(7)**	1	386
Ellwood, G.F. 2001 **(8)**	1	25
Fenwick, P., and Fenwick, E. 1995 **(9)**	7	31,32,32-33,33 (2),35,193
Green, C. 1968 **(10)**	1	121
Grey, M. 1985 **(11)**	3	37,37-38,80-81
Hampe, J.C. 1979 **(12)**	1	260-61
Hyslop, J.H. 1918 **(13)**	1	620
Jung, C.G. 196 **(14)**	1	92
Kelly, E.W., Greyson, B., and Stevenson, I. 1999-2000 **(15)**	1	516

Kübler-Ross, E. 1983**(16)**	1	210
Lawrence, M. 1997**(17)**	1	117
Lindley, J.H., Bryan, S., and Conley, B. 1981**(18)**	2	109,110
Manley, L.K. 1996**(19)**	1	311
Moody, R. 1975**(20)**	4	93,94 (2), 95-102
Moody, R., and Perry, P. 1988**(21)**	4	170-71,171,172,173
Morris, L.L., and Knafl, K. 2003**(22)**	2	155,156
Morse, M.L. 1994**(23)**	4	62,67,67-68,68
Morse, M.L., and Perry, P. 1990**(24)**	3	6,25-26,152-53
Myers, F.W.H. 1892**(25)**	2	180-194,194-200
Near-Death Experiences: The Proof. February 2, 2006**(26)**	1	
Ogston, A. 1920**(27)**	1	383
Rawlings, M. 1978**(28)**	7	5,56-57,57-58,75,77-78,79-80,99
Ring, K. 1980**(29)**	2	50,51
Ring, K. 1984**(30)**	1	44
Ring, K., and Cooper, S. 1999**(31)**	9	4,6-7,7,51,61,83,101-2,108-9,109-20
Ring, K., and Lawrence, M. 1993**(32)**	3	226-27,227,227-28
Ring, K., and Valarino, E.E. 1998**(33)**	11	59,60-61(2),62,62-63,63,64,224-25,226(3)
Rommer, B. 2000**(34)**	2	5-7,7
Sabom, M. 1982**(35)**	10	64-69,69-72,73-74,87-91,94,99,104,105-11,111-13,116-18
Tutka, M.A. 2001**(36)**	1	64
Tyrrell, G.N.M. 1946**(37)**	1	197-99
van Lommel, P., van Wees, R., Meyers, V., and Elfferich, I., 2001**(38)**	1	2041
Wilson, 1987**(39)**	1	163-64
	Total 107	

Appendix 9
Guide to Further Research

Here I list bibliographies, websites, journals, and books for further research, especially for those who are doing academic research. Thus, I suggest primarily studies of multiple NDEs, rather than inspirational books where an individual writes his or her own experience.

This is an exciting topic to research and would be ideal for those doing masters theses or doctoral dissertations. Put in a year or so of intense research and you can get your hands around the field. But I'd encourage you to not rush the study. Many aspects of NDEs require not only reading, but reflection. Read a couple of chapters of a meaty study, then take time to reflect upon the data. Allow your mind to roam outside of your intellectual comfort zone. Ask among your trusted friends and relatives about people within their trusted circles who've experienced NDEs. Interview them. Then reflect upon their experiences and ask them follow-up questions. You may come up with insights that have yet to be explored. It's truly a fascinating field of study!

Video

The Day I Died: The Mind, the Brain, and Near-Death Experiences, 2002, co-produced by the British Broadcasting Company (BBC) and TLC. This video can serve not only as a personal introduction to NDEs, but also as a tool to acquaint nurses, counselors, doctors and students with NDEs. It's very well done. In this video you'll find personal interviews with NDEers such as Pam Reynolds and one who was born blind. You'll meet researchers van Lommel, Greyson, Parnia, Fenwick, Blackmore, and Sabom. I found it on YouTube, but the low quality of the YouTube copy took away from the effect. You can order the original here:

http://ffh.films.com/id/11685

or get a 40 percent discount if you join the International Association for Near-Death Studies here:

http://iands.org/resources/educational-materials/30-the-ultimate-nde-video.html

Interviews

At http://www.skeptiko.com, Alex Tsakiris interviews key writers on all sides of the mind/body, natural/supernatural debate. Tsakiris asks excellent questions, doesn't shy away from controversy, and offers both audio and print versions – free of charge. Concerning NDEs, he's interviewed such writers as Nancy Evans Bush on distressing NDEs, Raymond Moody, Melvin Morse, Jan Holden, Eben Alexander, Chris Carter, Pim van Lommel, Jeffrey Long, Sam Parnia, Susan Blackmore, G.M. Woerlee, Penny Sartori, Peter Fenwick, etc.

Books (I'm listing these in order of recommended reading for researchers, although this will vary depending upon the purpose of your study.)

Life After Life, **Raymond Moody, M.D., 1975** - This book first popularized the NDE and remains a great place to start for an eye-opening introduction. Here students can read portions of a large number of NDEs to get a feel for the typical elements and what the "remarkable convergence" is all about.

As a young student, Moody didn't believe in life after death. Then he heard a presentation by a local psychiatrist who claimed to have died, come back to life, and was convinced he'd experienced life on the other side. As a philosopher (earned Ph.D.) and physician in training (he'd later complete his degree in psychiatry), Moody applied his restless mind to interviewing over 150 people about their NDEs, coining the phrase "near-death experience."

Since Moody was among the first in recent history to study NDEs, his subjects' experiences can hardly be explained away as being caused solely by expectations of an NDE-like experience.

Two weaknesses: First, Moody notes that his subjects, while diverse in their beliefs prior to their NDEs, were all from America. Researchers would later compare NDEs in other cultures. Second, he admits that the study was largely anecdotal. He interviewed people who claimed to have the experience, but didn't indicate that he tried to verify their claims of corroboration with medical records, corroborating testimony, etc.

***The Handbook of Near-Death Experiences: Thirty Years of Investigation,* edited by Janice Miner Holden, EdD, Bruce Greyson, MD, and Debbie James, MSN, RN, 2009** - If you want to do serious research and have a high tolerance for scholarly detail, save yourself a lot of time by acquiring the standard reference book in its field. You'll meet the key researchers, find the most important studies, and read summaries of the current state of research (as of 2005).

Some of the most respected NDE researchers provide chapters summing up research on pleasurable experiences, distressing experiences, children's NDEs, non-western NDEs, corroborating evidence (e.g., veridical perception), explanatory models, and practical recommendations for doctors, nurses, psychologists, hospice workers, and others who treat and counsel NDErs. The thorough documentation not only gives it authority, but also helps researchers plot a course for future study.

(Note: If the price is outside of your research budget, urge your library to purchase a copy. I checked it out free through interlibrary loan and took copious notes.)

For those exploring the evidential value of NDEs, note particularly Chapters 5 ("The Near-Death Experiences of Western Children and Teens"), 7 ("Census of Non-Western Near-Death Experiences to 2005"), 9 ("Veridical Perception in Near-Death Experiences"), and 10 ("Explanatory Models for Near-Death Experiences").

***Consciousness Beyond Life,* Pim van Lommel, M.D., 2007** - Serious students of NDEs will want to acquaint themselves with some of the prospective NDE studies in the clinical setting. Van Lommel offers one of the most recent studies and his book is not only well-written, but also brings earlier studies to bear in drawing his conclusions.

This respected cardiologist began his practice as a naturalist, but became convinced that his resuscitated patients were very much alive outside their bodies while their brains shouldn't have been capable of consciousness. While Moody interviewed people about their past experiences (a *retrospective* study), van Lommel interviewed, in a clinical setting, both his patients reporting NDEs and a control group of similarly diagnosed patients who did not report NDEs, making it a *prospective* study.

Additionally, van Lommel re-interviewed both groups over the years to compare their long-term life changes (a *longitudinal* study). These aspects made van Lommel's study much more scientifically rigorous than Moody's. Van Lommel documented his sources very well and showed an exceptional command of the relevant literature in the field.

Readers lacking sufficient patience and motivation may fail to work their way through the entire book. While Moody writes for a more popular audience, van Lommel *attempts* to write for the average Joe, but obviously has fellow physicians in mind when he throws around phrases like myocardial infarction.

Recollections of Death: A Medical Investigation, by **Michael B. Sabom, M.D.** - If you want to study NDE research in chronological order, read Dr. Sabom's study immediately after *Life After Life*. Sabom, a cardiologist, began his interviews in 1976, a year after the release of Moody's book.

It all began when Sabom attended a seminar on *Life After Life*, presented by a psychiatric social worker, Sarah Kreutziger. Being the only physician present, he was asked for his opinion. He replied simply, "I don't believe it."[1] But Kreutziger challenged him to ask his cardiac patients about their experiences and he was shocked that the third patient he asked reported a NDE.[2]

Recognizing that Moody's interviews were rather casual and unsystematic, Sabom decided to do a prospective study (he also did retrospective interviews, but evaluated them separately) of his patients in the clinical setting. He assumed that, contra Moody's report, he'd find a variety of widely divergent experiences, and that he could discredit their supposed visual recollections of their surgeries (from outside their bodies), since he knew the intricate details.[3] In sum, Sabom stated, "I suppose if someone had asked me what I thought of death, I would have said that with death you are dead and that is the end of it."[4]

After his first year of interviews, he started changing his mind.[5] By the end of his study (five years total), after interviewing 32 patients who described in detail their own resuscitations, he was convinced that they had actually left their bodies.

A great value to Sabom's study is that he approaches it, not just as a physician, but as a skeptical investigator. He consistently checks patient's stories against their medical records and interviews attending physicians and nurses to corroborate stories.[6] He excluded any patients with psychiatric illness or significant mental impairment.[7] He asked very detailed questions about the medical procedures they claimed to have seen outside their bodies, and noted how different procedures were used with different patients.

Further, he set up a control group of patients who didn't experience an NDE, asking them to describe what they thought a resuscitation would be like. In this way, he could compare the accuracy of both groups and judge how likely it would be for patients to guess the correct details.

Consistent with his approach, Sabom's chapter on naturalistic explanations includes not only discussions of physiological explanations such as anoxia and hypoxia, but also shows why it's unlikely that patients consciously or subconsciously fabricated their stories.[8]

Some people suspect that NDE researchers may make things up or fudge their data to get attention and try to publish a bestseller. But this seems highly unlikely for Sabom. At the time of publication, he taught Cardiology at Emory University's prestigious school of medicine. Publishing a bogus book based on bogus data would be a sure way to lose face and potential advancement in such an institution. He also published many articles on NDEs in peer-reviewed journals, so that his work was open for critique and replication among his peers.

Overall, the book was well written, well argued, and well organized.

Science and the Near-Death Experience, **Chris Carter, 2010** - The foreword by Neal Grossman, long-term philosophy professor at the University of Illinois, comes out blasting with the verbal equivalent of an M-16 machine gun. He's hopping mad that so many of his colleagues hold tenaciously to their naturalistic paradigms, while refusing to look at the evidence for paranormal activity. According to Grossman, NDE research hasn't been examined and found wanting; rather, it's been found uncomfortable and left unexamined.

After the foreword, author Chris Carter turns down the heat and coolly weighs documented evidence for and against the validity of near-death experiences. He does a fantastic job of bringing together much of the research done prior to 2010. His undergraduate and graduate degrees from Oxford prepared him well to do serious research. It is a great book for dealing with naturalistic objections to the validity of NDEs.

Dying to Live: Near-Death Experiences, **Susan Blackmore, 1993** - Blackmore was at one time a Senior Lecturer in Psychology at the University of the West of England, having studied psychology, physiology, and parapsychology. She is an outspoken atheist and arguably the leading authority on naturalistic explanations of NDEs. In *Dying to Live*, Blackmore sets forth a case for her naturalistic "dying brain hypothesis."

Her two-page preface comes across strident and opinionated (e.g., "Science tells us that death is the end....") making a fascinating contrast to professor Grossman's strident introduction to Carter's book ("...science has in fact already established that consciousness can exist independent of the brain...").

Fortunately, Blackmore quickly settles into research mode and begins analyzing the data, making some helpful contributions to the discussion along the way. For an extended discussion of *Dying to Live*, see Appendix #5.

Light & Death, **Michael Sabom, M.D., 1998** - While Blackmore examined NDEs through the lens of atheism, *Light & Death* peers through the lens of Christianity. Sabom's first study slowly shifted his worldview from "when we die, we die" to "there's an afterlife," while leaving his readers to make their own decisions about most religious implications. This second study finds a Sabom who's adopted a more decidedly Christian worldview,[9] addressing questions of religious significance, such as:

- Do NDErs report connections between prayer and their NDEs?
- Are miraculous healings associated with NDEs?
- Do NDEs lead people toward New Age expressions of faith, and away from institutional religion, as some researchers have reported?
- What does the Bible teach about issues related to NDEs?
- Is it possible that some beings that appear benevolent in NDEs are actually malevolent beings masquerading as angels of light?

To answer these and other questions, he interviewed 160 patients, mostly from his own practice. Forty-seven of these had near-death experiences and the rest were used for a baseline comparison.[10]

From an evidential perspective, highlights of the book include the first full description of the Pam Reynolds case[11] and his testing of the thesis that NDEs tend to lead people away from traditional religion (he concludes that they don't).[12]

Proof of Heaven, **Eben Alexander, M.D., 2012** - The above books study multiple NDEs. But there's value in reading full accounts of a few deep experiences written by NDErs themselves. An NDE occurs in the context of someone's life – a context which isn't typically explored in studies of multiple NDEs. Why begin with Alexander?

Imagine that scientists decided to send someone to the other side who had impeccable credentials to report back on what he experienced. Alexander would be their man. He taught academic neurology at Harvard for 15 years.

He wrote over 150 articles/chapters in academic medical literature. Although he had never studied NDE literature, he firmly believed that NDEs were produced solely by the brain, having nothing to do with God or heaven. When he slipped into a coma, he was at home and had no idea he was in danger of dying (thus no influence from expectations). He also experienced hallucinations, so that he could reflect upon the differences between the two.

Alexander wrote, not to satisfy every skeptic by examining detailed arguments pro and con. Instead, he wrote a very personal story of his experience and how it destroyed his naturalistic paradigm. I'm seeing more and more that in dealing with worldviews, rational people can look at the same data and draw diametrically opposed conclusions. Thus, the need to examine how people make paradigm shifts. Alexander's case is fascinating to explore in that regard. Additionally his experience contains a couple of instances of corroboration (e.g., seeing a deceased relative he'd neither met nor seen a picture of).

Return from Tomorrow, **by George G. Ritchie, M.D., 1978** - In addition to sending a neurologist, scientists would want to send an accompanying psychiatrist, to make sure they covered all mental/brain activities. George Ritchie was a respected Psychiatrist, his story having historical significance in that he was the first to expose Moody to NDEs. Ritchie was trying to recover from pneumonia when his bodily functions ceased and he was declared dead. (He'd later show students at the University of Virginia his death certificate.) Like Alexander, he wasn't expecting death and thus had no expectation of an NDE. Corroboration included an out-of-body trip to a city he'd never visited, which he later travelled through and recognized.

Beyond Death's Door, **Maurice Rawlings, M.D., 1978** - Dr. Rawlings is a respected cardiologist who believed that death was the end of life until he repeatedly resuscitated a patient who, panic stricken, claimed he was going to hell each time he died. This harrowing experience forced Dr. Rawlings to reexamine the basis of his naturalistic assumptions and to encourage his patients to talk about their near-death experiences. He concluded that near-death experiences were indeed visits to the other side and that hellish experiences were underreported due to patients suppressing uncomfortable memories. Serious researchers were slow to acknowledge frightening NDEs, but eventually began to study them. Rawlings interprets these experiences from a conservative Christian worldview.

Evidence of the Afterlife: The Science of Near-Death Experiences, Jeffrey Long, MD, with Paul Perry, 2010 - Dr. Long, a radiation oncologist, has gathered over 3,000 (and growing) first-hand accounts of NDEs on his website: http://www.nderf.org.

While he's studied thousands of such experiences, he did an extensive survey of over 600 of his earliest participants, so that he's able to provide data based on larger numbers than most studies. For example, he can report that 76.2 percent felt "incredible peace or pleasantness."

Other benefits of his web-based approach include:

- Reports from people who might be reluctant to share in a face-to-face interview.
- A global sampling. An assistant found over 250 volunteers to translate reports written in a multitude of languages.[13]
- The opportunity to examine the questions ourselves to make sure they're not worded to create a certain outcome, since the survey is standard for all participants.
- The ability to avoid the problem of interviewers either consciously or unconsciously encouraging embellishment, since subjects aren't interviewed personally.[14]

Although Long writes in a journalistic style for a popular audience, he often documents his sources and shows familiarity with the scholarly literature on NDEs. He considers the evidence for both spiritual and naturalistic explanations, coming out clearly on the side of believing in life after death.

Each type of study has its strengths and weaknesses. A weakness of anonymous surveys is that it's difficult to corroborate people's reports. Thus, they open themselves to the criticism of being "merely anecdotal." Yet, this is the nature of any large survey, such as a Gallup report.

To minimize fraudulent claims, Long used the common technique of wording the same question in different ways (redundancy), to catch inconsistencies. Also, he noted that there was little incentive to make up a story. NDErs receive no money and full names aren't attached, so they're not getting publicity in hopes of landing on talk shows. The survey is quite extensive, so that it's quite a commitment of time for someone to submit a false report. Still, even with all the safeguards, we can't be 100 percent sure that some fraudulent stories haven't slipped through. In surveys of this nature, researchers assume that the high number of overall responders will protect against the results being significantly skewed.

From the beginning of the book, Long tells his audience that NDEs have convinced him that there's life after death. His unbridled enthusiasm will come across to some as bias or lack of sufficient skepticism. For example, he pretty much accepts each report at face value, accepting that if someone claims they saw something specific while out of body, that this qualifies as evidence. I think his book would have been strengthened by showing more reserve in his evaluation of such testimonies, such as writing,

> "If this person's telling the truth, this is marvelous evidence for the afterlife. Since it's similar to reports that prospective researchers such as Sabom corroborated with patient records and eye-witnesses among his colleagues, I have a general trust in such reports."

The Near-Death Experiences of Hospitalized Intensive Care Patients: A Five-Year Clinical Study, Dr. Penny Sartori, 2008 - When Sartori heard her first NDE report from a patient, she dismissed it as wishful thinking.[15] It was only later that she found the serious literature on the subject and became intrigued.

Dr. Sartori presents the results of her study of patients in an intensive therapy unit who reported NDEs, so that it's broader than just cardiac patients. She researched under the supervision of two British experts on NDEs – Professor Paul Badham and Dr. Peter Fenwick. It's the UK's first ever long-term prospective study (overwhelmingly Welsh patients). It's thorough – 564 pages and painstakingly documented – covering not only her prospective study, but additionally the history of NDEs (48 pages), a discussion of physiological and psychological explanations (60 pages) and much rumination about implications of the study.

One of her purposes was to investigate "possible physiological or psychological factors that could be the cause of the phenomenon."[16] In her data analysis she carefully recorded the treatment, including arterial blood gas levels, heart rhythm, drugs, etc. She found .8 percent of all the patients reporting NDEs/OBEs, including 18 percent of cardiac arrest patients.[17]

Sartori shows a thorough mastery of the NDE literature throughout. Her bibliography of almost 500 publications, current up until about 2006, offers a wonderful source to guide further study.

It's helpful, from an evidential standpoint, that she included full interviews in her appendixes, not only of the NDEs, but also hallucinations. Her description of hallucinations from the patients in her study[18] showed the random and bizarre nature of hallucinations, as contrasted with NDEs. She noted, "The patients who had an NDE in addition to hallucinations, or had hallucinated in the past, were able to distinguish between the two experiences."[19] "Interviewing a total sample also reduced the risk of bias and ensured that no experience was overlooked."[20] This kept the "file drawer effect" at bay, whereby researchers are tempted to discount experiences that don't fit their hypotheses and report only the ones that fit.

She was very careful to explore all the possibilities of patients being able to get at the supposed veridical perception from natural means. This made the experiences she deemed compelling all the more powerful.

Note: If the price is outside of your budget, either urge your library to purchase a copy, or borrow it through interlibrary loan.

Irreducible Mind: Toward a Psychology for the 21st Century, **Edward F. Kelley, et.al., 2009** - Eben Alexander recommends this book "for those still stuck in the trap of scientific skepticism," praising its "rigorous scientific analysis." At 800 pages, it's thorough. I recommend it because the data that challenges naturalism goes beyond NDEs. This book, by academic heavyweights in the fields of psychology and psychiatry, covers NDEs, but also related phenomena such as mystical states of consciousness, extreme psychophysical influence, the empirical study of the mind-body problem, and memory.

***The Light Beyond: New Explorations by the Author of Life after Life,* Raymond A. Moody, 1988** - After his research for *Life after Life,* Moody compiled over a thousand new case histories of people with NDEs. He shares parts of these stories and gives us his latest thoughts. He brings us up to date (as of 1988) with other academic research, introducing us to the main players. The latter was particularly interesting and valuable to me. It's intriguing and enlightening to see how physicians and researchers get pulled into this field.

***Paranormal: My Life in Pursuit of the Afterlife,* Raymond A. Moody, 2012** - Moody spent a lifetime studying near-death experiences. In this book he gives his mature reflections from a biographical perspective, which I find fascinating and enlightening. Moody grew up in non-religious household where his father (a surgeon) was a staunch philosophical naturalist and had no patience for talk about the paranormal. Moody's philosophical studies (particularly Socrates) piqued his interest in the afterlife and led him to present his conclusions very tentatively, lest they be shot down later by further research and reflection.

***Glimpses of Eternity: Sharing a Loved One's Passage from This Life to the Next,* Raymond Moody, with Paul Perry, 2010** - Not all NDEs are private. Often, entire families share the experience, including parts of the life review, with a dying loved one. This experience allows corroboration from several independent sources, which is a significant evidential leap forward from having to trust one individual's personal testimony of an essentially private event. Furthermore, some report seeing deceased relatives that nobody present knew were dead at the time.

Moody collected many such cases through the years and finally put together his thoughts on them in this book. While Moody shares many stories and sometimes tells that he independently verified it with all who were involved, the skeptic side of me would prefer that he tell us in every case how he went about verifying the stories. If he played the role of the detective a bit more, such as Sabom did in his studies, I think he could strengthen his case.

Yet, since research has shown that lying and embellishment don't tend to be a problem in this field, it will be easy for some to pretty much take these stories at face value.

Other Researchers

Many researchers have studied and written extensively about NDEs. Consult my endnotes to find many great books and journal articles. A few others who deserve special mention are neuropsychiatrist Peter Fenwick, Britain's leading clinical authority on NDEs; Pediatrician Melvin Morse, who studied childhood NDEs, Kenneth Ring, Professor Emeritus of Psychology at the University of Connecticut, Bruce Greyson, Professor of Psychiatry at the University of Virginia; and Psychiatrist Elisabeth Kübler-Ross.

A Collection of Recommended Books

The *International Association for Near-Death Studies* offers a bibliography of 56 books. While not comprehensive, it's especially valuable in that it contains most of the older foundational works. A great place to start!

Journals

The NDE is no stranger to professional literature. The *Journal of Near-Death Studies* (originally titled *Anabiosis*), today in its 30th volume (four publications per year comprise each volume), is a peer-reviewed journal dedicated to the study of NDEs. If your local library doesn't carry it, ask your librarian about options with inter-library loan, which is free in our system. I had to go through a local university to get the most recent volumes through its inter library loan as pdfs. Other volumes were available at Georgia Tech.

The editors commit themselves to "an unbiased exploration of these issues and specifically welcome a variety of theoretical perspectives and interpretations that are grounded in empirical observation or research." I'd recommend any serious researcher to browse every issue.

Other journals with relevant research include *Resuscitation, Lancet, Journal of Nervous and Mental Disease, General Hospital Psychiatry, Journal of the American Medical Association, Journal of Scientific Exploration, Omega, Neurology, Brain, Death Studies,* and the *Journal of Humanistic Psychology.*

If you aspire to exhaustive research, consider joining the International Association for Near-Death Studies (currently $30 for the first year), and receive a free index to the periodical literature on NDEs, from 1877 to 2005. This database of almost 900 scholarly and popular articles, with article summaries, is searchable by 135 NDE topics.

Each journal article typically cites scores of other articles worth perusing. Look particularly for review articles, which sum up the scholarly research on a subject to date.

Helpful Websites

http://iands.org/home.html - The International Association for Near-Death Studies offers links to scholarly articles, a collection of free articles, and a newsletter. It recommends over 60 books and is home to the *Journal of Near-Death Studies.* It's a good place to start for those wanting to follow the serious research, offering free articles on both sides of the debate. It also contains over 200 NDE accounts that people have submitted to their site.

http://www.nderf.org - Site on near-death experiences by radiation oncologist Jeffrey Long. A helpful source for browsing over 3,000 accounts of NDEs that people have posted from around the world.

http://www.near-death.com/evidence.html - Scientific Evidence for Survival. Helpful introductions to various personalities, books, and articles on NDEs and related subjects.

http://www.skepdic.com/nde.html - Critiques NDEs from a naturalistic perspective.

http://www.infidels.org/library/modern/keith_augustine/HNDEs.html   - Another critique from a naturalistic perspective. Since the writer documents his sources, this is a good place to find articles and passages that can be taken to support naturalistic explanations.

http://nhneneardeath.ning.com - The Near-Death Experience Network is both a resource center and social network for those who've had NDEs. Offers a helpful list of resources on the right column of the home page.

Acknowledgements

I especially want to thank those scholarly researchers and empathetic listeners who dedicated significant portions of their lives to researching, reflecting upon, and publishing about a phenomenon that fifty years ago was typically ignored or attributed to mental illness.

Thanks to those who shared with me their near-death experiences. I withheld most of their names to protect their privacy.

Thanks to the knowledgeable and patient librarians at Kennesaw State University, Georgia Tech, and the Cobb County library system for their help in locating and securing journals and books that weren't available on local shelves or through the university databases.

Thanks to Carole Maugé-Lewis for her professional design work and to Tracy Hefner for her keen editing skills.

Special thanks to those who gave candid input on my early ideas and manuscripts: Dr. Ken Walker, Dr. Peter Schaefer, Dr. Roger Rochat, Dr. Jeffrey Long, Dr. Robert McGinnis, Eddie Bishop, Jeff Ciaccio, Allen Massey, Lisa Russell, Alberta Sequeira, Boomy Tokan and Katherine Wilson.

Thanks to David Blackburn for his tips on the nature of legal evidence.

Thanks to family members who gave valuable input – Cherie, Ann, Andrew, Benji, Mark, Paul, David, Richard and Angela.

Endnotes

Preface

1) Michael Sabom, *Light & Death* (Grand Rapids, Michigan: Zondervan Publishing House, 1998), 37-47; 184-190.

Chapter 1

1) Todd Burpo, *Heaven is for Real* (Nashville: Thomas Nelson, 2010).

Chapter 2

1) Raymond A. Moody, *Life After Life* (New York: Bantam Books, 1975).
2) Raymond A. Moody, *Paranormal* (New York: HarperCollins, 2012), 33.
3) Ibid., 62.
4) Ibid., 56ff. Dr. George Ritchie's experience was quite extensive, dramatic, and definitely worth a read. It significantly impacted his life. His 1978 book about his NDE, *Return from Tomorrow* (Waco, Texas: Chosen Books), is well-written, brief (124 pp.) and compelling.
5) Ibid., 64.
6) Ibid., 68ff.
7) Although Moody popularized NDEs, he was far from the first to study them. Prior to the publication of *Life After Life*, over 25 authors published over 30 articles on NDEs in Western scholarly periodicals. J.M. Holden, J. M., and R. Christian 2005b, The field of near-death studies through 2001: An analysis of the periodical literature, *Journal of Near-Death Studies* 24:21-34. Referenced in J.M. Holden, B. Greyson, D. James, 2009, *The Handbook of Near-death Experiences: Thirty Years of Investigation* (Santa Barbara, California: ABC-CLIO, LLC).
8) Pim van Lommel, *Consciousness Beyond Life* (New York: HarperCollins, 2010), viii. See also p. 310 - "That death is the end used to be my own belief."
9) Ibid., xiii.
10) Pim van Lommel, Ruud van Wees, Vincent Meyers, Ingrid Elfferich, Near-death experience in survivors of cardiac arrest: a prospective study in the Netherlands, *Lancet* 358: 2039-2045 (2001).
11) *Consciousness Beyond Life*, xii.
12) Ibid., 284.
13) The *Index to NDE Periodical Literature* collects these titles (up until 2005) and makes them searchable by 135 NDE-related topics, an invaluable resource for those aspiring to exhaustive research. Find it here: http://iands.org/research/index-to-nde-literature-1877-2005.html.
14) *The Handbook of Near-Death Studies*, 7.

Chapter 3

1) Pim van Lommel, *Consciousness Beyond Life* (New York: HarperCollins, 2010), 9. An Australian telephone survey of 673 people found nine percent claiming to have NDEs. M. Perera, *et al.*, Prevalence of Near-Death Experiences in Australia, *Journal of Near-Death Studies*, 24 (2) (2005), 109-115.
2) In Sartori's study, all but two of the NDErs "would not have disclosed their experiences had they not been asked." Penny Sartori, *The Near-Death Experiences of Hospitalized Intensive Care Patients* (Lewiston, Queenston, Lampeter: The Edwin Mellen Press, 2008), 245. Sabom noted that most of his

patients were very reluctant to share their NDEs, fearing that people would think they were crazy. "Many had been unable to discuss it with their closest friends or relatives for fear of ridicule…." (Michael B. Sabom, *Recollections of Death* (New York: Harper & Row, 1982), 11,25.

3) I took these from the reports in Moody's *Life After Life*, van Lommel's *Consciousness Beyond Life*, and my personal NDE interviews.

4) *Consciousness Beyond Life, 63-65,173;* Jeffrey Long, *Evidence of the Afterlife (New York: HarperOne, 2010),* *8,35,64,65.*

5) *Consciousness Beyond Life,* 150-153.

Chapter 4

1) Raymond A. Moody, *Life After Life* (New York: Bantam Books, 1975), 153-157.

2) Michael B. Sabom, *Recollections of Death* (New York: Harper & Row, 1982), 151-178.

3) Pim van Lommel, *Consciousness Beyond Life* (New York: HarperCollins, 2010), 105-135.

4) Penny Sartori, *The Near-Death Experiences of Hospitalized Intensive Care Patients* (Lewiston, Queenston, Lampeter: The Edwin Mellen Press, 2008), 59-120.

5) Chris Carter, *Science and the Near-Death Experience* (Rochester: Inner Traditions, 2010), 5-102. Carter suggests that this is the primary objection and devotes almost 100 pages to discussing it. Atheist Susan Blackmore, ostensibly looking at the data in an unbiased manner, shows her naturalistic colors in her preface when she states: "Of course, this comforting thought [the prospect of eternal life] conflicts with science. Science tells us that death is the end…." *Dying to Live* (London: Prometheus Books, 1993), xi.

6) For extensive discussions of this, see *Science and the Near-death Experience,* 6-102; *Consciousness Beyond Life,* 179-263.

7) Some naturalists tend to lump all such assertions together, dismissing any paranormal claims as akin to beliefs in fairies and elves. To many naturalists, talk of independently existing minds and other worlds seems so absurd that they may refuse to take NDE research seriously. Note the tone of this statement by neurologist Kevin Nelson: "Under the guise of science, researchers have claimed that near-death and out-of-body experiences 'prove' that mind exists separate from the physical brain. Such a claim is the most extraordinary in all of science, surpassing even the dramatic assertion that other intelligent life exists in the Milky Way, our galaxy." *The Spiritual Doorway in the Brain* (New York: Dutton, 2011), 260. Yet, does his critique of NDE research show a greater commitment to objective science? Not in my view. See my critique of Nelson's book in Appendix #6.

8) *Consciousness Beyond Life,* 273.

9) Carter, 72, quoted from Koestler, *The Roots of Coincidence* (New York: Vintage Books, 1973), 77.

10) Carter, 59, as quoted from *The Roots of Coincidence,* 51. For more on our present understanding of electrons, see quotes by Einstein and others in *Consciousness Beyond Life,* 221. Also see http://education.jlab.org/qa/history_03.html - on not being able to see electrons. http://mwolff.tripod.com/see.html - a helpful visual of the wave structure of an electron. http://discovermagazine.com/2005/jun/cover - on how electrons can be in more than one place at once (non-location). "As the photons accumulate on the film, the same old interference pattern of alternating bright and dark stripes gradually appears, defying common sense. In this case, there is only one thing each photon can interact with – itself. The only way this pattern could form is if each photon passes through both slits at once and then interferes with its alternate self. It is as if a moviegoer exited a theater and found that his location on the sidewalk was determined by another version of himself that had left through a different exit and shoved him on the way out." "…quantum theory has never yet failed to predict the outcome of any experiment."

http://wiki.answers.com/Q/Can_you_see_an_electron Can you see an electron? "No. It is far, far too small to be 'seen' in any way in which we 'look' at other stuff. Light, which is the medium for seeing things in the normal sense, is too 'large' for the tiny electrons. We see things because the things we are looking at reflect light. The reflected light is what we form images with. Electrons are too tiny to reflect light." http://www.preservearticles.com/201012302042/can-we-see-electron.html "Similarly, we don't see the electrons directly, but in fact, we see their 'foot-prints' – bursts of light on a fluorescent screen, effect on a photographic film, etc. These foot-prints confirm their existence." http://www.physicsforums.com/showthread.php?t=145501&page=3 - "The electron *is* not a wave, and the electron *is* not a particle. The electron *is* not the current model of wave-particle duality we have today. These models only represent a limited aspect of our perception of electrons with respect to the measurement devices we use. We have no access to knowledge of what the electron really *is…*" "The electron is thus not perceived in any apparent shape." http://en.wikipedia.org/wiki/Wave%E2%80%93particle_duality - Helpful article on wave-particle duality.

Read more here: http://wiki.answers.com/Q/Can_you_see_an_electron#ixzz1vDv8At8v.

11) James Jeans, *The Mysterious Universe*, first published in 1930 by Cambridge University Press, reprinted most recently in 2007 by Kessinger Publishing, 137.

12) Here's a great place to find a collection of naturalistic arguments concerning NDEs, often with documentation: http://www.infidels.org/library/modern/keith_augustine/HNDEs.html.

13) Maurice Rawlings, *Beyond Death's Door* (Nashville: Thomas Nelson, 1978), xi,21.

14) This seems to be an important distinction, which is often overlooked. Near-death experiences are *near* death, not *final* death. As such, we have no reason to expect that all people should have such an experience if they experience clinical death. Also, we have no reason to think that such an experience represents the final resting place of a person after death.

15) http://www.infidels.org/library/modern/keith_augustine/HNDEs.html#imagery

16) Raymond A. Moody, *The Light Beyond* (New York: Bantam Books, 1988), 22. See also Carter, 210, noting that the relatives seen are almost always deceased.

17) Another form of this argument would be to object, "This is just an example of God of the Gaps!" By this they are saying that science will one day explain it, just as it once explained how storms at sea were caused by weather patterns rather than ocean gods. But regarding explaining NDEs, this appears to be a statement of faith rather than science, for truly objective scientists should hold theories that fit best with our current observations. As I write, the Big Bang Theory is held by the overwhelming scientific population. Why? Because it's the best theory to account for several key observations over the last century. Of course, a scientist could say, "I don't believe in the Big Bang. I believe that future observations will lead to a better theory." But if there's no evidence for this, then it's a faith statement rather than a scientific statement, a prime example of an observation that Einstein once made of fellow scientists: they're typically poor philosophers.

Sure, the evidence for an afterlife through NDEs may be overturned by later studies, but at the present, the evidence weighs in for an afterlife. "But the overwhelming progress of science teaches me to wait for a naturalistic explanation!" some object. So what you're saying is, "Science has explained a lot of things naturalistically. Therefore, if science continues to move forward, everything will one day be found to have a naturalistic explanation." But that's quite a logical and evidential leap. Isn't that precisely the attitude that's hindered scientific progress over the centuries? Rather than taking seriously the observations that pose a problem with the old paradigm, we assume that later experiments will prove the old paradigm to be true. This was well argued by Thomas Kuhn in *The Structure of Scientific Revolutions* (Chicago: University of Chicago Press, 1996). Rather than trying to keep fitting odd pieces (anomalies) into our comfortable paradigms, we should occasionally step back and see if all the pieces make more sense in a new paradigm.

18) According to Keith Augustine, "In fact, most NDE reports are provided to researchers years after the experience itself. Ultimately, all we have to go on is after-the-fact reports of private experiences. The constant reconstruction of memory makes it difficult to know just what NDErs have actually experienced." http://www.infidels.org/library/modern/keith_augustine/HNDEs.html

19) Rawlings' first exposure to an NDE came from a patient with cardiac arrest whose heart kept stopping after each resuscitation. The patient told Rawlings, each time he regained consciousness, what he was experiencing. (Rawlings, 17-22) Prospective studies typically interviewed patients while they were still in the hospital. In Sartori's study, some of her patients reported their NDEs immediately after regaining consciousness. (Sartori, 260-264) Sabom interviewed those in his prospective study "as soon after the event as possible." (*Recollections of Death*, 11)

20) Bruce Greyson tested the theory of embellishment by interviewing 72 NDErs 20 years after their initial interviews. "Contrary to expectation, accounts of near-death experiences…were not embellished over a period of almost two decades. These data support the reliability of near-death experience accounts." B. Greyson, Consistency of near-death experience accounts over two decades: Are reports embellished over time? *Resuscitation* 73:407-11 (2007). M.L. Morse concludes, "Unlike ordinary memories or dreams, NDEs do not seem to be rearranged or altered over time." Near-death experiences of children, *Journal of Pediatric Oncology Nursing* 11:139(1994).

21) According to Keith Augustine, "the study of NDEs tends to attract researchers who already believe that NDEs provide evidence for survival. NDEs seem to be a natural lure to survivalists, since they offer the prospect, at least, of bolstering such researchers' belief in survival after death and of offering them hints about what exactly is going to happen to them when *they* die. Thus it is hardly a revelation that many of the researchers investigating the phenomenon are confident that NDEs point toward the reality of survival of bodily death." http://www.infidels.org/library/modern/keith_augustine/HNDEs.html I found no evidence for this statement in the NDE researchers I studied. In fact, I found quite the opposite.

22) *Consciousness Beyond Life*, 310.

23) *Beyond Death's Door*, 17, back flap.

24) *Recollections of Death*, 157.

25) Ibid., 156.

26) *The Near-Death Experiences of Hospitalized Intensive Care Patients*, 6.

27) Bruce Greyson, "Commentary on 'Psychophysical and Cultural Correlates Undermining a Survivalist Interpretation of Near-Death Experiences,'" 140. Cited in *Science and the Near-Death Experience*, 200.

28) According to Keith Augustine, "Background knowledge also surely plays a role. Personal experience and media portrayals make it easy for us to imagine what a hospital scene should look like (Rodabough 109). Even specific details about people are fairly predictable in a hospital setting." http://www.infidels.org/library/modern/keith_augustine/HNDEs.html

29) *Science and the Near-Death Experience*, 219, 220.

30) *Recollections of Death*, 83ff.

31) "*A priori* expectations, where the individual makes sense of the situation by believing they will experience the archetypal near-death experience package, may also play a crucial role." Dean Mobbs and Caroline Watt, There is Nothing Paranormal about Near-Death Experiences, *Trends in Cognitive Sciences*, Vol. 15, Issue 10, 447-449 (2011).

32) *Consciousness Beyond Life*, 149. "This is borne out by Greyson's study, in which the subjective data of resuscitated patients show that most of them did not even realize that they had had a cardiac arrest. The situation is comparable to fainting. When people regain consciousness after fainting they have no

idea what happened."

33) Elisabeth Kübler-Ross found that when people are confronted with a terminal prognosis, their first stage typically involves denial. *On Death and Dying* (New York, Simon & Schuster, 1969), 51ff.

34) Another example of the unexpected is that, in one-third of the cases where people encounter the deceased, "the deceased person was either someone with whom the experience had a distant or even poor relationship or someone whom the experiencer had never met." Greyson, Kelly and Kelly, *The Handbook of Near-Death Experiences, (Westport, Connecticut: Praeger Publishers, 2009), 231.*

35) Greyson, Kelly and Kelly, *The Handbook of Near-Death Experiences,* (Westport, Connecticut: Praeger Publishers, 2009), 215.

36) In Exhibit #3 I go much deeper into how NDEs typically differ from our cultural expectations. Appendix #1 discusses the common elements throughout cross-cultural studies of NDEs. Moody's observations confirm this. *Life After Life*, 59.

37) *The Handbook of Near-Death Experiences*, 115-120. Janice Miner Holden, Ed.D., Jeffrey Long, M.D., and B. Jason MacLurg, M.D. review the literature on these potential variables and conclude that they make no statistically significant difference. They conclude, "For now, the best answer to the question, 'Who has NDEs, how often, what kind, and with what aftereffects?' is probably that NDEs appear, for the most part, to be equal opportunity transpersonal experiences." "…research has not yet revealed a characteristic that either guarantees or prohibits the occurrence, incidence, nature, or aftereffects of an NDE. Perhaps the conclusion of research so far – that everyone is a potential NDEr – is the most mysterious, provocative, and important message for readers to take away." *The Handbook of Near-Death Experiences*, 133.

38) *Science and the Near-Death Experience*, 172-176; *Consciousness Beyond Life*, 116.

39) People have often made grandiose claims that there's a "striking similarity" [Juan Saavedra-Aguilar and Juan Gomez-Jeria, A Neurobiological Model for Near-Death Experiences. *Journal of Near-Death Studies* 7:205-222 (1989), 209, 217] and "vast clinical and surgical literature" [Michael Persinger, "Modern Neuroscience and Near-Death Experiences: Expectancies and Implications. Comments on 'A Neurobiological Model for Near-Death Experiences.'" *Journal of Near-Death Studies* 7:233-39 (1989), 234] demonstrating the similarity of NDEs and the experiences of those with, for example, temporal lobe epilepsy, electrical stimulation of the temporal lobe, and transcranial magnetic stimulation. Yet, Persinger (1989) gave only one reference for his claim – a paper by Janice Stevens [Sleep is for Seizures: A New Interpretation of the Role of Phasic Events in Sleep and Wakefulness, in M.B. Sternman, M.N. Shouse, and P. Passount (Eds.), *Sleep and Epilepsy* (New York: Academic Press, 1982), 249-64 (1982)], who made no reference to the supposed vast literature. Concerning his claims to have replicated "all of the major components of the NDE" (Persinger 1989, 234) with transcranial magnetic stimulation, the actual experiences that were even close were very vague, such as "I experienced thoughts from childhood." [Michael Persinger, Near-Death Experiences and Ecstasy: A Product of the Organization of the Human Brain? In S. Della Sala (Ed.), *Mind Myths: Exploring Popular Assumptions about the Mind and Brain*, (Chichester, England: John Wiley, 1999), 85-99.] Researchers tried to replicate Persinger's experiments using his own equipment, but failed, concluding "Suggestibility may account for previously reported effects" [P. Granqvist et al, "Sensed Presence and Mystical Experiences are Predicted by Suggestibility, Not by the Application of Transcranial Weak Complex Magnetic Fields." *Neuroscience Letters*, 379:1-6 (2005),1; see also M. Larsson et al., Reply to M.A. Persinger and S.A. Koren's Response to Granqvist et al., Neuroscience Letters, 380:348-50 (2005)]. For a more comprehensive look at these claims and rebuttals, see *The Near-Death Experiences of Hospitalized Intensive Care Patients*, 87-95 and *The Handbook of Near-Death Experiences*, 219,220.

40) P. Fenwick 1997, "Is the Near-Death Experience N-methyl-D-aspartate Blocking?" *Journal of Near-Death Studies* 16:43-53; *The Near-Death Experiences of Hospitalized Intensive Care Patients*, 86.

41) *The Near-Death Experiences of Hospitalized Intensive Care Patients*, 91. Also noted and discussed in *Light & Death*, 181; Ernst Rodin, Comments on 'A Neurobiological Model for Near-Death Experiences, *Journal of Near-Death Studies* 7/4 255-259 (Summer, 1989).

42) For example, see Dean Mobbs and Caroline Watt, There is Nothing Paranormal about Near-Death Experiences, *Trends in Cognitive Sciences*, Vol. 15, Issue 10, 447-449, 18 August 2011.

43) See B. Greyson, E.W. Kelly, E.F. Kelly, Explanatory Models for Near-Death Experiences, in *The Handbook of Near-Death Experiences*, 217.

44) Sartori has an especially good discussion of both hypoxia and anoxia in *The Near-Death Experiences of Hospitalized Intensive Care Patients*, 59-68.

45) *Life After Life*, 163.

46) See *Consciousness Beyond Life*, 115, *Science and the Near-Death Experience*, 167. In *The Handbook of Near-Death Experiences*, 115-133, Janice Miner Holden, Jeffrey Long, and B. Jason MacLurg review the literature on these potential variables and conclude that they make no statistically significant difference.

47) *Science and the Near-Death Experience*, 162-168; *Consciousness Beyond Life*, 114-116; 144-148. In two of Sartori's cases, blood was taken "at the precise time of the NDE or OBE." "Both patients were receiving oxygen therapy continuously and their levels of oxygen were normal during the time of their experiences." "Neither set of results support the anoxia or hypercarbia theories" (Sartori, 280). Sabom also had a case where his patient reported seeing, from outside his body, a needle being inserted into his groin. This was done for a blood gas analysis, which showed his oxygen level to be above normal and his carbon dioxide level lower than normal, the opposite of what you'd expect if NDEs were due to hypercarbia or anoxia. (*Recollections of Death*, 178)

48) Maurice Rawlings, *Beyond Death's Door* (Nashville: Thomas Nelson Inc., 1978), xii.

49) *Science and the Near-Death Experience*, 164ff., *Consciousness Beyond Life*, 146-148.

50) *Science and the Near-Death Experience*, 168.

51) Sabom argues this regarding experiments inducing hypercarbia. "Were these experiences which were reported by Meduna's patients and which resembled the NDE caused by the high levels of carbon dioxide *per se* or were they due to some other mechanism associated with the patient's CO2-induced near-death condition?" *Recollections of Death*, 178.

52) *The Handbook of Near-Death Experiences*, 225. Bruce Greyson is Professor of Psychiatry and Neurobehavioral Sciences at the University of Virginia Medical School and has authored over 100 publications in peer-reviewed medical journals. He has been prominent in near-death studies for decades. Edward Kelly is research professor in the Department of Psychiatry and Neurobehavioral Sciences at the University of Virginia. Emily Williams Kelly is research assistant professor in the Department of Psychiatry and Neurobehavioral Sciences at the University of Virginia.

Another strong point against physiological explanations is that each of them confuses and disorients the mind rather than heightens its activities. According to Parnia and Fenwick, "Any acute alteration in cerebral physiology such as occurring in hypoxia, hypercarbia, metabolic, and drug induced disturbances and seizures leads to disorganized and compromised cerebral function ... [and] impaired attention," whereas "NDEs in cardiac arrest are clearly not confusional and in fact indicate heightened awareness, attention and consciousness at a time when consciousness and memory formation would not be expected to occur." S. Parnia, P. Fenwick. Near-death experiences in cardiac arrest: Visions of a dying brain or visions of a new science of consciousness? *Resuscitation* 52:8 (2002). Found in *The Handbook of Near-Death Experiences*, 228.

53) *Science and the Near-Death Experience*, 160,161; *The Handbook of Near-Death Experiences*, 218,219.

54) Sartori (*The Near-Death Experiences of Hospitalized Intensive Care Patients*) kept careful records of drugs given to both patients with and without NDEs. Of those who experienced NDEs, 26.7% were given

no sedatives and 66.7% weren't given painkillers.(235) Only 6.67% of the NDErs were given both painkilling and sedative drugs. "If drugs were the cause of the NDE then a higher percentage would be expected."(235) A large percentage of her total sample (including those who experienced NDEs and those who didn't) was given painkilling, sedative drugs or had a general anesthetic. "Less than 1% of this sample reported a NDE…." (232, 281) After noting that almost all of her patients who had hallucinations (as opposed to NDEs) had been given painkilling and sedative drugs (only one had a hallucination without being given drugs, but this one suffered from severe sleep deprivation)(237), Sartori concluded, "This strengthens the argument that drugs contribute to confusional experiences as opposed to causing clear, precise reports of NDEs."(237) "…drugs inhibit the NDE, or the recall of it, as opposed to causing it; this is acknowledged by Blackmore (1993, 40-41) and Greyson and Stevenson (1980)." "In some of the most vivid NDEs no drugs were administered at the time of the experience."(Sartori, 281)

55) G.O. Gabbard, and S.W. Twemlow, *With the Eyes of the Mind: An Empirical Analysis of Out-of-Body States* (New York: Praeger, 1984); B. Greyson, Near-death experiences precipitated by suicide attempt: Lack of influence of psychopathology, religion, and expectations. *Journal of Near-Death Studies* 9:183-188; H. J. Irwin, *Flight of mind: A Psychological Study of the Out-of-Body Experience* (Metuchen, NJ: Scarecrow Press, 1985). T.P. Lock, and F.C. Shontz, Personality correlates of the near-death experience: A preliminary study. *Journal of the American Society for Psychical Research* 77:311-18 (1983); K. Ring, 1980. *Life at Death: A Scientific Investigation of the Near-Death Experience*, (New York: Coward, McCann & Geoghegan, 1980). See also *Recollections of Death* and *The Handbook of Near-Death Experiences*, 216.

56) Dr. Sabom rejects the possibility of both conscious and unconscious fabrication for several reasons. First, he corroborated stories with family members, medical personnel, and medical records. He also noted that most of the patients weren't acquainted with NDEs, and the few who were familiar often pointed out how theirs differed from the ones they'd heard about. They were also very reluctant to share, since there wasn't an upside to their telling their stories. The downside was they feared being referred to a psychiatrist. Finally, there's much evidence of long-term life changes associated with NDEs. Why would a fabricated story radically change a life? *Recollections of Death*, 156-160.

57) Janice Miner Holden, Jeffrey Long, B. Jason MacLurg, Characteristics of Western Near-Death Experiences, in *The Handbook of Near-Death Experiences*, 133.

58) *The Handbook of Near-Death Experiences*, 232.

59) Sartori reviewed the literature very well in her 60 page discussion of naturalistic explanations (*The Near-Death Experiences of Hospitalized Intensive Care Patients*, 59-119). She concluded, "Despite the many reductionist arguments, the NDE remains unexplained in such terms." Pim van Lommel's review of the literature on naturalistic explanations also concluded that naturalistic explanations had failed. (*Consciousness Beyond Life*, 105-135) Note other literature reviews in *The Handbook of Near-Death Experiences*, and *Light & Death*, 175-191.

60) The author of this study demonstrated no knowledge of the extensive literature in peer reviewed journals on this subject. If he didn't want to take the time to examine these studies himself, he should have at least referred to the summaries of studies found in *The Handbook of Near-Death Experiences, The Near-Death Experiences of Hospitalized Intensive Care Patients, Consciousness Beyond Life*, and *Science and the Near-Death Experience*. Here's the article: http://www.scientificamerican.com/article.cfm?id=peace-of-mind-near-death

Other critiques of near-death studies often show the same lack of familiarity with the scholarly NDE literature. See, for example, the 1989 textbook by Michael C. Kearl, *Endings: A Sociology of Death and Dying*, (New York: Oxford University Press, 1989), 493-496. This 500+ page textbook on the subject of dying dedicates only four pages to near-death experiences, referencing only Moody and Kübler-Ross and concluding that it's all a matter of faith. This is a horrific oversight, seeing that *The Journal of Near-Death Studies* (formerly *Anabiosis*) had started its bi-yearly, peer reviewed publication in 1981 and many studies had been done before this text was written, including Sabom's prospective study in book form by 1982.

Chapter 5

1) Raymond A. Moody, *Life After Life* (New York: Bantam Books, 1975), 99.

2) Pim van Lommel, *Consciousness Beyond Life* (New York: HarperCollins, 2010), 21.

3) "Hornell Hart (1954) analyzed 288 published OBE cases in which persons reported perceiving events that they could not have perceived in the ordinary way. In 99 of these cases, the events in question had been verified as having occurred, and the experience had been reported to someone else *before* that verification occurred." J.M. Holden, B. Greyson, D. James, 2009, *The Handbook of Near-Death Experiences: Thirty Years of Investigation* (Santa Barbara, California: ABC-CLIO, LLC), 223. H. Hart, ESP projection: Spontaneous cases and the experimental method. *Journal of the American Society for Psychical Research*, 1954, 48:121-46); *The Handbook of Near-death Experiences* also mentions E.W. Cook, B. Greyson, and I. Stevenson, Do any near-death experiences provide evidence for the survival of human personality after death? Relevant features and illustrative case reports. *Journal of Scientific Exploration*, 1988, 12:377-406; E.W. Kelly, B. Greyson, I Stevenson, 1999-2000. Can experiences near-death furnish evidence of life after death? *Omega*, 1999-2000, 40:513-19.

4) For example, see *Life After Life* (28,98,99,100); *Consciousness Beyond Life* (19ff.,38,173-178,298); Chris Carter, *Science and the Near-Death Experience* (Rochester: Inner Traditions, 2010), 119, 120,219,265-267,156,171,216; Penny Sartori, *The Near-Death Experiences of Hospitalized Intensive Care Patients* (Lewiston, Queenston, Lampeter: The Edwin Mellen Press, 2008), 267-274, 297-301. Michael Sabom [*Recollections of Death* (New York: Harper & Row, 1982), 27] found 32 of his patients having veridical experiences. He did an especially good job of corroborating reports with medical records, nurses, doctors, and family members.

5) Several of these instances have been mentioned in the NDE studies I read. Sartori mentions and documents deathbed visions where people "report meeting relatives or friends who they did not know to be deceased at the time they saw them."

6) Ring addresses NDEs with corroboration in *The Handbook of Near-death Experiences*, p. 231, referencing K. Clark, in B. Greyson and C.P. Flynn, Eds., *The Near-Death Experience: Problems, Prospects, Perspectives* (Springfield, Illinois: Charles C. Thomas, 1984) 242-55; Ring and Lawrence "Further Evidence for Veridical Perception During Near-Death Experiences," *Journal of Near-Death Studies* 11:223-29, (1993); Sartori, Badham, and Fenwick, "A Prospectively Studied Near-Death Experience with Corroborated Out-of-Body Perceptions and Unexplained Healing, *Journal of Near-Death Studies* 25:69-84 (2006). Sartori notes that "NDErs have also reported discovering solutions to problems or possessing knowledge previously unknown following the NDE," citing K. Ring, *Heading Toward Omega: In Search of the Meaning of the Near-Death Experience* (New York: William Morrow, 1984), 165-92.

7) Susan Blackmore suggests that a part of these claims can be attributed to guessing. *Dying to Live* (Buffalo, NY: Prometheus Books, 1993), 115.

8) "Perhaps they're just good guesses" some will say. But several studies (such as Sartori's and Sabom's prospective studies) tested this with control groups who did not have NDEs. In van Lommel's research, among his NDErs, "92 percent were completely accurate, 6 percent contained some error and only 1% were completely erroneous." (*Consciousness Beyond Life*, 20)

9) Penny Sartori, *The Near Death Experiences of Hospitalized Intensive Care Patients: A Five-Year Clinical Study*, (New York: The Edwin Mellen Press, 2008) 212-215. She concluded, "…this research has demonstrated that those who reported OBEs gave more accurate descriptions of events and equipment used than those who were resuscitated, but did not report a NDE/OBE. This lends further support to the possibility of consciousness existing apart from the brain."(273,274) See also P. Sartori, P. Badham, and P. Fenwick, A Prospectively Studied Near-Death Experience with Corroborated Out-of-Body Perceptions and Unexplained Healing, *Journal of Near-Death Studies* 25:69-84, (2006), 3. Cardiologist Michael Sabom also tested the hypothesis that out of body "observations" were merely retrospective reconstructions. Twenty-five of his cardiac patients who did not have NDEs were asked to guess about what happened in their procedures. Eighty percent made at least one *major* error. Furthermore, Sabom noted that among the patients who reported veridical perception, that their observations were often specific for their particular resuscitation and would not have accurately described the resuscitation of another one of his patients. Example: one reported seeing doctors give him a "shot in the groin," which was accurate for his procedure, but wasn't done in other cases where patients reported veridical perception (*Recollections of Death*, 83-87,113,114).

10) Michael Sabom, *Light & Death* (Grand Rapids: Zondervan, 1998), 12.

11) *Consciousness Beyond Life*, 19,158. As Greyson, Kelly and Kelly put it in their review of explanatory models, "The real challenge of explanatory models of NDEs lies in examining how complex consciousness, including thinking, sensory perception, and memory, can occur under conditions in which current physiological models of mind deem it impossible (*The Handbook of Near-death Experiences*, 234).

12) *Consciousness Beyond Life*, 161-204. Note this reprise article by Worlee against van Lommel - http://www.neardeath.woerlee.org/setting-the-record-straight.php.

13) R.H. Sandin, *et al.*, Awareness during Anaesthesia: A Prospective Case Study, *The Lancet*, Volume: 355   Issue: 9205   pp. 707-711 (Feb. 26, 2000).

14) Ibid.

15) "Unresponsiveness is thought to almost universally occur at the time of cardiac arrest, as a consequence of a precipitous drop in cerebral perfusion. The first action that Basic Life Support (BLS) and Advanced Life Support (ALS) trainees are taught to perform is to check for unresponsiveness. It is theoretically possible, however, to maintain awareness following cardiac arrest if cerebral perfusion is maintained by the use of highly effective chest compressions and in the presence of adequate oxygenation. Reports of such retained awareness during cardiac arrest in the literature are sparse." Shailesh Bihari and Venkatakrishna Rajajee, *Neurocritical Care*, Prolonged Retention of Awareness During Cardiopulmonary Resuscitation for Asystolic Cardiac Arrest Neurocritical Care, Volume 9, Number 3, Pages 382-386 (2008).

16) Pim van Lommel, Setting the Record Straight: Correcting Two Recent Cases of Materialist Misrepresentation of My Research and Conclusions, *Journal of Near-Death Studies*, 30(2),107-119, Winter 2011. When a patient's EEG (measuring brain activity) has been monitored during cardiac arrest, it flat-lines after an average of 15 seconds (113). Thus, "it seems rational to assume that all 562 survivors of cardiac arrest in several recently published prospective studies on NDE should have had a flat EEG, because no patient had been resuscitated within 20 seconds of cardiac arrest onset." Now it's true that a flat-line EEG doesn't rule out any brain activity whatsoever. Some kind of electrical activity that an EEG can't register may continue somewhere deep within the brain. Yet, consciousness can be maintained only when large portions of the brain (e.g., the brainstem, cerebral cortex, hippocampus and thalamus) are functioning properly and working together. Since the EEG shows primarily electrical activity in the cortex, a flatline EEG indicates an unconscious state. "The issue is not whether there is any non-measurable brain activity of any kind whatsoever but whether there is

measurable brain activity of the specific form, and in different neural networks, as regarded by contemporary neuroscience to be the necessary condition of conscious experience. And it has been proven in several studies in patients with induced cardiac arrest that there was no such measurable and specific brain activity during cardiac arrest." (115) Neither does such unified brain activity occur during deep sleep or successful anesthesia(116). A publication by the National Institutes of Health (2010) puts loss of consciousness during cardiac arrest at 10 seconds http://www.nlm.nih.gov/medlineplus/tutorials/heartattack/ct139105.pdf (p. 7). According to Dr. Sam Parnia, "an alternative explanation is that the experiences reported from cardiac arrest, may actually be arising at a time when consciousness is either being lost, or regained, rather than from the actual cardiac arrest period itself. Any cerebral insult leads to a period of both anterograde and retrograde amnesia. In fact memory is a very sensitive indicator of brain injury and the length of amnesia before and after unconsciousness is a way of determining the severity of the injury. Therefore, events that occur just prior to or just after the loss of consciousness would not be expected to be recalled. (Do Reports of Consciousness during Cardiac Arrest Hold the Key to Discovering the Nature of Consciousness? *Medical Hypotheses* 69(4):933-937)

17) Greyson, Kelly and Kelly (*The Handbook of Near-Death Experiences*) have a particularly good discussion of the hypothesis that NDEs occur as the brain shuts down or as brain function returns, on pp. 229-231 of their chapter, Explanatory Models for Near-Death Experiences. In brief, patients' memories from just prior to loss of consciousness or just after regaining consciousness are either completely absent or confused. (M.J. Aminoff, *et al.*, 1988. Electrocerebral accompaniments of syncope associated with malignant ventricular arrhythmias. *Annals of Internal Medicine* 108:791-96 (1988); S. Parnia, and P. Fenwick, 2002. Near death experiences in cardiac arrest: Visions of a dying brain or visions of a new science of consciousness? *Resuscitation* 52:5-11. See also *The Handbook of Near-Death Experiences*, 230.)

While partial awakening has been reported in 0.1 to 0.3 percent of general surgeries, the experiences are "generally extremely unpleasant, frightening, and painful and not visual – extremely different from NDEs. (*The Handbook of Near-death Experiences*, 230) Yet, the patient reported that, during her NDE, her vision "was brighter and more focused and clearer than normal vision" and that her hearing "was a clearer hearing than with my ears." (*Light & Death*, 44) Sartori dismisses the suggestion that blood flow during CPR gives the brain enough blood to sustain partial consciousness. (*The Near Death Experiences of Hospitalized Intensive Care Patients*, 68,69) Sartori later has an extended, documented discussion on "When did the NDE/OBE occur?" (260-264). She concludes, "This research confirms Fenwick's point; it appears that consciousness can exist independently of a functioning brain." (264)

18) This remarkable NDE was originally published in *Light and Death*, 37-47; 184-190. It was discussed further in van Lommel, 173-178; see also *The Handbook of Near-death Experiences*, 191-193, where Holden examines the criticisms of this NDE by Augustine and finds them wanting. Augustine holds that since 2 out of 1000 patients experience some type of awareness during anesthesia, that she could have overheard some of the conversations. But those rare cases are typically explained by someone being under-anesthetized. In this case, her anesthesia was deep and closely monitored in three different ways. Also, the constant, loud clicking in the molded ear plugs would rule out anything being heard, whereas the eye coverings would keep her from seeing anything. Augustine maintains that she consolidated a coherent memory over a period of three years by things she learned over time. But van Lommel and others found that people's NDE stories stayed consistent from the first report in the hospital setting to years later when followed-up upon. There's no tendency toward embellishment. While other challenges have been forwarded against this case, in my opinion, they always fall short. For a good back and forth debate on this case, see G.M. Woerlee, Could Pam Reynolds Hear? A New

Investigation into the Possibility of Hearing during this Famous Near-Death Experience. *Journal of Near-Death Studies*, 30: 3-25 (2011), and responses by Hameroff and Carter in the same journal.

19) Vivid consciousness should not occur during general anesthesia or cardiac arrest, since the mind is quickly and severely impaired. For example, cardiac arrest causes instantaneous circulatory arrest, so that blood flow to the brain ceases. Even if certain low-level brain activity could remain, it isn't sufficient for conscious experience. Yet, "in five published studies alone, more than 100 cases of NDEs occurring under conditions of cardiac arrest have been reported" (*The Handbook of Near-death Experiences*, p. 227.) According to Sam Parnia and Peter Fenwick [Near-Death Experiences in Cardiac Arrest, *Resuscitation* 52:5-11 (2002)], "…NDEs in cardiac arrest are clearly not confusional and in fact indicate heightened awareness, attention and consciousness at a time when consciousness and memory formation would not be expected to occur." According to Greyson, Kelly and Kelly, "An analysis of 520 cases in our collection showed that 80 percent of experiencers described their thinking during the NDE as 'clearer than usual' or 'as clear as usual.' Furthermore, in our collection, people reported enhanced mental functioning significantly *more* often when they were actually physiologically close to death than when they were not" (*The Handbook of Near-death Experiences,* p. 229). The 11-year-old I interviewed told me very specifically the colors of the flowers he saw in his NDE and even what colors he *didn't* see in his NDE. It was a very vivid experience, with a very vivid, intact memory. It appeared from my conversation that he could retrieve the scenes from his NDE and review them at will, although when he experienced them he had stopped breathing and lay unconscious under a pile of snow. Nelson (*The Spiritual Doorway to the Brain*) argues, "The characteristics of near-death experiences measured by the Greyson scale…combine to tell us that wide expanses of the brain are engaged during these experiences." (p. 117) Yet, such "wide expanses" should be picked up easily on an EEG. According to Nelson, the brain is "*alive* and *conscious*" during NDEs." (132) See also p. 214 – he believes that "part of the dreaming brain erupts in a brain already awake," creating "experiences that are realistic and memorable." Yet, this again seems to require a fully functioning brain, which is clearly contraindicated in cardiac arrests and general anesthesia.

20) According to Sabom, unlike dreams, "The NDE…is perceived as stark reality both during the experience and later in reflection. In addition, the extreme variability of dream content from person to person and from night to night contrasts with the consistency of events in the NDE. It is thus unlikely that the NDE can be explained as being a dream" (*Recollections of Death*, 166). Let's imagine that I'm feeling jittery and take a Valium to relax me. In about an hour I'm feeling very relaxed and fall asleep on my couch. Now it's quite possible that, going to sleep in such a relaxed state, I might have a dream that features relaxation as I picture it, such as reading a book on a porch in a mountain chalet or building a sandcastle on a beach. What we don't hear is that everyone who takes Valium has extremely similar dreams with one or more of 15 common elements.

Example: We don't find reports that 90% of the people taking Valium have dreams that begin with lying on rafts in a swimming pool, chatting with their best friends who are also on rafts, followed by a walk to an ice cream shop where they sip a milkshake and talk to the proprietor about relaxing life events. Then they walk toward the restroom and find themselves transported to a mountain chalet, where they choose a book from a seemingly endless bookshelf and sit on a porch overlooking a trout stream. Instead, the variety of dreams produced in a relaxed state could be seemingly endless.

21) *Life After Life*, 21. Dr. Sartori's patients were from the UK, almost entirely Welsh. She reported, "The NDE reports from this sample were consistent with other Western accounts of NDEs documented in the literature. There were no features culture specific to a Welsh population." Penny Sartori, *The Near-Death Experiences of Hospitalized Intensive Care Patients* (Lewiston, Queenston, Lampeter: The Edwin Mellen Press, 2008), 225.

22) Maurice Rawlings, *Beyond Death's Door* (New York: Thomas Nelson, 1978), xiii.

23) *Consciousness Beyond Life*, 143. Among Dr. Sartori's patients who had deep NDEs, "…none of the patients claimed to be familiar with NDEs prior to their hospital admissions" (Sartori, 266).

24) *Consciousness Beyond Life*, xii.

25) *Life After Life*, 175.

26) See, for example, *Recollections of Death*, 116,162. One person would suddenly lose consciousness mid-sentence. Another was hit from behind by a car.

27) *Consciousness Beyond Life*, 147. Sabom's study concluded, "A person's age, sex, race, area of residence, size of home community, years of education, occupation, religious background, or frequency of church attendance did not seem to affect whether he or she would or would not encounter an NDE during a near-death crisis event. Moreover, knowledge of the NDE prior to the near-death crisis event did not appear to predispose the person subsequently to report an NDE following a crisis event." (*Recollections of Death*, 57,61)

28) *Consciousness Beyond Life*, 147.

29) Sartori discounts wishful thinking as a cause by citing seven patients who explicitly spoke of being surprised by the content of their NDEs. *The Near-Death Experiences of Hospitalized Intensive Care Patients*, 215,216, 274,275.

30) *Consciousness Beyond Life*, 19.

31) *Life After Life*, 105. One NDEr in Sartori's study reported seeing someone who might have been Jesus, but he didn't expect Jesus to look that way at all. "I don't know who he was; he might have been Jesus for all I know but that's not what I'd expect Jesus to look like, his hair was scruffy and needed a good combing! His eyes were piercing and bright, it's as if I was drawn to look at his eyes." *The Near-Death Experiences of Hospitalized Intensive Care Patients*, 192. See also *Science and the Near-Death Experience*, 111,115,117,105,107,124,264,219.

32) *Life After Life*, 77-84.

33) Jeffrey Long, *Evidence of the Afterlife* (New York: HarperOne, 2010), 17.

34) *Recollections of Death*, 50. For details of conversations on the other side and how they each had closure, see 210,211; also *Light & Death*, 23,67,68,111,112,114.

35) http://www.nderf.org.

36) Ibid.

37) See, for example, *Consciousness Beyond Life*, 71-79.

38) Melvin Morse, *Closer to the Light* (New York: Villard Books, 1990), 3-21.

39) M. Morse, (1983). A near-death experience in a 7-year-old child. *American Journal of Diseases of Children (1960)*, *137*(10), 959-961.

40) *Closer to the Light*, 18-21.

41) Melvin Morse, writing in *The Light Beyond*, Raymond Moody (New York: A Bantam Book, 1988), 108.

42) M. Morse, D. Conner, D., D. Tyler, D. (1985). Near-death experiences in a pediatric population. A preliminary report. *American Journal of Diseases of Children (1960)*, *139*(6), 595-600; M. Morse, P. Castillo, D. Venecia, et al. "Childhood Near-Death Experiences." *American Journal of Diseases of Children* 140 (1986): 1110-1113; *Closer to the Light*, Melvin Morse and Paul Perry, 1990, Villard Books, NY, 1990.

43) Serdahely "concluded that adult retrospective accounts were indistinguishable from contemporary pediatric NDEs" (W.J. Serdahely, 1991). A comparison of retrospective accounts of childhood death experiences with contemporary pediatric near-death experience accounts. *Journal of Near-Death Studies* 9:223. "In terms of NDE content, even though every experience is unique, the NDEs of children and teens follow a consistent pattern that appears to be little different from the pattern experienced by adults…. Neither do children's experiences appear to be affected by cause of near-death crisis, age,

gender, religiosity, or any other demographic variable. One distinction appears to be that children are almost always accompanied into the light" (*The Handbook of Near-Death Experiences*, 92,105).

44) According to Richard Bonenfant, "Children's accounts are often informative simply because they report exactly what they see without great concern over the rational interpretation of their observations." R.J. Bonenfant, A Child's Encounter with the Devil, *Journal of Near-Death Studies* 20:95(2001). From *The Handbook of Near-Death Experiences*, 91.

45) *Consciousness Beyond Life*, 75,76.

46) Ibid., 72.

47) *Science and the Near-Death Experience*, 254-268.

48) Ibid., 254, 255. Another line of evidence could be exploring NDEs in which a person is surprised to encounter a person on the other side that he didn't know had died. Bruce Greyson cites 29 cases in his article, "Seeing Dead People Not Known to Have Died: 'Peak in Darien' Experiences," *Anthropology and Humanism*, Vol. 35, Issue 2, pp. 159–171, (2010). Greyson also notes, "In our collection of 665 NDEs, 138 (21 percent) included a purported encounter with a deceased person, whereas only 25 (four percent) included a purported encounter with a living person." To use these as evidence for the afterlife, it seems we'd need to discover what percentage of NDEs include an encounter with a person not known to have died. If the amount is smaller than four percent, then couldn't the people not known to have died be merely a subset of those living persons who were seen?

49) *Science and the Near-Death Experience*, 257.

50) Ibid., 256.

51) Ibid., 258.

52) Deathbed visions may also serve as a sort of evidential bridge from near-death experiences to final-death experiences. Some researchers note that since NDEs are by definition experienced by people who don't remain finally dead after their experience, that we must make the unwarranted assumption that at a person's final death they'll experience some of the same features as the NDE. Of course, the only way to know this with 100% certainty would be to experience final death ourselves, but the deathbed vision would give us an indication from those who are at the point of entering their final death state.

53) See especially Raymond A. Moody, *Glimpses of Eternity* (New York: Guideposts, 2010).

54) Ibid., 13,14.

55) *Glimpses of Eternity*, 77,80,81.

56) From personal interview with Bucky.

57) *Life After Life*, 5,6.

58) *Consciousness Beyond Life*, vi.

59) *Beyond Death's Door*, xii, xiii.

60) *Consciousness Beyond Life*, 310. Why would they lie? Put yourself in their place. Having just gone through such a trauma, they're obviously afraid that sharing such a wild experience will cause people to think they've gone a bit whacko. No wonder they're very hesitant to share. One of the men I interviewed shared his NDE with his wife, but even though his surgeon was a Christian, he didn't tell him. Although he works with a men's ministry in a church, he's reluctant to tell people there. He's not sure why he's so reluctant – he simply is. But all this hesitation to share argues strongly against someone making it up to get attention.

This is very different from a TV evangelist telling about his miraculous answered prayer. Now maybe it indeed happened to the evangelist, but since he's got everything to gain from such a dramatic testimony, I question it. But for the patient with no religious TV show, whose body is in bad shape and risks having his sanity questioned, there's no apparent motive for making up such an event.

61) *Life After Life*, 89.

62) Ibid., 85.

63) *Consciousness Beyond Life*, 39.

64) Ibid., 23.

65) See especially K. Ring, and S. Cooper, 1999. *Mindsight: Near-death and out-of-body experiences in the blind.* Palo Alto, CA: Institute of Transpersonal Psychology." Van Lommel reports on the blind NDE in *Consciousness Beyond Life*, 19,23-26,39. Sartori states, "The reports [of the blind seeing] were considered to be genuine due to the similarities between NDEs in the blind and the sighted, the sincerity of the experience and in some cases, the corroboration of witnesses." *The Near-Death Experiences of Hospitalized Intensive Care Patients*, 100, commenting on Ring and Cooper, 68.

66) http://www.newdualism.org/nde-papers/Ring/Ring-Journal%20of%20Near-Death%20Studies_1997-16-101-147.pdf Kenneth Ring and Sharon Cooper, Near-Death and Out-of-Body Experiences in the Blind: A Study of Apparent Eyeless Vision, *Journal of Near-Death Studies*. "There is no question that NDEs in the blind do occur and, furthermore, that they take the same general form and are comprised of the very same elements that define the NDEs of sighted individuals. Moreover, this generalization appears to hold across all three categories of blindness that were represented in this study: those blind from birth, those adventitiously blind, and those severely visually impaired."

"The second issue, and the one that was the driving force of this study, was whether the blind claim to have visual impressions during their NDEs or OBEs. On this point, too, our data were conclusive.

Overall, 80 percent of our respondents reported these claims, most of them in the language of unhesitating declaration, even when they had been surprised, or even stunned, by the unexpected discovery that they could in fact see. Like sighted experiencers, our blind respondents described to us both perceptions of this world and otherworldly scenes, often in fulsome, fine-grained detail, and sometimes with a sense of extremely sharp, even subjectively perfect, acuity."

What do the blind "see" in their normal dreams (as opposed to their NDEs)? "(1) There are no visual images in the dreams of the congenitally blind; (2) individuals blinded before the age of 5 also tend not to have visual imagery; (3) those who become sightless between the age of 5 to 7 may or may not retain visual imagery; and (4) most persons who lose their sight after age 7 do retain visual imagery, although its clarity tends to fade with time."

67) Ibid., 125.

68) *Consciousness Beyond Life*, 24-26.

69) Ibid., 26.

70) Ibid., 152.

71) Ibid., 55. The study comes from C. Sutherland, *Transformed by the Light: Life after Near-Death Experiences* (Sydney, Australia: Bantam Books, 1992).

72) *Life After Life*, 84.

73) Ibid., 84,85.

74) *Consciousness Beyond Life*, 40.

75) *Life After Life*, 105.

76) Ibid., 65.

77) Ibid., 84.

78) *Consciousness Beyond Life*, 152; Sabom had the same results when comparing his NDErs with his control group – *Light & Death*, 95-97.

79) (http://en.wikipedia.org/wiki/Illusory_superiority)

80) To prove you're not just dreaming that you're reading, or to prove that we're not in a fabricated

delusion like "The Matrix," all we can say is that we have a vivid apprehension of people and leaves and grasshoppers through our senses. And if you think about it, you can't really go beyond that "vivid apprehension." You may say, "Yes, but I talk to other people who have the same vivid experience of this physical world and we can do physical experiments which prove that it's real." Sure, but if this were all a dream world, those people and experiments would all be a part of your dream. It's merely because it seems qualitatively different from a dream – it *seems* real – that you're very confident that you're reading a book rather than merely dreaming that you're reading a book.

81) But let's take this a step further, starting with an analogy. Let's say you're trying to make a decision between two cars to buy, and in your opinion, the typical reports don't give you enough information. So the salesman pulls out a study showing a nonbiased consumer report of the last 500 people who bought these cars. Ninety percent reported that they're really glad they purchased car #1 after one year.

So what's your verdict? Even without driving the car yourself for a year, wouldn't you be wise to accept the experience of the 90 percent? Is accepting the experience of multitudes of NDErs really so different, even though we've never experienced one?

82) For the sake of brevity, I've ignored the contributions of Swiss-born psychiatrist Elizabeth Kübler-Ross. When she moved from Switzerland to New York City in 1958 to complete her education, she winced at the deplorable state of the dying. Rather than dying surrounded by friends and family, they typically died in lonely hospital rooms, surrounded by blinking lights and beeping machinery. Doctors often failed to engage them, viewing death as their failure to heal. Optimistic Americans didn't want to think about death.

Kübler-Ross forced us to examine the death experience and emotionally engage the dying. Her work helped bring about both hospice and professional counseling for the dying. She also listened to patients when, close to the point of death, they suddenly became very alert and told of a beautiful place of reunion with deceased loved ones. As a respected scientist, Kübler-Ross was honored with 18 honorary doctorates. She taught physicians and academics about death and dying and wrote over 20 books. As she taught, she exposed them to the near-death experience.

Chapter 6

1) Kenneth Ring surveyed three university classes (111 students), which covered the topic of NDEs. After the courses, most students reported a decreased fear of death, a stronger belief in life after death, a more spiritual orientation, a stronger belief in the purposefulness of life, and a strengthened view of God. [The impact of near-death experiences on persons who have not had them: A report of a preliminary study and two replications. *Journal of Near-Death Studies* 13:229 (1995).] Whereas some of van Lommel's patients in Holland became "spiritual," but showed less interest in traditional religion, Sartori reported of her patients (overwhelmingly Welsh): "All patients reported an increased tendency to pray, go to church, and read the Bible." *The Near-Death Experiences of Hospitalized Intensive Care Patients*, 244.

2) *Consciousness Beyond Life*, 284.

3) *Life After Life*, 58,59.

4) *Consciousness Beyond Life*, 284.

5) *Life After Life*, 64.

6) Ibid., 59.

7) Ibid., 59.

8) *Consciousness Beyond Life*, 34.

9) Ibid. 29.

10) Susan Blackmore, *Dying to Live* (Buffalo, NY: Prometheus Books, 1993), xii.

11) *Consciousness Beyond Life*, 35.

12) Ibid., 55.

13) *Life After Life*, 65.

14) Ibid., 63.

15) *Consciousness Beyond Life*, 151.

16) Steve Sjogren, *The Day I Died* (Ventura: Regal Books, 2006), 31. The wife of one of Sartori's patients reported this change in her husband. "[He] is very different since the experience; he is very loving towards me. Before he used to do as he pleased and go out driving in the car whenever he wanted without giving me a second thought. Now, he won't go out unless I want to go out too. He is far more considerate and I feel like he's more loving and affectionate" (*The Near-Death Experiences of Hospitalized Intensive Care Patients*, 293).

17) *Life After Life*, 65, 93.

18) In one of my personal interviews, the NDEr talked with three celestial beings, explaining to them why he felt that he needed to return for his family. Moody shared an experience where an elderly aunt was ill and the family kept praying for her to recover. Finally, the aunt told a family member that she'd seen the other side and wanted to stay there, but their prayers were hindering her from going over. She died shortly after they stopped praying for her recovery. (Ibid., 81)

19) *Consciousness Beyond Life*, 151.

20) Ibid., 53.

21) Ibid., 151.

22) Ibid., 152.

23) *Consciousness Beyond Life*, xiii.

24) Ibid., 29. As Moody stated, "almost everyone remarks upon the *time-lessness* of this out-of-body state." *Life After Life*, 47.

25) *Life After Life*, 43.

26) *Consciousness Beyond Life*, 21.

27) One described it "as if I was seeing with all-knowing eyes. (Ibid., 36)

28) *Life After Life*, 143,144.

29) *Consciousness Beyond Life*, 29-31.

30) Sartori notes, "Research (Grey 1987, Fenwick and Fenwick 1996a, Ellwood 2001, Rommer 2000) has served to highlight that negative NDEs are just as real as the pleasant ones and can occur in the absence of anesthetics" (*The Near-Death Experiences of Hospitalized Intensive Care Patients*, 18). She further states, "Religious beliefs and prior knowledge do not appear to influence the experience as cross-cultural studies reveal a similar pattern regardless of content of the experience or cultural beliefs" (23). "There are cases that have both pleasant and frightening components; they may begin as frightening and convert to pleasant (Bonenfant 2001) or vice versa (Irwin and Bramwell 1988)" (24). In her study, "13.3% had 'frightening' NDEs, consistent with three other studies which found 12.5% (Grey 1987), 15% (Atwater 1992) and 18% (Rommer 2000). See *The Handbook of Near-Death Experiences*, Chapter 4, for a good review of the literature on distressing NDEs.

31) According to *The Handbook of Near-Death Experiences*, 70, although nine studies with 459 experiencers found no accounts of distressing NDEs, "12 other studies involving 1,369 experiencers produced the accounts of 315 people (23%) who reported NDEs ranging from disturbing to terrifying or despairing." For a recent book dedicated to distressing NDEs, see *Dancing Past the Dark: Distressing Near-Death Experiences*, by Nancy Evans Bush (2012).

32) *Consciousness Beyond Life*, v.,vi.

33) The atheists I read don't claim to have a slam dunk argument for atheism. After all, how could you ever prove with any degree of certainty that there is no God? Instead, they make the more humble claim that they see no strong evidence for the existence of God. In a discussion such as this, it should (if all people were objective) take only one strong line of evidence to move an honest seeker from atheism to theism. This can happen with scientific theories. Reference the white swan theory being decimated by the sighting of one black swan.

Appendix 1

1) Raymond Moody, *Paranormal* (New York: HarperCollins, 2012), 47,48.

2) Ibid., 63.

3) Ibid., 77.

4) I found this NDE on www.nderf.org. Dr. Alexander reported that his "companion" during his NDE appeared at first in human form, wearing a beautiful dress, then as an "orblike ball of light," then later returned to human form. *Proof of Heaven* (New York: Simon & Schuster, 2012), 68.

5) *The Handbook of Near-death Experiences: Thirty Years of Investigation* (Santa Barbara, California: ABC-CLIO, LLC), 140-148.

6) Jeffrey Long, *Evidence for the Afterlife* (New York: HarperOne, 2010), 9.

7) For instance: NDE #1307 on www.nderf.org – like a "movie of myself and of my entire life…" "I could sense the real meaning of these relationships." "I had a sense of love and gratitude towards the persons appearing in my flash back." "This panoramic review of my life was very distinct, every little detail of the incidents, relationships were there – the relationships in some sort of distilled essence of meaning. Persons were life-like, living pictures, with all their personality, inner selves." NDE #2136 – went through the life review like a powerpoint. NDE #2913 – experienced life events going by in quick succession.

8) From www.nderf.org.

9) Ibid., NDE #49.

10) Ibid., #1828.

11) Ibid., #116.

12) Ibid., #1720.

13) Ibid., #1465.

14) Ibid., #2838.

Appendix 2

1) Charles Q. Choi, Peace of Mind: Near-Death Experiences Now Found to Have Scientific Explanations, *Scientific American*, September 12, 2011, p. 127. I often find such assertions in NDE literature, by both survivalists and naturalists, suggesting that all the NDE elements have been replicated by natural means. Yet, every time that I check their documentation, the experiences seem very different in many respects. For example: 1. Melvin Morse, David Venecia, and Jerrold Milstein, Near-death experiences: A neurophysiological explanatory model. *Journal of Near-Death Studies* 8:48, 1989 (from Handbook, pp. 217,218) - "…all the reported elements of NDEs can be produced in the office setting" with inhaled carbon dioxide. 2. M.A. Persinger, 1989. Modern neuroscience and near-death experiences: Expectancies and implications. Persinger comments on "A neurobiological model for near-death experiences." *Journal of Near-Death Studies* 7:234 (1989) – "a vast clinical and surgical literature…indicates that floating and rising sensations, OBEs, personally profound mystical and

religious encounters, visual and auditory experiences, and dream-like sequences are evoked, usually as single events, by electrical stimulation of deep, mesiobasal temporal love structures." Persinger went on to claim that through using transcranial magnetic stimulation, he had produced "all the major components of the NDE, including out-of-body experiences, floating, being pulled towards a light, hearing strange music, and profound meaningful experiences" [*The Handbook of Near-death Experiences: Thirty Years of Investigation* (Santa Barbara, California: ABC-CLIO, LLC), 220]; 3. Saavedra-Aguilar, J.C., and Gomez-Jeria, J.S., 1989. A neurobiological model for near-death experiences. *Journal of Near-Death Studies* 7:209 - "The list of mental phenomena seen in temporal lobe epilepsy and stereotaxic stimulation of the temporal lobe includes all the NDE phenomena." (*The Handbook of Near-death Experiences,* 219) 4. Michael Shermer, executive director of the Skeptics Society, stated in a March 2003 article, Demon-Haunted Brain, published in *Scientific American,* "Neuroscientist Michael Persinger, in his laboratory at Laurentian University in Sudbury, Ontario, for example, can induce all these perceptions [out-of-body experiences] in subjects by subjecting their temporal lobes to patterns of magnetic fields" (http://www.michaelshermer.com/2003/03/demon-haunted-brain). Shermer goes on to quote van Lommel's study as delivering "blows against the belief that mind and spirit are separate from brain and body," when in fact van Lommel's study gave strong evidence *opposing* this thesis. See van Lommel's response to Shermer here: http://www.nderf.org/NDERF/Research/vonlommel_skeptic_response.htm.) 5. Susan Blackmore claims that "all the components of the NDE can occur under other conditions, under the influence of drugs, stress, or even during dreams." *Dying to Live* (London: HarperCollins, 1993), 49. 6. Dr. Kevin Nelson claims that "Lempert's team compared the experience of their subjects to Moody's descriptions of the near-death experience. Surprisingly, they found *"no real difference* [emphasis his] between the two types of experience." [*The Spiritual Doorway to the Brain* (New York: Dutton, 2011), 124] This is quite a claim. From Nelson's description, Lempert has practically reproduced NDEs with induced fainting. Yet, as I show in Appendix #6, a perusal of Lempert's study shows significant differences in almost every respect. It would seem that this claim has taken on the status of a stubborn urban myth in the NDE literature that needs to be thoroughly researched. Every time I look up the cited sources and study the original data, the stark differences between NDEs and the reported naturalistic experiences become apparent.

2) *Trends in Cognitive Sciences*, Volume 15, Issue 10, 447-449, 18 August 2011.

3) "…Here in Spain the paper was mentioned in "Cuarto Milenio", a popular TV show on parapsychology, in a radio program "MIlenio 3", in one of the main newspapers, "el ABC", and in "el Mundo". Guess what the headline was in all of them: "The Science Finally Explains the NDEs. There is nothing paranormal about them"? The French newspaper "le Figaro" publishes a similar review of this paper. So does the Russian "Коммерсантъ". (From the discussion at the end of this interview: http://www.skeptiko.com/165-dr-caroline-watt-defends-there-is-nothing-paranormal-about-near-death-experiences/.)

4) *Life After Life*, 156-177.

5) *Science and the Near-Death Experience*, 150-215.

6) *Consciousness Beyond Life*, 105-135.

7) Penny Sartori, *The Near Death Experiences of Hospitalized Intensive Care Patients: A Five-Year Clinical Study* (New York: The Edwin Mellen Press, 2008), 57-120.

8) *The Handbook of Near-death Experiences: Thirty Years of Investigation* (Santa Barbara, California: ABC-CLIO, LLC), 213-234.

9) http://www.skeptiko.com/165-dr-caroline-watt-defends-there-is-nothing-paranormal-about-near-death-experiences/

10) As Pim van Lommel stated in a published reply to Mobbs and Watt, "I am deeply concerned that articles like Mobbs' and Watt's are passing the peer review process when the authors did not even acknowledge…existing literature that contradicts their stated position." *Journal of Near-Death Studies*, 30(2), Winter 2011.

11) *The Handbook of Near-Death Studies*, 7.

12) *Journal of Near-Death Studies*, vol. 30, no. 2, Winter 2011, Pim van Lommel, Guest Editorial; Setting the Record Straight; Correcting Two Recent Cases, 108,109.

13) http://www.skeptiko.com/165-dr-caroline-watt-defends-there-is-nothing-paranormal-about-near-death-experiences/

14) In Chapter 4 I didn't mention Mobbs' and Watt's explanation of the feeling of being dead, since it's not commonly argued. They note that the brain can fool people into thinking they're dead. It's called Cotard syndrome. They cite a case in which a patient was diagnosed with epilepsy and encephalitis. Yet, her conviction that she'd died was completely irrational, since she could touch her body and note that she was physically walking around and talking to living people. She was delusional. She didn't know how she supposedly died, but suggested it may have been when she had the flu a few weeks prior. She also reported hallucinating disco music, moving walls, and the feeling of water running down her left forearm. R. McKay, L. Cipolotti, Attributional Style in a Case of Cotard Delusion, *Consciousness and Cognition*, 16 (2007), 353.

Reading the details of the study confirms that her experience was very, very different from NDErs rationally concluding that they must have died, based upon such empirical data as hearing a doctor pronouncing them dead, seeing their lifeless bodies from a distance, walking through people, seeing heavenly beings, meeting God, etc.

Not only is Cotard syndrome very different from the NDE experience of death, but Mobbs and Watt fail to connect the syndrome with NDEs. They admit that "why delusions such as Cotard syndrome occur is unknown." So what data compels us to believe that Cotard syndrome would likely occur during a near-death event? Simply noting that some delusional people think they're dead in no way proves that the NDE experience of feeling dead is illusory.

15) *Dying to Live*, 34.

16) *Dying to Live*, 39.

17) Mobbs claims in a reply to criticism that he read Holden's chapter on Veridical Experiences and that it presented only one case study of veridical perception. (Response to Greyson, et al. There is nothing paranormal about near-death experiences, Dean Mobbs, *Trends in Cognitive Sciences*, September 2012, vol. 16, no. 9), p. 446. Yet, Holden's chapter was a review of the literature on the subject, not an attempt to present details of individual studies. She documented her chapter meticulously and pulled together documentation for over 100 examples of NDEs with corroboration in 43 different NDE studies.

18. http://www.skeptiko.com/165-dr-caroline-watt-defends-there-is-nothing-paranormal-about-near-death-experiences.

19. http://www.skeptiko.com/165-dr-caroline-watt-defends-there-is-nothing-paranormal-about-near-death-experiences.

Appendix 4

1) Raymond A. Moody, *The Light Beyond* (New York: Bantam Books, 1988), 18; Note also Michael B. Sabom, *Recollections of Death*, 145, 184-186 on the nature of the evidence. See also Moody in *Life After Life*, 177-186.

2) Moody's autobiography, *Paranormal* (New York: HarperCollins, 2012), yields insight into why he was so reluctant to declare that NDEs offered proof of heaven and God. First, as a philosophy student at the University of Virginia, he was impressed by Socrates' unique ability to help people see that their positions weren't as solid as they thought. Thus, he eschewed dogmatism, knowing that strong opinions could often be overturned. He certainly didn't want to give people a false assurance of heaven, only to have that hope overturned by future research. Second, he knew that NDEs were not experiences with a person's final death. They were something intermediate. Thus, what people experience in a *near*-death experience doesn't necessarily tell us about a person's *final* death experience. Third, Moody had a very uncomfortable relationship with his father, who didn't believe in God and wouldn't even listen to arguments for anything paranormal. According to Moody, "I feared my father greatly – I still do" (228). Perhaps he wanted to please his father by remaining publically skeptical. Fourth, he wanted *Life After Life* to be accepted by the scientific and specifically the medical community. Knowing that his first book didn't give adequate evidence for the afterlife, he decided to let the stories speak for themselves rather than try to sensationalize them with his own superlatives and dogmatic conclusions. Instead, he determined to simply get the stories out there and start the scientific process by delineating the typical elements of NDEs, hoping this would inspire others to a more rigorous scientific study of NDEs. It worked. (46,81,100-103,118)

3) Large scale clinical studies aren't as conclusive as one might think. For example, one study found that as much as 90 percent of carefully conceived, rigorously controlled, large-scale medical studies are eventually either overturned or extensively revised. http://well.blogs.nytimes.com/2010/10/18/questioning-the-results-of-medical-research) Dean Mobbs, coauthor of "There is nothing paranormal about near-death experiences," suggests in response to criticism of his article that NDE researchers should use "gold standard" techniques like double blind studies ("Response to Greyson et al.: there is nothing paranormal about near-death experiences," *Trends in Cognitive Sciences*, Sept. 2012, Vol. 16, no. 9, 446). Yet, double-blind studies aren't always practical, even in medicine. For example, to conduct a double-blind study to determine if open heart surgery is effective, researchers would need two sets of patients with severe arterial blockage. One set would be cut open and have a bypass performed. The other set would be cut open but not have a bypass. Neither group would know who actually had the bypass. Obviously, it's not practical to do double-blind studies to test open-heart surgeries. Other forms of evidence must be used in such cases.

The meaning of "scientific evidence" shifts from field to field. "Scientific evidence has no universally accepted definition but generally refers to evidence which serves to either support or counter a scientific theory or hypothesis. Such evidence is generally expected to be empirical and properly documented in accordance with scientific method such as is applicable to the particular field of inquiry. Standards for evidence may vary according to whether the field of inquiry is among the natural sciences or social sciences" (http://en.wikipedia.org/wiki/Scientific_evidence).

The following article describes how medical decisions should (and do) incorporate legal evidence, although medicine often prides itself on being based upon entirely scientific evidence. Medicine is "an art of probabilities, or at best, a science of uncertainty. One can better practice medicine by using other evidentiary standards in addition to the scientific. To employ only the scientific standard of proof is inappropriate, if not impossible; furthermore, as this review will show, its application in medicine is fraught with bias." http://www.lewrockwell.com/miller/on-evidence-medical-and-legal.pdf - Donald W. Miller, Jr., M.D., Clifford G. Miller, Esq., On Evidence, Medical and Legal, *Journal of American Physicians and Surgeons* Volume 10 Number 3 Fall (2005).

4) See John C. Lennox, *God's Undertaker* (Oxford: Lion Hudson, 2009), 32ff, on the difficulties of defining science and the scientific method. Also, p. 38 concerning considering all available empirical

evidence to infer to the best explanation.

5) In science, "anecdotal evidence" has been variously defined as:

- "information that is not based on facts or careful study"
- "reports or observations of usually unscientific observers"
- "casual observations or indications rather than rigorous or scientific analysis"
- "information passed along by word-of-mouth but not documented scientifically"

See a good discussion of "anecdotal" here: http://en.wikipedia.org/wiki/Anecdotal_evidence.

Sartori distinguished her evidence from anecdotal: "The fact that I was working with these patients at the time they [the NDEs] occurred enhances their authenticity. They were not anecdotal reports, but were elicited at the time, or within a few days of occurrence." *The Near Death Experiences of Hospitalized Intensive Care Patients: A Five-Year Clinical Study*, (New York: The Edwin Mellen Press, 2008), 300.

6) Pim van Lommel, *Consciousness Beyond Life* (New York: HarperCollins, 2010), 139,140,150-153.

7) See, for example, the results of van Lommel's prospective study, utilizing a control group. Ibid., 149-153.

8) Dr. Long found that of the NDErs who shared their stories anonymously on his website, 8.5% said they had never shared the experience with another person. *Evidence of the Afterlife*, Jeffrey Long (New York: HarperOne, 2010), 35. According to Sabom, "Many had been unable to discuss it with their closest friends or relatives for fear of ridicule...." *Recollections of Death* (New York: Harper & Row, 1982), 11.

9) *The Near Death Experiences of Hospitalized Intensive Care Patients: A Five-Year Clinical Study*, 327.

10) As Cambridge Mathematician and Philosopher of Science John Lennox suggests, some gaps science closes; others it opens. See his discussion in *God's Undertaker* (Oxford: Lion Hudson, 2009), 188-192.

11) *The Handbook of Near-death Experiences: Thirty Years of Investigation* (Santa Barbara, California: ABC-CLIO, LLC.), 7.

12) Karl Jansen argues this in The Ketamine Model of the Near-Death Experience, *Journal of Near-Death Studies*, 16 (1) (1997), p. 5.

13) Raymond A. Moody, *Paranormal* (New York: HarperCollins,2012), 243,244.

14) Ibid., 244-246.

Appendix 5

1) Susan Blackmore, *Dying to Live* (New York: Prometheus Books, 1993), 3.

2) Ibid., 22,39,261.

3) Ibid., 62, etc.

4) Ibid., 244.

5) Ibid., 113-135,262.

6) Ibid., 49.

7) Ibid. I appreciate that Blackmore typically expresses appropriate tentativeness, rather than dogmatically proclaiming that she's proven a scientific connection. For example, "It implies that there may be a phase.... During this state they might be able to hear what was going on...." (59) "From this evidence I would now like to try to piece together an idea of which experiences should occur under which conditions. The evidence is pitifully inadequate at the moment...." (62) "It is certainly dangerous to speculate about specific mental processes on the basis of global brain processes. However, bearing in mind this is pure speculation, an interesting possibility arises." (63) She also appropriately mentions where her hypothesis needs further testing. Concerning her explanations for the tunnel experience, she states, "As far as I know, this has not been tested." "This has never been

tested...." (87) "This, too, awaits testing." (90) Concerning the life review, she notes that the main prediction "would be hard to test directly," but might be indirectly tested. (217)

8) Janice Miner Holden, Bruce Greyson, Debbie James, editors, *The Handbook of Near-Death Experiences: Thirty Years of Investigation* (Santa Barbara, California: ABC-CLIO, LLC), chapter by Holden, Long and McClurg, 132,133.

9) Ibid., 43,49.

10) Ibid., 67-93.

11) Jeffrey Long, *Evidence of the Afterlife* (New York: HarperOne, 2010), 9.

12) From www.nderf.org. One of the people I interviewed described the tunnel as being multicolored, like the multicolored breath mint Certs. Blackwell actually did her own survey in India to try to find NDErs with tunnel experiences. But her survey has been criticized on two grounds. First, the survey was published in an English paper that's read largely by westernized people. Secondly, upon closer inspection, what they reported as tunnels may have not been like the tunnels reported in the West. *The Handbook of Near-Death Experiences*, 140, 150-152. Sartori has an especially good discussion on the tunnel experience and Blackmore's arguments concerning it – Penny Sartori, *The Near Death Experiences of Hospitalized Intensive Care Patients: A Five-Year Clinical Study*, (New York: The Edwin Mellen Press, 2008), 62-66.

13) *Dying to Live*, 180.

14) Michael Sabom, *Light & Death* (Grand Rapids: Zondervan Publishing House, 1998),184.

15) *Dying to Live*, 136-164.

16) Ibid., 163. Blackmore continues to use this as a basis for explaining NDEs. Toward the end of her book, she writes, "My conclusion is that the NDE brings about a breakdown of the model of self along with the breakdown of the brain's normal processes. In this way it can cut right through the illusion that we are separate selves. It becomes obvious that 'I' never did exist and so there is no one to die." (p. 259)

17) See *Dying to Live*, chapter 7 and especially the conclusion on p. 164.

18) Ibid., 224.

19) Ibid., Chapter 11.

20) Ibid., 242,243,253.

21) If the NDE truly demonstrated a breakdown of the illusion of self, then I'd predict that NDErs would report a lessening of importance of self. Yet, NDE studies find the opposite effect. Sartori references H.J. Irwin, The Near-Death Experience as a Dissociative Phenomenon: An Empirical Assessment. *Journal of Near-Death Studies*, 12(2), 95-103 (1993), finding that the sense of identity is heightened, not diminished. K. Ring found NDErs reporting an increased sense of purpose and greater self-confidence. [*Heading Toward Omega: In Search of Meaning of the Near-Death Experience* (New York: William Morrow, 1984) referenced in *The Handbook of Near-Death Experiences*, 43. Moody's subjects (*Life After Life*, 90,93,96) reported a feeling of special importance or destiny, the sense that they've received a special favor of God or fate, a stronger assurance of life after death. They tend to lose their fear of death, not because they believe the self never existed, but because of their "new or strengthened belief in survival of bodily death." Many believe in heaven and a joyous reunion with their creator. They're determined to find His will for their lives. (*Life After Life*, 96; *The Handbook of Near-Death Experiences*, 45,46) See also *Reflections on Death*, 22 – "I was fully in control of my mind" sounds more like *heightened* than *dissolved* identity.

Blackmore's interpretation of the positive changes being due to the breakdown of the illusion of self during the NDE isn't borne out by the research that suggests the experience "revealed to them a transcendent reality and brought them face-to-face with a divine presence." (*The Handbook of Near-*

Death Experiences, 57) "It is as though the creator of the universe has given them a precious gift of life, and this life takes on special importance and is endowed with a unique mission" (58).

22) We could go further with this line of observations that cut against Blackmore's hypothesis. In what way can we say that Hitler was *wrong* to kill innocent people? If we truly have no choice (as Blackmore believes), then there isn't a true right and wrong, there just *is*. If "I" don't exist, then why does she continue the book by using subjects like "we"? How can she transition to the next chapter by saying "*we* need to understand the mental models created by the dying brain" and "*we* have to ask what model of self was being constructed at the time." (emphasis mine) Unless I've misunderstood Chapter Seven, *there is no "we."* For if "I" and every other "I" don't exist, then there can be no "we" as a collection of individuals. And on what grounds should we trust our powers of reasoning if they're merely part of a fallible construct?

23) If the dissolution of self is the most important part of the experience, why don't I find NDErs reporting this loss of self and its importance? According to Blackmore, upon returning to consciousness their brains immediately reconstructed another model of self. (259) Although this would successfully explain the contrary evidence provided by NDE reports, it would also render our primary data for exploring NDEs – the personal reports – practically useless as data with which to build our theories.

Thus, Blackmore's defense of the dissolution of self as the reason for life change seems extraordinarily weak.(247ff.) Rather than survey people and ask them what aspect of their experience changed them, she assumes most of them have misinterpreted what changed them and suggests that it's the "loss of self" experience, which she's yet to prove is a part of the experience. To bolster her claim, she quotes a man who came out of his experience with the "dissolution of self" explanation. Yet, Blackmore admits that his experience was drug induced (probably morphine) and not a classic NDE. (254,255) She seems to have totally left her research at this point. For a good general discussion of Blackmore's psychological arguments, see *The Near Death Experiences of Hospitalized Intensive Care Patients*, 95-98.

24) *Dying to Live*, 113. See also her summary on pp. 262,263.

25) http://www.newdualism.org/nde-papers/Ring/Ring-Journal%20of%20Near-Death%20Studies_1997-16-101-147.pdf, K. Ring and Sharon Cooper, Near-Death and Out-of-Body Experiences in the Blind: A Study of Apparent Eyeless Vision, *Journal of Near-Death Studies*.

Appendix 6

1) Kevin Nelson, *The Spiritual Doorway in the Brain* (New York: Dutton, 2011), 5.

2) Ibid., 260.

3) Ibid., 67.

4) Ibid., 214,218.

5) Ibid., 3,4.

6) Ibid., 4.

7) Ibid., 9.

8) Ibid., 200,270.

9) "We found that NDErs do indeed have more psychic abilities than the normal population. And we are not talking about a slight increase in abilities here. People who have had near-death experiences are four times more likely to have psychic experiences than those who have not had them." Melvin Morse with Paul Perry, *Transformed by the Light: The Powerful Effect of Near-Death Experiences on People's Lives* (Raleigh, NC: Ivy Books, 1993), 91.

10) See the questions he asked. (Nelson, p. 201) Another potential problem is that he studied a specific subset of NDErs: "each believed at the time" of the NDE "that his or her life was in immediate danger." (p. 200) So why didn't he simply choose people who shared NDEs? Well, his hypothesis is that fear is "the fundamental link" to many of our spiritual experiences. (p. 160) So, apparently he wanted to choose only NDErs who were experiencing fear at the onset of their NDEs. Yet, other NDErs have suddenly passed out, apparently without any fear or expectation of possible death. For example, concerning the patients that van Lommel studied,

> "Most patients experienced no fear of death preceding their cardiac arrest; its onset was so sudden that they failed to notice it."(36.5)

It's quite possible that Nelson ended up with a large number of cases where people *thought* they were going to die, but weren't actually near death. This could bias the sample toward people who are more prone to dissociate from their bodies during extreme danger.

11) *The Spiritual Doorway in the Brain*, 128-131.

12) See, for example, B. Greyson, E.W. Kelly, E.F. Kelly, Explanatory Models for Near-Death Experiences, in *The Handbook of Near-Death Experiences*, 217. See also Chris Carter, *Science and the Near-Death Experience* (Rochester, Vermont: Inner Traditions, 2010), 164-168.

13) Here's another example. Foundational to Nelson's hypothesis is his belief that mind functions are produced by the brain. But again, he never considers contrary evidence. While he relies upon the research of neurosurgeon Wilder Penfield, is Nelson aware that after a lifetime of brain research, Penfield concluded that the mind is separate from the brain? According to Penfield, "For my own part, after years of striving to explain the mind on the basis of brain action alone, I have come to the conclusion that it is simpler (and far easier to be logical) if one adopts the hypothesis that our being does consist of two fundamental elements." W. Penfield, *The Mystery of the Mind* (Princeton NJ: Princeton University Press, 1975), 80. See also pp. 39,47,48,85.

14) *The Spiritual Doorway in the Brain*, 124.

15) Syncope and near-death experience. (1994). *The Lancet*, 344(8925), 829-829. Retrieved from http://search.proquest.com/docview/199043829?accountid=11824; Lempert, T., Bauer, M. and Schmidt, D. (1994), Syncope: A videometric analysis of 56 episodes of transient cerebral hypoxia. *Annals of Neurology*, 36: 233–237.

16) For example, in an examination of reports of tunnel vision and "dreamlets" in studies of fighter pilots experiencing g-force, the actual descriptions are often very different from the brief summaries that people try to use to show similarities. See Chris Carter, *Science and the Near-Death Experience* (Rochester, Vermont: Inner Traditions, 2010), 172-176.

17) *The Spiritual Doorway in the Brain*, 132. In fact, Nelson argues that the characteristics of NDEs "combine to tell us that wide expanses of the brain are engaged during these experiences." (117) But wouldn't such vivid consciousness, if it's indeed produced solely by the brain, show up on an EEG?

18) Ibid., 146.

19) Ibid., 144-146.

20) Ibid., 148.

21) Ibid., 148.

22) Ibid., 211,212.

23) In an endnote, Nelson comments on his skepticism toward paranormal claims: "Extraordinary claims, however, require extraordinary evidence." (p. 116) "When it comes to believing in the paranormal, I start with the yardstick provided by David Hume on miracles that violate the laws of

nature: I believe in the paranormal only if not believing would mean having faith in something even more miraculous." (p. 267)

On one hand, this seems like a sound approach, in the sense that when someone exclaims, "It was a miracle!" we should look first to possible natural explanations. So a person claims that prayer miraculously put her cancer in remission. But what percentage of people with that type of cancer go into remission? If 5%, then couldn't her remission be adequately explained by her being in that 5%?

Yet some seem to take this principle too far, not accepting anything as "extraordinary evidence." David Hume, for example, holds that proving the resurrection of Jesus would actually provide no evidence whatsoever for his divinity. After all, perhaps science will one day provide a reasonable naturalistic explanation, as it has for so many other supposedly miraculous occurrences. And besides, is there some law of logic that tells us that if someone pulls off a resurrection, he's therefore divine? Perhaps the resurrection merely shows that Jesus was a great magician?

Using Hume's approach, it's evident that nothing could ever provide sufficient evidence for a paranormal event. For him, the evidence for the normal functioning of natural laws is so overwhelming that you could never have sufficient evidence that the laws had been violated.

But it seems to me that evidence from NDEs is indeed extraordinary, to the extent that naturalistic explanations indeed become more "miraculous" than supernatural explanations. Sure, it's possible that science may in the future show how, in a near-death experience, people born blind report seeing and people wake at the moment of a distant relative's death and sense their presence or share their trip to another dimension. But to me, in the light of all currently available scientific evidence, believing in a naturalistic explanation requires more blind faith than believing that there's more to this life than our natural laws can explain. I'd suggest that committed naturalists might never see the extraordinary nature of the evidence for the paranormal. Why? Because of the power of their paradigm – viewing evidence through their naturalistic-colored glasses.

24) Eben Alexander, *Proof of Heaven* (New York: Simon & Schuster, 2012). For more on Nelson, note a review of Nelson's book: Rudolf H. Smit & Titus Rivas, *Book Review, The Spiritual Doorway in the Brain: A Neurologist's Search for the God Experience*, by Kevin Nelson, *The Journal of Near-Death Studies*, vol. 30, #2, (Winter, 2011). The following article critiques two of Nelson's journal articles on the subject he expanded upon in his book: Does the Arousal System Contribute to Near-Death and Out-of-Body Experiences? A Summary and Response, by Jeffrey Long and Janice Miner Holden. *Journal of Near-Death Studies*, 25(3) (Spring 2007).

Appendix 7

1) Raymond Moody, *Paranormal* (New York: HarperCollins, 2012), 60,61.

2) Ibid., 94,95.

3) Blackmore notes that "visions of the world's future" are relatively rare. *Dying to Live*, (Buffalo, NY: Prometheus Books, 1993), 30.

4) http://www.skeptiko.com/112-gary-habermas-skeptical-of-near-death-experience-spirituality

5) One of Sartori's patients reported an interesting event in this regard. A being on the other side told him to warn a relative to not believe all that a medium was telling her because some of it was lies. Interestingly, he didn't even know that she had been consulting a medium. Penny Sartori, *The Near-Death Experiences of Hospitalized Intensive Care Patients* (Lewiston, Queenston, Lampeter: The Edwin Mellen Press: 2008), 178-180.

6) Pim van Lommel, *Consciousness Beyond Life*, (New York: HarperCollins, 2010), 56-58.

7) Michael B. Sabom, *Recollections of Death* (New York: Harper & Row, 1982), 139-141.

8) Ibid., 140.

9) *The Near-Death Experiences of Hospitalized Intensive Care Patients*, 244.

10) Ibid., 252,253; J.M. Holden, B. Greyson, D. James, editors, *The Handbook of Near-Death Experiences: Thirty Years of Investigation* (Santa Barbara, California: ABC-CLIO, LLC., 2009), 319,320.

11) *The Near-Death Experiences of Hospitalized Intensive Care Patients*, 304.

Appendix 8

1) P.M.H. Atwater, *Children of the New Millennium* (New York: Three Rivers Press, 1999).

2) R.J. Bonenfant, "A child's encounter with the devil: An unusual near-death experience with both blissful and frightening elements," *Journal of Near-Death Studies*, 20:87-100 (2001).

3) R.J. Brumblay, Hyperdimensional perspectives in out-of-body and near-death experiences, *Journal of Near-Death Studies*, 21:201-21 (2003).

4) K. Clark, Clinical interventions with near-death experiencers. In B. Greyson and C.P. Flynn (Eds.), *The Near-Death Experience: Problems, Prospects, Perspectives* (Springfield, IL: Charles C. Thomas, 1984), 242-55.

5) F.P. Cobbe, *The Peak in Darien* (London: Williams & Norgate, 1882).

6) E.K. Cook, B. Greyson, and I. Stevenson, Do any near-death experiences provide evidence for survival of human personality after death? Relevant features and illustrative case reports. *Journal of Scientific Exploration* 12:377-406 (1998).

7) R. Crookall, *Case-Book of Astral Projection* (Secaucus, NJ: University Books, 1972).

8) G.F. Ellwood, The Uttermost Deep: The Challenge of Near-Death Experiences (New York: Lantern Books, 2001).

9) P. Fenwick and E. Fenwick, *The Truth in the Light: An Investigation of over 300 Near-Death Experiences* (London: Headline, 1995).

10) C. Green, *Out-of-Body Experiences* (Oxford, England: Institute of Psychophysical Research,1968).

11) M. Grey, *Return from Death* (New York: Arkana, 1985).

12) J.C. Hampe, *To Die is Gain: The Experience of One's Own Death*, Trans. M. Kohl (Atlanta: John Knox Press,1979).

13) J.H. Hyslop, Visions of the dying: Class 1. *Journal of the American Society for Psychical Research* 12 (10): 585-626 (1918).

14) C.G. Jung, *Synchronicity: An Acausal Connecting Principle*. Trans. R.F.C. Hull. In H. Read, M. Fordham, G. Adler, and W. McGuire (Eds.), *The Collected Works of C.G. Jung*. 2nd ed. Vol. 8, *The Structure and Dynamics of the Psyche* (Princeton, NJ: Princeton University Press, 1969, orig. pub. 1952), 417-531.

15) E.W. Kelly, B. Greyson, and I. Stevenson, Can Experiences Near Death Furnish Evidence of Life after Death? *Omega* 40 (4): 513-19 (1999-2000).

16) E. Kübler-Ross, *On Children and Death* (New York: Simon & Schuster,1983).

17) M. Lawrence, *In a World of Their Own: Experiencing Unconsciousness* (Westport, CT: Praeger, 1997).

18) J.H. Lindley, S. Bryan, and B. Conley, Near-Death Experience in a Pacific Northwest American Population: The Evergreen Study. *Anabiosis: The Journal for Near-Death Studies* 1:104-24 (1981).

19) L.K. Manley, Enchanting Journeys: Near-Death Experiences and the Emergency Nurse. *Journal of Emergency Nursing* 22 (4): 311-16 (1996).

20) R. Moody, *Life After Life* (Atlanta: Mockingbird Books, 1975).

21) R. Moody, and P. Perry, *The Light Beyond* (New York: Bantam Books,1988).

22) L.L. Morris, and K. Knafl,. The nature and meaning of the near-death experience for patients and critical care nurses. *Journal of Near-Death Studies* 21:139-67 (2003).

23) M.L. Morse, Near-death experiences and death-related visions in children: Implications for the clinician. *Current Problems in Pediatrics* 24:55-83 (1994).

24) M.L. Morse, and P. Perry, *Closer to the Light: Learning from the Near-Death Experiences of Children* (New York: Villard Books, 1990).

25) F.W.H. Myers, On indications of continued terrene knowledge on the part of the phantasms of the dead, *Proceedings of the Society for Psychical Research* 8:170-252 (1892).

26) Near-Death Experiences: The Proof. February 2, 2006, Feb. 2. Article scanned from *Daily Express*, London. Retrieved February 2006 from http://farshores.org/p06ndetp.htm.

Ogston, A. *Reminiscences of three campaigns* (London: Hodder & Stoughton, 1920).

27) M. Rawlings, *Beyond Death's Door* (Nashville: Thomas Nelson, 1978).

28) K. Ring, 1980.

29) K. Ring, 1984.

30) K. Ring, and S. Cooper, *Mindsight: Near-Death and Out-of-Body Experiences in the Blind* (Palo Alto, CA: William James Center for Consciousness Studies, 1999).

31) K. Ring, and M. Lawrence, Further evidence for veridical perception during near-death experiences. *Journal of Near-Death Studies* 11:223-29 (1993).

32) K. Ring, and E.E. Valarino, *Lessons from the Light* (New York: Plenum, 1998).

33) B. Rommer, *Blessing in Disguise: Another Side of the Near-Death Experience* (St. Paul, MN: Llewellyn Publications, 2000).

34) M. Sabom, *Recollections of Death: A Medical Investigation* (New York: Simon & Schuster, 1982).

35) M.A. Tutka, Near-Death Experiences: Seeing the Light. *Nursing* 31 (5): 62-63 (2001).

36) G.N.M. Tyrrell, 1946.

37) Pim van Lommel, R. van Wees, V. Meyers, and I. Elfferich, Near-death experience in survivors of cardiac arrest: A prospective study in the Netherlands. *Lancet* 358:2039-45 (2001).

38) Wilson, *The After Death Experience: The Physics of the Non-Physical.* (New York: William Morrow, 1987).

Appendix 9

1) Michael Sabom, *Recollections of Death* (New York: Harper & Row, 1982), 3.

2) Ibid., 4.

3) Ibid., 7,83.

4) Ibid., 2.

5) Ibid., 156-158.

6) Ibid., 54,68,71,72,73,77,78,90,93,94,98,99,103,110,112,113.

7) Ibid., 7.

8) Ibid., 156-160.

9) Michael Sabom, *Light and Death* (Grand Rapids: Zondervan, 1998), 193,194.

10) Ibid., 22,33.

11) Ibid., 37-51; 184-191.

12) Ibid., 131-142.

13) Jeffrey Long, *Evidence of the Afterlife* (New York: HarperOne, 2010), 43.

14) Ibid., 22,23.

15) Penny Sartori, *The Near-Death Experiences of Hospitalized Intensive Care Patients* (Lewiston, Queenston, Lampeter: The Edwin Mellen Press, 2008), 6.

16) Ibid., 122.

17) Ibid., 143.

18) Ibid., 216-224.
19) Ibid., 275.
20) Ibid., 131.

Index

ABOUT THE AUTHOR

J. Steve Miller is the founder and president of Legacy Educational Resources, providing global resources for teachers of life skills in public schools, churches, and service organizations at www.character-education.info. A self-styled "wisdom broker," he collects wisdom from many fields and packages it for teachers and writers via his published books and the Web.

Steve is an educator, entrepreneur, and speaker, having taught audiences from Atlanta to Moscow. He's known for drawing practical wisdom from serious research and communicating it in accessible, unforgettable ways. His wife, Cherie, and their seven sons continually remind him what works and what doesn't. Connect with him at www.jstevemiller.com.

OTHER BOOKS BY J. STEVE MILLER

Richard Dawkins and His God Delusion: A Preliminary Critique of His Truth Claims - In his best-selling book, *The God Delusion*, Richard Dawkins makes many claims concerning the existence of God and the viability of religion. This brief critique takes several of Dawkins' main contentions and subjects them to research and analysis.

According to Dr. Henry F. Schaefer III, one of the most distinguished living physical scientists, specialist in quantum and computational chemistry, and author of over 1000 scientific publications, "I welcome this thoughtful and easily digested response to the insubstantial attacks on God by the world's most popular atheist."

Social Media Frenzy: Why Time Consuming Facebook, Twitter & Blogging Strategies May NOT Work for Your Business - Consider These Alternative Social Networking Initiatives - How can businesses and individuals harness the power of social media without expending excessive time and effort? Miller contends that in many, if not most situations, the time consuming strategy of trying to build a social media following will waste much time and result in few sales. He supports this position with research and practical examples. "Solid, well reasoned and sound." – Amazon review.

Enjoy Your Money! How to Make It, Save It, Invest It and Give It: The Adventures of the Counterculture Club - A film producer called it "the money book for people who hate money books." Well researched, but written in story form, this award-winning book makes a great gift for high school and college graduates. "Had I read this book in my 20's, I'd be financially independent today. It's a remarkable blend of fabulous research with clear and lively writing. You'd pay an expert quite a sum for this caliber of counsel. That's why I say that the best investment you make this year just might be this book. Your second best investment will be the copies you buy for your children." - Dr. Dwight "Ike" Reighard, former Executive Vice President and Chief People Officer, HomeBanc

Sell More Books! Book Marketing and Publishing for Low-Profile and Debut Authors: Rethinking Book Publicity after the Digital Revolutions - Can low-profile, not-yet-famous authors get published and sell lots of books? This multiple award winning book says "Yes!" and tells how.

"…a comprehensive guide to marketing a book…[a] well-written, engaging resource that's loaded with specific tips…. Brimming with creative ideas, *Sell More Books!* should prove to be a low-profile author's best friend." - ForeWord Reviews

Printed in Great Britain
by Amazon

MARITIME
NORFOLK

Further details of Poppyland Publishing titles can be found at
www.poppyland.co.uk
where clicking on the 'Support and Resources' button will lead to pages
specially compiled to support this title.

POPPYLAND
PUBLISHING

The schooners *Commerce* and *Ellis* unloading coal on Cromer beach about 1870. Both vessels have a derrick rigged between the masts to hoist the baskets of coal from the hold so that they can be tipped out into the waiting carts.

MARITIME NORFOLK

Part One of a contribution to
the maritime history of Nelson's
county

Robert Malster

The replica cog *Lisa von Lübeck* makes her way up the channel to King's Lynn in 2009 – though with no sails set, the 13th century sailor might be mystified as to how she is making such a good speed.

Opposite page: The long Norfolk coastline remains a busy seaway, whether it be for the pleasure sailor or the working vessel.

Maritime Norfolk is the first part of Robert Malster's pioneering study of the maritime history of the east of England and covers the coast and inland waterways from the Fenland to Caister. A companion volume provides the story of the port of Yarmouth.

The paddle tug *Marie* bringing a schooner into Wells.

ISBN 978 0 946148 97 4

Published by Poppyland Publishing, Cromer NR27 9AN

Picture credits:

Adrian Woods	141 (top)
Chris Taylor Photo	106 (top)
David Cleveland	78, 134, 163
Frank Muirhead	131 (top)
Jack Patten	40
Jane Inglesby	187
Michael Softley	61, 78
Michael Stammers	71

Norfolk Museums and Archaeology Service 50, 98 (bottom), 105 (bottom), 109 (bottom)

Norfolk Record Office	130
R.E.Pestell	176-177, 179 (top)
RNLI, Hunstanton	57 (lower border)
Paul Damen	205
Paul Russell	57 (bottom), 83, 204 (middle)
Philip Vicary	149, 152

Poppyland Photos   iv, v (top), viii-ix, x, xi (bottom), xvi, 10, 16, 27, 43, 47, 48, 58, 64 (bottom), 80, 87, 97, 99 (bottom), 100, 104, 106 (border), 109 (top), 112, 129, 131 (bottom), 132, 133, 134 (top), 136 (top), 137, 140, 141 (bottom), 144, 155 (top), 157, 160, 161, 171, 172 (bottom), 179 (bottom), 182, 183, 189, 200 (border), 204 (top & bottom), 210, 211 (border), 219, 242

Poppyland Collection   xi (top), 99, (top), 102, 105, 108 (main), 114-117, 120, 130, 135, 137 (bottom), 155 (bottom), 170, 178, 180, 181, 188, 192, 206

Port of Lowestoft Research Society   45 (top)

Robert Aldwin   153

Robert Malster   ii-iii, v (bottom), xi (top), xiv, xv, 2, 3, 6, 7, 8, 11, 12, 13, 14 (top), 18, 26, 31, 37-40, 44, 45 (bottom), 46, 52-54, 56, 63, 64 (top), 675, 67, 68, 69, 72-75, 88, 90, 92, 93, 98 (top two), 103, 104 (top & bottom), 122-127, 158, 165, 168, 172 (top), 173, 174, 184, 185, 190, 191, 193-195, 200 (main), 201, 202, 209, 210 (main), 216, 217, 221-237, 240

Scira Offshore Energy Ltd. xiii (bottom), 119

Theo Stibbons   14 (bottom), 15, 57 (top),

Printed in Turkey by Latitude Press Ltd.

Contents

Preface

This book had its genesis sixty years ago when spritsail barges could be seen towing up the river to Norwich behind either the steam tugs *Gensteam* and *Cypress* or one of the black-hulled motor coasters belonging to F.T. Everard & Sons, of Greenhithe; when a visit to Yarmouth would reveal steamers from the Baltic unloading deals that had been brought across the North Sea stacked above the deck as well as stowed in the hold; and when steam and motor drifters from Scotland taking part in the autumn herring fishing crowded Yarmouth harbour, giving the erroneous impression that one might be able to cross the river by stepping from one to the other.

In 1950 I went 'down below' in a Lynn shrimper, trawling for shrimps, and then three years later I spent a night on 'the Knoll' fishing for herring in the drifter *Harold Cartwright* during the Home Fishing. I never achieved my ambition of becoming mate of a sailing barge, but my interest in maritime affairs had been well and truly aroused. Over the years I researched the history of the fishing industry and sought information about the sailing vessels that brought fruit from the Levant and from the Azores, collected shipbuilders' half-models and tools for the Maritime Museum for East Anglia in the old Sailors' Home at Yarmouth, and spent hours scanning nineteenth-century newspapers to discover the early history of the lifeboat service.

Many people encouraged my activities and fed me with first-hand information about the beach companies and local shipping affairs. To attempt to list those to whom I am indebted is to risk forgetting some who should be acknowledged.

One who gave me unstinting help was Philip Rumbelow; he introduced

me to John 'Skipper' Woodhouse at Caister, his brother David and his father Joe Woodhouse, who told me what it was like to sail in the beach company's yawl. Innumerable other people, including fellow-members of the old Norfolk Nautical Research Society, gave me invaluable support in one way or another. My good friends David Cleveland and Peter Stibbons have had a hand in my work, and so has Peter Allard. Edward Paget-Tomlinson proved a stalwart friend and helper, and through him I met others who gave me the advantage of their knowledge. Mike Stammers, late of the Merseyside Maritime Museum, David Higgins, Peter Northeast, Jack Patten, David Butcher, Jill Freestone and many other friends have encouraged and helped me over the years. Mrs. Susan Ranson read the draft and made many useful suggestions.

I would need a multitude of pages to list all those who have assisted me in researching the story of east coast shipping; I thank them all, and hope they will forgive me for not mentioning each of them by name.

I have already told the story of trade on the rivers in *The Norfolk and Suffolk Broads*, published by Phillimore in 2003, but certain friends persuaded me that the present book would be incomplete without reference to the commercial exploitation of the inland waterways. To a great extent the inland navigation was an integral part of the coasting and overseas trade, and so deserves a place here.

To those who hoped that the result of all this work would have been so much better than it is, more of a scholarly work or more readable, I apologise for my shortcomings. And for the inevitable errors, which I am sure are mine and not theirs, I crave forgiveness.

In conclusion, I dedicate this book to all those seamen and fishermen who sailed from Norfolk ports and found their way about the North Sea and other waters by lead-line and compass, making an immeasurable contribution to our history.

The sailing barge *Juno*, built of steel in north Norfolk as a charter vessel, lying in Blakeney harbour, where she is based. She serves as a reminder of the days when sailing traders lay all along the quay.

Introduction

Norfolk is a maritime county with a long coastline facing the North Sea, or the German Ocean as it was known until Anglo-German naval rivalry in the early years of the twentieth century rendered that name politically incorrect. For hundreds of years the North Sea, far from being an eastern frontier to the region, has served to link East Anglia closely to the continent of Europe and to Scandinavia.

Waves of settlers crossed from Europe far back in history. Nobody has recorded how they came, but it must have been by boat across the Narrow Seas. Once the land bridge that linked Britain and Europe in the time that elephant and rhinoceros roamed the plains of eastern England had been submerged there was no other way. Many must have perished on the offlying banks or in the surf on the beaches, but others survived to set up home on the welcoming shores of Norfolk and Suffolk and to give their genes to a new generation of East Anglians.

The Saxons came by sea; the Danes came the same way; and immigrants who came from the Low Countries in later centuries likewise made the short sea crossing from their erstwhile homeland to the new. Little wonder that for centuries residents of East Coast towns considered themselves closer to Amsterdam than to London.

Much more than that, the sea was for many Norfolk men the highway to the rest of the world, to Africa, India, North and South America and to Australia and New Zealand. Ships from Norfolk ports carried products of many kinds to Europe and to the wider world and returned with cargoes of citrus fruit and other foodstuffs as well as with the raw materials of British industry.

After some 150 years of railway travel and half a century of popular air travel the importance of travel by sea has been half-forgotten. The great passenger liners that carried colonial administrators and civil servants to India, port out and starboard home so as to be on the shady side during those most trying days passing through the Arabian Gulf, have gone; posh is a word that has lost its meaning. The sea is little more than something on which yachtsmen find their pleasure, though the construction of a new outer harbour at Yarmouth might suggest that even today seaborne trade has a part to play in Britain's economic well-being.

Archaeologists have shown that the Babingley River was navigable in the Middle Ages, and while we know almost nothing about the craft that sailed up that west Norfolk river or around the coast we do know that water transport was of great importance in those times. Foot travellers might still have been

Opposite page: Blakeney Quay at the end of the nineteenth century with a ketch-rigged coaster, the *Bluejacket*, alongside. The wooden Blakeney Fairway buoy serves as a reminder that the channel into Blakeney was already marked by buoys in the seventeenth century when Captain Greenville Collins published a chart of the approaches to the port.

Four Sheringham fishermen, 'Potter' Hardingham, John 'Tar' Bishop, Elijah Farrow and 'Belcher' Johnson, pose for the photographer in 1910. Note the elaborate patterns of their woollen ganseys.

striding out along the surviving Roman roads, but when it came to moving goods around it made much better sense to load ten or twenty sacks of corn into a boat and send it coast-wise to its destination than to hang two sacks on a packhorse and send it cross-country.

We know that passengers as well as goods travelled by water in the fourteenth century, for it is recorded that thirty-eight men and women lost their lives on 19th October 1343 when a boat called the *Blitheburghesbot*, on its way upriver from Yarmouth to Norwich, sank in a storm near Cantley; the report of the inquest is to be found in the city records of Norwich. And in the fifteenth century the Abbot of St. Benet-at-Holm in the parish of Horning went to court to seek to safeguard his right of passage downriver from his manor of Heigham, the corporation of Norwich having obstructed the River Wensum by building the New Mills.

It was a nineteenth-century antiquarian who introduced the fiction that St. Benet's was established in the middle of the marshes to provide solitude for the monks. In reality it was built right beside the main highway of trade in the area, the River Bure, and far from being an isolated place ignored by the medieval inhabitants the abbey was much visited not only by those affluent gentry who gave so generously in hopes of later advantage but also by the ordinary people of the district. They came to the two fairs held each year on the Fairstead outside the abbey gates, and for the most part they probably came by river.

St Benet's and the mill tower which now stands within its walls.

Caen stone for the construction of Norwich Cathedral and, in smaller quantities, for the building of parish churches came by sea from France. It was carried up the river from Yarmouth by square-sailed keels, under the watergate at what we now know as Pulls Ferry and up a canal into the Lower Close.

There is a story, too, that the stone for the building of the great abbey at Bury St. Edmunds was brought up the Gipping to Rattlesden and then carried the last twelve miles or so to the site of the abbey by waggon. The more obvious way might have been to have shipped the stone into the Great Ouse and up the Lark, but Lynn was then held by the Bishop of Norwich and that might have proved awkward for the abbot, who presided over an establishment that did not owe allegiance to the diocesan supremo. One can imagine the boatmen laboriously damming the river behind their barge and then waiting several days for the water to rise sufficiently for them to make further progress, the skipper commenting with asperity that 'the ol' abbot'll hev ter wait fer 'is stoon. Do he want it sooner, he'll hev ter ask his guv'nor fer a miracle.'

Many tales are told of streams that were navigable in the Middle Ages, and some at least of them are possibly true. The River Wissey, a tributary of the Great Ouse, was navigable as far as Oxborough Hithe, and the Nar was made navigable from Lynn up to Narborough in the eighteenth century, while it is said that 'lighters, keels and other boats of considerable burthen' had in former times been able to reach Bungay even before the navigation of the Waveney was improved under an Act of Parliament of 1670. That was all before drainage authorities were set up to remove water from the rivers to the sea as expeditiously as possible in the interests of the farmers and arable production.

In his book on the archaeology of the Civil War Peter Harrington remarks how different was the geography of seventeenth-century England from that of today in terms of communication. Saying that the road network was vastly different and that places and routes – particularly rivers – that are secondary today were of critical importance in the centuries leading up to the industrial revolution, he points out that the placing of parliamentarian forts and batteries in the Fens needs to be explained in terms of the situation in the 1640s; their siting is puzzling when considered from a present-day point of view.

Around the coast there were towns and villages that carried on a lively and profitable trade through their tiny harbours or, in the absence of any creek or river mouth, over their beaches. The town of Cromer was once a significant ship-owning port, and places as small as Mundesley, Bacton and Palling once had a thriving maritime trade.

The East Anglian coast has throughout history been vulnerable not only to invaders but to the sea itself. Sandy beaches and soft cliffs of clay, chalk and gravel are easily eaten away by the waves, and the material eroded by wave

Pulls Ferry at Norwich, in a Victorian magic lantern slide. The Caen stone was carried on a channel which ran through the archway.

The newly constructed wind farm on the Sheringham Shoal is one of many which will eventually take their place in the North Sea. A variety of specialist vessels have been involved in constructing the farm.

F.T. Everard's mulie barge *Cambria* at the Baltic Wharf, Norwich, about 1950. Alongside her is the Great Yarmouth Shipping Company's steam lighter *Opal*, built at Gainsborough on the Trent in 1896, and ahead of her are two dumb lighters, one laden with coal for Norwich gasworks.

action is carried by longshore drift and deposited elsewhere to form new shingle spits, salt marshes and sandbars which might in course of time be embanked and drained by man. The sandbanks off the east coast are constantly changing in the same way, to the peril of seafarers who find well-used channels silting up and new banks appearing where once was deep water.

The discovery of a Bronze Age construction, revealed by erosion of the underlying peat, off Holme-next-the-Sea at the mouth of the Wash in 1998 demonstrated how the sea had invaded what was once dry land. Not far away the embanking of marshes north of King's Lynn is just one instance of how man has in much more recent times sought to win land from the sea. And the new channel of the Great Ouse in the same area provides an illustration of how man has been prepared to alter the natural course of a waterway for his own benefit.

Those who dwelt in the coastal towns and villages and went to sea were a race apart from the men who followed the plough. Their life was very different from that of inhabitants of inland places, who though they might move around in the course of their lives generally had nothing like the wealth of experience of the seafaring fraternity. Those who sailed deep sea saw sights and experienced dangers that were quite unknown to the great majority of men and women who lived on the land. No wonder sailors' yarns were regarded as far-fetched and even flights of fancy.

What extraordinary things the mariner might bring back with him from a voyage to the Mediterranean or to the Tropics! The little museum that grew up in the Sailors' Home on the front at Yarmouth once had on display a monkey with a fish's tail, the two stitched together by some dusky-skinned seamstress so neatly that few realised they were being hoodwinked.

There is a bond between seafaring men that can sometimes transcend the barriers that ordinarily divide people of different nationalities. A Danish seaman, Theodor Neilsen, arrived at Wells in a three-masted schooner in the early 1900s, married the daughter of the Wells pilot and in 1910 joined the Wells lifeboat crew. So well did he integrate with the local seafaring community that he was appointed coxswain in 1933, serving with distinction throughout the Second World War and retiring in 1947. He gained an MBE in 1940 for a special wartime service when he led a group of four fishing boats from Wells, Blakeney and Brancaster on a secret mission to the French coast at the time of the Dunkirk evacuation.

In much the same way a young Dutch seaman, Adriaan Serruys, arrived in Norwich in the coaster *Venus* in the 1950s, married a local girl and settled in the city. He found work with a Norwich scrap metal merchant, eventually took over the business, became a millionaire when the scrap business was sold and used the money to build up a hotel and sports club business. The Dutch diminutive of his name, Arri, was soon changed to the English Harry, and by the time he died in 2005 he was one of the best-known and best-liked business people in the city.

Something has been lost from the coastal communities since the virtual collapse of the fishing industry and the decline of the British Merchant Navy. A *Punch* cartoon from the early twentieth century humorously exemplifies the gulf between the seafarer and the inhabitant of an inland town. An Edwardian lady with fur around her neck and umbrella in her hand is anxious not to miss the train home, and she consults an elderly fisherman. 'Can you please tell me the *exact* time?' she asks the gansey-clad old salt, receiving the reply "alf ebb.'

The gulf between the seafarer and the landlubber, as portrayed by *Punch* in its issue of 12th December 1906.

Miss Binks (breathless, hurrying to catch London train after week-end trip). "Can you please tell me the exact time?"
Old Salt. "'Alf ebb."

The Wash   1

It is no more than twenty miles as the gull flies between the Norfolk seaside resort of Hunstanton and the old port of Boston, 'Botolph's Town', on the River Witham. To travel from one to the other by land one has to undertake a much longer journey by way of King's Lynn, the Cut Bridge, Cross Keys Bridge and Fosdyke Bridge, and then northwards from Sutterton; by the time one reaches the Lincolnshire town one will have driven not far short of fifty miles. In between Hunstanton and Boston is the Wash, a shallow and treacherous inlet of the sea that provided an access to several ports but at the same time proved a trap for many a ship and a grave for countless seamen.

The old *North Sea Pilot*, published in 1905, in describing a course from the Humber to Cromer, tells of the perils of the Wash. 'The deep bight between the Humber and Cromer, the upper part of which is indifferently termed Lynn Deep and the Wash, is for the most part occupied by numerous and dangerous sands, some skirting the main, whilst others lie out a considerable distance in the offing; through these sands the several rivers which have their outlets in the Wash find their way at low-water. The rapidity of the tides in this deep bight, the low character of its shores, and the mist which almost constantly prevails, render this the most difficult portion of the navigation on the eastern coast, and consequently a more than common degree of vigilance is necessary when navigating in the locality.'

That, in a nutshell, is the Wash from a seaman's viewpoint. Not a pleasant place in which to be, particularly when a nor'easter is piling up steep breaking seas and sending the sleet scurrying before it. Many a ship's master has attempted in vain to grope his way out of this trap, only to feel the keel of his vessel grind on the unyielding sand and to experience his ship breaking up under him.

The tidal streams run strongly and the rise and fall of the tide can be more than 20ft. I remember going out from the Fisher Fleet in a Lynn shrimper in 1950 and seeing the great expanse of water stretching apparently unbroken from the Norfolk coast over to Lincolnshire at high water, but as we towed our trawl in one of the channels the colour of the water changed; then the sands emerged from the surface and before long the distant view was obscured by what seemed to be rolling hills of yellow sand on which the cocklers lay aground between the tides. Not for nothing does the *North Sea Pilot* warn that 'careful attention must be given to clearing marks and bearings . . . as well as a frequent use of the lead.' To underline its warning it points out how vessels from the Lincolnshire coast bound to Lynn have, for want of such

Opposite: Tradition has it that Edmund, patron saint of East Anglia, landed at Hunstanton on the corner of the Wash. St. Edmund's Point is prominent in this aerial view, in which the white-painted former lighthouse also stands out sharply.

A little billy-boy sloop, its
gear lowered, is moored in
the River Nene at Wisbech,
linked with the shore by
a plank that appears to be
some 40ft. long.

precautions, crossed the Lynn Deep and been wrecked either on the Roaring
Middle or on the Norfolk shore.

The sea and the land merge almost imperceptibly when the weather is
misty, as it often is, and one can well imagine how the Wash used to overflow
much that is now farmland in days before the sea banks were thrown up to
hold it at bay. Much has been changed by man's efforts to drain the fenland
and bring it into production. The Romans were probably the first to attempt
to keep out the tides during the 400 years that they governed Britain, and
generation after generation has kept up the fight since their time.

In the thirteenth century Boston, on the western shores of the Wash with
the River Witham (pronounced with a soft *th*) forming a natural harbour
very suitable for the small ships of that period, was possibly the second port
of England after London, with Lynn not far behind. The biggest import of
all was wine, Boston importing nearly 500,000 gallons in 1300-01, most of
it from Gascony. The popularity of wine from the region lying between the
Pyrenees and the River Garonne dated back to the marriage of King Henry
II to Eleanor of Aquitaine in 1152, and Gascony remained a possession of the
kings of England for three hundred years.

It is impossible to say when the fenland rivers were first used for transport,
but there is no doubt that for many hundreds of years the Great Ouse and
other waterways carried cargoes inland from the great port of Lynn, adding
substantially to its commercial importance. Archaeologists generally accept
that there was trade along the waterways in Roman times, William Stukeley
suggesting in the nineteenth century that the Car Dyke in Lincolnshire was
intended to carry grain to the Roman troops in the north. Coming to a later
period, Dorothy Summers in her magisterial study of the Great Ouse observes
that while there is a lack of evidence to indicate the extent to which the river
was employed for transport before the Norman Conquest, it is unlikely that
the potentialities of the river as a means of communication were ignored.[1]

There are strong indications that the Danes used the Great Ouse to
penetrate far inland when raiding in England during the ninth and early tenth
centuries. There are a number of earthworks near the river to bear witness
to the presence of the Danes at that time. The most interesting of them, at
Willington, about five miles east of Bedford, appears to have been a base in
which the Danes perhaps overwintered, with an outer harbour and a smaller

inner harbour, together with what might have been a dock for repairing or even building their boats.[2]

Stone and timber for the building of the various monasteries must have come by water. The monks appear to have aided the supply of these necessities by excavating canals to supplement the existing waterways. The cartulary of Ramsey Abbey contains an agreement made between that abbey and Sawtry Abbey near Peterborough in 1192 by which the monks of Sawtry were to close up all the channels they had made in the marsh between Whittlesey and Ugg Mere, 'except the great channel which runs from Whittlesea Mere to Sawtry, which shall remain open, for by it the monks of Sawtry bring stones and such necessaries for the building of their monastery and of their other offices'. Stone from the quarries at Barnack near Stamford was used in the cathedrals of Peterborough, Ely and Lincoln, in the abbeys of Ramsey and Crowland, and in the churches of many parishes in the fenland, and water transport was clearly used to carry it to wherever it was needed. In the middle of the eleventh century Ramsey Abbey agreed to render 4,000 eels a year at Lent to the abbey

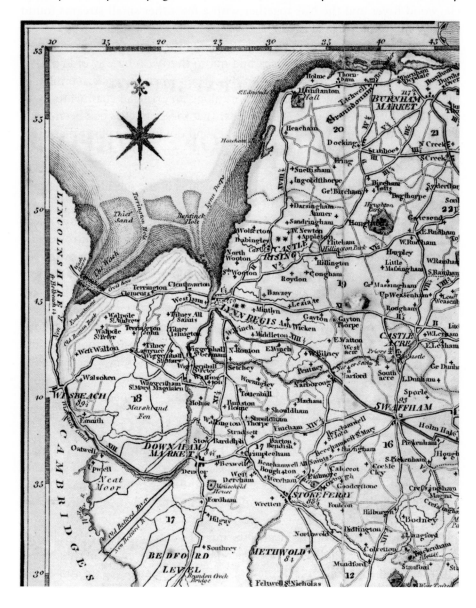

The coasts of the Wash and the Fenland rivers from a map published in *The Norfolk Tour*, 1824. The indentation north of Wisbech and the Wash Way can be seen clearly.

of Peterborough in return for building stone from Barnack.[3]

Many other things needed by monastic houses such as that at Ely also came by water, from the port of Lynn, including wax from Paris and the Baltic, Spanish iron and nails, and luxuries such as cloves, mace, figs and raisins, nuts and sugar.[4]

The fourteenth-century rolls of the sacrist of Ely show that he and his fellows used the fenland waterways as their normal everyday means of transport, since mention of boats and boat-hire occurs again and again in the accounts.[5] Over the centuries there have been many changes in the fenland rivers, some natural and many as the result of man's interference. In the eleventh century most of the rivers, including the Great Ouse and the Nene, found their way to the sea by way of Wisbech, which Professor Eilert Ekwall suggests derived its name from the River Wissey. These rivers meandered across the fens in a somewhat haphazard manner, sometimes breaking their banks and spreading across the surrounding countryside to produce bogs and lakes of considerable proportions. The Wisbech outfall was the major outlet to the sea, and only the Gaywood River and the Nar together with a few other small streams found their way into the Wash at Lynn.

Exactly how and when the western branch of the Great Ouse came to flow from Outwell along the Well Creek and out to the Wash by way of Lynn is a matter for conjecture. Nor is it known for certain when the eastern branch of the Great Ouse was diverted at Littleport along an artificial channel to reach the outfall at Lynn, though it is fairly clear that these changes had been made by the mid-thirteenth century. What is beyond doubt is the effect that these changes had on the development of the port of Lynn and on the navigation of the fenland waterways.[6]

By the time the religious and political tensions of the seventeenth century burst out into internecine conflict in the 1640s the trade of the fenland waterways had developed to the point at which the waterways became of major strategic importance. As Peter Harrington has pointed out, control of the waterways and of the bridges across them was vital in the Civil War, when the parliamentarian forces constructed a number of earthwork fortifications to safeguard certain strategic points.[7] Best known of these is the Earith Bulwark built by the Eastern Association to protect the crossing over the Great Ouse and the Old Bedford River near St. Ives. Another such fort was thrown up at Horsey Hill near the crossing of the River Nene between Peterborough and Whittlesey, and a third south-east of March guarded the gunpowder magazine for the Isle of Ely that was established nearby. Other earthwork fortifications on the western frontier of the Eastern Association have been recorded but have been obliterated by development.

In spite of considerable difficulties the Ouse was made navigable to Bedford in the seventeenth century and there was a flourishing inward trade in coal and outward in corn by the end of that century. In 1830 it was said that Bedford had 'a tolerable trade in grain, coals and timber by river navigation', and Cambridge, while primarily a university town, 'unavoidably secures an extensive trade in coals and corn, particularly oats and barley owing to its advantageous situation on the head of the inland navigation from Lynn'. Pigot's directory of that year noted that Marsh and Swann's boat left Cambridge every Saturday morning for Lynn, but that was clearly far from being the full extent of the town's trade. The Lynn boat called at Ely, from where lighters operated by Abraham Johnson, William Law and Thomas Smith ran 'occasionally' to Cambridge, Lynn, Bury St. Edmunds, Northampton, Huntingdon and intermediate places.

An early attempt was made to operate a steamboat service between Lynn and Cambridge when in 1824 the 72ft. sternwheel steamer *Union* began running with passengers, but it is probable that she did not survive for long.

March benefited from its position on the Nene 'facilitating the conveyance of coal, corn, timber and the produce of the gardens (which are here numerous) to Cambridge, Lynn, Peterborough, and various other places'.[8] Although references to river trade are not easy to find there is enough in contemporary directories to indicate that the fenland waterways were as busy as any other water highways. As late as 1892 there were boat and barge owners at Chesterton, just outside Cambridge, and at Chatteris, Ely, March and Whittlesey, while even in the 1920s – by which time steam tugs were being used to tow the lighters – there were still three barge owners at work.

The Corporation of Cambridge was always very much aware of the importance of its river trade, and fought a losing battle with the 'adventurers' who drained the fens and sought always to remove the water as quickly as possible, often to the detriment of the navigation. It was surely no coincidence that Stourbridge Fair, once one of the largest and most important trading fairs in the country, lasting for six weeks in September and October each year, was on land verging on the Cam; not only goods but people were conveyed to the fair by water.

The importance of inland navigation to the university town might have diminished in the course of the nineteenth century, but Cambridge's waterborne trade had by no means come to an end. In 1879 Kelly's directory speaks of 'a considerable trade in corn for the supply of the town and for the London markets . . . there are also iron and brass foundries, a tobacco manufactory, brick and tile works, curriers' works, breweries, maltings, some large flour mills, and in the immediate neighbourhood several extensive nurseries'. Though nothing is said of the river trade, it is clear that these industries must have depended to some extent on carriage by water even if the great days of the barges had passed.

Barge traffic was by no means confined to the main rivers. The Little Ouse, which has its confluence with the Great Ouse at Brandon Creek (some thirteen miles below the town of Brandon), was made navigable in the late seventeenth century so that it supplied the borough of Thetford with coal and carried corn down to Lynn, while the River Lark was made navigable in the early part of the following century to supply Bury St. Edmunds. The 'coal river' as it was sometimes called was of great importance to Bury, but in 1802 the *Ipswich Journal* reported that the town was short of coal owing to Lynn being 'ill supplied' and because a lack of water during the autumn had made the navigation from Lynn uncertain and difficult.

On the Little Ouse and elsewhere on the river navigations water levels were controlled by staunches, or as the locals pronounced the word, 'staanches'. These consisted of a barrier athwart the river with a lifting gate which could be raised by a winch operated by a large wheel at one side. The staunch held up a head of water in the reach above, and when there were barges to go up

Parts of the lode system of the Cam and the Ouse can be seen today as drainage ditches, as here at Swaffham Prior, some remain navigable.

Brandon staunch on the Little Ouse allowed lighters to sail up to Brandon and Thetford. It was typical of the staunches found elsewhere on the Fenland rivers.

or down the river the gate would be raised, allowing water from above to flow downriver. Barges going down would ride the torrent of water pouring through the staunch; those going upriver would have to wait until the water level had dropped sufficiently for them to be hauled through the staunch against the flow, after which the gate would be dropped so that the water above the staunch gradually deepened and the barges could proceed upriver to the next staunch. Brandon staunch, a mile or so below Brandon Bridge, was the last of the Little Ouse staunches to remain in working order

At Isleham, some three miles east of Soham and just north of Soham Lode, there were quarries which furnished clunch, a hard chalk widely used in the area as a building stone. 'The village and neighbourhood are famous for the production of limestone, great quantities of which are sent to Wisbech, Peterborough and other parts by Mr. George Frederick Robins', says Kelly's 1892 directory; Mr. Robins is described as a timber, coal and general merchant, limeburner and farmer. A bank of limekilns in one of the Isleham chalkpits has been preserved in the middle of a modern housing development now occupying the pit. Stone or clunch was also quarried at Burwell. Further north both the Wissey and the Nar were at one time navigable for some part of their courses, enabling John and Robert Marriott at Narborough to carry on a considerable business in coal, timber, corn and malt through the wharf at the head of the Nar.

On the eastern fen edge villages such as Burwell, Reach, Swaffham Bulbeck and Bottisham were reached by lodes, artificial cuts made to link the villages with the River Cam. At the head of Swaffham Lode, more than three miles long, is the hamlet of Commercial End which even today bears witness to the extent of this inland port's trade. Former maltings and warehouses, now converted into residences, as well as fine houses once inhabited by well-to-do merchants are clustered around the now-silted quay at the head of the lode,

from which cargoes of locally grown corn were once despatched to Lynn for loading into coasting vessels for Newcastle and elsewhere. Pigot's directory is somewhat dismissive of Swaffham Bulbeck but cannot avoid appraising one establishment, that of Messrs. Giblin and company, as being 'justly classed amongst the first and most respectable general merchants in the county'. Charles and Henry Giblin were both designated 'esquire', removing them from the ranks of the mere tradesmen; Giblin and company were listed as limeburners and merchants.

The typical local craft such as might have been built by John Mansfield at Swaffham Prior in the 1830s were double ended, clinker built with rather wide elm planking, and with a distinctive curved stem and sternpost. The smaller fen boats, used to carry the products of the fenland such as turf (peat), osiers for basketmaking and sedges and rushes to local markets, were no more than about 20ft. in length; the largest of the fen lighters were as much as 50ft. long, with a beam of 10ft. or more. The lighters had three stout beams, one amidships and one at each end, fastened with hefty knees.

The design was quite different from that of craft used for similar purposes elsewhere. There is just one qualification to this statement: the lighters employed on the Stour Navigation were clearly of the same kind, and must have been introduced to the Suffolk river by a fenland boatbuilder. As with so many other double-ended boats, the design is said to be derived from a Scandinavian original, but this is, I think, unproven.

For the most part the fenland lighters were towed by horses, though this proved difficult in cases where the landowners were opposed to the passage of horses along the banks. Professor H.C. Darby quotes a report to the House of Commons in 1777 that between 4th May 1776 and 3rd February 1777 as many as 2,692 boats and lighters had 'passed on the Hundred Foot River', and they had been hauled by 1,265 'pretty large horses'. It was said that the

Fenland lighters moored at Thetford about 1900. In 1845 the town was said to import coal and timber and to export corn, wool and other agricultural produce by way of the Little Ouse.

damage to the banks was all the greater because the horses 'did not draw in a right line, one behind the other, but obliquely, and so cover a larger space'.[9] In some places the horses had to walk along the barrier bank with a very lengthy towline spanning the low-lying 'washes' between the bank and the waterway.

Though the figures given to the House of Commons in 1777 would indicate that most lighters travelled in pairs, in later days at least gangs of up to eight were quite common. The bow of each lighter was closely linked to the stern of the one ahead by a 'seizing chain' and each lighter was fitted with a pole that projected over the stern of the lighter ahead, the outer end being fastened by a rope that could be manipulated to swing the pole as needed to steer around bends. The second lighter in the gang had a longer 'steering pole' with 'fest ropes' at its outer end that were used to steer the vessel, there being no rudder on the lighter; in effect the second lighter acted as a rudder. *The South-East Prospect of the City of Ely* drawn by Samuel and Nathaniel Buck and published in 1743 clearly shows a gang of four lighters drawn by two horses whose burden seems to be considerably lightened by the squaresail set on the leading vessel. In this case the haling path is close beside the river and the towline appears to be reasonably short.

Because the college grounds came right down to the river in the Cambridge Backs it was impossible to have a haling path on the bank. Instead there was a submerged path in the middle of the river along which the unfortunate horses had to wade. This path can be seen in use in an Ackerman print of Clare College; a man is standing on the back of the horse, which is up to its flanks

A gang of lighters being towed by a pair of horses at Ely, from Samuel and Nathaniel Buck's *South-East Prospect of the City of Ely*, 1743.

in the water and with a very short towline to the leading lighter of a gang. This lighter has a mast on which could be set a sail; it is lowered to pass under the bridge.

Most lighters had a large unobstructed hold, but one in each gang, the 'house lighter', had a cabin in which the lightermen could live when away from home. The third lighter in the gang shown on the Ackerman print appears to be a house lighter since it has a smoking chimney. It is said that the gangs also had a 'horse lighter' in which the horses could be carried on those stretches of river where it was not practicable for them to tow, or perhaps when the wind was in the right quarter for the leading lighter to set its squaresail.

It was not only on these inland waterways that horses were employed for towing: in the days when small seagoing ships traded up the Welland to Spalding they were towed up by horses. Larger vessels unloaded at Fosdyke Bridge, some eight miles below the town.[10]

The present Fosdyke Bridge carries the busy A17 trunk road, that fearfully inadequate link between the Midlands and Norfolk, over the Welland, whose channel runs to the north-east by way of Fosdyke Wash to join with that of the Witham. Between Long Sutton and Walpole Cross Keys the road runs an almost-straight course alongside the trackbed of the former Midland and Great Northern Joint Railway, and the two shared the Cross Keys swing bridge over the Nene at Sutton Bridge. Today the Nene flows on for another three miles below the bridge before emerging into the Wash at Crabs Hole, but it was not always like that.

Even as late as the 1790s when Thomas Donald and Thomas Milne were surveying their one-inch map of Norfolk there was a deep indentation to within five miles of Wisbech, and near where Cross Keys Bridge now carries the A17 over the River Nene there was a two-mile 'Wash Way' across Cross Keys Wash that was fordable only at low water. Perhaps it was thereabouts that more than five hundred years earlier King John's baggage train was overwhelmed by the tide and the crown jewels lost. Even in the nineteenth century it was said that the passage was extremely dangerous without a guide, and lives were sometimes lost in attempting to ford it.

Most helpfully the mapmakers date the Common Marsh Bank to 1791 and also show the 'Old Roman Sea Bank'[11] between West Walton and Clenchwarton. After perhaps 1,500 years the boundary had been moved but half a mile, but since the time of the map the outfall of the Nene has been moved some five miles seaward and a considerable extent of marsh has been drained and brought under cultivation.

The Port of Wisbech

Until the river was straightened and the outfall improved in 1830 the Nene had an eagre like that in the Trent or the better-known Severn bore. About 1680 Ralph Thoresby set down in his diary his impressions of the eagre, which seems to have impressed him greatly.

> This morning, before we left Wisbech, I had the sight of an Hygre or Eager, a most terrible flush of water, that came up the river with such violence that it sunk a coal vessel in the town, and

such a terrible noise, that all the dogs in it did snarl and bite at the
rolling waves, as though they would swallow up the river, the sight
of which (having never seen the like before) much affected me,
each wave surmounting the other with extraordinary violence.[13]

Perhaps the seven boats that were revealed by workmen engaged in
deepening the river in 1635 had been victims of the eagre. The seventeenth-
century historian William Dugdale in his book *Monasticon Anglicanum* tells
us that the sunken boats were lying on a stony bottom that was eight feet below
the then bed of the river, but marine archaeology had not then been thought
of and we have no record of their design or of their probable date.[14]

That was not by any means the only time attempts were made to deepen
the river and improve both the navigation and the drainage. In the mid-
eighteenth century it was said that seagoing vessels were unable to get up to
the town quays and were having to lie in Sutton Wash some distance below
the town and transfer their cargoes to lighters, but efforts to improve the
outfall by making a new cut met with a great deal of opposition. When a new
channel was excavated 'the works were demolished by a misguided multitude,
under the impression that they were protecting the interests of the Wisbech
navigation', and when the cut was eventually completed towards the end of the
century it proved of limited value.[15]

Those were the days of windpower, both at sea and ashore. It is recorded
that in the eighteenth century the areas of low-lying land drained by the Nene
depended on some sixty windmills to raise water from the drainage ditches
to the river level and that seven mills in Wisbech were engaged in pressing
seed to extract the oil, a somewhat noisy process when the stamps were in
operation pounding the seed. Perhaps it was one of these, or a predecessor,

The grand riverside housing
of North Brink today speaks
of the wealth there once was
in shipping.

that the Swiss scholar Dr. Casaubon saw when he came to Wisbech in 1611, but like so many writers he gives no description, merely saying 'we saw a mill where they make oil from rape seed, the supply of which is very great in this town'. Windmills were once used for various tasks besides grinding grain into meal.

At the beginning of the nineteenth century John Rennie, the well-known Scottish engineer, was asked by the Corporation of the Bedford Level to give his opinion on the Wisbech outfall and the drainage of the Nene washes. In his report, made in 1814, he recommended the cutting of a new channel from the mouth of Kinderley's cut to Crabs Hole in connection with other improvements higher up the river. Implementation of his plan was delayed by the economic situation following the end of the Napoleonic Wars, but in the 1820s the scheme went ahead in conjunction with the building of an embankment and bridge across Sutton Wash promoted with great determination by Lord William Bentinck. In spite of implacable opposition from the people of Wisbech and the agricultural community of the surrounding area work began on the scheme in 1827 and was completed in 1834. Construction of the two-mile embankment employed some 900 men and 260 horses.

The effect of the new outfall on the port of Wisbech must have startled those who had opposed the work. Whereas in 1805 the tonnage handled had amounted to less than 30,000 tons, by 1840 it was 109,885 tons and by 1849 over 150,000 tons. As the number and size of ships using the port increased a company was formed to operate steam tugs, three of which were in use on the Nene by 1850. Sadly the company did not prosper, and in that year the wooden paddle tugs *Middlesboro'*, *Samson* and *Don*, all of them built on the Tyne, were advertised for sale.[16]

There might have been tugs to bring ships through the largely wooden Cross Keys Bridge and up the narrow channel to the quays, but when the vessels had berthed there were few facilities for unloading them. The coal might have been loaded on the Tyne by means of chutes that could deposit a wagon load in the hold in a few moments, but at ports like Wisbech it had to be shovelled into baskets and hoisted out using a rope passing over a single block secured to a spar above the hatches; in seamen's terms a single-whip purchase. Deals from the Baltic were carried ashore by timber porters along a bouncing plank laid between the hatch coamings and the quayside.

Mobile cranes such as are used today for swinging ashore packaged timber

Wisbech as it appeared in 1756 with lighters and other craft on the River Nene, from a plate in *The History of Wisbech and the Fens*, 1849.

imported from Scandinavia were unknown, and straddle carriers were not even envisaged by the timber merchants of the eighteen-fifties. In the more flourishing ports such as Wisbech there was what was often termed The Crane, that name with its capital letters and definite article being an indication of its rarity. At Wisbech the New Crane was erected in 1845 to replace the Old Crane which mouldered on a section of river bank that had for years been slowly subsiding into the Nene. A print entitled *The New Crane and Wharf* printed from a copper plate paid for by John Whitsed, who as Mayor in 1845 laid the foundation stone of what was called the Crane Warehouse, fails to show anything resembling a modern crane. Only a close examination under a magnifying glass reveals the jib of a small crane such as would in later years grace many a railway goods yard, and one cannot discern even the 'plain deal partition' said to have been erected around it 'as an invitation to bill-stickers'.[17]

During the seventeen-nineties, no doubt about the time the original crane was installed, Wisbech merchants decided that the construction of a canal from the town to the Old Nene at Outwell would open up the fenland navigations to goods imported through Wisbech. An Act was obtained in 1794 and the five-and-a-quarter-mile canal was completed two years later at a cost of £16,500, but the venture did not prove profitable. Expenditure on clearing silt that threatened to block the Wisbech lock, and on repairs, continued to erode profits for many years. The opening of the Wisbech & Upwell Tramway in 1883-84 brought a further decline in trade, though it was not until 1922 that the last barge was seen on the canal, which was formally abandoned four years later.

In 1865 there were fifty-six trading vessels registered at the port of Wisbech,[18] including two steamers, the *Great Northern* and *Newton Colville*, both of which belonged to Wisbech merchant Richard Young, who was elected Mayor of Wisbech in 1858 and held that office for five succeeding years. A Victorian 'self-made man', he also owned six sailing vessels at that time, the largest of which were the barque *Walsoken*, 370 tons, and the full-rigged ship *Osborne House*, 365 tons, named not after the Queen's residence in the Isle of Wight but after the owner's Walsoken home.

Between about 1837 and the time of his death in 1871 Richard Young owned no fewer than forty-three vessels, about half of them steamers. Sometimes

The New Crane at Wisbech which replaced the Old Crane in 1845, from an engraving in *The History of Wisbech and the Fens*. The jib of the crane can just be seen beyond the building with a tower.

he held shares in partnership with others, as with the schooner *Elizabeth Huddleston*, acquired in 1837 by him in association with Thomas Greeves of Tydd St. Giles and Thomas Rawson of Long Sutton, who was the master.[19] This vessel was sold after four years to George Prest and Richard Bouch.

Young's ships were by no means confined to the coasting and home trades. The *Richard Young*, a 298-ton barque built at Wisbech by Cousins in 1849, sailed to Venice in 1852, from there to Constantinople, and then brought a cargo of Russian grain from Taganrog on the Sea of Azov to Amsterdam, arriving home at Wisbech towards the end of the year. She left again three days before Christmas for Oran, and the following year was sailing to Ceylon before bringing a cargo of barley from Constantinople that was unloaded at her home port. Her next voyage was again to Ceylon. The *Richard Young* was lost in Norwegian waters in 1864.

In 1853 one of Young's vessels, the 300-ton barque *City of Peterborough*, took out to the Cape of Good Hope a cargo of coal for the coaling of Brunel's steamer *Great Britain*, sailing from Sunderland to the Cape in 81 days. Twelve years later she was lost with all hands in a furious storm in Table Bay in which seventeen vessels were sunk or driven ashore.

While taking a prominent part in public life in the Fenland, Young was also well known in London business circles, being a director of the Great Eastern Railway and taking a particular interest in the establishment of that company's continental steamer services from Harwich. In 1871 a new paddle steamer for the Harwich-Rotterdam service was named *Richard Young*; the following year she was the first vessel to sail along the New Waterway to Rotterdam.

A number of the vessels sailing from Wisbech were built on the banks of the Nene. There were three shipbuilders at work in 1830, Joseph Dean, John Henson and Isaac Waddingham; Henson was followed by other members of his family in the course of the nineteenth century, the last of them to work at the trade being David John Henson, who was still operating the yard in the 1890s. Among the Wisbech-built vessels was the oddly named schooner *Six H's to the Queen*, launched in the year of Queen Victoria's coronation.

A delightful story is told by Arthur Oldham about the building of a little schooner by Henson in 1856. During the building a redstart was found to have built its nest among the stern framing. The nesting bird was jealously protected by the workmen and was allowed to hatch its eggs and feed its young without interference. When the time came for launching it was decided to give the vessel the appropriate name of *Redstart*.[20]

A sizeable fleet of little ships, several of them sloops, was owned by John T. Smith, who lived in Nene Parade, Wisbech. He had five sloops, two schooners and the ketch *Bluejacket*, which was built at Walsoken, a Wisbech suburb, in 1860 and was later owned in north Norfolk. Downriver at Sutton Bridge a timber merchant, George Prest, owned a small fleet of which the largest at 247 tons was the brig *Sarah Richardson*, built in 1839.[21] One of his vessels, the schooner *Zuma*, built at Grimsby in 1856, was still afloat at the end of the century, owned in Goole; she was eventually lost in a gale at Saltfleet on the Lincolnshire coast.

With the arrival of the railways from 1847 onwards maritime trade through Wisbech fell away by as much as a half, although the railway companies had

This *View of Wisbech from the Horse-shoe* shows two post wind-mills on the river bank, one of them apparently derelict, and the big eight-sailed tower mill. The two steamers at left are possibly the tugs introduced without much success in the 1840s. A gang of Fenland lighters is passing.

grandiose plans to develop the port of Wisbech as a serious rival to Lynn. Much money was spent on constructing new quays with railway access and in 1850 Robert Stephenson & Co. replaced Lord William Bentinck's Cross Keys Bridge with a hand-operated swing bridge that would serve to carry the railway as well as the road over the Nene; that bridge was itself replaced in 1897 by a third bridge constructed by the Midland & Great Northern Railway a hundred yards upstream of the Stephenson bridge. The 1897 bridge, which originally carried railway and road side by side across the river and now serves only road traffic, is listed at Grade II* as a building of historic importance.

It was just below Cross Keys Bridge that the Sutton Bridge Dock Company, largely promoted by the Great Northern Railway, began in the 1870s to excavate a rail-served dock from the marshland of Cross Keys Wash. The dock

Frozen up in the river at Wisbech in 1981.

Whilst dock and cranage facilities continue at Wisbech, much of the trade has moved downriver to near Cross Keys bridge at Sutton Bridge. The town has developed marina facilities for the leisure yachtsman.

opened on 14th May 1881, but the very next day there were clear signs that the project had not been properly designed and constructed and that the dock was doomed. First the entrance lock began to leak, and then the following month the dock wall collapsed; it was never rebuilt. Three ships that were in the dock were extricated only with considerable difficulty; there is a story that a ship is still entombed in the silt within the dock, but that is no more than legend.

A century later there were wharves at what was by then known as Port Sutton Bridge, operated by Fenland District Council and handling quite large ships bringing a variety of cargoes. Ill luck struck again in December 2000 when the mv *Lagik* arrived from Norway with a 2,250-tonne cargo of steel products. She was being swung prior to berthing when she grounded and became wedged across the river on a falling tide. Had a tug been standing by to assist in swinging her all might have turned out well, but there was no tug and the 300ft. vessel's stern was lodged firmly on one bank; the *Lagik* broke in two as the tide fell, and there she lay effectively blocking the river. She had to be broken up as she lay. The port of Wisbech was closed for forty-four days.

Though overshadowed by the major port of King's Lynn, Wisbech occupied a useful position for the export of grain and potatoes grown on the Fen farms. Considerable quantities of farm produce were brought down the rivers to be exported in seagoing ships from the Wisbech quays, and in 1934 plans were drawn up for widening the Nene all the way to Northampton, some eighty miles from the sea. It was a project that proved all too enterprising for the depressed 1930s, but twenty years later a few Thames barges with auxiliary engines were trading to Peterborough. I recall the Rochester sprittie *Thyra*, owned by the London & Rochester Trading Co. Ltd., unloading at a riverside flour mill at Peterborough, seen from the train as I returned to camp during my period of National Service about 1950.

Commercial shipping still sails up the Nene to Wisbech as well as to Sutton Bridge, and since 2000 Fenland District Council has developed the Wisbech Yacht Harbour with 128 berths, some of them reserved for visiting yachts.

King's Lynn   2

When the early settlements of Lynn were first laid out on land reclaimed from the *llyn*, the lake through which the Gaywood River, the Nar and the Little Ouse drained into the Wash, the town plan was greatly influenced by the waterways or 'fleets' which carried drainage into the main river and also served to allow small craft to navigate up to quays in the heart of the town. Although there was never the kind of network of waterways that one finds in some Dutch towns there was in the early days a series of channels in the north end of the town connecting with the Gaywood River, which later became known in its lower reaches as the Fisher Fleet, the harbour used by the town's fishermen.

The town was laid out on part of the Gaywood estate, owned by the bishops of Norwich. Herbert de Losinga, the bishop who moved the see to Norwich, set up a Benedictine priory at Lynn, which was already the site of an embryonic settlement of salters and merchants by the end of the eleventh century. It is said that the waste products of salt production dumped on the mud at the edge of the *llyn* provided the foundation for some of the earliest buildings, and sandy hillocks to the north of the modern town bear witness to the scale of later salt production.

Bishop's Lynn, as it was then known, developed around the Saturday Market Place and the priory church of St. Margaret, the Purfleet providing a good harbour for trading vessels owned by the early merchants who were attracted to the new settlement. By 1200 there was a further settlement, the Newland, centred on a second market place to the north, the Tuesday Market Place, and merchants were erecting substantial houses with attached warehouses behind the quays, with a street running between the houses and the quay. The typical property had a short range along the street backed by a longer range at right angles to the frontage, the house usually being accessed by a passage from the street cut through the frontage.

Until the changes in the fenland rivers that gave Lynn the advantage over Wisbech at some time in the Middle Ages Lynn's inland trade must have depended as much on transport by land as on water carriage, yet the returns of King John's Custom of 1203-05 show that Lynn and Boston were at that time the wealthiest ports in the country after London and Southampton, with a significant trade with the Low Countries. Lynn's street pattern seems to show that the town then carried on a good deal of trade by road.[1] It would be interesting to know a great deal more about the early trade of the Wash ports, but there is little hope that we shall learn very much from such records as exist from the early period.

Opposite: The Hanseatic warehouse in King's Lynn, constructed in 1475, is the only surviving Hanseatic building in England. It is located on St. Margaret's Lane.

A mid-nineteenth-century plan of King's Lynn showing the river frontage and the fleets before the construction of the docks at the north end of town.

Lynn built up a great trade in corn brought down the fenland waterways from the vast hinterland. There was also a significant export trade in salt from the saltpans around the Wash, and in cloth of Lincoln green and Stamford scarlet as well as lead from Derbyshire. The biggest import was wine, and there was also an important trade in timber, wax, pitch, resin, copper and steel from the Baltic, Prussian beer and bow-staves, Arctic squirrel, beaver and sable skins from Russia, Norwegian hawks and falcons, Flemish cloth, swords and helmets from Cologne, dyes from Picardy, linen and canvas, figs, raisins, dates, olive oil and Cordovan leather from Spain. A Spaniard, John de Ispania, was mayor of Lynn at the end of the thirteenth century.

The chamberlains' accounts of Newcastle-upon-Tyne show the extent of Lynn's trade with that port, to which Norfolk merchants sent cargoes of barley and other cereals and from which they shipped a good deal of coal.[2] In the years 1508-11 the chamberlains' accounts show ninety-seven Lynn ships arriving on the Tyne, a dozen carrying barley, eight with malt and seven with stones; exactly what kind of stones is not explained, but possibly they were building stones from the Barnack quarries brought to Lynn by the fenland waterways. The seventy other vessels were either 'empty' or in ballast.

The town authorities imposed a toll on incoming shipping for the deposition of ballast on special 'shores' which had to be maintained at the town's expense. Ships owned in Newcastle did not have to pay the ballast toll, but all other vessels discharging ballast did, regardless of any favoured status in respect of other tolls. Those who dumped their ballast wherever they thought they might get away with it were fined, if they were caught; three men of Dunwich were fined in 1509.

Lynn ships sailing to the Tyne and mentioned in the accounts for 1508-11 were the *Anttony*, *Balyaye*, *Buttell*, which several times delivered cargoes of hemp and 'cabylls' – cables presumably made by a Lynn ropemaker – *Clement*, *Cristoffer*, *Davy*, *Jamys*, *Jennett*, *John*, *Lennertt*, *Mary*, *Mary Fortune*, *Margett*, *Mighell* and *Trinite*.

That is fifteen names, but there were clearly some names that were shared by more than one ship. There were probably at least three vessels belonging to Lynn sharing the name *Cristoffer* at that time. One of them, skippered by John Robyns until about May 1510 and then by John Foster, visited Newcastle nine times in the period and each time left with 20 chaldrons of coal, a Newcastle chaldron then being approximately 21cwt.

A larger *Cristoffer* whose master was first William Chamberlayn and then Robert Berry made five voyages to Newcastle and left each time with 34 chaldrons of coal, while another vessel of the same name skippered by John Manerston made two trips in June and July 1511, leaving the Tyne each time 'with 9 hundred fiche'. There also appear to be at least two other small vessels of the same name belonging to Lynn at the same time, to say nothing of the *Cristoffer* of Burnham, the *Cristoffer* of Grimsby, the *Cristoffer* of Yarmouth and not a few others sharing the name.

Research into sixteenth-century shipping can prove confusing at times.

The Iceland fare

An important part of Lynn's trade in the Middle Ages was the summer trade with Iceland, which had by the Union of Kalmar in 1397 been united with Norway, Sweden and Denmark, the latter country becoming in time the dominant partner. The trade was almost entirely in salt and wind-dried fish, for the Icelanders had little else to exchange for the goods they needed, the grain and other food that kept them alive through the long winter, the fish hooks that enabled them to catch cod and ling, and the cloth to make clothes that kept out the bitter cold. England, with an increasing population, needed the fish that was eaten on Fridays and on the other fast days ordained by the pre-Reformation Church.

If tradition be true one of the very first to sail from Lynn to Norway and Iceland was Brother Nicholas de Lenn, a Franciscan friar from Lynn who is said to have made the voyage in 1360 and to have produced charts which he presented to Edward III on his return.[3] If indeed he did make charts they would have been crude and primitive ones, not such as would be suitable for navigational use, for this was long before the first real sea charts were drawn. There might be something in Richard Hakluyt's story that Brother Nicholas sailed to Iceland, but the fable that he landed in Iceland and, using an astrolabe for navigation, travelled overland to the North Pole can hardly be more than an unwarrantable gilding of the lily.

During the fourteenth century English fishermen were voyaging afar in search of good fish to feed the growing population, guided by 'needle and by stone': the magnetic lodestone and the magnetised iron needle which the navigators inserted into a straw and floated in a bowl of water to form a primitive compass. Among those who found their way to northern waters were certain 'fishers of salt fish of Cromer and Blakeney' who carried on their trade 'on the coasts of Norway and Denmark'.[2] Hakluyt declared that the men of Blakeney were fishing off Iceland in the days of King Edward III, in the middle of the fourteenth century, and while there is no surviving evidence to prove their presence in Icelandic waters at that date they were certainly fishing off the Norwegian coast by that time. Whether or not we believe Hakluyt's assertion, we can be sure that by 1412 east coast fishermen were voyaging to the Vestmann Islands off the south coast of Iceland, where the seas abounded in cod and ling.[5] These men from Blakeney and Cromer and other Norfolk ports understood deep-sea lining and were quite prepared to defy the orders of Henry V's government forbidding direct trading with Iceland; as well as catching their own fish they were happy to barter with the Icelanders, exchanging essential supplies of food and goods for fish caught by Icelandic fishermen and dried in the wind on wooden racks.

The Icelanders' attitude to the arrival of English fishermen was approving, for in 1412 the annalist recorded sorrowfully 'No news from Norway to Iceland'; the hoped-for supply ship had failed to arrive. When a strange ship appeared off Dyrholm isle the men who rowed off to it were by no means sorry to discover 'fishermen out from England', for the fishermen were able to provide at least some of the victuals they required. The next year 'thirty or more' fishing doggers arrived off the Vestmann Islands.

The fishermen's ventures paved the way for English merchants who left

England in the early spring and spent the summer in Iceland, returning between July and September. The kind of ship in which the Lynn merchants voyaged to Iceland may be seen in a pew end from the church of St. Nicholas at Lynn now in the Victoria and Albert Museum. In place of the single mast and squaresail of earlier ships this early-fifteenth-century vessel had two masts with a squaresail on the mainmast and a three-cornered lateen sail on the mizzen; the mainmast has a stout fighting top and the 'castles' fore and aft are no longer mere appendages but form an integral part of the hull.

The East Anglian fishermen used hand-lines as much as 90 fathoms (540ft.) long to catch the cod, handling them either from the deck of the ship or from small boats launched from the ship. At the end of the line was a large lead weight to take the line to the bottom, and just above the lead was a stick called by the fisherman a chopstick bearing two lines and baited hooks.

Alternatively, when fishing in shallower inshore waters they would set long-lines many hundreds of feet in length, buoyed at each end and held fast by a number of small anchors. Every fathom and a half along its length was fitted a short line known as a snood bearing a baited hook. Large numbers of cod might be taken on long-lines, and at the beginning of the sixteenth century the Icelandic Althing complained that the use of long-lines by English fishermen was preventing fish from reaching the very shallow coastal waters fished by the Icelanders.

Not only did the English ships catch their own cod, which were salted down on board and packed into barrels, but they also traded with the Icelanders for their wind-dried cod or stockfish. The stockfish trade was one that benefited both the English fishermen and merchants and the Icelanders, yet it was also one that produced diplomatic problems for those taking part. Iceland was of course a long way from Norway and even further from Copenhagen, where the king and the government seemed sometimes to forget the needs of the Icelanders, who were dependent on the supply ships that made survival possible in the isolated wastes of that far-off island.

The Danish king decreed that trade with Iceland was to be carried on only through the staple port of Bergen, on the rocky west coast of Norway. This preserved the trade to his own subjects, but when Copenhagen forgot its responsibilities to the distant island community nobody need be surprised that the islanders ignored the rules and were happy to welcome foreign ships whose captains were prepared to sell them the supplies they so much needed. As English trade expanded and the clothiers of East Anglia sought markets for the cloth they wove in towns such as Hadleigh, Lavenham and Long Melford it was inevitable that the merchants and shipmasters of a port like Lynn should be attracted to those northern waters.

At first the merchants had the blessing of King Eric, who was prepared to issue letters allowing them to sail into his dominions with their wares without paying toll, but as the trade grew he took steps to restore the monopoly of Bergen. There he had the support of the merchants of the Hanse, that confederation of north German town states that operated a 'factory' on Bryggen, the quay built out into Bergen Fjord, and sought to establish its own trading monopoly. In 1415 King Eric wrote to Henry V of England complaining of damage caused by English fishermen trading with Iceland. That year a royal proclamation prohibiting trade with Iceland 'except in accordance with ancient custom' –

through Bergen – was read in sixteen east coast ports, including Lynn.

All the same, as Professor Carus-Wilson says in her account of the Iceland venture, the arbitrary decrees of distant kings in London and Copenhagen could not put a stop to business that in Iceland was equally opportune to both parties. Feeling abandoned by their own government, the Icelanders took matters into their own hands and welcomed those who came to trade with them, seeking only to regulate the trade and to counter the lawlessness of those fishermen who caused trouble either ashore or afloat. Thus encouraged, more and more English merchants forsook Bergen and took part in a direct trade with Iceland. It was not long before Lynn had its recognised body of 'merchants of Iceland' who in 1424 elected two of their number for taxing the merchants, as did 'merchants of Norway', 'merchants of Prussia' and other merchants.

This did not at all suit the merchants controlling the staple port of Bergen, who found the Bergen trade declining as English merchants sailed direct to Iceland. They employed their influence to oppose any relaxation of the staple restrictions and seem to have made great efforts to confine all trade to themselves.

A new Danish governor, Hannes Palsson, was sent by King Eric to Iceland in 1420. With him there went a large retinue of Danes, who set about collecting the king's taxes and quickly made themselves unpopular with the native Icelanders. The new governor established a market in the Vestmann Islands, fixed the prices to be charged there, and proceeded against those merchants who built houses in the islands and settled there throughout the year in contravention of the licences they had been given.

During that same year Stephen Schellendorp, a German who might perhaps have been sent by the Hanse merchants, arrived in Iceland. Whether or not he was indeed an agent of the Hanse, he certainly played their game, writing a letter to King Eric in which he alleged that English merchants had acquired so firm a footing in Iceland that if nothing were done to prevent their operations there the island would surely cease to be a Danish possession.

Popular history tells of unruly Englishmen who fought with the Icelanders, committing murder, causing mayhem and performing acts of piracy that brought shame on the name of England. Schellendorp's obsequious letter with its declarations of disinterested service to the Danish crown not unnaturally stirred up trouble. The English fishermen and merchants, aware of the risks they ran in visiting Icelandic waters, went prepared for a hostile reception; when they landed they did so fully armed and in battle array, and those who opposed them were killed. When in 1425 Palsson and his companion Balthazar van Dammin tried to arrest the marauding English ships in the Vestmann Islands they were repelled by archers. Not only that, they were themselves captured and carried off to England, where Palsson composed a furious condemnation of the English interlopers, setting down one by one all the thirty-seven crimes they were alleged to have committed during his five years of office.

It is to this almost interminable complaint of the deeply injured governor that we owe the whole of our evidence of the misdeeds of the English in Iceland during the first quarter of the fifteenth century, says Professor Carus-Wilson, who examined the list in detail and found that many of the allegations concerned the operations of mariners from Hull. Nobody from either Lynn or Bristol appears in the list, leading her to conclude that most of the merchants probably carried on a peaceful trade to the advantage of all concerned.

The popular view that this was a shameful episode when English seamen and fishermen fought with the Icelanders does not accord with Professor Carus-Wilson's considered opinion that on the whole it was not the Icelanders whom the English attacked but rather the Danish officials who tried to claim exorbitant taxes from the traders. English resistance to the officials and even the kidnapping of Palsson seems to have been applauded by the Icelanders, if one is to judge from their annals. When the governor was captured and borne off to England the annalist set down his astringent comment: 'Few were sorry at that.'

It was not to be expected that King Eric would accept the Icelandic opinion, however, and when the time came for the ships to set forth the next year his decree that all ships sailing to Iceland without his permission were to be called to account was read – in an English translation – in a Congregation at Lynn. The Lynn merchants were forbidden to set sail, an ordinance forbidding the voyage being read out by the Common Clerk in February 1426. The Congregation 'ordained that all persons frequenting Island [Iceland] should be summoned to come to the Gild Hall before the Mayor and Community, and be there forbidden to navigate to Island under pain of forfeiture of goods and deprivation of liberty'. There were those among the seafaring community of Lynn who saw no good reason for abandoning their intended voyage, but a little later, after the Council of England had considered Palsson's diatribe, Thomas Beaufort, Duke of Exeter, forbade the Iceland voyage, and this prohibition was also read out in a Congregation. The Mayor of Lynn took quick action, arresting a vessel that was about to sail for Iceland.

In other ports the authorities were less diligent, and that autumn a London vessel put in at Lynn on its return from Iceland. What the Lynn seamen said about that is not recorded, but the cocky captain, John Vache, apparently made disparaging remarks about those who had been so easily frightened off the Iceland voyage. When Vache was taken before the town authorities no less a person than the Mayor himself told how Vache had called the Lynn merchants traitors. Vache was made to eat his words, swearing upon the gospels that he had never used the words complained of, before he was released from custody.

Immigration from Iceland was not unknown, though the manner in which men and women left their homes for England is quite unknown. A more or less contemporary source says that the starving Icelanders were willing to sell their children into slavery to obtain food for those who remained, but it is not beyond possibility that adventurous Icelandic youngsters were quite willing to stow away on the English ships in the hope of finding a better life and a new home in England; economic migration is by no means only a twenty-first-century phenomenon. However they came to this country, the five boys and three girls found at Lynn in 1429 were ordered to be returned home the following year when the Iceland fleet set out in the spring. How they were to get home when King Henry forbade any 'by the audacitie of their follie' to trade with Iceland except through the staple port of Bergen need not concern us.

Truth to tell, neither the decrees of the Danish king nor the ordinances of

Henry V were sufficient to stamp out the trade with Iceland that had been so firmly established by merchants from Lynn and other ports. It was a trade that was as vital to the Icelanders as to the men of Lynn, and it increased rather than diminished in the 1430s and 1440s, sanctioned by licences issued by the respective kings. Each year the English ships gathered around the Vestmann Islands, 'where is the best fishing of all Iceland', fishing with long-lines bearing hooks by the hundred and, as the Icelanders complained, preventing the fish from approaching nearer the shore where they fished from their small boats.

In the latter half of the fifteenth century the dynastic struggle between the houses of York and Lancaster not only created dissension and unrest at home but had a damaging effect on overseas trade. Although forty years earlier the men of Lynn seem not to have been guilty of any of the crimes of which Hannes Palsson complained so passionately, in 1467 they do seem to have been involved when the governor, Bjorn Thorleifson, was 'smitten to death' by English traders. The governor's wife seems to have been a force to be reckoned with; she donned a coat of mail and led an avenging force against the English, many of whom were killed, and she also persuaded King Christian in distant Copenhagen to act against the aggressors. Four ships belonging to Lynn were seized in the Sound the following year and sequestered as compensation for the outrage.

The involvement of Lynn is strongly implied in King Christian's reply to the English king's representations. The Danish king wrote 'to the mayors and rulers of all cities and towns in England except those of Lynn' saying that he was retaining certain Lynn ships which had, as he put it, fallen into his hands to satisfy the relatives of the innocent dead. He was willing to grant safe conduct for any English ships other than those of Lynn, and added for good measure that if any had lost their possessions through Lynn's crime they must seek redress from Lynn and not from him.

Such conflicts did nothing to improve relations between England and Denmark. The situation deteriorated further when English traders found themselves not only at odds with the Danish king but also with German rivals, both the Hanseatic merchants at Bergen and other Germans seeking to infiltrate the Iceland trade. Eventually the Iceland fleet was being ordered to gather in the Humber and to proceed in convoy under the protection of the king's ships. In 1484 Richard III commanded those who voyaged to Iceland 'Remember that ye dessever not, without tempest of weder compelle you, but that ye keep you togeder, aswele going into the said parties as in your retourne unto this our realme, without any wilfull breche to the contrarie, upon payn of forfeiture of your shippes and goodes.'[7]

Notwithstanding the conflict of interests the Iceland trade went on. Having received yet another complaining letter from his cousin the king of Denmark, Henry VII in 1491 addressed a letter to the Earl of Oxford giving instructions that fishermen visiting Icelandic waters should 'take noo thyng but that they truly pay or agre for, and friendly entrete our seyd cousin's subjects without eny robbyng or exstortyng them in their bodyes nor goodys'. In other words, pay for what you take and don't drive too hard a bargain.

An Anglo-Danish treaty of 1490 eased restrictions on Englishmen visiting Iceland, and in succeeding years English merchants, including those from Lynn, continued to trade with Iceland, ever, one hopes, bearing in mind the king's orders. England's troubled relations with the Scots proved a problem for those taking part in the trade with Iceland, however. In 1523 Lord Surrey informed Cardinal Wolsey, who as Henry VIII's Chancellor was in charge of foreign affairs, that 'the Scotts entende to set forth vi or vii ships to the Ilonds to mete with the Islonde flete in retornyng homwards, wich if they do a mervelous domage shall ensue, and the costs of Norfolk and Suffolk undone and all Inglond shalbe destitute of fish next yere'.[8] The reference to the East Anglian coast is significant; in 1528 a list of English vessels engaged in the northern fisheries shows that no fewer than 149 ships voyaged to Iceland that year, and the majority of them were from ports in Norfolk and Suffolk.

It seems that the importance of the stockfish trade decreased somewhat when Henry VIII declared himself head of the Church of England and the new Protestant Church placed much less weight on the old rules of fasting. In 1533 only 85 ships went to Iceland, and by the early 1550s the Iceland fleet had been reduced to a mere 43 ships, much to the bitterness of the impoverished East Anglian ports, says Evan Jones.[9]

Ill-judged legislation aimed at regulating the market in white fish seems to have damaged the trade, though in 1565 a muster roll of Norfolk indicates that the county then had at least 33 ships employed in trading with Iceland, about half of the total number engaged. The decline was reversed at the beginning of the seventeenth century, it being claimed in 1632 that Iceland 'is the greatest fishing in the Kingdom and exceedeth the Newfownd Land and herring fishings'. England's population was growing apace and the trade with Iceland helped to provide the food needed to support this growth, fish prices rose and the fishing became increasingly profitable.

Again, however, taxation threatened to kill the goose that laid the golden egg. Charles I, always short of funds, increased the toll he took from ships returning from Iceland and also raised the duty on salt, at the same time removing the concession that allowed fishermen to claim back the duty imposed on salt imported from Biscay if that salt was used in the curing of fish.

The Civil War period, during which Lynn was besieged and taken by the Parliamentary forces, caused a further setback to the trade, though the fishery did recover in the days of the Commonwealth, when the Iceland fleet sailed under the protection of naval vessels such as the *Marigold*, which convoyed a fleet in 1654. However in 1662 we read complaints that the East Anglian cod fisheries were in severe decline and that fishermen preferred to 'let their vessels lie and rot in haven than to undergo much pain and peril for that which would not at their return quit cost in any proportion because their fish turn to no account'.[10]

In 1702 it was reported that no ships had been sent on the Iceland voyage from Yarmouth in the previous two years, though that port had earlier with Lynn been one of the principal participants in that trade. Recalling that the Iceland fishing had formerly employed 10,000 men, a writer stated that there were at the beginning of the eighteenth century not a thousand taking part. The Icelandic fishery was effectively finished, the principal cause being the tax on salt.

A House of Commons report on the state of the British fisheries in 1785 at last accepted that the salt taxes had devastated the trade. A Yarmouth shipowner, John Shelly, was quoted in the report as saying that there had once been 'a fishery carried on from Yarmouth upon the coast of Iceland, which employed about 200 vessels – that the fish usually caught there were cod, taken with hand lines, and were dry-salted in the hold of the vessel – that the reason why that fishery is not now carried on is, that, except in the fishery for herrings, the duty for all the salt not expended in the curing of fish must be paid, or the salt destroyed.'[11]

Lynn's other trades

The Hanseatic League, that extraordinary free trade community of nearly two hundred towns in northern and western Europe with which English merchants trading with Iceland came into conflict, was trading with Lynn from the thirteenth century onwards and established a trading 'factory' or steelyard in St. Margaret's Lane in the fifteenth century. The steelyard was built in the 1480s on land reclaimed from the river and acquired by the king for the use of the Hanse merchants as a result of the signing of the Treaty of Utrecht in 1475 which ended a period of conflict between England and the League; it is the only property of the Hanseatic League to survive in Britain, though it has its counterpart in the Norwegian port of Bergen.

With the collapse of the Hanseatic League the complex of buildings was sold in 1751 to one of Lynn's leading merchants, Edward Everard, who built a new house on the St. Margaret's Place end that incorporated some parts of the medieval building. The warehouse ranges survived the changes and near the end of the twentieth century were restored to provide a home for the Weights and Measures Department of the county council, a not inappropriate use for what is so often called the Steelyard.

Everard was not the only well-to-do resident of his generation to build himself a fine residence. The street running north from the Saturday Market Place, Queen Street, contains a number of stylish Georgian houses, or in most cases older houses restyled with Georgian fronts, the grandest of which is the brick-built Clifton House, re-fronted in 1708, with its tall tower from which its owner could perhaps watch for his ships coming upriver.[12] Old prints of the river front show that there were once other lookout towers in the town, but only that of Clifton House survives.

A good idea of the extent of one commercial property in St. Margaret's Place can be gained from a newspaper advertisement addressed 'To Merchants in General' in 1821 which referred to Lynn as 'the Second Coal Port in England'.[13]

> This Estate has a peculiar advantage, having one of the best births [sic] in the harbour for vessels, and corn may be spouted from the granaries, by which a very considerable expence in porterage is to be saved; and vessels from 300 to 500 tons burthen may load and unload there. Besides the above advantages, this Estate gives an opportunity of carrying on a most extensive foreign and inland trade, as by the River Ouze [sic] commerce may be extended into seven inland counties; and from the works now carrying on above Lynn, it is expected that vessels of any burthen may enter the harbour, and from thence transport merchandize to all parts of the world.

A carte-de-visite photograph of King's Lynn by E. Bullock, portrait, landscape and architectural photographer, of St. James Street, Lynn. About a dozen vessels, mainly brigs, are moored head to the flood tide in the river, while another brig lies in the mouth of the River Nar. Two large wooden cranes stand on the Boal Quay.

The advertisement goes on to mention that the wine vaults that formed part of this property would hold 300 pipes of wine, a reminder that there were very extensive cellars under many of the town's waterside properties. Henry Hillen, the Lynn historian, speaks of that part of the town along the river being honeycombed with underground stores.[14] The wine trade had been a most important one from medieval times onwards, as many as 332,560 gallons being imported in 1801.

Lynn was a busy port in the eighteenth and early nineteenth centuries, with a thriving trade with the Baltic, from which came both timber and deals. The Russian port of Memel, now Klaipeda, Lithuania, was often crowded with British ships, and in about 1824 traders in Lynn put forward a proposal for the establishment of an English church there for the use of visiting British seamen. Timber was also imported into Lynn from Danzig and from St. Petersburg, while many cargoes of linseed came from Riga, now the capital of Latvia.

A stretch of the medieval town wall that was narrowed and refaced as part of poor relief work around 1817 contains a number of ballast stones from the Baltic. It seems likely that a shipload of ballast from the Baltic was used in the refacing.[15] A Lynn man, Thomas Wale (1701-96), having served a six-year apprenticeship to Lynn merchant William Allen, was sent out to represent his master in Riga, and in due course he became a successful merchant himself. Wale spent almost his whole life in Riga, where he had a flourishing business, returning to Lynn as a septuagenarian. It seems that among the wares that he sold in the Baltic port were pale ales and porter brewed by Everard's brewery in Lynn, for Lynn ales were widely distributed both in the Baltic and in the Netherlands in the eighteenth century.[16]

Perhaps the finest reminder of Lynn's status as a trading port in the seventeenth and eighteenth centuries is the impressive building, described by one architectural historian as 'one of the most perfect buildings ever erected', that stands beside the Purfleet. Known today as the Custom House, it was designed by Lynn merchant, architect and artist Henry Bell and built in 1683 as 'an Exchange or place of meeting for Merchants & others for conference in Trade & Comerce' (sic).

Seamen and navigators

Also beside the Purfleet and close to the Custom House there now stands a statue of Captain George Vancouver (1758-98), an officer of the Royal Navy who has left an indelible mark on the map of North America as a result of his work in producing accurate charts of the coastline of what are now British Columbia and the State of Washington. Canada's third largest city now bears his name, and so does the large island that lies offshore opposite the city.

The youngest son of a Lynn family of Dutch origin, he began his seafaring career in 1772 as a midshipman on board Captain James Cook's ship, HMS *Resolution*. He served with Cook on his second and third expeditions and was commissioned lieutenant in 1780, having survived a skirmish with Hawaiian natives similar to that in which Cook was killed.

Those two long voyages with Cook provided the young Vancouver with an outstanding apprenticeship, preparing him well for his future career. Not the least valuable part of this training was the instruction he received from the astronomer William Wales in observing, surveying and drawing. It was during the second of those voyages that Vancouver first saw the north-west coast of America, on which he was to accomplish his own great achievements in later years.

In 1788 a fur trader named John Meares set up a trading post at Nootka Sound, on the shore of what later became known as Vancouver Island, thus attracting the hostile attentions of Spanish officials who claimed the whole western American coast from Cape Horn to latitude 60 degrees north, the area that we now call Alaska. There was great excitement when news reached England of the seizure of Meares' ships, and the government prepared for war with Spain, which in the wake of the French Revolution was unable to count on French support.

Spain gave way and agreed not only to return the trading post at Nootka Sound but conceded that the British had a right to peaceful exploitation in the Pacific so long as they did not come within ten leagues of Spanish settlements. Vancouver was given command of HMS *Discovery*, a former merchant ship built at Whitby in 1764, and sent off to the Pacific in 1791 with orders to make a detailed survey of the coast from California to Alaska, and to meet the

A statue of Captain Vancouver stands outside the former Custom House on the quay, and nearby is a memorial to some of the other seamen associated with Lynn, including James Burney, Samuel Cresswell and William Hoste.

Spanish commissioner Juan Francisco Bodego y Quadra at Nootka Sound and arrange the settlement of the Nootka Convention agreed by the two countries the year before.

As commander of the two-ship expedition – the other was HMS *Chatham* – he seems to have attracted the enmity of more than one of his subordinates, who on their return to Britain sought to blacken his name; possibly it was due to them that he has a reputation as a severe disciplinarian, irascible and quarrelsome. That reputation fits uncomfortably with his good relationship with the natives of Hawaii, where his ship wintered during the four-year expedition, and with the cordial friendship that grew up between him and Juan Francisco Bodego y Quadra.

The Spanish naval officer, who had been born in Lima, Peru, in 1743, had already surveyed large parts of the coast, and there is little doubt that Vancouver recognised in him a fellow spirit. His work resulted in a very fine set of maps, and in a rare instance of amiable co-operation he allowed Vancouver to make use of them in his own exploration.

When Vancouver proposed that England receive possession of Nootka and that Neah Bay serve as a free port for both Britain and Spain Quadra politely declined his suggestion. There was, however, no falling out; both agreed on one thing, the name of the island, which they decided should be Quadra and Vancouver Island. It is a little sad that the name of this delightful Spanish gentleman was in the course of time dropped and largely forgotten.

While the diplomatic side of his mission might not have been as successful as he might have wished, both Briton and Spaniard leaving it to their respective governments at home to reach a compromise, Vancouver's other task was carried out with such thoroughness and skill that the charts he produced were still in regular use a century later. And while Vancouver's use of the Spaniard's work is reflected in the many Spanish placenames appearing on his own charts, he also added many more names that commemorate his friends and those who voyaged with him in the *Discovery* and the *Chatham*.

Much of the survey work was carried out by the first lieutenant of the *Discovery*, Lieutenant Peter Puget, and other members of the ship's complement in small pulling and sailing boats which could operate inshore and in shallow waters. The southern stretch of the inland sea on which lie the modern towns of Seattle and Tacoma he named Puget's Sound 'to commemorate Mr. Puget's exertions' while an island in the approaches to that inland sea he named Whidbey Island after Joseph Whidbey, master of the *Discovery*. Vashon Island he named after his friend Captain James Vashon.

It was Joseph Whidbey who discovered the deepest fjord in North America that provided an important route to Skagway during the Klondyke Gold Rush between 1897 and 1899 and named Lynn Canal by Vancouver, remembering his birthplace. It is a natural fjord with a depth of some 330 fathoms, not a canal in the normal sense. In the approaches to the Lynn Canal is Chatham Strait, named after HMS *Chatham*.

It is notable that Vancouver enjoyed generally excellent relations with the indigenous peoples both in Hawaii and on the American coast, following Cook's example by noting details of their languages and showing considerable sensitivity to their customs and way of life. In his journal he made many observations on the native peoples, on their houses, their canoes, the clothes they wore, the food they ate and on their language that have since proved valuable to those who study aboriginal people.

Having paved the way for British exploitation of the American north-western seaboard Vancouver returned to Britain in 1795 by way of Cape Horn, thus completing a circumnavigation of the globe. His work had worn him out; he died at Petersham in Surrey in 1798 at the age of only forty, leaving it to his brother John to complete the journal of his explorations, published as *Voyage of Discovery to the North Pacific Ocean and Round the World in the Years 1791-95.*

Another notable seaman from the Lynn area was Captain Sir William Hoste, who was born in 1780 at Ingoldisthorpe, between Sandringham and Hunstanton, and was sent to a boarding school in Lynn at the age of seven. He later moved to the Paston School at North Walsham, where Horatio Nelson had been a pupil years before. William's career was determined for him by his father, a sporting parson, who contrived by social influence or by bribery to have his name entered in the books of the *Europa* as a captain's servant when he was five; he did not, of course, go to sea at that age, but when he was twelve arrangements were made for him to join the *Agamemnon*, of which Nelson had been given command. The necessary introduction had been made by Thomas Coke, of Holkham Hall.

Nelson seems to have taken to the lad, appointing him to be what the Navy called 'the captain's doggie' – his errand-boy – and directing him to sling his hammock in his own quarters below the poop deck, joking that he must be looked after as carefully as a rare zoological specimen. The other captain's servants, including Nelson's stepson Josiah, were accommodated in far less comfortable quarters on the orlop deck, deep down in the bowels of the ship.

The *Agamemnon* was sent to the Mediterranean, where William had his first taste of action when Nelson, with young Hoste at his side, boarded and took a small vessel moored under the cliffs of Corsica. Some time later William's father received a letter from Nelson, who told him 'You cannot receive much more pleasure in reading this letter than I have in writing it, to say that your son is everything which his dearest friends can wish him to be, and is a strong proof that the greatest gallantry may lie under the most gentle behaviour. Two days ago, it was necessary to take a small vessel from a number of people who had got on shore to prevent us; she was carried in high style, and your good son was at my side ...'

The Custom House beside the Purfleet, the Mariners' memorial on the quayside and the plaque to Sir William Hoste in St. Margaret's church.

Wiliam Hoste remained happily with Nelson until the attack on Tenerife in the Canary Islands in which Nelson received a serious wound that resulted in his losing his right arm. One of the first documents signed by Nelson with his left hand was a certificate of Hoste's provisional promotion to lieutenant. While Nelson returned in the *Seahorse* to recuperate in England young Hoste remained in the *Theseus* enforcing the blockade of Cadiz. His promotion was in due course confirmed.

He was still serving in the *Theseus* when that ship took part in the destruction of the French fleet in Aboukir Bay, leaving a French army stranded in Egypt. In due course he obtained command of his own ship, and at the time of Trafalgar was in command of HMS *Amphion*, a 36-gun frigate launched at Mistley on the Stour in 1798 and a favourite ship of Nelson's. To his great regret he missed that battle because his old captain, now the commander-in-chief, had sent him on a special mission to Gibraltar and Algiers.

Hoste heard the devastating news of the death of his patron and friend when he arrived back at Gibraltar more than two weeks after the encounter. 'I have just time to say that I am as well as a man can be, who has lost the best friend he ever possessed,' Hoste told his father in a hasty letter.

Captain Hoste and the *Amphion* continued to serve in the Mediterranean, and five years later led the frigates *Amphion*, *Active*, *Cerberus* and the smaller *Volage* against a far superior French force at the battle of Lissa. As the British ships beat towards the enemy, who were to windward, Hoste called his signal midshipman and told him to make the signal 'Remember Nelson'.

Sailors manning the guns on the weather decks of the frigates sprang into the rigging and cheered; in spite of the French superiority in numbers the victory was Hoste's. The visitor today to St. Margaret's church at Lynn will see there the memorial to William Hoste on the wall.

The Arctic whalers

A public house named The Greenland Fishery long remained as a reminder of the whaling that used to be carried out by vessels from Lynn in the seventeenth and eighteenth centuries. Henry Hillen regarded the 'whale fishery' as the successor to the Iceland stock-fish trade that had been so profitable in an earlier period.

He recorded how the banks of the River Nar in the southern part of the town, the parish of All Saints, were lined with blubber yards containing huge coppers in which the blubber of whales and seals was tried down or boiled to yield the train-oil that was so important a means of illumination before the introduction of mineral oils in the nineteenth century. On the eastern side of the river there was a long warehouse whose roof is said to have been largely supported by whale bones rather than the normal timber rafters.

A French visitor, Francois de La Rochefoucauld, was given a somewhat rosy account of the whaling trade when he toured East Anglia in 1784. Among the ships in the harbour he saw one that was, he said, built in a peculiar way. 'I was told it was built for whaling,' he wrote. 'Lynn sends out five of these. Each is manned by a crew of forty-five and carries on its deck six long-boats, very lightly built, for launching into the sea. Their voyages last eight or nine months, and they catch one, two or three whales. It is known that in a single voyage the merchants cover the cost of fitting out the vessel and sometimes the cost of its construction.'[17]

Hillen suggests that Lynn had been sending ships northwards after whales in the seventeenth century, but it was in the 1750s that the Greenland whaling trade began to expand both in England and in Scotland, aided by bounties provided by the government to encourage the fitting out of the ships.[18] Lynn's participation in the trade was boosted by an Act of Parliament passed in 1771 'for the better support and establishing of the Greenland Whale Fishery,' and in spite of the great cost of fitting out the ships the Lynn owners found that whaling was a lucrative business.

The whalers left their base in the Nar in March for the Davis Strait, the broad passage between the west coast of Greenland and Baffin Island, or for the seas to the east of Greenland. There they had to face not just the ordinary hazards of the seaman but also pack-ice that might crush any ship caught in it, blizzards, thick fog and Arctic seas brought up by gales sweeping down from the pole. On the way north they might put in to Lerwick in the Shetlands, where the crews were allowed ashore for a last drunken carousal before the ships made their departure for the Arctic.[19]

The men aboard the whale-ships might never cross the Line but the new members of the crew had their meeting with Neptune, Mrs. Neptune, the barber and all his other attendants on May Day, by which time the ships were usually at the edge of the ice. Part of the ceremony was the hoisting of a garland made from the ribbons given by the men's sweethearts – or stolen from any female met with in the streets of Lynn on a man's way down to the ship. That garland remained aloft until the ship's return to port, by which time the colourful ribbons had been bleached by the weather.

The hunt for the Greenland whale was carried on in double-ended pulling boats 26-28ft. in length and with a breadth of about 5ft.9in. The oars, usually six, were held by rope grommets and single tholes. Each boat carried six, sometimes seven, whale lines each 120 fathoms (720ft.) long, but these were insufficient by themselves and as soon as a harpooner had struck a whale a signal to the ship brought other boats to the scene to join their lines to those of the first. The Greenland whale when struck would dive and take out the line; if the length of line were insufficient the whale would be lost. It was not unknown for a strong whale to have four or more boats towing behind it.[20]

The whale usually remained under water for thirty or forty minutes, and during that time it might have taken out 700 fathoms of line. Sometimes the whale sought refuge under the ice, coming up to breathe in a gap among the pack-ice. In such a case a boat's crew would have to land on the ice and attempt to kill the whale from the ice-floe.

Once a whale was dead it had to be towed back to the ship, where it would be cut up while it was moored alongside. The blubber, the thick layer of fat that lay beneath the skin, was cut off and hoisted aboard the whaler, then cut up into chunks and stored in barrels which would be stacked in the hold. Flensing or flinching, the cutting up of the dead whale, was an extremely dirty task, and in bad weather it could be a dangerous one as well.

The master of one Lynn whale-ship, Captain Cook, of the *Archangel*, had a very narrow escape from a polar bear in 1788 when the bear charged him and began to hug him. With Captain Cook on the ice was the ship's surgeon, but he was forty yards away when the bear seized the master. Captain Cook called to him to shoot the bear; it was his only chance. The surgeon took careful aim and killed the bear, undoubtedly saving the captain's life.

Several ships were caught in the ice and seriously damaged in 1789, when the Lynn whaler *Balaena* returned with six 'fish'. Six years later the *Balaena* again had six whales, the *Experiment* had seven and the *Form* three. The *Balaena* was wrecked in Baltasound, on the island of Unst in the Shetlands, in a gale in 1796, and for some years only the *Fountaine*, Captain J. Phillips, and the *Experiment*, Captain John Baines, sailed from Lynn. In 1809, when the *Fountaine*, *Enterprise* and *Experiment* went north the first-named ship captured fourteen whales, two unicorns (narwhal) and three seals, which together yielded 340 butts of blubber.[21]

The return of the whale-ships to Lynn in July or August brought a day

Lying at a quay close to the South Gate in the early years of the twentieth century is a Yarmouth fishing craft converted to a coasting trader. She might be the dandy *Leader*, built at Yarmouth for Isaac Shuckford in 1860, which at the turn of the century was owned by Fairfax Hardy Mason, who lived in Lynn's Purfleet Street; if the identification is correct, she has been re-rigged as a ketch.

of festivity to the town. Hillen gives an interesting and lively account of the event.

> For weeks the arrival of the mysterious whalers was daily anticipated, and when at last, with royal yards aloft, they silently glided past the battery on the Fort and entered the harbour, the bells of St. Margaret's rang out their merriest peal, whilst the whole exulting town turned out to celebrate the event. Excited crowds rushed eagerly along the banks of the river as the ungainly vessels, decorated with flags of all kinds, and with garlands of evergreens from the far-distant land, appeared.
>
> For months past the coopers had not been idle, as was evident by the long tiers of new casks, ready to receive the precious liquid, then burnt in clumsy lamps. How suddenly their hammers dropped to the ground as the pleasing rhythm of the bells announced the return of the brave adventurers, and, while horses with tow lines helped the vessels along the eastern side, the agile coopers, unconscious of their begrimed faces, joined the weather-beaten harpooners who were straining at ropes on the opposite bank. And, as the ships crept wearily towards their restful berths, beside the blubber-house, oh how the good folk rejoiced in the success of the enterprise, whilst groups of girls and boys stared with undisguised astonishment at the high-piled deckloads of gigantic bones; and counting the stock of enormous jaws, they could scarcely repress their tears, as they remembered the startling predicament in which poor Jonah found himself.

With the ships safely berthed in the Nar the rendering down of the blubber could begin, and a very smelly process that was. As Hillen put it, 'the ill-smelling vapour, carried by an attentive south-west wind, soon permeated every nook and corner of the adjacent neighbourhood.'

Those who could afford to do so left the town until the work was done and the stink faded. Those who could not made the best of a bad job, declaring that the smell was good for their health.

Compared with certain other ports such as London, which fitted out ninety-one whalers in 1788, and Hull, which that year had thirty-six, Lynn's participation in the whaling trade was relatively insignificant, but for some years the Greenland voyage did contribute to the prosperity of the town's merchants.

War and other problems

The wars with Revolutionary France seriously curtailed the trade of Lynn: the North Sea was infested with French privateers, which captured and sank many British ships trading with the Continent as well as many more taking part in the coasting trade, and they also inflicted losses on the whaling fleet. Hardly less damaging to trade was the system of impressment under which merchant seamen were seized by the press gangs for service in the Royal Navy. In 1779 the gentlemen of Lynn gave an amateur performance at the town's theatre 'for the benefit of the wives, widows and families of the impressed men for His Majesty's Sea Service, belonging to Lynn and the Environs'.

The war brought large numbers of prisoners, mainly French, who were housed in prisons at Yaxley and Stilton near Huntingdon and later at a specially constructed prisoner-of-war camp at Norman Cross near Peterborough. In 1797 six transports arrived at Lynn with 900 French prisoners who were taken in lighters to the barracks at Stilton, and two years later more prisoners came in four transports under the escort of the gun-vessels *Wrangler* and *Manley*, both of them converted merchant ships. Other prisoners, French and Dutch, passed through the town from time to time, and were lodged overnight in a warehouse at the King's Staithe.[22]

It was not only the hostile operations of the Dunkirkers that led to a downturn in trade, for the River Ouse which formed the harbour of Lynn presented considerable difficulties to the shipping that used it. The serpentine channel was subject to silting and was obstructed in places by sandbanks that were blamed by the townspeople on the draining of the Bedford Level and the establishment of Denver sluice – though the 'blowing up' of the sluice in 1713 did not result in any improvement in the harbour. To the north of the town the river took a wandering course through the marshes to the Wash, the broad-spreading channel encumbered with shifting sands and shallows that proved a particular hindrance to the bigger vessels using the port. The rise and fall of spring tides was said to be about 15ft., but when there were gales from the north-west the tide could rise as much as 20ft. and the town's streets would be flooded. Even as late as 1924 some buoys that had been lying on the Common Staithe were carried up by a flood and deposited in the street.

Large vessels could take days to navigate the few miles from the Wash up to Lynn, and craft were almost as likely to be wrecked within the harbour as at sea. One of the handicaps they faced was an eagre similar to that in the Nene at Wisbech, a tidal wave that was liable to overwhelm small boats and to drive larger vessels from their moorings. It was banished by later improvements to the channel of the Ouse.

Those that were set adrift were liable to go aground either on the islands of sand and mud that divided the channel in two or on the low shores, if they did not come into collision with other moored craft. An eighteenth-century plan of the harbour shows not only the two mid-river sandbanks, the larger of them a mile long, but also a long curving spit off West Lynn that reduced the width of the channel to a mere hundred yards at its narrowest point. These banks were under water at high tide but stood several feet above the surface as the tide fell.

A severe nor'-westerly March gale created havoc in the harbour in 1820, when almost every one of the ships moored there broke adrift. Some drove upriver towards St. Germans; some grounded in the river; and one was driven over the North Sea Bank on to the fields beyond. Two vessels were lost on the Breast Sand in the Wash; those who survived from their crews were forced to walk four miles up to their middles in water to reach the shore after spending seven hours in the rigging.[23]

Until by-laws were made in 1831 for the regulation of shipping using the port, masters simply anchored their vessels wherever they liked 'and the selfishness which generally guided their actions caused great trouble', to quote the historian Henry Hillen. To improve matters the Corporation of Lynn provided a number of dolphins, wooden constructions to which ropes could be fastened, and laid a number of heavy chains on the river bed with lighter chains attached, to which ships could be moored. There were also buoys to which stern moorings had to be made fast so that the vessel did not swing with the tide. One of the by-laws stipulated that when a craft left the moorings the chain should be attached to the buoy and not merely slipped into the water to fall to the river bed.[24] Old photographs show tiers of vessels large and small moored in this way in midstream.

When various proposals were made in the later eighteenth century to remedy the state of the Ouse they were met with controversy and opposition: some opponents painted a dire picture of Lynn sinking beneath the waters or being washed away by the tide; others were of the opinion that on the contrary the channel would run dry, destroying Lynn as a port. Eventually a new channel, the Eau Brink Cut, was made between St. Germans and Lynn to cut off a wide bend in the river and provide a less impeded passage for water draining from the fens to the south. The map produced by Thomas Donald and Thomas Milne and published by William Faden in 1797 shows the proposed cut and the sea walls that would isolate the old channel beginning where the River Nar entered the Ouse.

Finished at last in 1821, the Eau Brink Cut was crossed by a new timber bridge more than 800ft. long with two lifting spans in the middle which were raised to allow the steam packet *Swiftsure* to pass through on the opening day but seem hardly ever to have been lifted thereafter. Some fifty years later the wooden bridge was replaced by one of wrought iron, which was itself eventually replaced by a modern bridge carrying the A47 over the river; the iron piers of the 1873 bridge long remained as a reminder of the Victorian Cut Bridge.

The emigrant trade

The years following the end of the Napoleonic Wars were disastrous for British agriculture, and many families in the East Anglian countryside were reduced to a state of near-starvation because there was no work for the men on the farms. Some of the farmers as well as their labourers found themselves in dire trouble and decided to seek a better life in what were then referred to as 'the colonies'. In April 1830 the *Suffolk Chronicle* reported that 'a number of persons, most of them presenting the appearance of great poverty, passed through Bury in waggons, on their way to embark at Liverpool for the United States of America.' Not all headed for Liverpool, for each year in the 1830s ships sailed from Lynn with emigrants

The vessels that carried emigrants from Lynn were not passenger ships but were small cargo ships, some at least of them owned by Lynn merchants, temporarily converted with wooden bunks and tables in the hold for the accommodation of the emigrant families. Unlike some of the ships sailing from other ports, the Lynn vessels were fitted up in a way that enabled the families to have a fairly reasonable standard of living on the voyage and the Lynn captains had some consideration for the comfort and wellbeing of their passengers. Not only did the Lynn shipmasters have a good reputation for looking after their passengers on the voyage, they were renowned for assisting them to find accommodation on their arrival in Quebec and helping them move on from there if they wanted to do so.

No doubt that is why when the curate-in-charge of Great Dunham, near Swaffham, was arranging the emigration of some of his parishioners in 1836 he found that Oxley, English & Oxley of Lynn were charging a premium rate of £5 15s. each for adults, children half price, for the voyage to Quebec in the *Hero*. The Great Dunham emigrants went by way of Yarmouth, where Isaac Preston & Son were offering a special reduced rate of £3 for a passage to the same place.

An advertisement in the *Norwich Mercury* in 1837 specifically mentioned that Captain John Long, master of William English's ship *Anne*, had received special thanks from his passengers the previous year:

> Fine A1 Copper Fastened Ship Anne, burthen 400 tons, John Long, master . . . will be fitted up in the same commodious manner as last year (when the accommodation and treatment of the Passengers, were returned by a unanimous testimony of their approbation and thankfulness) and will Sail for Quebec in April next.[25]

The *Anne* sailed from Lynn on 20th April 1837 and arrived at Quebec on 9th June.[26] It seems that the claims made in the advertisement might not have been exaggerated, for as the passengers were embarking the *Norwich Mercury* commented that 'It is but justice to all concerned in this ship to say that in no vessel engaged in the same employment has greater attention to the accommodation and comforts of the passengers ever been evinced. We have read letters received from the emigrants who went in her last year, overflowing with gratitude to the owner, the captain, and the seamen for the kind treatment and ample provisions they enjoyed during their voyage.' Happy indeed those emigrants who sailed from Lynn!

The departure of one vessel is described for us by the *Norwich Mercury* of 26th May 1832, which tells us that 'On Tuesday last the *Ardwell* of this port [Lynn] broke ground with 84 emigrants for America, all of whom appeared to be amongst the class of respectable labourers, and from whose statement it would seem that nothing, save a want of employment to procure the common necessaries of life, could have influenced them to quit their native shores.'

The departure of the *Ardwell* was delayed for several days by adverse winds, and she lay on the West Lynn side of the harbour awaiting her chance to slip down into the Wash. During that time some 'benevolent individuals' raised a subscription to buy the emigrants tea, sugar, rice and other good things to help them on their way. When the *Ardwell* did get under way there were hundreds of spectators on the shore to watch her slip down the Ouse; the emigrants waved and shouted to those ashore, and it was quite clear that they were in good spirits as they embarked on a new life on the far side of the Atlantic.

The *Ardwell* did not always uphold the Lynn vessels' reputation for giving the emigrants a comfortable passage, for in 1836 it was reported in the local newspaper that the vessel had been at sea for nine weeks and the provisions were exhausted when the *William*, from Bathurst, New Brunswick, fell in with her off the Grand Banks. The captain of the *William* passed over what

Having unloaded its cargo
at the Boal Quay a billyboy
ketch sails down the Ouse
on its way to sea.

Most were launched from yards around the Humber or on the Yorkshire and Lincolnshire waterways, but they were by no means confined to that area. Wakefield on the Calder was the birthplace of ketches like the *Jehovah Jireh*, built in 1859, rebuilt in 1885 and wrecked on the Yorkshire coast with a cargo of Yarmouth herring in barrels in 1903, while Knottingley on the Aire had four yards building vessels such as the schooner *Zoar* of 1862, owned by William Worfolk, a Knottingley shipbuilder, and the ketch *Joshua* of 1864, which was still trading at the end of the century.

Some were small enough to trade up the Yorkshire rivers and canals, others were of a size that confined them largely to coastal trading to ports around the Wash and further afield. The 50-ton ketch *Yarburgh*, built at Louth in Lincolnshire in 1831 and trading up the Waveney to Beccles in the 1840s, was 58ft. long with a beam of 16ft. and a depth of 8ft. She was run down by the steamer *Odessa* off the Spurn in 1873. Rather larger was the ketch *Woodland Lass*, built at Yarmouth in 1851, which measured 73½ tons and was 63ft. in length with a 16ft. beam and a depth of 8½ft.

Differences in rig do not always provide a guide to the size of a billyboy. There were two vessels named *Eva*, both registered at Goole at one time, and it is interesting to compare the entries in the *Mercantile Navy List*. While the ketch *Eva*, built at Allerton on the River Aire in 1872, measured only 49 tons the sloop *Eva*, built at Mexborough on the Dearne and Dove Canal just north-east of Rotherham in 1854, had a registered tonnage of 54. The

Two billyboy schooners in
the Ouse at King's Lynn
about 1905, both of them
moored fore and aft to
buoys. The further one has
a gaff aloft with a cargo-
handling block suspended
from it, and both still have
square sails on the foremast.
Marriott's Warehouse, now
known as the Green Quay
Warehouse, obscures the
west front of St. Margaret's
Church, and just to the left
of it is a tall malt kiln.

ketch *Eva* had passed to Lowestoft registry by 1899, when she was owned by a London corn factor with an address in Mark Lane.

From Lincoln and Ely there came in the 1840s two little sloops with the resounding name of *Bounty of Providence*, both of them registered at Boston. Surprisingly other billyboys were built much further to the south, at Southwold – where the little schooner *Heart of Oak* was launched in 1836 – and at Woodbridge, where William Taylor built the sloop *Charlotte* in 1843 and another billyboy sloop, the *Laura*, the following year. One billyboy is recorded as having been built at Fingringhoe on the Colne, where the *Excelsior* was launched in 1855.

With their ungainly hulls and relatively inefficient sailplans their sailing qualities were at best unremarkable. The usual method of progress was to sail while the tide was in the vessel's favour and then to anchor when the tide turned; it is said that on one occasion it took two billyboys three weeks to accomplish a trip from the Humber to Yarmouth with a cargo of Yorkshire coal.

Frank Carr tells a story that originated with Harold Cox, of Woodbridge, who had at one time been mate of the ketch-rigged billyboy *Brilliant* of Goole, an old-timer built at Leeds in 1841 and still sailing as the twentieth century dawned.[32] The *Brilliant* was wallowing along one day when the boy had an idea of catching some mackerel. He got some hooks and a piece of ropeyarn and cast them over the side. Presently the skipper came on deck and spied the fishing gear.

'What've you got that ropeyarn over for, boy?' he wanted to know.

'Thought I'd catch a fish, skipper.'

'D'you know that's stopping her a knot an hour, boy?'

'How fast do you reckon she's going then?'

'Oh, about three knots.'

'Well then skipper, I'll hang a couple more over and stop the old – altogether!' retorted the youngster, nipping smartly forward to avoid the skipper's hand.

Though they were outclassed by the boomie barges built at Ipswich and Littlehampton and elsewhere towards the end of the nineteenth century the billyboys traded all round the coast carrying non-perishable cargoes to the shallow, difficult north Norfolk ports, to Yarmouth and Lowestoft, into the Alde and Deben and many another river. Their crews were small, sometimes just the older members of the skipper's family.

In 1858 the Grimsby sloop *Queen* was on her passage from London to Boothferry in Yorkshire with a cargo of manure, perhaps the sweepings of the London streets, when she was caught in a storm and cast on to Yarmouth beach. The skipper had with him his wife and three children, the eldest five and the youngest a baby of fourteen months.

The unfortunate master was swept overboard with one of his sons in his arms and the oldest boy died in his mother's arms as they clung in the rigging after being driven from the cabin by the cargo when the bulkhead gave way. Only the mother and her baby survived; they were eventually taken from the rigging by a boat that put off from the shore. Not only was the mother penniless but she was also homeless, for she told the local coroner that she had been sailing with her husband for ten years and the *Queen* was her home.

That was not an exceptional case, for a few years later smacksmen who

The Alexandra Dock at Lynn in the 1930s with the regular steamer from Rotterdam unloading. The tug *Ely* is taking a number of coal-laden barges out of the dock on the way to the beet sugar factory at Ely, and in the foreground are rafts of imported timber.

boarded the sinking billyboy schooner *Wesleyan* off Beachy Head got a shock when they entered the cabin and found the skipper's wife with five children huddled around her and a three-month-old baby in her arms as naked as the day he was born. They dragged the frightened children away from their mother and threw them into the smack's boat. Then, after getting the children and their mother safely to the smack, they returned for the crew.[31]

'We could see from the way the schooner acted in the sea that her time was getting short,' one of the smacksmen recalled later. 'The captain seemed like a man out of his mind – he wouldn't get into the boat, and told us that the schooner was all he had in the world, that he should go home to an empty house, for even his bedding was aboard of her, and that he would stop and go down with her.'

One can imagine the skipper's feelings of despair, but the smacksmen had time neither to sympathise nor to argue with him. They could feel the schooner, laden with blocks of stone from Portland, settling down. They caught hold of the miserable captain, dragged him to the side and hove him into their boat. They had time only to follow him into the boat and cut the painter with an axe before the billyboy went down by the stern.

Disaster struck the billyboy ketch *Evening Star* on 21st October 1905 when she was run down by the ss *Tangermunde* about two miles below Lynn. The *Evening Star*, which had been built at Mexborough in Yorkshire in 1873 and was registered at Hull, was owned by her skipper, Captain Charles Hartley, whose home was in Carmelite Terrace, Lynn. Captain Hartley and the cook, Frederick Sanford, went down with the ship, which was torn open on the starboard side near the stern, but the 66-year-old mate, Harry Harrod, although hampered by his seaboots, swam for the shore. He almost made it; it was thought that he was so exhausted when he reached the shore that he did not have the strength to haul himself up the bank, and he drowned with the others.

The remains of the *Evening Star* mouldered away on the mud near the Pilot House at Lynn for many years, and I was able to take a photograph of what survived in the late 1940s.

Shipbuilding

Although Lynn was not particularly noted as a shipbuilding centre, some at least of the vessels trading from the port were built in shipyards on the bank of the Ouse or on the River Nar. One of the shipyards was close to St. Ann's Fort, and it was probably on this yard that a shipbuilder named Brindley built a number of warships for the Royal Navy in the late eighteenth and early nineteenth centuries. He launched the gunboat *Tigress* – originally known simply as *No. 45* – in 1797, the ship sloop *Victor* in 1798, and the gunboats *Furious* and *Griper* in 1804. A similar craft, the *Shamrock*, which became a surveying vessel in 1817, was built by a Lynn builder of the name of Larking in 1811-12.[34]

The great majority of ships built at Lynn were, however, merchant vessels. Possibly it is a reflection of the inadequacy of the Lynn yards for the fitting out of large vessels that the full-rigged ship *Colville*, built by William Bottomley on his yard near the South Gates, was on her way to London under jury masts when she drove on to the Sunk Sand off Harwich in March 1824. The crew left her in a boat and were picked up by the Colchester smack *Ino*, but one of them died of exposure. After being abandoned by her crew the *Colville* drove over the sands and was taken into Ramsgate by a salvaging smack.

A directory of 1830 names three boatbuilders in the town as well as William Bottomley and William Richardson, shipbuilders.[35] Bottomley launched a number of vessels including the three-master *Marlborough*, which was destined for the West Indies trade when he launched her in 1822; she was still sailing out of Liverpool in 1857. Several thousand people are said to have watched the launch of the barque *Westmoreland* from his yard in 1832, and the historian Hillen names thirteen vessels, including several of considerable size, built on that yard between 1845 and 1856 by Bottomley and his successors, Reynolds and then William Shipp. Like his contemporaries William and Thomas Rolin, Shipp was a shipowner as well as a shipbuilder, operating the snow *Harcourt* which he built in 1856.[36]

The importance of the shipping trade in the mid-nineteenth century is reflected by the list of shipowners in an 1855 directory which includes no fewer than forty-seven names. Nonetheless, many of the ships built in the Lynn yards went to other ports; the 414-ton barque *Young England*, launched in 1853, was sailing between Shields and India a few years later, while the snow *Calypso*, built in 1848, was sailing between London and Australia.

In the 1850s a shipbuilder named James Seals established a yard at West Lynn on the other side of the Ouse from King's Lynn and in 1857 built a patent slip on which to haul vessels out for repair. The slipping of the first vessel, the schooner *Eliza* – one of two schooners of that name registered at Lynn – was 'celebrated by the firing of guns,' according to a report in a local newspaper.[37]

Wrecks

Two wrecks in 1850 serve to indicate the impact that such events could have on a wide range of townspeople in a place like Lynn. The loss of the brig *Atlantic*, belonging to Robert Simms, a Lynn coal merchant, on the Roaring Middle during a gale attracted only mild criticism of the crew who abandoned

The billyboy ketch *Evening Star* beached at Lynn after being in collision. Her remains were still to be seen slowly mouldering away fifty years later.

The disintegrating wreck of the *Evening Star* on the Ouse foreshore near the Pilot Office at Lynn in 1950.

Possibly a converted ship's
boat in the Purfleet, 1975.

the ship when it was thought they might have saved her had they remained aboard, but the stranding of the London trader *Talisman* on the Inner Knock off the Lincolnshire coast was said to have caused considerable alarm among local tradesmen as her cargo included goods required for the annual Mart, then a trading fair rather than a pleasure fair with roundabouts and sideshows. 'The loss of this vessel will fall very heavily on some of the tradespeople of the town, who had large quantities of goods on board, some of whom had not had them insured,' observed the *Norwich Mercury*, reporting both events in the same column of the same edition.[38]

Shipwreck was all too common an experience for seamen in the age of sail, and many a widow was left to mourn a husband drowned at sea, many an orphan left destitute by the loss of a father whose ship had been cast ashore in a storm. In an attempt to alleviate the plight of such people the Lynn Shipwrecked Seamen's Society was established in 1822.

There were regular traders operating between Lynn and Hull, London and other ports. In the 1840s William Clifton owned a half-dozen sailing vessels running weekly between Lynn and London, the *Edward, Eugene, Fairy, Gem, Navarino* and *Volusia*, and there were also vessels sailing monthly to Newcastle.[39] Sailing vessels always had the disadvantage of being subject to the weather, and a good breeze from the wrong direction could all too often have an adverse effect on the schedules of these traders.

The problem of getting up the river against an adverse wind was largely solved in the early 1830s when two wooden paddle tugs were acquired by a local owner and set to work assisting ships into the port. The idea of using steam vessels to bring ships into port was scoffed at by many in the town's mercantile community, but those early tugs did well even if they had to reduce their charges when a third tug introduced competition in the 1840s.[40]

The advent of steam also produced competition for the regular traders. By 1845 the steamer *William IV* was running a weekly service between Lynn and London and the *Cambridge, Jupiter* and *Lord Nelson* were sailing regularly to Hull and Gainsborough. The owners of the *Cambridge* were pioneers of the holiday cruise, in 1845 taking her off the service to Hull in order to operate a cruise from Lynn and Yarmouth to Rotterdam in July of that year. She was advertised to arrive at Rotterdam early in the morning, 'giving Passengers an opportunity of leaving there by First-class Steamers to view the Splendid Scenery on the Rhine or to visit Waterloo, Brussels and Antwerp' before returning to Lynn a week later. A brass band was hired to entertain the passengers on the voyage.[41]

Reclamation, improvement and legal hold-ups

The shallow Wash with its many sandbanks has long attracted the eyes of those who wished to emulate the Dutch and add many productive acres to the land of Britain. In 1837 Lord William Bentinck put forward a scheme for reclaiming the Wash and employed Sir John Rennie to report on the possibilities. Rennie suggested that the four fenland rivers, the Witham, Welland, Nene and Great Ouse, should be redirected into a single combined outfall and that the shallow area of water should be embanked and reclaimed with a view to bringing it eventually into agricultural production. By combining the four rivers the drainage of the low-lying land would be improved and at the same time navigation would be greatly enhanced by providing a much deeper and straighter channel to the sea.

There was certainly a great need for the approaches to the port to be improved: when in 1845 two vessels, the *Aboyne* and the *Symmetry*, took the ground as they sailed upriver it was remarked that 'scarcely a week passes without some mishap'.[42] Only a few weeks later the Lynn and Hull steamer *Jupiter* went ashore as she was coming up the channel on a Saturday evening, and it was thought at the time that she would not be refloated until the next spring tides.

At an Admiralty inquiry held at Lynn Town Hall in 1849 by Captain Washington and Captain Vetch, Rennie described plans for a new channel between Lynn and the Wash that was intended to improve the approaches to the port. The need for change was underlined by the evidence of William Armes, who described himself as a merchant but obviously had had considerable experience of the sea earlier in his life. He was a Pilot Commissioner and secretary of the Lynn Maritime Association.[43]

'The present channel is extremely circuitous, and the tides frequently set across the channel so as to cause frequent delays in getting up from the roads to the harbour,' he told the inquiry. 'The channel is very dangerous. With regard to the detention of vessels in the channel, the first vessel I took charge of had the good fortune to make the voyage [presumably from the Tyne] in four days. It was a vessel of 300 tons burden.

'After I got to the Lynn roads I was then seven days getting into the harbour from the sea.'

Armes explained that he had arrived at a neap tide, and had had to wait for a spring tide before he could get upriver to Lynn. That was in about 1830; he added that conditions had improved somewhat since that time, but the only thing that would remedy what he called the 'badness of the channel' was a new cut to the sea.

By the river at King's Lynn in the 1970s.

'It is not only the question of time,' he went on, 'but the damage done in the present channel to the shipping.'

As though to bear out what he said the same newspaper that carried an account of the Admiralty inquiry contained an item recording that 'On Thursday last, a vessel was, from the state of the channel, laid ashore, immediately opposite the town, and it was expected would go over before the return of the tide. Lower down the channel there were also two other vessels in a similar situation from the same cause.'[44]

Besides the very necessary improvements to navigation it was estimated that an area of 150,000 acres might be reclaimed, and this great area of land was to be known as Victoria County after the young queen who had just ascended the throne. It was a visionary scheme, but like all such enterprises it had its detractors. Expressing the hope that a new Ouse outfall proposed in 1845 would solve the problems the port was facing, the *Norwich Mercury* commented 'How it could ever have been opposed by any of the merchants of the place has always been a mystery to us, seeing that little short of their actual existence depends upon it.'

An Act of Parliament was obtained in 1846 for a much smaller project involving a two-mile cut to carry the Ouse from Lynn to the Wash, another

Lynn fishing boats in the Fisher Fleet at high water about 1950. The *Baden Powell* on the inner berth is a yoll, built by the Worfolks about 1902 and reputedly the first boat they built after moving to Lynn. The *Boy Herb*, LN145, is a shrimper; the trawl beam can be seen laid along the starboard side.

The Wash smack *Freda & Norah* in Lynn Docks about 1950. Built at Boston by Gostelow, she had been working under power since before 1930.

The bows of the smack *Freda & Norah*.

cut through a sandbank known as the Vinegar Middle, and the reclamation of a mere 32,000 acres north of the town. Even this enterprise met with difficulties, not least through the death of Lord William Bentinck, and it was not until 1850 that a contract was awarded to Peto & Betts, one of the leading British civil engineering contractors of that time headed by Samuel Morton Peto and Edward Betts.

Work was to have been completed in three years, but it was held up by legal action instituted by the Eau Brink Commissioners whose intervention caused a delay of some sixteen months. The commissioners objected to the contractors using the tidal flow to scour the cut and insisted that the whole thing should be dug out, a dam being constructed at each end to prevent the water from flowing into the excavation. When the contractors flooded the new channel, apparently in an attempt to pre-empt the opposition, the commissioners went to the Court of Chancery to obtain an order stopping the work.

Eventually the legal hold-ups were overcome, but several more Acts of Parliament were needed before the work could be completed towards the end of the century. Storms and high tides created havoc with the embankments and reclamation proved a long-drawn-out operation, as did the task of removing the wreck of the 2,300-ton steamer *Wick Bay* which broke her back after going aground near the Daseley beacon in the approaches to the port. A special parliamentary Act had to be obtained to sanction the spending by Lynn corporation of some £20,000 on the removal of the wreckage, which threatened to block the channel. Such was the burden placed on the ratepayers of the borough by the *Wick Bay* disaster that in 1897 the King's Lynn Conservancy Act was obtained setting up the King's Lynn Conservancy Board, which from then on had responsibility for lighting, buoying and beaconing the port – and for removing wrecks.

The docks

Notwithstanding the difficulties and delays, the effect of the new channel on the port of Lynn did prove beneficial. A King's Lynn Docks and Railway Company[45] was formed in 1865 to build a dock in the north of the town, and this was opened in 1869 by the Prince of Wales, later King Edward VII, who named it the Alexandra Dock after the Princess of Wales. A second dock, the Bentinck Dock, was opened in 1884.

Whereas in the River Ouse ships had to lie aground beside the quays, within the enclosed docks they could remain afloat whatever the state of the tide outside in the river, where at spring tides there is a rise and fall of more than 20ft. The construction of the docks and the bringing of the railway into the dock area enabled Lynn to meet the challenges of the twentieth century.

The Bentinck Dock was equipped with seven hydraulic cranes intalled at the time the dock was opened and not replaced by electric cranes until 1959. On the opposite side of the dock was a hydraulic coal hoist that was used in the early 1900s for loading ships with coal brought by railway from the Nottinghamshire and Derbyshire coalfield; it was damaged in an air raid during the Second World War but was still in operation, sometimes being used for bunkering coal-fired steamers, in the 1950s.

The port of Lynn had been quick to take advantage of the spread of the railways, the Lynn & Ely Railway opening a harbour branch from Harbour Junction, South Lynn, in 1846. A swing bridge was built over the River Nar, or Friars Fleet, in 1854 when the line was extended on to the Boal Quay; a second manually operated swing bridge over the Mill Fleet carried it on to the South Quay.

With the construction of the docks a quite extensive system of lines was laid out by the King's Lynn Docks & Railway Company, approached by a level crossing over Pilot Street. This network made it possible for inward cargoes to be forwarded by rail with the least delay.

In the early days of the oil industry wooden barrels of paraffin for heating and lighting were brought to the town by rail, and as the trade developed cargoes were brought by tanker to storage tanks on land belonging to the Docks & Railway Company. The first such cargo came in the Anglo-American Oil Company's 715 gross ton coastal tanker *Tioga* in 1925. Other companies subsequently established depots on the dock estate, and during the Second World War the Lynn installations, operated in wartime by the Petroleum Board, handled many millions of gallons of aviation fuel destined for East Anglian airfields.

When the war ended in 1945 Lynn was quick to restore trade with German ports, and in particular with Hamburg. In the 1960s the German coasters *Alster* and *Fink* were running a regular service between Lynn and Hamburg, taking vegetables grown on the fields of Marshland, cans of fruit from a Lynn cannery and a variety of other export cargoes to the Elbe and returning with combine harvesters and other agricultural implements for sale to British farmers. As the trade with Hamburg built up a new vessel, given the name of *Lynn*, was built at Emden in 1968 for the service.

An important trade at Lynn for many years was the import of phosphates, the raw material of the artificial fertilizer industry. The West Norfolk Farmers' Manure & Chemical Company built a large works to the south of the town in 1872, and many of the cargoes unloaded at the Boal Quay went there. In 1937 the 5300-ton MV *Halingdal*, one of the largest vessels to trade to Lynn, lay at the Boal Quay to unload a cargo of phosphates from the Pacific island of Nauru, the first such cargo to arrive in Britain from that source.

The docks were taken over by the British Transport Commission in 1948 and are now operated by Associated British Ports, which are also responsible for Lowestoft and Ipswich. They now handle some 750,000 tonnes of cargo a year.

The excavation of the docks cut off the head of the Fisher Fleet, in which lay the town's fishing boats. The fishermen who sailed from the Fisher Fleet lived in the North End, the area that had been known in the thirteenth century as the Newland. Spread out around St. Nicholas' Church, the North End was a very distinctive part of town whose atmosphere has been encapsulated by Frank Castleton in his book *Fisher's End*. The flavour of the area is preserved in the museum at True's Yard.

Fishing at Lynn

Fishing was in the nineteenth century a quite important industry in the Wash, with vessels working from Boston, Wisbech and the Fisher Fleet at Lynn. In the 1870s there were 150 sail of boats, a third of them decked craft, working from Lynn, with 500 men and boys employed in the local fisheries. The principal

The Lynn shrimper *Lily May* under sail about 1937. Note that the mainsail is loose footed, being attached to the boom only at the clew.

The underwater lines of a shrimper are well shown in this photograph of one laid on the mud in the Fisher Fleet.

A cockle boat, used to ferry cockles from the sands to the larger boat lying afloat. Note the absence of a midships thwart to facilitate the handling of a load of cockles. On the transom is carved 'A. Rake & Sons Lynn'; Alfred Rake was listed in a 1937 directory as a shellfish merchant. The *Rob-Pete* in the background is a shrimper.

landings were then of eels, shrimps, oysters and mussels; 4,452 tons of mussels were sent to market in the winter of 1874-75.

There were races for local fishing craft in the annual Lynn Roads Regatta. The course was from the Common Staithe at Lynn downriver, round the Lynn Well lightship and back, though in 1850 when a dozen boats took part the course had to be shortened owing to light winds. The boats were divided into three classes, the winner in 1850 being the *Lady of the Lake*, one of the first-class smacks; second was *Honour*, one of the second-class boats. Another competitor was the *John Thomas Wigner*, named after the town's Baptist minister.

Largest of the craft at Boston and Lynn were those known to the fishermen as smacks, carvel-built counter-sterned boats of about 50ft. with raking stern-post and completely decked. Probably the last of these smacks was the *Freda & Norah*, BN154, which I saw in Lynn docks about 1950. Built by Gostelow at Boston at the beginning of the century, she had had a motor for at least twenty years when I saw her and no longer carried sails.

There must have been something about her lines that impressed itself on my memory, because years later I was driving along a road in the south of England when I saw a boat standing in a public house car park which I knew at once was the *Freda & Norah*. She had apparently been acquired by the owner of the public house as a 'feature' to attract attention to his pub, and in my case it succeeded, for I turned back to have a closer look. Some time later I heard that the smack had deteriorated to the point at which it was decided to make a bonfire of her on 5th November, but she was saved by some enthusiasts from the Humber who removed her for preservation. What has become of her since is uncertain.

It is possible that this type was copied from the larger type of Colne smack built at Wivenhoe and Rowhedge. Not only were such smacks built on the Colne for the Lynn fleet but some of the vessels from the Colne were sold to Lynn in their old age, while it is probable that some of the Essexmen migrated to the Norfolk port at some time in the nineteenth century. No doubt they came to exploit the oyster beds in the Wash which provided a source of cheap food until fished out about 1860.

Among the Colne smacks that joined the Lynn fleet was Lemon Cranfield's celebrated *Neva*, built on the Harrises' yard at Rowhedge and probably the most successful of all the Essex smacks in the annual regattas on the Colne. Captain Cranfield spent his summers in charge of crack racing yachts and his winters fishing his home waters in the *Neva*, which was paid for out of his share of the winnings of the Fife-built cutter yacht *Neva* in the 1876 season. The smack seems to have been sold to Lynn on Captain Cranfield's death and appears in a 1912 list as LN198. She was still fishing out of Lynn in the early 1930s, when news of her survival was brought to Rowhedge by Colne platers and shipwrights who had found employment at the King's Lynn Shipbuilding Company yard at West Lynn.[46]

It might seem strange that boats were built so far away, but it would appear that there was no boatbuilder working at Lynn until the Worfolks moved to the town in the early years of the twentieth century, although there had been three in the town back in 1830. The Worfolk family came originally from the Humber area; a William Worfolk was a shipbuilder at Knottingley in the 1860s and owned the 81-ton billyboy schooner *Zoar*, which had been built in 1862.

Smaller craft known as shrimpers, about 35ft. in length, worked from the

A contrast in sterns: a view of the double-ended yoll *Baden Powell* and the broad transom of the *Boy Herb*.

Fisher Fleet. Like the smacks they had a good rake to the sternpost to enable them to tack easily up or down the narrow channels they had to negotiate on the way to the fishing grounds. Cutter rigged, like all the Wash fishing boats, the shrimpers were decked, with a large well aft of the mast. Most of this type had a flat counter in contrast to the elliptical counter of the big smacks. As their name suggests, they were used for shrimp trawling and were also employed in cockling, for which they were put aground as the tide fell so that the crew could go out on the sands raking out the shellfish into nets which were piled into the well. When cockling, a boat of about 12-14ft. was usually towed behind and used for landing on the sand as soon as an area appeared above the water.

Today a fishing fleet continues to trawl the channels between the flats of the Wash.

There was also a third type in use at Lynn, known by the fishermen as yolls or yawls. These were clinker built and double-ended, with a foredeck and narrow side decks, and a long well similar to that of the shrimpers. Towards the end of the nineteenth century when the beach companies of the Winterton-Yarmouth area were going out of business a Lynn fisherman bought a small beach yawl from one of the companies and converted it for fishing, giving it a single mast and the usual Wash cutter rig, with a bowsprit set to port of the stem.[47] There is a Francis Frith photograph of the South Gates at Lynn, taken about the turn of the century, and there sitting on the mud is what can only be this first of the Lynn yolls, with a local cockle boat tied up beside her.

Also in the Frith photograph is a Yarmouth dandy, the *Leader*, built at Yarmouth in 1860 as a herring drifter but converted into a cargo vessel when acquired by Fairfax Hardy Mason, who had an address in Purfleet Street, Lynn. She was not alone among Yarmouth fishing boats in being used later in life for cargo carrying.

With its relatively shallow draught and long straight keel the converted yawl was particularly suited to cockling, and it seems that a number of other fishermen decided to have similar boats built for this trade. Two of these were still working from the Fisher Fleet about 1950, the *Baden-Powell* and the *Edward VII*. Their names would indicate that they were built about 1902, and it is said that the *Baden-Powell* was the first boat built by the Worfolk brothers after moving to Lynn.

I suspect that G.S. Laird Clowes might have made an entirely understandable error when he wrote in the 1937 Science Museum historical review and catalogue of British fishing and coastal craft that these double-ended boats were known at Lynn as luggers, remembering that the yolls from which they sprang were indeed rigged with dipping and standing lugsails. When I was making my inquiries at the Fisher Fleet about 1950 I never heard them referred to as anything but yolls.

All three of the Lynn fishing boat types shared a peculiarity in their sail arrangement. Instead of the boom having the usual fitting to the mast it had a crutch which rested on a wooden saddle fitted around the mast. The mainsail was not laced to the boom but was set loose-footed.

The traditional craft gradually forsook sail as motors were installed, and they were replaced by modern steel motor fishing vessels from about 1950 onwards. In 1959 the timber staging of the Fisher Fleet, installed as long ago as 1877, was replaced by a concrete structure in a £24,000 scheme.

Now shellfish from the Wash are handled by local companies that operate modern processing plants and distribute it far and wide, in contrast to the local markets supplied by the old sailing smacks, yolls and shrimpers.

North-west Norfolk 3

The eastern shore of the Wash is a fascinating place that has changed a great deal over the centuries. At North and South Wootton new farmland has been gained from the Wash, extending as much as two miles beyond the one-time coast. Significantly, one area of the new fields is shown on the map as Vinegar Middle, the name of a bank which once threatened ships entering the port of Lynn; nearby is the isolated remnant of Wootton Old Creek. In contrast, further north what was once, long ago, dry land is now tidal mud and sand flats.

Man has been living in the area for thousands of years, and has left many signs of his activities. It is an area that is remarkably rich in terms of archaeology, and perhaps the most remarkable find of all is the early Bronze Age timber circle that was revealed by erosion of the peat bed off Holme-next-the-Sea in August 1998. Although dubbed 'Seahenge' by the press when news of its discovery broke early the following year, it is not strictly speaking a henge monument at all; it consists of a ring of split oak timbers sunk a metre into a foundation trench and when first erected standing probably two metres above ground, with an inverted oak bole in the middle. The split timbers were set with the bark to the outside, and there was no gap between them to form an entrance.[1]

The upper part of the timbers was severely eroded as the peat was washed away by the tides, but it was found that the buried section had been preserved so well by the wet conditions in the surrounding peat that tool marks were still visible after some four thousand years; dendrochronology and radiocarbon dating revealed that the timbers had been felled in 2050 and 2049 BC. What has not been revealed so far by the archaeologists' investigations is the use to which this strange structure might have been put.

I was staying at Old Hunstanton at the time the archaeological investigation was going on, but heeded the appeal of those concerned and did not trudge across the sands to gaze at this wonderful discovery and take photographs. When the archaeologists scored a publicity disaster by using a chainsaw to obtain a sample of timber for dating and New Age enthusiasts clambered over the exposed timbers in protest at the English Heritage plans to excavate them and remove them to safety I kicked myself; I would have done far less harm than they were doing to this extraordinary monument from the distant past.

Altogether this find caused a considerable stir. Local people were indignant at its summary removal, and letters appeared in the *Eastern Daily Press* saying that the timbers should be reburied where they were found; they had, the writers said, been under the sea for four thousand years without being harmed, and they should stay there.

Opposite: An aerial view of Holme-next-the-Sea, where the Roman road known as the Peddars Way now meets the sea. Presumably coastal erosion has removed the ferry port for which it was heading and from which a ferry operated to the Lincolnshire coast.

The feature at Holme-next-the-Sea that has become known, somewhat confusingly, as Seahenge. It is neither a 'henge' not was it constructed in the sea. It is now conserved at the King's Lynn Museum.

The timbers had not, of course, been submerged for anything like four thousand years. Their position out on the sands was evidence of the change in the coastline over that period. When the structure was erected it was probably in a woodland setting some distance from the sea. Had they been left where they were the timbers would certainly have been destroyed by erosion, and the decision to remove them to Flag Fen near Peterborough for conservation and research was perfectly proper.

Perhaps 'Seahenge' was clearly visible when the Romans marched this way to take ferry across the Wash on their way to Lincoln and York, for two Roman roads have their northern end at Holme, though they might have terminated originally at some point that is now out at sea. The Icknield Way, sometimes said to have been a Roman adaptation of a much more ancient long-distance route from East Anglia into Wessex, can still be traced between Ringstead and Holme; confusingly the Peddars Way and Norfolk Coast Path is diverted off the Peddars Way and on to what is clearly a section of the Icknield Way just to the north of the six-sailed windmill at Ringstead.

Where it has not been transformed into a modern road the Icknield Way is a typical Roman road, some fifteen feet wide and with a ditch at each side. The Peddars Way, some 1400ft. to the east, on the other hand, is a much more prominent highway, with a width in some places of as much as thirty feet, perhaps more. The modern road named Peddars Way runs into Holme past detached houses, the more modern ones having their gardens set back to respect the original width of the road.

Why did the Romans have two roads running almost side by side? Is the Peddars Way something more than just a road linking Colchester and Lincoln by way of a ferry from Holme to the Lincolnshire shore? There can be no doubt that it was an official creation imposed on the landscape, and there is a suggestion that it marked a boundary, perhaps between two sections of the Iceni tribe, one group centred on Caistor-by-Norwich (Venta Icenorum) and the other looking west towards the Wash, perhaps with an administrative centre in the Fens at Stonea, near March.

Along the line of the Icknield Way is a group of wealthy villas, different from the general pattern of known Roman housing in Norfolk. There is one at Snettisham and others to the south, spaced out along the edge of the higher ground. Who lived in them, and how did they make their living?

The assumption is that these were farmhouses occupied by Romano-British farmers who cultivated the better land on the west-facing slopes and kept cattle on the poorer land to the east, but it seems very likely that they were also quarrying the local ironstone from the heathland at their back and smelting it in the vicinity. There are pits on Roydon Common and elsewhere from which one can pick up nodules of almost pure iron; were those deposits far richer before the ironstone was exploited in Roman times?

In David Dymond's *The Norfolk Landscape* is a map of the area showing Roman sites in North-west Norfolk; among them are at least eighteen ironworking sites in the area. One is led to ask whether these villas might not have been the homes of ironmasters rather than farmers; more likely they were inhabited by men who combined the two occupations and no doubt took part in maritime trade through the little ports of the Wash.

Could it have been their industrial prowess that made the Iron Age inhabitants of this area wealthy enough to possess the fabulous gold and silver articles found at Ken Hill, Snettisham, in 1948 and subsequent years?[2] Rainbird Clarke described the original hoard of coins and ornaments discovered during ploughing as 'probably the most important group of antiquities ever recorded from Norfolk'. The gold, electrum and silver torcs or necklets from the Snettisham hoards, now on display in the British Museum, indicate that the Iron Age inhabitants of this area included some wealthy individuals who could afford the best things in life.

There is evidence of an even earlier prosperity: White's 1854 directory refers to 'brass instruments, in the shape of hatchet heads, with handles to them, usually denominated *celts*,' having been dug up at Snettisham 'at various periods', and it is notable that the area has produced an extraordinary number of hoards of Bronze Age axeheads. The first on record was found in 1779, and more recent finds were made in 1930, in 1948 and in 1962. Significantly, perhaps, many of the axes were damaged or worn out, and it might be that they represented a craftsman's stock of material gathered for melting down.

No doubt access to the sea was always important in this area. A number of streams flow down from the high ground occupied by the Icknield Way and Peddars Way, and some at least of these formed small harbours where they ran into the Wash. Faden's map of Norfolk, printed in 1797, marks Snettisham Harbour and Heacham Harbour, though it seems unlikely that these were being much used by that time. Also on the map is the Babingley River, which was certainly navigable up to Castle Rising and beyond in medieval times. Investigation of this river as part of the Sedgeford Historical and Archaeological Research Project has revealed that in the Middle Ages the river was being used for navigation as far inland as Fring, clear evidence being found of navigation works on the river.

It seems likely that there was once another haven to the south of Heacham and Snettisham, for Dersingham is mentioned in a letter written in 1577 by William Heydon to Nathaniel Bacon, the second son of Sir Nicholas Bacon, Lord Keeper in the reign of the first Elizabeth. At the time they were both serving on a Commission concerning piracy, and Heydon mentions 'serten pirates at Dasyngham, which kepe as evell or worse evell than thosse which wee have taken in hande.' It is interesting that his spelling of the placename approximates closely to the pronunciation used today by some local people.[3]

The household and privy purse accounts of the Lestranges, lords of the manor of Hunstanton, contain a number of items concerning shipping at Hunstanton. Sir Nicholas le Strange seems from the accounts to have owned a ship, perhaps the one from which coal was landed by boats in 1519. Having been landed on the beach, the coal had to be carried in baskets to the coalyard. Boats were also used to load the same or another ship with barley. The landing place would presumably have been the gap at Old Hunstanton where the lifeboat house was built more than 300 years later; New Hunstanton, a mile or so to the south, was a creation of a later member of the Lestrange family in the nineteenth and twentieth centuries.

Ships were still landing cargoes on Hunstanton beach in the mid-nineteenth century, but by then neither Heacham nor Snettisham harbour was in use; at both places small ships were beached on the sands and unloaded their cargoes between the tides. Snettisham seems to have been quite a busy place, for cargoes of shingle were loaded off the beach and taken to Lincolnshire for repairing the roads. The lord of the manor, who rejoiced in the name of Henry L'Estrange Styleman Le Strange, took a payment of 10d. a ton for his shingle.

This trade in ballast was still being carried on by the Snettisham Shingle Co. Ltd. in the 1920s and by the Etna Stone & Shingle Co. (Snettisham) Ltd. in the 1930s, when some of the vessels carrying the material to the Humber were 'beetles', former landing craft built during the First World War for the ill-fated Dardanelles campaign. The flooded pits from which the shingle was extracted latterly now attract large numbers of wildfowl, and the sparse remains of a loading jetty can be seen quite near the hides of the RSPB reserve.

The seaside bungalows which sprang up along the Snettisham shore in the first half of the twentieth century provided a summer weekend refuge for people from far afield, and in the years of housing shortage after the Second World War became year-round homes for those who could not find more suitable accommodation. When a tidal surge struck the east coast on the night of 31st January/1st February 1953 the occupants of these dwellings were trapped as the sea swept over the shingle bank, engulfing the bungalows and

A postcard view of Hunstanton lighthouse and the wireless station after the light had been discontinued and the lantern removed.

Hunstanton lighthouse about 1905, by which time the tower had been painted with red and white bands. The small building to the right of the lighthouse is an Admiralty wireless telegraphy station, one of a number installed around the coast to communicate with naval vessels.

drowning twenty-five people. One of those who died was nineteen-year-old Peter Beckington, who was swept away as he struggled through the icy water in a vain attempt to save his elderly neighbours; he was awarded a posthumous Albert Medal for his gallantry.

Another award, that of the George Medal, went to American airman Reis Leming for his work in rescuing people from bungalows at Hunstanton South Beach that same night. Pushing a rubber dinghy ahead of him, the 6ft. 3in. airman saved the lives of at least twenty-seven people before himself collapsing from exposure and exhaustion. His own comment on his action was 'Shucks, it wasn't much.'

The Hunstanton lifeboats

Considering the difficulties of navigating the Wash it is hardly surprising that when the Norfolk Association for Saving the Lives of Shipwrecked Mariners was formed in 1823 it very quickly decided to station a lifeboat at Hunstanton. The boat, which does not seem to have been given a name, was built by John Skelton at Scarborough and was ceremonially launched at Hunstanton in July 1824. We know nothing of her design, but she was apparently a pulling (rowing) and sailing boat because a report of the launching states that she was 'furnished complete with all necessary stores, oars, sails, anchors, &c. for the sum of £95'; she is said to have been 28ft. in length and 8ft. 3in. beam, and to have had a crew of twelve.[4] A house was built for her at Old Hunstanton, presumably on much the same site as the lifeboathouse that today accommodates an Atlantic inshore lifeboat.

The boat was described in glowing terms when the annual meeting of subscribers was held at Hunstanton in July 1831, and the boat was launched to give trips to those attending, but very little was recorded about her work. No details have survived of any services by that first Hunstanton lifeboat, which seems to have been withdrawn by 1843.[5] The Coastguards had a boat which they kept in the lifeboathouse after the lifeboat had been withdrawn, and it is thought that these men carried out some lifesaving services, but there seem to be no records of their operations.

Having taken over the existing stations operated by the Norfolk Association for Saving the Lives of Shipwrecked Mariners (often abbreviated to the

Norfolk Shipwreck Association) in 1858, the RNLI decided in 1867 to open a new station at Hunstanton. The lifeboat sent to the new station was a 32ft. self-righter built by the Thames yard of T.W. Woolfe & Son, the cost of £253 being defrayed by the licensed victuallers of Great Britain, who continued to support the Hunstanton station until its closure in 1931. The boat was named *Licensed Victualler* at a launching ceremony in the summer of 1867: an engraving in the *Illustrated London News* shows gentlemen on horseback and ladies in open carriages driving out into the shallow water to obtain the best possible view of the launching.

The *Licensed Victualler* was soon in action. On 18th November 1867 she picked up the sixteen-man crew of the Swedish barque *Thetis* who had abandoned their vessel after she had grounded on the Woolpack Sand in the mouth of the Wash. Not long afterwards she rescued fifteen people from the German steamer *Harmonia* which had been driven aground in a very strong gale.

The self-righting boats, developed from the design which had won the Northumberland prize for Yarmouth boatbuilder James Beeching in 1851,

Bare-footed children enjoying a day on the beach watch with interest as the Hunstanton lifeboat *Licensed Victualler* is launched by horses from Caley Hall Farm on August Bank Holiday, 1910. Among the launchers at this practice is a Coastguardsman, in naval uniform.

were disliked by many of the Norfolk fishermen and beachmen, who preferred a beamier and more stable boat that they said was less likely to turn over in the first place. Their distrust of the self-righters seemed to be confirmed when the *Licensed Victualler* capsized as she put out on service one stormy day in 1867, fortunately without the loss of any of her crew.

In spite of that accident the boat continued to serve for twenty years at Hunstanton, and then in 1887 she was replaced by a slightly larger self-righter from the same builder which served until 1900. In that year a 35ft. self-righter was delivered from the Thames Iron Works at Millwall on the Thames which was, like her two predecessors, named *Licensed Victualler*. Between them the three lifeboats saved 117 lives.

At Old Hunstanton the lifeboat had to be hauled through a narrow gap in the sand dunes to reach the shore, and then, as the tide goes out a long way, it was sometimes necessary to take the lifeboat on its carriage a considerable distance before it could be launched. The horses that hauled the lifeboat on its carriage came from one of the local farms, an arrangement that usually worked well. Two farmers took it in turn to provide a team of horses, and when a vessel, later reported to be the Blakeney ketch *John Lee*, was seen on the Woolpack during a November gale in 1897 this arrangement led to disaster. One team of horses was sick and could not take part in launching the boat, and the owner of the other team refused to provide his horses as he insisted that it was not his turn. It took some time for the coxswain to overcome the farmer's obduracy, and by the time the lifeboat was on its way to the scene the wrecked ship had gone to pieces and all the crew had drowned.

The relatively narrow wheels of the lifeboat carriage tended to sink into soft sand and it was possible for the carriage to become stuck, making it impossible to launch the boat. In an attempt to overcome this problem one of the Institution's district inspectors of lifeboats, Lieutenant-Commander Henry Gartside-Tipping, designed a wheel with a number of hinged plates which effectively formed a moving roadway on which the carriage travelled. Lieutenant-Commander Gartside-Tipping lived in Norfolk at Geldeston and was very active locally as a yachtsman in the years before the First World War, in which he died on active service. Tipping's plates, as they became known, were fitted to the Hunstanton carriage and proved most valuable.

The third *Licensed Victualler* was one of the first lifeboats to be called to the assistance of an aircraft when it went out on 26th October 1914 to a Sopwith seaplane from the Royal Naval Air Station at Yarmouth which had suffered engine failure. It was also one of the first to be launched by tractor, for when just after the First World War the RNLI decided to experiment with the use of caterpillar tractors a 35hp Clayton tractor was sent for trials at Hunstanton and Brancaster.

During the trials at Hunstanton the tractor became completely submerged after the driver and the Institution's deputy surveyor of machinery had been 'rescued' from the bonnet of the tractor by the lifeboat. At that stage the carburettor, magneto, sparking plugs and ignition were unprotected, and when the flywheel threw water over the sparking plugs the motor stopped. However, after the tractor had been rescued by seventy or eighty volunteers as the tide dropped and the electrical system was dried out and the oil changed it proved possible to restart the motor and the tractor moved off under its own power. As a result of that experience the ignition system was protected from the water and the tractor was rendered submersible. When the trials came to a successful end in 1921 the Institution left one of the specially adapted tractors at Hunstanton, where it remained until the station closed down in 1931.

The last recorded service launches of the *Licensed Victualler* took place on 9th May 1916 when four men were saved from the Goole ketch *Panther*, a billyboy which went ashore at Heacham and broke up. The cargo of coal was strewn along the beach, to the benefit of local residents who made good use of it in the following weeks. After landing the rescued men the lifeboat went out again to render assistance to the London-registered *Pursuit*, a schooner built at Wells in 1861, which oddly enough was then owned in Knottingley where the *Panther* had been built in 1870. In the remaining fifteen years of her life the *Licensed Victualler* seems to have carried out no effective services.

Hunstanton's flanking lifeboat station to the west was Skegness, which was opened by the Lincolnshire Coast Shipwreck Association in 1830 and taken over by the RNLI in 1864. During the years of pulling and sailing boats whose area of operation was severely limited the two stations would not have come

Hurried adjustments are made during trials of the 35hp Clayton tractor at Hunstanton in 1921. Two such tractors were tried out at Hunstanton in that year and another was sent to the station for permanent duty in 1923, making this one of the first stations to exchange horses for a tractor.

into contact at all, but with the building of a motor lifeboat, the Liverpool type *Anne Allen*, for Skegness in 1932 it became possible for the Skegness boat to cover the whole of the Wash. No doubt the building of a motor lifeboat for the Lincolnshire station was taken into consideration when the RNLI decided in 1931 to close that at Hunstanton.

When in 1979 a D-class inshore rescue boat (IRB) was sent to Hunstanton the crew soon established links with their colleagues on the Lincolnshire side of the Wash. The lifeboathouse built in 1900 for the third *Licensed Victualler* was leased from the Le Strange estate to house the IRB. Intended primarily to deal with yachting and bathing mishaps which were becoming increasingly frequent, the inflatable inshore rescue boats were initially on station only in the summer months. The 16ft. D-class IRBs were not considered robust enough for use in winter conditions, but when in 1982 an Atlantic 21 semi-inflatable inshore lifeboat was supplied Hunstanton became an all-year station.

Most of the services performed by the D-type IRB were to assist people in small boats and to search for people reported in trouble in the water, but on 12th August 1981 the boat was launched following a report of a child being run down by a speedboat off Heacham. What had actually happened was that the sole human occupant of the speedboat had fallen overboard and been severely injured by the propeller. The boat, unoccupied except for a dog, continued to circle at high speed.

Helmsman Alan Clarke realised that the uncontrolled boat could possibly hit a bather and or run ashore and injure someone on the beach. It was vital that it should be stopped, but attempts to bring the IRB alongside the speedboat were unsuccessful. Eventually crew member 'Ossie' Osborne managed, at the third attempt, to leap aboard as the IRB was held alongside the speedboat for a few seconds, and he was able to bring the boat under control. He said later that he had been more frightened of the dog than he was of having to leap from one boat to the other.

The first service of the Atlantic 21 came on 2nd April 1982 when a Jaguar from RAF Coltishall crashed into the Wash five miles south-west of Hunstanton. The service proved very different from that performed by the

Licensed Victualler in 1914, when the pulling and sailing boat landed the pilot of a seaplane who was able to spend the night as guest of the coxswain, John Colman Riches. The Atlantic 21 and its crew spent six hours in the area searching for the pilot of the Jaguar and recovering pieces of wreckage, and then spent the following three days assisting in the salvage of the shattered aircraft.

The crew became used to liaising not only with their fellow lifeboatmen from Skegness but with RAF and USAF helicopters both in exercises and in actual rescue operations. The nature of lifeboat operations was changing radically, and an entirely new type of craft was deployed at Hunstanton in 2003 when the RNLI sent one of its first hovercraft to the station.

The decision to introduce hovercraft to the lifeboat fleet was taken by the RNLI executive committee in 2001 following year-long trials with a twin-engined hovercraft propelled by two airscrews in protected housings at the stern. The trials, which included a visit to Hunstanton, confirmed that hovercraft could work over different terrains and that the volunteer crews could be trained to 'fly' them.

They are particularly useful in estuaries and areas like the Wash where there are extensive sandbanks and mudflats and coastal salt marshes that are not accessible by boat. Many of the calls to the inshore lifeboat involved people cut off by the tide either on the sandbanks or on marshes.

The first RNLI hovercraft to go on station went to Morecambe at the beginning of 2003 and was called out when thirty Chinese cockle gatherers were overwhelmed by the tide in Morecambe Bay. The second, later named *Hunstanton Flyer*, went on service at Hunstanton in the spring of that year and quickly proved its worth when it was launched to the aid of nine stranded children.

On first arriving at Hunstanton it was accommodated in a fenced-off enclosure at the head of the gap, but a hangar was built for it beside the lifeboat shed in 2004 at a cost of £100,000. The craft itself cost £122,000, which compares oddly with the £253 cost of the first *Licensed Victualler* in 1867.

By 2005 the RNLI had six hovercraft in service, at Morecambe, Hunstanton, Southend-on-Sea and New Brighton and two in the reserve fleet.

Hunstanton's first Atlantic 21 lifeboat.

Alan Clarke, Hunstanton's first Atlantic 21 helmsman. The *Spirit of America* is towing the motor launch *Traddlers Two* into Brancaster Harbour.

The go-anywhere lifeboat: the hovercraft crossing the beach near the lifeboat station at Old Hunstanton. The first RNLI hovercraft came to Hunstanton for trials in 2001 and one was put on station there two years later.

North Norfolk 4

All along the north Norfolk coast there is a string of little ports approached by narrow, shallow channels which served to bring little sloops and ketches to their modest quays. Although today they appear insignificant, especially when seen at around low water, some of them were of great importance in the Middle Ages and retained their economic vitality into the nineteenth century.

Furthest west of this group is Thornham, whose rather unimpressive harbour is reached from the village by Staithe Lane. From seaward it is accessed by a narrow channel through the sands that is scoured by water draining from a network of twisting channels in the salt marshes between Thornham and Titchwell. White's directory of 1845 mentions 'a warehouse at the head of a small creek from Brancaster bay, navigable for small vessels which bring in coals and take out corn', and years ago a little watercolour turned up in a saleroom showing one of these small vessels lying beside the black shed that White glorified as a warehouse.

Three miles to the east lies Brancaster, whose rather more imposing harbour is sheltered by the sands stretching out from Scolt Head Island, like Blakeney Point a spit of sand and shingle built up by longshore drift. Brancaster Staithe used to be what W.A. Dutt called 'the headquarters of the orth Norfolk mussel fishery',[1] the shellfish being brought from the scalps in those flatbottomed boats that were once so much a feature of this coast. Rumour has it that these were developed from the dories salvaged from a French fishing vessel wrecked on the north Norfolk coast in the nineteenth century, but some experts dismiss this tale as mere folklore and point out the similarity of the mussel boats to flatbottomed boats used in other areas of shallow water, such as the Somerset flatners.

The Brancaster lifeboats

From 1874 to 1935 there was a lifeboat station at Brancaster, opened by the RNLI with the idea of closing the fifteen-mile gap between the stations at Hunstanton and Wells. In the days of pulling and sailing lifeboats the area of cover could be severely limited by wind and tide, and so large a gap between stations would in some circumstances render it impossible to give assistance to a casualty.

The self-righting lifeboat *Joseph and Mary* was sent by rail to Hunstanton station, where a team of horses took over and hauled her, on her carriage, to Brancaster by road. On the day of her naming by Mrs. Simms Reeve, the wife

Opposite: Whilst much of our story is of trade and fishing, the increased leisure use of the maritime environment comes in many forms. The harbour-master at Wells-next-the Sea a hundred years ago would not have imagined that his successor would one day be supervising hundreds of enthusiastic swimmers taking part in the annual Wells triathlon.

of the chairman of the station committee, the boat was taken in procession through the decorated village and down the lane to the boathouse, where the naming took place, followed by a service of dedication. It was a festive occasion for the village.

The *Joseph and Mary* remained at Brancaster for eighteen years, though in 1879 her name was changed to *Lily Bird*. Her first service was performed on 8th November 1874, when the local oyster smacks were caught out by a sudden heavy nor'westerly gale while dredging in Brancaster Bay and she went out to escort them back to harbour. Three times the following year she was called to assist vessels that had grounded on the Burnham Flats, which stretch for miles along the north Norfolk coast and proved a trap for shipping, particularly in northerly gales. In all three cases the vessels were assisted off and eventually taken into King's Lynn.

The lifeboathouse was about a mile north of the village of Brancaster and rather more than two miles from Brancaster Staithe, where many of the crew lived. The distance that the crew and launchers had to run when the call came proved a distinct disadvantage, and this was recognised by the RNLI, who in 1888 agreed to allow the crew five shillings each for an exercise rather than the normal four because of the time it took them to reach the boathouse.

The following year when the lifeboat was called out to a steamer on the Woolpack Sand one of the crew, twenty-eight-year-old Henry Southerland, decided that as the tide was in and there was no boat available in which he could row across the harbour he would swim across. Having done that he tramped across the marsh and along the dunes to the boathouse and, still in his wet clothes, took his place in the boat. The steamer had floated off the sand by the time the lifeboat arrived. Henry Southerland caught a chill, and that developed into pneumonia from which he died some time later. Taking into consideration the enthusiasm he had shown, the RNLI granted his widow £25, a sum that was in 1889 not as insignificant as it now seems.

One of the most difficult services undertaken by the Brancaster lifeboatmen came on 18th April 1892, when the Prussian brig *Felix* of Stettin went on the Burnham Flats in a strong northerly wind while on her way to Wisbech with timber. It took the lifeboatmen more than four hours to find the wreck, which was by then on her beam ends with the seas breaking over her. The Brancaster men managed to save the captain, who had lashed himself to the head of the mainmast, but the other seven men had been washed overboard or had fallen from the rigging before the lifeboat arrived. By the time the lifeboat reached her station the crew had been at sea for more than eight hours.

Such long services were by no means exceptional. In August 1892, when the steamer *Mogador* was seen in a dangerous position some nine miles from Brancaster, the *Lily Bird* spent nine and a half hours on service. The steamer had been on Burnham Flats but had refloated by the time the lifeboat reached her. Coxswain Thomas Lane was asked by the master of the steamer to go on board and take charge. With the lifeboat in tow he navigated her into deep water, eventually handing her over to a Lynn pilot.

At the end of 1892 the *Lily Bird* was replaced by another self-righter built at Dumbarton by R. McAlister & Son. This boat, the *Alfred S. Genth*, spent twenty-four years on the station. Like her predecessor she was transported by rail to Hunstanton and then taken on her carriage to Brancaster.

The ten and eleven-hour services of the *Lily Bird* just described pale into insignificance beside that carried out by the *Alfred S. Genth* on 2nd-4th February 1900, the longest service performed by any of the Brancaster lifeboats and the first for Robert Loose as coxswain. He had taken over from Thomas Lane in the autumn of 1898 when Lane retired after twenty-three years in charge of the boat and another two as second coxswain.

The *Alfred S. Genth* was launched at 10.15am on the 2nd to investigate reports of a vessel off Thornham making signals that could not be deciphered in the poor visibility. A strong east nor'east wind was raising a rough sea as the lifeboat sailed to the west. The lifeboatmen found the Welsh schooner *Edwin*, owned in the slate port of Portmadoc, abandoned near the Burnham Flats, having apparently refloated on the rising tide after going aground there. The lifeboatmen searched for the crew, who had taken to the boats, but could find no trace of them, so they boarded the schooner and prepared to salvage her. At that point a King's Lynn pilot cutter came on the scene with the crew of the *Edwin*, who had been taken out of their boats by the pilots.

With the schooner's crew back on board, plus some of the Brancaster men and a King's Lynn pilot, and with the *Alfred S. Genth* standing by, the *Edwin* was taken into Lynn. The lifeboat got back to Brancaster at 11.15am on the 4th; the crew had endured forty-nine hours in an open boat with little to drink and eat.

Robert Loose remained coxswain until reaching retirement age in 1908, when his place was taken by his son William. Robert had joined the crew in 1879, became bowman in 1891 and second coxswain three years later, then coxswain in 1898, and during his twenty-nine years as a lifeboatman he never missed a launch, either a practice or a call on service. William did not quite equal his father's service, though he remained coxswain until the station was closed in 1935. The Loose family was much involved with the Brancaster lifeboats, William's brother Robert becoming bowman in 1919 and other members of the family being in the crew at various times.

The first motor lifeboats came into service between 1904 and 1906, and

The Brancaster lifeboat *Winlaton* being launched by one of the early launching tractors in the early 1920s.

in 1914 there were investigations into the possibility of providing a motor lifeboat somewhere on the north Norfolk coast. However, it was not until 1923 that a motor lifeboat was sent to Cromer and 1936 that one was sent to Wells. When a new boat was built for Brancaster by S.E. Saunders at Cowes in 1916 it was again a pulling and sailing boat, a 35ft. self-righter named *Winlaton*. Like both her predecessors the *Winlaton* was launched from a carriage that was hauled by borrowed farm horses, but during the First World War difficulties arose over the loan of horses and in 1923 a Clayton petrol-engined tractor took the place of the horses.

As the coasting trade declined and the number of sailing craft decreased the call-outs became less frequent. Indeed, the *Winlaton* performed only one effective service during her time on the station, and that was when the boat was on a practice launch on 12th March 1919. The coxswain saw that a Wells fishing boat that had been gathering seed mussels in the Wash for re-laying in Wells harbour was in trouble about half a mile from the shore and took the *Winlaton* to her assistance. Lifeboatmen helped to jettison some of the mussels to lighten the boat and one of the crew, Harry Loose, helped get the boat into Brancaster harbour while the lifeboat landed a seasick boy from the fishing boat.

The *Winlaton* was launched on 17th December 1925 when the Whitby steamer *Glenaen* went aground in thick fog about half a mile to the west of Scolt Head while on her way to Wells. Coxswain Loose suggested to the master that he should lay out a kedge so that the vessel could haul herself off at high water, but the master was told by some local fishermen who had already boarded the steamer before the lifeboat came up that he should refuse the lifeboatmen's assistance. The skipper took their advice, which proved disastrous, for the wind increased to gale force and pushed the *Glenaen* up the beach; it was two months before she could be refloated, with considerable difficulty and effort.

Altogether the three lifeboats at Brancaster were launched on service thirty-two times, saved thirty-four lives and assisted to save five vessels.

Maltings and mills

Between Brancaster village and Brancaster Staithe is the site of the Roman fort of Branodunum, most northerly and probably least known of the Saxon Shore forts that were built along the south and east coasts during the Roman occupation of Britain. 'Numerous urns, coins, &c. found here are preserved in the cabinets of the curious,' says the 1845 directory. Very little of the fort can be seen today except from the air, though one can with difficulty still trace the outline of the walls in a field on the north side of the coast road, the A149. From the air one can make out not only the outline of the rectangular fort with its rounded corners but also the cropmarks of the streets of the civilian town which lay to the east and north-east of the fort, and perhaps also to the west. In the seventeenth century the walls were still standing 12ft. high, and the ditch surrounding the fort survived, but in 1770 the remains were systematically demolished. That is to say, they were torn down to provide building stone for use in the surrounding area, and in particular in the construction of a malthouse that was said to be the largest in England, able to wet 420 quarters of barley each week. When the premises came up for sale at the Globe Hotel in King's Lynn in 1847 they were described as 'that substantial-built Dwelling-house, with good arched cellars, 2 counting houses, granaries for upwards of 5,000 quarters of corn, extensive warehouses for oil cakes and guano, foreman's cottage, coach house and stable under a double roof of 312 feet by 31 feet, adjoining a quay with exclusive rights and reservoir, sluice for scouring the Creek, at which the vessels lie for receiving or discharging their cargoes . . . The above described premises were originally constructed for a malting, with steeps for 420 quarters of barley per week, floors and kiln to work the same, and could, if required, be again adapted to that purpose, and are particularly noticed . . . as being the largest in England.'

The largest in England? That, of course, was before the building of multi-storey maltings at Yarmouth, Oulton Broad, Snape, Ipswich, Mistley and elsewhere in the second half of the nineteenth century. By 1845 that impressive malting had gone out of use for its original purpose, and it was demolished in 1878. Stones from the Roman fort survive in other buildings at the staithe, and can also be found in the parish church half a mile up the road.

The 'sugar-stones' as Dutt calls them seem to have come from quarries at or near Castle Rising, and one wonders whether they were brought to Brancaster overland or, more likely, by sea. This whitish limestone was also used in Roman buildings elsewhere in Norfolk, and can be seen reused in quantity in the church at Reedham, apparently having been taken from a nearby Roman site that was obliterated in the nineteenth century.

From the Peddars Way the modern Norfolk Coast Path runs along the edge of the marshes to Holkham and Wells, crossing over the little River

Overy Staithe at high water, showing warehouses and maltings towards the left, about 1905.

A North Norfolk canoe or flatbottom showing the broad heel to the transom that provided buoyancy when carrying a heavy load of mussels.

Burn on the way. Whether the river gave its name to the Burnhams or took its name from the settlements is debatable. The river once powered two mills between Burnham Overy Staithe and Burnham Overy Town, each of them having an associated windmill – a combination of power sources that was by no means uncommon in Norfolk. The connection between the tarred brick tower mill built by Edmund Savory beside the coast road in 1816 and his watermill on the crooked bend at the bottom of the hill is not obvious, but nobody can miss the fact that at Union Mills a little less than a mile upstream the watermill and the associated windmill belong together, for the two buildings are linked. According to an advertisement of 1825 the windmill, built by Thomas Beeston in 1814, 'is by improved machinery rendered capable of working the flour machine in the water mill when required, by which much manual labour is dispensed with'.[2] The windmill was gutted by fire in 1935, but since the conversion of the two mills into a five-bedroom

Traditional lines are still seen in the the vessels of Burnham Overy Staithe, whether for fishing or tripping.

house it has been topped with a fair replica of the original ogee cap.

At Burnham Overy Staithe, at the head of Overy Creek and a rather tortuous channel from Holkham Bay, there is now very little sign of the trade that used to be carried on there. We read that in 1845 the channel from Holkham Bay was 'navigable for vessels of 60 or 80 tons up to the Staith, where the spring-tides rise 9 or 10 feet, and where a considerable trade in coal and corn is carried on, as well as in oysters, of which there is an excellent bed in the offing, where 5 boats and 15 fishermen are regularly employed'.[3] Some twenty years later there was a resident shipping agent, Captain William Sturley, and five master mariners and two pilots at the staithe, as well as the establishment of Richard Dewing & Company, maltsters and corn and coal merchants.[4] Richard Dewing was the owner of two small vessels, the schooner *Overy Packet*, built at Wells in 1839 by J.H. Parker, and the sloop *Heroine*, launched in 1851. The 1854 directory reveals that there were 'extensive malting establishments worked for some of the London breweries'; those maltings were obviously sending their malt away to the Thames by sea. The fields of Norfolk and Suffolk produced some of the best malting barley grown in the country, so the presence of quite large maltings even in these small ports need by no means surprise us.

Malt is the basic raw material of the brewing trade and is also used in baking. Malting is the controlled germination of grain, mainly barley, during which the starch in the grain is changed into a material that can be turned into sugar in the brewer's mash tun. In the old floor malting process the grain was first 'wetted' in the steep, being allowed to absorb water for some time, and was then spread fairly thinly on the germinating floor, where it was turned daily to aerate it and to prevent the rootlets from matting together as they grew. At just the right moment the germination was brought to an

A small coasting ketch at Overy Staithe about 1912.

end by taking the green malt from the malting floor and drying it in a kiln (pronounced kell in East Anglia). The maltster's skill was displayed in his choosing exactly the right moment for the transfer of the green malt to the kiln and in determining the right amount of time in the kiln and the heat applied during kilning. Different kinds of malt for the production of different beers require varying treatment, different degrees of heat.

In the kiln the green malt was spread on a floor constructed in such a way that heat could pass through it from the furnace below and through the drying malt. At one time a woven horsehair mat was used for spreading the malt on; later perforated clay tiles were produced with quite large holes in the underside and patterns of much smaller holes on the upper side, while some later maltings had kiln floors of wedge-shaped wire. An iron and brass founder at Wells, John Woods, developed a cast-iron malt-kiln tile that was basically similar to the clay tile made in a number of brickyards in East Anglia.

John Woods and Samuel Woods were partners in J. Woods & Son at the Glebe Ironworks in Theatre Street in 1883, both of them living close to the works, but by 1890 the firm had been taken over by Jabez James Cornish of the north Norfolk Iron Works at Great Walsingham. The Walsingham foundry had been established by Henry Cornish some time before 1830, and both that and the Wells branch survived into the 1920s but closed down during the Depression. The Walsingham foundry subsequently reopened, but finally expired several years ago.

Wells-next-the-Sea

Malting was particularly important in Wells, where there were extensive ranges of maltings in the streets running down to the quay. One gets a flavour of nineteenth-century Wells from the advertisement for the sale of Mr. Thomas Gibbons' property in 1822, he having been one of the unfortunate merchants and tradesmen of the town who had been declared bankrupt at a particularly bad period for business. 'We grieve to learn that every merchant in this respectable sea-port has recently experienced the sad reverse of fortune to such a degree as to be either declared insolvent, or voluntarily to discontinue business. – There is not now a merchant in business in the place . . .' the Norwich Mercury reported at the end of 1831.

> Gibbons' 'valuable estates' included his 'spacious Dwelling House and offices, malt-house, granary, yards, stable, gig-house, cart-lodge, and other appurtenances thereto belonging . . . adjoining the Tuns Inn' and another malthouse and granary, coalhouses and other premises near the quay. With them went 'the cinder-yard and gangway for shipping corn, &c. directly opposite to the said granary'. As a reminder of his social status, the advertisement informs us that with the house went 'a very commodious Gallery Seat in the Church'.

Gibbons was not only a maltster and merchant but also a shipowner. He had the brigs *Three Friends* and *Mary* and the sloops *Wellington*, *Success* and *Dolphin*, all of which were 'lying at Wells Quay . . . and fit for sea' at the time of the sale.

An advertisement of 1834 for two Wells-built vessels, a 60ft, sloop and a rather bigger brig. The date at the foot of 29th January 1334 is clearly a misprint.

To be SOLD by Private Contract, A Round Sterned Carvel-built SLOOP, length aloft 60 feet, depth 8 feet 4 inches, breadth 16 feet 7 inches, admeasures 73 tons, carries 80 Chaldron of Coals, 510 Quarters of Barley, or 110 Tons Dead Weight at 8 feet water. Is well calculated for the Port of Norwich, or any Dry Harbour, was built at Wells under particular inspection, and of the very best materials, is between two and three years old, and was in December last refitted with all New Sails, Standing and Running Rigging, Masts, Yards, Boom, Gaft, &c.&c. Sails remarkably fast, and only wants Provisions to proceed to Sea.
Also, a very superior BRIG, length aloft 64 feet 8 inches, breadth 20 feet 4½ inches, depth 11 feet 0½ inch, admeasures 114 tons, carries 125 Chaldrons of Coals, or 165 Tons Dead Weight at 10½ feet water. Was built at Wells under particular inspection, and of the very best materials, is six years old, Copper Fastened to her brim, is well found in every respect, has now undergone thorough Caulking and Refit, and wants only Provisions to proceed to Sea.
The above Vessels are now lying in the Port of Wells, and can be inspected by applying to Mr. R. Parker, Lloyd's Agent, or any information given to letters post-paid.
Wells, Jan. 29, 1334.

It might have been a bad period for trade, but the auctioneer could not resist reminding potential bidders of the advantages of investing in the town, 'Wells being a very excellent port for trade, a good harbour, and within ten miles of one of the first corn markets in the county'.

Some of the old maltings survive, converted to other uses, but no longer does the aroma of curing malt permeate those narrow streets as it once did. In the mid-nineteenth century some of the Wells maltings were operated by Robert J. and Randall Brereton, maltsters and merchants whose business had been established at Blakeney earlier in the century.

At that time Frederick Smith was a miller and merchant at Ryburgh Magna, combining those trades with farming, but by the late 1870s the firm of Frederick & George Smith had expanded into Dereham and Wells while retaining a foothold in what was becoming known as Great Ryburgh. It was F. & G. Smith who in the early part of the twentieth century built the massive brick granary on the east end of Wells quay that remains such a landmark, though converted into flats whose residents have been heard to complain of the disturbance caused by fishermen departing on their lawful occasions in the early morning.

In 1880 the firm acquired an iron paddle tug, the *Marie*, which had been built at Milton in Kent in 1875, using her to tow vessels up the channel to the quay and out again after they had loaded from the company's granaries. In her early life the *Marie* had twin funnels abreast, but somewhere about 1910

The town of Wells from the bank built in the mid-nineteenth century by the Earl of Leicester. Prominent in this view are the kilns of maltings lying beyond the quay.

The schooner *Minstrel*, built at Wells by Henry Tyrrell in 1847, at Wells quay towards the end of the nineteenth century. Owned in mid-century by Thomas Thirtle Mack, merchant and farmer of Burnham Overy, she had by the time of the picture come into the hands of John Savory, miller, merchant and maltster, also of Burnham Overy.

Regatta day at Wells at the beginning of the twentieth century. Just beyond the tug *Marie* can be seen the large brick granary built in 1904 by F & G Smith of Great Ryburgh and Wells.

The *Marie* precedes a large steam coaster down the channel on the top of the tide; a steel sailing vessel with a rather attractive figurehead is moored alongside the quay.

The *Marie* is followed away from the quay by a white-hulled Dutch tjalk.

Taken just minutes after the preceding photograph, the tug and the Dutch barge make their way down the channel towards the sea; the boat towing astern of the tjalk might well be the pilot's.

A barquentine and, in the distance, a steam coaster at Wells quay about 1900. In the foreground is a whelker, a type of boat developed from the Shannock or crab boat for use in fishing for whelks.

she was reboilered by Frederick Savage at King's Lynn and reappeared with a single funnel.

The purchase of a steam tug did much to overcome the handicap of a long approach to the quay and a difficult channel that almost dries out at low water. In 1845 William White referred to Wells somewhat unkindly as 'formerly one of the most incommodious seaports in England' but qualified his criticism by remarking that the harbour was being improved under the terms of a Harbour and Quay Act obtained the year before. The commissioners appointed to carry out the work are said to have borrowed £22,000 and to have spent £10,000 on the construction of a 250yd. stone quay alone.[5] The building of the new quay and the improvement of the approach channel went hand-in-hand with improvements to the town streets and the erection of a gasworks.

One of the commissioners was Henry Tyrrell, a draper in High Street whose son, Henry Thomas Tyrrell, had just acquired the shipyard previously operated by John Hammond Parker, one of two yards then active in the area east of the quay.

In 1847 Tyrrell launched the 151-ton brig *Countess of Leicester*, which when first registered at Wells was owned by a half-dozen of the more affluent men of the area, including the builder's father, who described himself as a merchant of Wells. He and farmer George Wiseman of Burnham Overy Staithe each owned sixteen shares, the other four each having eight shares; they were James Hull, who was in partnership with Henry Hull as corn, coal and coke merchants at Burnham Overy Staithe, Thomas Thirtle Mack, who was in business as a corn and coal merchant at Overy Staithe but had a house and a farm at Burnham Thorpe, William Mack, a farmer at Burnham Norton, and John Groom, who owned a farm at Great Walsingham.

Such a division of ownership between a number of people was quite normal; so long as no accident befell her a trading vessel such as the *Countess of Leicester* could be a good investment for a man with money to spare. All those who took shares in the new brig had already invested in other locally registered vessels.

Named after the wife of Thomas Coke, Earl of Leicester, the son of the well-known agricultural improver who did so much to promote the agricultural revolution of the eighteenth century, the new brig attracted quite a lot of attention on the day of her launching. The *Norfolk Chronicle* reported that 'it was a beautiful morning and a great concourse of people present . . .'. Most unusually we can enjoy the scene through a peepshow-type model that was most likely made to commemorate the occasion.

The model is a remarkable evocation of a small shipyard of the Victorian period. It represents the *Countess of Leicester* on the launching ways, flags flying and a large gathering of people on board awaiting the moment she will be released to glide into the water of Wells harbour. On an adjacent berth is a vessel in frame, probably the 58-ton schooner *Minstrel* which was launched the following August; she was still trading at the end of the century, owned by John Savory, the Burnham Overy miller.

Beyond the building berths, in the background as it were, are three small weatherboarded buildings with pantiled roofs. One houses the sawpit, with the top sawyer steering the pitsaw through a log and other workmen sharpening their tools on a large grindstone; another houses the pitch boiler, and the third

A contemporary model of Henry Tyrrell's shipyard with the brig *Countess of Leicester* on the left, ready for launching, and the schooner *Minstrel* in frame. It is thought to have been made by Henry's brother Joseph John, who was an accomplished artist.

is the blacksmith's shop. And in the middle ground are little groups of men at work and Tyrrell himself, in top hat and holding a mould under his right arm, giving instructions to one of the men.

It has been suggested that the model might well have been made by Tyrrell himself; but it is more likely to have been made by Henry's brother Joseph John, who was a boy of fourteen at the time the *Countess of Leicester* was launched. Joseph John was the artist of the family and painted some excellent pictures that still survive in private hands in Wells.[6] Parts of the model are fastened together with sealing wax with a decorative capital T impressed into it, which is suggestive of family involvement. Tom Dack, who lent the model to the Maritime Museum for East Anglia, inherited it from his father T.H. Dack, who was apprenticed to the Wells boatbuilder Frederick Whitaker, who in his turn had served his time with Tyrrell.

In 1854 Tyrrell built, under Lloyd's special survey, what was probably the largest vessel to be launched into Wells harbour, the 335-ton barque *Guadalete*, for London owners. In 1857 she was sailing between London and Cadiz.[7] He gave up the tenancy of the shipyard in 1863 and in March 1864 he was appointed a Lloyd's surveyor, retiring in 1881. He died at Wells ten years later.

There is no evidence of when shipbuilding had begun at Wells. The shipyard that had been operated by Nicholas Everitt was clearly well established when it was advertised for sale early in 1796; it had a 'store house, blacksmith's shop, counting house, a large steam boiler for setting planks, stable and other conveniences . . . very eligibly situated near the Quay.'[8]

By the beginning of the nineteenth century there were at least two yards at work, and for a time at least a third yard on the north side of the harbour channel. During the latter part of the eighteenth century one of the ship carpenters of Wells was a woman, if M.J. Armstrong's *History and antiquities of the county of Norfolk* (1781) is to be believed. 'Elizabeth Clayton, near forty years of age, from an early propensity towards masculine employments, has continued to dress and work in the capacity of a ship carpenter for many years. She drinks, swears, chews tobacco and keeps company only with the workmen. She is a strong and healthy person and will employ her tongue, or fists, as much to the danger of an opponent as the boldest man. She earns

Wells quay in the Edwardian period with a steam coaster, a billyboy and another steam vessel alongside.

nine shillings per week, and, as yet, has not been prevailed on to enter into the matrimonial state.'

She died in 1805 at the age of sixty, still unmarried; the *Norfolk Chronicle* recorded that 'she was a strong and robust woman, and never permitted anyone to insult her with impunity'. It would indeed be good to know more of this redoubtable working woman.

It is interesting to discover that between 1814 and 1826 the Wells shipbuilders launched twenty-eight ships, and that in the same period thirteen small vessels were built at Blakeney. It might be that the Wells builders to some extent enjoyed the patronage of the Coke family of Holkham Hall, for in 1832 'a fine vessel of 70 tons burthen . . . was built entirely of oaks of Mr. Coke's own planting at Holkham' – and a report of the launching states that 'Mr. Coke and his son were present at this ceremony'.[9]

Several of the vessels launched from John Lubbock's yard were ordered by Robert and Randall Brereton, who were maltsters and merchants with premises at Wells Quay and at Blakeney. When the brig *Henry & Elizabeth* was launched in 1832 it was specifically announced that she was intended for the Mediterranean and Baltic trade, an indication that the Breretons were not building up their fleet merely to carry their own malt to the London breweries.

A leading Wells owner, Joseph Haycock, who operated as a corn, coal and oilcake merchant on the Quay, numbered among his six ships listed in an 1865 register the largest vessel registered at Wells at that time, the 889-ton full-rigged ship *Agamemnon*. Built at Sunderland in 1855, she had been engaged in the China trade before she came to the Wells register. One might imagine her lying at the quay at Wells, her spars towering above the quayside houses as she unloads a cargo from the Orient; but it would be no more than imagination, for she must have been far too big ever to enter her home port. Haycock also had the barque *Orkney Lass*, built at St. Monance in Fife in 1848 and formerly owned in Liverpool, which at 319 tons would probably also have been unable to berth in Wells. Both vessels were classed A1 at Lloyd's.

Another Wells owner with a considerable fleet was Joseph Southgate, whose home was in the Buttlands. In 1865 he had eight vessels, five of them of over 100 tons. Biggest of his vessels was the brig *Abdiel*, 135 tons; he also had the brigantine *Greek Slave* and the schooners *Crest of the Wave* (1854),

An early aerial photograph of Wells taken in the 1920s, with the quay in the middle of the picture. Just inland from the quay can be seen some of the big maltings that contributed much to the port's trade.

Ellen (1854), *Julia* (1843), *Mary Ann* (1838), *Mystery* (1851) and *Nile* (1859). Another Southgate, the Wells postmaster Francis Southgate, had the schooner *Enchantress* (1852).

With so many vessels belonging to the port there was no shortage of work for tradesmen such as Edmund Cawston, the mastmaker at East End, and the ropemakers Robert Baker and William Thurgar. Every seaport as well as many an inland town had at least one ropewalk, a long and narrow open space in which the ropes could be laid up; that is, the twine could first be twisted into strands and the strands could then be twisted together to form a rope.

We get some idea of the scale of ropemaker Thomas Samuel Fox's business from the advertisement of the sale that resulted when he became bankrupt in 1832. The ropewalk was 124 fathoms (744ft.) long and there were rope, hemp and tar houses, wheel-houses in which the turning machinery was housed, and cartsheds and other buildings at one end.[10] Fox had taken over the business from a G. Suckling in 1821, but ropemaking on the site went back at least to about 1780.[11] One wonders if Fox had bitten off considerably more than he could chew, for when he came up for his examination at Norwich Guildhall with debts of £14,000 he was described as a house builder, brickmaker, lime burner and rope maker.

Fox was not the only person to find himself in financial difficulties in that year of 1832, because the shipbuilder John Hammond Parker was having to sell off his 'extensive stock of Oak, Elm and other Timber Planks, Deals, Pitch, Tar, &c.' to raise money with which to pay his creditors. The advertisement in the *Norwich Mercury* pointed out that this 'valuable stock' was 'lying immediately annexed to the water side, and consequently may be shipped at a very trifling expence'.[12]

Wells must have been a difficult harbour in the eighteenth century, when the harbour's mouth was off Holkham and the approach channel took a serpentine course across the sands to approach the quay. Just to the west of the channel was a sandbank named, ominously, Wreck Sand. There would certainly have been a need for buoys or marks of some kind to be provided to facilitate the navigation, and John Whormby, the eighteeenth-century clerk of Trinity House, reported stuffily in 1746 that there were 'several buoys and beacons maintained by a Haven Master, who seems to be only an officer of

The changing face of Wells:
Edwardian holidaymakers
taking a boat trip from
Wells beach. Just possibly it
is a Sunday School outing.

their own creation'. In fact the placing and maintenance of buoys and beacons had been authorised by an Act of Parliament of 1663. The harbour channel was joined by a little river flowing down across the salt marshes from Holkham on the west and by the East Fleet running across the salt marshes on the other side. Water draining from the salt marshes along these two channels on the ebb helped to scour the harbour channel, but already in 1780 the landowners, the Earl of Leicester and Sir Charles Turner, had thrown up banks with a view to draining the marshes at the back of the Marram Hills, the sand dunes that are today still such a feature of the area, now covered with pines planted by the Earl to stabilise the sand.

The Wells lifeboats

With the formation in 1823 of the Norfolk Association for Saving the Lives of Shipwrecked Mariners lifeboats were provided for a number of stations around the Norfolk coast. A station was established at Blakeney about 1824, and in 1830 it was decided to transfer the old Cromer lifeboat, built by Henry Greathead in 1804, to Wells. A boathouse was built for her 'at the westside of the entrance to Wells Harbour' not very far from the site of the present-day lifeboat station.

The decision might well have been prompted by the events of January 1830, when a number of vessels found themselves in peril off the north Norfolk coast and the Blakeney boat proved ineffective in giving them the assistance they needed.[13] The sloop *Nancy* of Perth spent several days riding off Blakeney with her mast and bowsprit carried away, and the steam packet *City of Edinburgh* lay off the port for a considerable time with her machinery broken down, but it seems that nobody from Blakeney was prepared to go to their aid. The *Nancy* was eventually got into Wells, but the lifeboat crew refused to take the

Blakeney boat out to the steamer, nor would they go to the aid of the sloop *Hope* when she grounded on the bar. It was left to the crews of the vessels in port, together with two survivors of a vessel that had been lost a few days earlier, to take out a boat and rescue the crew of the *Hope*.

It would seem that the lifeboat crew were thus shamed into taking the lifeboat out, but they turned back before reaching the steamer. The seamen who had gone to the *Hope* were joined by the men they had rescued in determining to take out the lifeboat to the steamer's aid, but when they went for her they found that the lifeboat had been 'removed from its usual place so that they could not have the use of her'.

It was boatmen from Wells who eventually managed to board the steamer and bring her into Blakeney Pit. In due course the *City of Edinburgh* was towed to London by another steamer so that her engine could be repaired, but that was not the end of the affair because the local pilots apparently put in a salvage claim and caused the steamer to be arrested in London.[14]

Though the boat seems to have remained in service at least until 1851, when it was listed in the Duke of Northumberland's report on lifesaving services around the coast, nothing seems to be recorded of any rescues she performed. In 1844 an Act of Parliament was passed to amend and extend an Act of 1835 that had set up a body of harbour commissioners; clause 114 stipulated that the commissioners had to provide an efficient lifeboat and crew and laid down penalties of two pounds for every day that the lifeboat was not available for use.

No doubt the commissioners considered that the provision of a boat by the Norfolk Shipwreck Association satisfactorily fulfilled this obligation, and it is not known whether or not they actually took a hand in the administration of the lifeboat station. By the time of the Northumberland report the boat was almost fifty years old and most likely worn out: it is probably safe to assume that there was no lifeboat at Wells when the national institution took over the Norfolk Shipwreck Association in the winter of 1857-58.

William Harman, a member of an old Wells family who compiled *Notes on the Fisheries, Ships and Wrecks of Wells-next-Sea*[15] when he was nearing ninety, does not record any lifeboat rescues in the 1860s though he does mention several wrecks in those years. In 1860 one of the Wells oyster smacks went down with all hands in a sudden storm, and then in November 1868 the local sloop *Rose in June* was wrecked at Holkham, the crew spending several hours in the rigging in bitter weather. The three men were eventually saved by four Wells fishermen, James Stacey and his brother David and two others, in a crab boat named the *Pet* which they took down to Holkham beach on a waggon. The *Rose in June* was owned by her master, Captain J. Brandford, and the Wells merchant Joseph Haycock. Within a month the Wells billyboy *Seaflower*, owned by her master, Captain T.W. Powditch, foundered off Wells in a December gale with the loss of the skipper and the crew of two, one of whom was his son.

Then the following October the billyboy sloop *Three Betseys* left the quay laden with barley for the Humber before a sou'westerly wind. Some three hours after she left the wind changed to nor'nor'west and increased to a very heavy gale. Next morning wreckage and sacks of barley from the cargo were found strewn all along the beach, the only evidence of the disaster that had befallen the vessel and her crew, Captain Ben Marsh, his brother Bircham and James Sampher. Just three days after the loss of the *Three Betseys* another Wells vessel, the schooner *Enchantress*, owned by J.B. Southgate, the Wells postmaster, was driven ashore at Holkham when on her way to Caen in Normandy with a cargo of coal. The crew of five were all lost.

After being rescued from the *Rose in June* in 1868 Captain Brandford took command of the schooner *Advance*. One afternoon in November 1870, the *Advance* was anchored in Wells Bay laden with barley for Wells, and when a nor'easterly gale came on that night she drove ashore at Holkham not far from where the *Rose in June* had been wrecked. Captain Brandford and his crew took to the boat, but it overturned, and the cook, Tom Beck, was swept away and never seen again; Captain Brandford and the rest of the crew managed to scramble ashore. After that Captain Brandford decided to give up the sea and left Wells for his native Yorkshire. Ill luck followed him, though, and he was drowned some years later while working as a lock keeper on one of the Yorkshire navigations.

There had already been moves to open a lifeboat station at Wells, the RNLI Inspector of Lifeboats having visited the town in August 1868 to discuss the matter with the harbour commissioners and others. He recommended that a station should be opened, and a 33ft. self-righter that was paid for by subscriptions from readers of a publication named *Penny Readings* was sent to Wells by rail the following year. *Penny Readings* had been founded by a surgeon from Bungay, Edward Burman Adams, and the lifeboat was named *Eliza Adams* after his wife. Built on the Thames by T.W. Woolfe & Son, the *Eliza Adams* was one of the standard self-righting pulling and sailing boats derived from the type that had won the Duke of Northumberland's premium for Yarmouth boatbuilder James Beeching in 1851. Although the Institution had not been entirely satisfied with Beeching's design, a considerable amount of development resulted in a boat that was then considered to be the most satisfactory lifeboat built up to that time. She was kept in a new boathouse on the west end of the quay for launching into the harbour, but it was thought that she could be taken to the beach instead, using the road atop the bank constructed by Lord Leicester in 1859.

The boat did not perform her first service until 30th September 1871, when she was called out in a nor'easterly gale to the Grimsby schooner *Commerce*, owned by a Lincoln brewer, which was on fire. Captain George Hill and his crew made the mistake of leaving the *Commerce* in the ship's boat and were all drowned when the boat capsized; Captain Hill's body was washed ashore, and was buried in Wells cemetery.

The north Norfolk coast could be a deathtrap when a gale from the north thrust vessels towards the shore, and it was not unknown for vessels to be lost without anyone ashore being aware they were in distress. On Maundy Thursday, 13th April 1876, it was an easterly gale accompanied by a blizzard that created havoc in the vicinity of Wells. As William Harman records, the weather never cleared all day and on the Good Friday morning five ships were seen lying on the shore. One of them was the little billyboy *John & Jane*, whose crew and the captain's wife had taken refuge in the rigging. As the tide dropped and the vessel dried out they climbed down and walked ashore. The cargo of rape seed was salvaged and taken up to Wells in the local boats to be dried on the malthouse kilns, but the *John & Jane* was sold as a wreck. After the seed had been dried it was sold to Hull and taken there by the Wells ketch *Dispatch*. Three of the other ships that were ashore at Holkham went to pieces, only the *Annie Rosette* of Goole being refloated; her cargo of linseed was carted up to Wells.

That same day the Yarmouth schooner *Cygnet*, laden with slate, went on the Bridgirdle off Burnham and all five crew members were drowned. Nobody ashore knew anything until some days later a number of Wells men sent down to salvage what they could from the *John & Jane* found the body of one of the crew washed up on the sand.

A particularly vicious nor'easterly gale on 29th October 1880 caused many shipping casualties not only in the vicinity of Wells but all along the East Anglian coast, sinking a score of fishing vessels and driving ashore no fewer than thirty-six trading vessels. At times the wind reached force eleven on the Beaufort scale, hurricane force, and at daybreak several vessels were seen being driven inshore, their sails blown to ribbons. First to strike the beach was the snow *Violet*, of Whitby, which was bound for Shields in ballast.

Being light she was driven well up the beach, and the crew were able to send a line ashore attached to a lifebuoy. Men on the beach, among whom was William Harman, made a heavier line fast to the buoy and the crew hauled it back, then used the lifebuoy to gain the shore one by one. The captain, a very short man of seventy or so, was the last man to leave the vessel, and he was given a bad ducking as he was hauled ashore.

'I think we ashore were a bit anxious to get him ashore and pulled him underwater, so it was a little while before he could regain his breath,' said Harman. When eventually he did recover his breath he was heard to utter the words 'Never no more!'

That was taken at the time to mean that he would never return to sea, but it was later discovered that it might have related to the advice he had been given by a Wells man that if he ever got caught in a storm off north Norfolk he should steer for Holkham Bay, where he would stand a good chance of being saved. That man was William Harman's father, with whom the captain had been shipmates years before. 'He seemed to know exactly where to come ashore to save their lives,' Harman said.

Next to come aground was the Whitby brig *Sharon's Rose* with about 400 tons of coal for Dieppe. Being deep laden she grounded some distance out, and the crew stuck to the vessel to await the arrival of the lifeboat. Third to strike was the brig *Lois*, of Littlehampton, which like the *Violet* was sailing in ballast. As she took the ground she swung broadside to the sea, and the crew took advantage of the lee she offered to get their boat out. The watchers on the shore held their breath, fearing that the boat would overturn in the breakers, but the crew got ashore in safety. Their ship became a total wreck.

Though the lifeboat was needed it seems that nobody gave the order to launch, and it was midday before the *Eliza Adams* was at last launched into the harbour. The crew had a stiff pull down the channel against the flood tide and it was another hour before they reached the *Sharon's Rose*. After a considerable struggle the seven men of the brig were taken into the lifeboat, which was towed back to the quay by the wooden paddle tug *Promise*.

The men rescued from the *Sharon's Rose* had just been landed and were being taken off by willing helpers in the town when another vessel, the 170-ton snow *Ocean Queen* of Sunderland, was seen in trouble to eastward of the harbour. The lifeboat was manned by the same crew, with a smattering of new men, and was towed down the harbour by the *Promise*, but the tug cast her off outside the harbour and returned to the quay because the tugmaster was worried that if he delayed there would not be sufficient water for him to negotiate the harbour. The *Eliza Adams* attempted to reach the *Ocean Queen*, whose sails were in ribands, but she was blown into shallow water where the lifeboat was unable to follow. The crew of the *Ocean Queen* remained on board their vessel and were able to walk ashore at low water.

The crew of the lifeboat took her about half a mile to seaward under oars, and then the coxswain, Captain Robert Elsdon, gave the order to set the sails.

Four wrecks lie on Wells beach after the gale of 29th October 1880 in which the Wells lifeboat *Eliza Adams* capsized with the loss of ten of her crew; only two survived. On the left is the brigantine *Albion*, and under her bowsprit can be seen the *Violet*, with the *Sharon's Rose* and the *Louis* to the right.

There was no hope of pulling back to the harbour through the sea that was running and against the strong ebb tide. The boat had reached the East Bight, a channel across Bob Hall's Sand that would bring them into The Run at the entrance to the harbour, when a heavy curling sea rose up on the starboard side.

The sheets were let go and the boat luffed up before the sea, but it broke over her and into the foresail, overturning her in an instant. She turned bottom up and failed to right herself for several minutes; it could be that the mainmast jammed in the sand and the boat only righted when the mast broke off. All the lifeboatmen were wearing cork lifebelts, but only two out of thirteen survived. One of them was Captain Thomas Kew, who found himself entangled in the boat's gear when she went over. When he freed himself he set off for the beach, but he would have been drowned had he not been dragged from the water by two Coastguards who were among those who saw the capsize.

Among the eleven men lost in the *Eliza Adams* that day were two pairs of brothers, Captain Robert Elsdon and John Elsdon and Samuel and Charles Smith. Ten of those lost were buried at Wells; the body of Charles Smith was never found. It was the worst accident that had occurred to a lifeboat belonging to the RNLI up to that time, and ten widows and twenty-seven orphans were left to mourn.

There was a feeling in the town that men already exhausted by their efforts in saving the crew of the *Sharon's Rose* should not have gone out a second time when the call came to the *Ocean Queen*. When Captain Kew was questioned about this at the inquest he replied merely 'I never heard them complain.'

The lifeboat that was built by Woolfe to replace the *Eliza Adams* was considerably larger, 37ft. long with twelve oars. The *Charlotte Nicholls* served only seven years and performed only one rescue before being sold out of service, apparently because some doubt was expressed about her self-righting capability. One wonders if that was a reflection of local feeling after the failure of the *Eliza Adams* to right herself properly, but nonetheless her replacement was another 37ft. self-righter, named *Baltic*. Oddly enough, she too lasted little more than seven years, perhaps because the crew had lost faith in the self-righting boats.

The main drawback, however, was the position of the lifeboathouse at one end of the quay a mile and a half from the sea. With a flood tide against her the boat could not be rowed down the harbour; at low water there was insufficient depth in the harbour to float her. In theory she could be taken to the beach on her carriage, but in practice this seems to have presented insurmountable difficulties.

Dissatisfaction with the situation of the boathouse and with the first *Baltic* herself was brought to a head by events in the autumn of 1893. A severe northerly gale struck the north Norfolk coast on the afternoon of 18th November and several vessels found themselves in distress in the vicinity of Wells, but after being launched into the harbour the *Baltic* just could not make headway against the gale. Although the oarsmen struggled manfully, they could make no progress down the harbour channel.

First to drive ashore was the laden collier *Duke of Cornwall*, which grounded between Wells and Blakeney. The crew of three were saved by the Coastguards from Wells. Then in the evening the Littlehampton-built ketch

barge *Lord Beresford*, one of a number of such barges belonging to the English & Continental Shipping Company, with a cargo of barley for Burnham Overy, parted from her anchors in Wells Bay and drove ashore on Holkham beach; the crew were forced to take to the rigging, from which they were eventually rescued. The barge was refloated later after the cargo had been unloaded and carted to Wells.

Worse was to come two days later, when the schooner *Hickman* of Goole, named after her Yorkshire owner, sank in the mouth of Wells harbour. The *Baltic* was launched in the early afternoon and made for the wreck, but progress was slow and she took an hour and a half to reach it. On the way the lifeboatmen saw a seventeen-year-old boy, on his first voyage, drop out of the rigging; his body was picked up on Cley beach several days later. The lifeboat was anchored to windward of the wreck, with the intention that she should be veered down, letting out the cable until she was in a position to take the *Hickman*'s crew on board. Unfortunately the anchor dragged, and she was blown to leeward of the wreck. An attempt was made to throw a grapnel into the schooner's rigging as the lifeboat was swept past, but just at that moment a big sea filled her and washed two of the crew out of her. They were both retrieved by their companions, but all hope of getting back to windward of the schooner was lost and the boat had to be beached at Holkham.

At that time twenty-two Wells men, mostly fishermen, had formed a salvage company which operated a boat named the *Friends*, with William Crawford[16] as coxswain. Fifteen of them manned the *Friends* and set off on the last of the ebb in hopes of saving the four men in the rigging of the *Hickman* at around low water. As they approached, Coxswain Crawford was heard to say 'It's now or never.' The ship was lying head to sea with her sails in tatters and with big seas breaking over her decks. At first the men in the boat got no answer to their hails and feared that all the crew had perished, but then they saw one object move, then a second and a third. A fourth man was lashed in the rigging, but he was dead.

The crew of the *Hickman* had suffered an horrendous experience as the vessel was driven up the North Sea from the Firth of Forth. Heavy seas had swept the decks, taking the freshwater casks and the boat overboard, and the sails had been blown out of the boltropes. The mate, lashed in the rigging, had died raving mad after he had witnessed the lifeboatmen's failure to reach them.

Having got the three survivors on board the salvagers proceeded up the Wells channel for about a mile, but that was as far as they could get at that stage of the tide. Looking at two of the survivors who were in a very bad way, Coxswain Crawford ordered four of the boat's crew (one of them William Harman) to take the rescued men across the sands towards Wells. It was clear that if they waited in the boat for the tide to make the two men would die before they reached Wells.

'The two exhausted men we simply dragged across a mile of sand, two of the boat's crew for each man, and the captain walked by our side,' said Harman. 'We managed to get them up to Wells beach, and the doctor was there to meet us, and a conveyance that took them to the King's Arms. They were attended by two doctors before they rallied.'

The RNLI made a monetary award to the crew of the *Friends* and considered

Opposite: 29th October 2005. The Wells lifeboat *Doris M Mann of Ampthill* slips from her carriage to take a wreath to the site of the tragedy, 125 years on. Present day crew and townsfolk then gathered at the harbour side memorial to recall the loss of life on the *Eliza Adams* lifeboat.

The outbreak of war in 1939 brought new work for the lifeboat, which was called out several times when aircraft were reported down at sea. Sometimes the *Royal Silver Jubilee* operated with an RAF air-sea rescue launch that was based at Wells Quay; the launch had a far higher speed than the lifeboat but was handicapped by the inability to leave harbour when the tide was low and by the difficulty of navigating the intricate channel to the sea. On one occasion the lifeboat was launched after a report of a Wellington bomber having come down in the sea; on the way out the lifeboatmen found the ASR launch in difficulties. The second coxswain went aboard the launch to act as pilot, and in spite of the darkness the launch succeeded in finding six airmen in a rubber dinghy. It was the RAF launch that brought the men back to Wells, but without the help of the lifeboatmen that rescue could not have been accomplished.

On 14th July 1942 the lifeboat was launched early in the morning after a report of a four-engined bomber ditched some three miles from the boathouse. The crew found the Avro Lancaster, belonging to No. 97 Squadron from Woodhall Spa in Lincolnshire, still afloat and standing on her nose, weighed down by the four engines; the whole of the tail and part of the port wing had broken away. Clinging to the underside of the port wing was one badly injured airman, still conscious and moaning with pain. He was lifted gently into the boat and attended by Dr. E.W. Hicks, the honorary secretary, who often went out in the boat when on such missions.

What of the rest of the crew? Coxswain Neilsen clambered up on to the wing and made his way to the fuselage, climbing inside to ascertain if any of the crew were still there. He found nobody. The lifeboat landed the injured airman before putting out again to search for others of the aircrew. Unhappily the rescued man died later in hospital, and the bodies of his six comrades were eventually recovered from the sea. For his action in searching the aircraft, regardless of the risk that it might at any moment roll over and sink, Coxswain Neilsen was given the Institution's thanks on vellum.

There was an echo of this event in 1995 when it was announced that an 87-year-old woman from Surrey had left £400,000 to the RNLI for use by the Wells station. It was thought that the woman's sweetheart had been the pilot of the Lancaster bomber.

The Wells lifeboat was launched on 5th May 1943 when an airborne lifeboat was dropped to a ditched aircrew for the first time. The airborne lifeboat, dropped by parachute from a search aircraft, was about twelve miles from Wells when its little petrol motor broke down and the *Royal Silver Jubilee* was sent to the rescue, but the much faster RAF launch reached the scene first and picked up the airmen from the broken-down boat.

Coxswain Neilsen was in charge of the *Royal Silver Jubilee* during the whole of her service at Wells. A Dane, he had arrived at Wells as a seaman aboard a three-masted schooner in the early years of the twentieth century, had married the daughter of the Wells pilot and settled in the town, joining the lifeboat crew in 1910. About the time of the Dunkirk evacuation in 1940 Neilsen led a flotilla of fishing boats from Wells, Blakeney and Brancaster on a secret mission to the French coast, and for this exploit he was made an MBE.

With the end of the war the RNLI decided to send a 35ft. 6in. Liverpool boat to Wells and handed the *Royal Silver Jubilee* and her sister boat *Rosabella* over to the Koninklijke Noord En Zuid-Hollandsche Redding-Maatschappij to assist the Dutch organisation in making good the ravages of the wartime occupation. The former Wells boat, renamed *Rosilee*, was stationed on the island of Vlieland, where she served until 1959. In 1953 the Dutch lifeboat service rebuilt her and replaced her petrol engines and Hotchkiss cone propeller by a diesel engine driving a normal external screw propeller.

The first of the twin-engined 35ft. 6in. Liverpool type boats to be completed for the RNLI, the *Cecil Paine* took up station at Wells in July 1945, shortly after the end of hostilities in Europe. Nonetheless, the immediate aftermath of war was very soon to affect the new boat when on the night of 7th January 1946 an attempt was made by six escaped German prisoners of war from the POW camp at Matlaske, between Holt and Aylsham, to start the lifeboat's engines after they had broken into the boathouse. They were recaptured by local police before they could go any further with their escape attempt.

Coxswain Neilsen retired in 1947, and his successor, William Cox, received the thanks of the Institution on vellum for his part in the rescue of five of the crew from the Turkish steamer *Zor* on 18th May 1955. The *Cecil Paine* was launched just after three in the afternoon to go to the aid of the *Zor*, which was on her way from Finland with timber for Hull when the deck cargo began to shift in worsening weather. She had anchored some six miles from the Dudgeon lightvessel. It was quite usual for timber ships to list, but the heavy list that the *Zor* soon developed boded ill. By the time the lifeboat reached her in the early evening the lifeboatmen could see through the hail and snow showers that she was at a 45-degree angle, and her windward side was awash. Boards from the deck cargo were cascading into the sea at every heave of the vessel and were floating away to leeward. Six people from the *Zor*, including the captain's wife, had already been taken aboard the steamer *Richmond Queen*, a 1600-gross-ton coaster belonging to the Queenship Navigation Company of Glasgow, which was standing by and intending to take the stricken vessel in tow.

The master of the *Zor* hoped it would be possible in spite of the gale that was blowing to save the vessel, and when Billy Cox manoeuvred the lifeboat alongside the listing steamer's lee side to take off five of his crew he and three others opted to remain on board. The lifeboat also took a second hawser to the *Richmond Queen*, the first one having parted, but it was all in vain.

The Wells lifeboat had to leave in the early hours of the morning because she was running short of fuel. She landed the rescued men at Wells, and it had to be left to the Sheringham lifeboat under Coxswain Downtide West to take off the master and the three crewmen just before the *Zor* went down. Coxswain West was also given the thanks of the Institution on vellum.

The *Cecil Paine* continued to serve at Wells until 1965, when her place was taken by the 37ft. Oakley self-righting boat *Ernest Tom Neathercoat*, which was at Wells for twenty-five years. The *Cecil Paine* was sold out of service in 1972 and continued her lifesaving work in Portugal with the Instituto de Soccoros a Naufregos.

Although the first lifeboat had been placed at Wells by the Norfolk Association for Saving the Lives of Shipwrecked Mariners in 1830 it was in 1969 that the RNLI celebrated the centenary of the station with the presentation of a commemorative vellum, marking a hundred years since the placing on station of the *Eliza Adams* by the Institution. In those years the lifeboats had been launched on service 180 times and had saved 118 lives.

When she first arrived the *Ernest Tom Neathercoat* had an open cockpit, but after a time she was given a canopy to provide a little protection for the crew on lengthy services like that to the German motor vessel *Nordenstedt* on 3rd September 1974, when she spent more than 12 hours at sea in a force nine gale and very rough conditions.

That canopy gave inadequate shelter when on 15th February 1979 the lifeboat was called to the Romanian cargo ship *Savinesti* in trouble in the North Sea with her engine broken down. The north-easterly wind was strong gale force nine gusting to storm force ten and heavy snow was reducing visibility at times to a matter of just a few yards; heavy rolling seas constantly struck the boat, putting the radar and other electronic equipment out of action and filling the cockpit time after time so that Coxswain David Cox had to reduce speed. The temperature was four degrees below freezing. Nevertheless the lifeboat with its soaked and frozen crew maintained course.

After three hours the lifeboat found the Romanian ship and stood by her as two other ships attempted without success to pass a towline. The intense cold and the constant drenching as heavy seas crashed on to the lifeboat were causing the lifeboatmen severe suffering, and David Cox asked if the bigger Humber lifeboat, a 54ft. Arun with enclosed wheelhouse, could relieve the Wells boat when it arrived on the scene. Meanwhile the Wells boat continued to stand by in the most appalling conditions.

One of the Wells crew said later that he found the cold so intensely painful that he would have been relieved if the lifeboat had capsized and never come up again. The sea was warmer than the biting cold of the blizzard.

When at last she was relieved by the *City of Bradford IV* from the Humber David Cox turned for home, but the return voyage was a nightmare for the eight lifeboatmen. They streamed the drogue to help hold the boat steady before the wind. Snow was blowing into the open cockpit, and one member of the crew was kept occupied clearing the screen and compass glass. They made landfall off Brancaster, but it still took the boat two hours to negotiate the final seven miles back to Wells. Visibility was so bad that a Wells fishing boat had to act as pilot to bring the lifeboat over the bar and into harbour.

Two of the lifeboatmen were suffering from frostbite and lost the feeling in their fingers; it took three weeks for the feeling to come back. All eight of them had to be helped ashore; they were rigid with cold and unable to walk. The town of Wells was cut off by snow for the next three days.

For that service, lasting some eleven and a half harrowing hours, David Cox was awarded the Silver Medal; Coxswain Brian Bevan of the Humber lifeboat gained the Bronze Medal. The other seven members of the Wells crew were given medal service certificates; it was certainly a callout they would never forget.

During the 1980s the *Ernest Tom Neathercoat* was given a folding wheelhouse which enclosed the cockpit. The structure had to be made to fold down because of the limited headroom in the boathouse, but it was still a modification that was greatly appreciated by the crew.

Whenever the *Ernest Tom Nethercoat* was away from her station for a periodical survey and overhaul the reserve Oakley *Calouste Gulbenkian* took her place. Built in 1961, this boat had been stationed at Weston-super-Mare

until 1969 when she joined the reserve fleet. She had a long stint at Wells in 1986-88 when the *Ernest Tom Neathercoat* went to a yard on the Medway for a complete rebuilding, and in that time the *Calouste Gulbenkian* was out on service four times, saving a Dutch yacht and her five crew on one of those services.

When her service at Wells came to an end in 1990 the *Ernest Tom Neathercoat* went to North Sunderland (Seahouses) in Northumberland for a spell and was then retired and taken to the National Boat Building Centre at Oulton Broad for display; she later returned to Wells and was on display not far from the lifeboat station until 2000. She has since been restored at a Stiffkey boatyard and in June 2012 returned to Wells once more, being placed back in the water by crane.

Her replacement in 1990 by the first production Mersey, a 12-metre carriage-launched craft powered by twin Caterpillar turbo-charged diesel engines giving her a speed of seventeen knots, twice that of her predecessor, necessitated big changes at Wells. The old boathouse, originally built almost a hundred years earlier, had to be rebuilt to accommodate the new boat and was extended to provide better facilities.

Built of aluminium, the Mersey *Doris M. Mann of Ampthill* was a major technological advance on earlier lifeboats. Before she entered service Coxswain-Mechanic Graham Walker and five other crew members spent a week at the RNLI training centre at Poole learning about the new boat and familiarising themselves with her handling. It was not only the new boat herself that they had to get used to; they had to learn about the sophisticated

At low water the difficulty of the channel for yachtsmen entering Wells is revealed; the salt marshes are a hazard to the unwary walker and frequently result in a call for the inshore lifeboat.

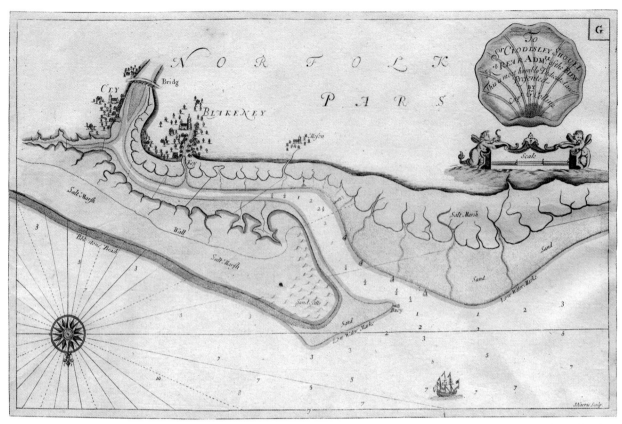

Captain Greenville Collins' chart of the approaches to Cley and Blakeney, 1693. Even at that date the entrance was marked by buoys, probably as a result of a local initiative. Appropriately Captain Collins dedicated this chart to Sir Cloudesley Shovell, 'Rear Admirall of the Blew,' who hailed from the village of Cockthorpe, just a few miles from Blakeney.

new equipment with which she was equipped, including not only radar but the most up-to-date communications and navigation systems. At the end of the course they sailed the new boat to her station.

Wells was one of the earliest RNLI stations to receive an inshore lifeboat, the first inflatable rescue boat being supplied in the summer of 1963. At first these craft were on station only during the summer months, the expectation being that they would be employed primarily in services to bathers and small boat sailors during the holiday season.

The Wells inshore boat was capsized by a freak wave off Morston in August 1968 after being called to search for a dinghy that had been reported missing. The two lifeboatmen succeeded in righting their inflatable and rowed ashore at Morston; the boat for which they had been looking had meanwhile returned safely to Wells.

Many of the calls to the inshore lifeboat have involved people who had become cut off by the tide when walking in the marshes, but a most unusual service was recorded in July 2006 when the ILB was launched to help two people and a horse stranded on a sandbar in Holkham Bay. One horse had already swum ashore after unseating its rider and the other was being held by the two riders as the tide rose around them.

The lifeboat first landed the two riders, leaving two crewmen to hold the horse, and then after the crew had obtained advice from the lifeboat operations manager's wife, herself an experienced equestrian, returned to the sandbar. The horse was persuaded to swim to the shore alongside the boat.

The pattern of calls is indicated by the record of services in 2010, when the all-weather lifeboat answered 12 and the inshore boat 23, nine of which were to people cut off by the rising tide. The record shows four people saved (people who might have lost their lives were it not for the lifeboat), 18 landed and 21 brought in.

The future of stations like Wells, where the all-weather lifeboat has to be launched across the beach by carriage, was indicated in 2006 when the RNLI's experimental FCB2 (fast carriage boat) underwent launching trials at Wells using two types of prototype carriage. Propelled by twin water jets powered by two Caterpillar C9 engines developing 550ihp each, the FCB2 is designed for a top speed of 28 knots. The prototype of what is now known as the Shannon class paid another visit to Wells in 2012. It is expected that Wells will be allocated one of the first of this new type when it becomes operational.

Cley and Blakeney

Following the improvements made to the harbour Wells was considered to be a place of safety in onshore gales; the entrance was marked by a series of buoys and beacons. However, in severe winter weather the trade of Wells was sometimes brought to a standstill, and the best refuge was Blakeney Harbour.[17] 'This is the only harbour of safety for shipping when caught in a gale of wind, dead on the coast, and is capable of receiving ships of 4 or 500 tons,' said a Blakeney man. 'A flag is hoisted on the Church Tower, as a signal when you may run for it, if the boats cannot get off; there will then be full nine feet over the bar.'

In the Middle Ages the twin ports of Blakeney and Cley-next-the-Sea, their harbours protected by the ever-growing shingle spit now known as Blakeney Point, were of considerable significance, both in terms of trade and in other respects from time to time. Graffiti on the arcade pillars of Blakeney church portraying medieval ships serve as a reminder of the voyaging of local seamen, who not only crossed the North Sea but found their way to Icelandic waters, as Hakluyt recorded. One can imagine a local seaman, bored by the droning voice of the parson, taking out his trusty knife and scratching those pictures of little single-masted vessels when he should by rights have been thanking God for his safe return from wherever it was the wind had blown him.

Not all that went on in those ports was strictly legal: when the fishing was bad the men of Cley turned to piracy for a living, and there is little doubt that smuggling was another of their accomplishments. It seems highly likely that these ports carried on a trade with Scotland in the fifteenth century, when relations between England and her northern neighbour varied like a chameleon on a piece of tartan; what might be perfectly legitimate intercourse when the two countries were on relatively friendly terms became an illicit trade when hostilities broke out.

In 1405 or thereabouts King Robert III of Scotland, a kindly man but by no means a strong enough ruler for his restless country, decided to send his surviving son James out of the country 'to learn French' – his eldest son had died unhappily. James was sent to the Bass Rock, and from there he took ship for France. In the vessel's hold as it sailed south were silver plate and other goods fit for the service of a prince, but there was no gun or 'crack of war' to defend that precious freight. Poor James was a bad sailor, the motion of the

The Cley channel at half tide soon after the First World War.

ship upset his head and his stomach, and the ship hugged the Yorkshire coast, the master hoping to find calmer water near the shore.

Meanwhile one Sir John Prendergast, described as an outlaw, slippery as an eel and tough as salt pork, had sailed from Cley in company, so it seems, with Robert Bacon of Cromer and others of the same kind. Nearly twenty years earlier the fishermen of those ports had protested, successfully, that their little ships were useless in warfare and should be excluded from royal service, but presumably for chasing fish and other prizes of the sea they were ideal. So it came about that at the end of March 1406 these little ships from north Norfolk lay off Flamborough Head, right in the way of the ship carrying James to France.

James was taken prisoner, and Sir John Prendergast and his merry men set course for London, where James was lodged in the Tower; he remained a guest, willing or unwilling, for almost twenty years. During that time he learnt not only French, for the fourth Henry was a linguist, but also how to govern a country in the English manner.

Thomas of Walsingham says that the capture happened 'by chance', but there are indications that it might not have been mere chance that Sir John and his ships were off the Yorkshire coast at just the right time to intercept James's ship; Henry IV seems to have prepared the Tower for the reception of an important Scottish visitor in February, at least a month before the interception. Those north Norfolk ports were not corporate towns with a corporation seeking to ensure that everything going on in the town was done by the book. Somebody wishing to hire shipping for some not entirely legitimate purpose might well choose such a place, where he could bargain directly with the seamen with no fear of interruption by a prying alderman.

Nearly two hundred years later, when Spain was endeavouring to subdue the rebellious people of the Netherlands, certain mariners of Blakeney were involved in piratical operations off the north Norfolk coast on the Spanish king's behalf, contrary to a proclamation by Queen Elizabeth I prohibiting English mariners to serve foreign princes. A little more than ten years before the departure of the Armada for its attack on England, Henry Carew and Thomas Hubbert obtained letters of marque from the King of Spain authorising them to seize ships belonging to the Netherlanders and to sell goods they seized; and they used the north Norfolk ports as their base.

As a justice of the peace Nathaniel Bacon, second son of Sir Nicholas Bacon, Elizabeth's Lord Keeper, sought to act against them. With another JP he rode over to Blakeney from Stiffkey, where he was building a fine new house for himself, but he found it less than easy to proceed against the malefactors when they sat tight aboard their ship in the harbour. Nathaniel and his fellow JP told the Privy Council that they had sought ways to apprehend Hubbert, 'but he is either hidd or fledd', adding that 'we thought it not convenient to use force about the taking of them in the ship'. The fact that Nathaniel's party was outnumbered was left unsaid.

The harbour of Cley, or Clay as the name used to be spelt and pronounced, was at one time much more extensive than it is now, stretching right up to the vicinity of the parish church of St. Margaret's, which lies more than half a mile from the town's later quays. The former extent of the Glaven only becomes evident in times of serious flooding when the water stretches across the valley so that the church looks out over a shallow estuary as it did seven hundred years ago. It was the building of a bank to enable land in the valley to be reclaimed for agricultural use in the seventeenth century that changed the topography of the area and also led to silting of the harbour.

The drainage operations of a Dutchman named Jan (or John) van Hasedunck on behalf of certain landowners about 1637 seem to have caused consternation among the merchants and shipowners of the Glaven ports, and during legal proceedings in 1638 it was said that 'the said new embankment made over the mayne channel between the great and little eyes' had excluded the inhabitants 'from their fishing in the said channel and cricks' and from the sea, 'their chief means of livelihood'. They complained that they were 'forced to beg and seek new habitations'.

The inhabitants of Cley and Wiveton petitioned the King, pointing out the effect the construction of the bank had had on the port's trade. Whereas in 1637 the importation of coal amounted to 1,043 Newcastle chaldrons, and 614 lasts of corn had been exported, the following year trade had dropped to 538 chaldrons of coal inwards and 226 lasts of corn outward, they declared. In 1637 thirty ships were entered in the customs house records, but in 1638 only fourteen were recorded.

To underline the importance of their harbour the local people told the story of a Danish ship, the *Jonas* of Husum, bringing 44 horses 'fit for His Majesties service' which was able to find refuge there on 10th April 1638. The ship, her ship's company and the cargo would all have been lost 'had they not in this haven been preserved for they were bound Eastwards and there is noe haven nearer then Yarmouth eastward which is about 30 miles distant'.

The petition seems to have had the desired effect and the bank was ordered to be removed, but it was no more than a rearguard action. In time the marshes were reclaimed and shipping was prevented from passing above Wiveton bridge.

Nonetheless Cley remained a place of business and trade for another two hundred years, even if Pigot's *Commercial Directory* of 1830 unkindly labelled it 'a place of little consequence in mercantile affairs, save what is derived from the importation of coals, and exportation of barley and malt'. Nevertheless the Customs House for the port of Blakeney and Cley remained at Cley until its authority was absorbed into that at Wells in the middle of the nineteenth century. The imposing three-storey Customs House itself survives, with a carved wooden panel over the door portraying smugglers engaged in their trade being surprised by an officer and a group of Revenue men on the quay

A view of Cley about 1900, with the windmill at work on the left of the picture. Perhaps the missing vanes in one sail are the result of a recent storm.

at Cley.[18] Smuggling was a very serious matter along the north Norfolk coast in the eighteenth century and in the first half of the nineteenth, as one might judge from the remarks of Daniel Defoe, who wrote of the coastal towns having 'a very considerable trade cary'd on with Holland for corn, which that part of the country is very full of: I say nothing of the great trade driven here from Holland, back again to England, because I take it to be a trade carryed on with much less honesty than advantage; especially while the clandestine trade, or the art of smuggling was so much in practice; what it is now, is not to my present purpose'.

That it could be a very violent business was proved by the affray that took place early one February morning in 1833 as the riding officer from Weybourne and a customs boatman were 'surveying their district' a few miles to the east of Cley. A terrier belonging to the riding officer began to bark, and when his master went to investigate he was overpowered by a group of smugglers who were clearly going about their illegal business. They took away his pistols and cutlass and handcuffed his hands behind his back, and then coolly went back to their work.

The boatman managed to run off and sought aid at the watch-house,

The decay of Blakeney's shipping trade is evident in this photograph of the harbour at the end of the nineteenth century, with two derelict vessels on the mud; the one already partly broken up is probably the *Newcastle Packet*. The ketch on the left is, however, still in commission; she is most likely the *Fiducia*. The tug *Comet* of Newcastle was built of steel at Middlesbrough in 1889 and was later acquired by Edward C. Turner, the Blakeney merchant, who was in partnership with Martin Fountain Page as Page & Turner, corn, coal, cake, seed and manure merchants and shipowners.

Warehouses running back from the quay are prominent in these two pictures from the early years of the twentieth century, both of which appear to show the same little lute-sterned ketch at Blakeney; she is possibly a Yarmouth fishing boat converted into a trading vessel.

where he alerted the chief officer, a Lieutenant Howes. The lieutenant and another man set out with the boatman in search of the smugglers, ignoring a partly loaded cart that had apparently been left deliberately to take their attention. They found the smugglers without much difficulty, for there were said to be 'upwards of one hundred men, with from twenty to thirty horses and carts, some empty and some loaded'. Even allowing for some pardonable exaggeration, the lieutenant and his two men were hopelessly outnumbered, yet undaunted they went into the attack. Lieutenant Howes 'himself broke two pistols about the faces of the smugglers, and ran a dirk through the arm of another, who got away with it sticking in his arm', and wounded several more with his cutlass.

The odds were shortened a little when it seems reinforcements came on the scene, though the newspaper account does not say who they were or where they came from. One of the approaching men apparently fired a signal shot which led the 'preventive force', all three of them, to give a loud cheer, at which the smugglers scattered and ran off, leaving five loaded carts, five horses and two prisoners in the hands of the preventive men. One of the men taken prisoner had had a pistol or musket ball pass through both his legs, one of

A billyboy ketch and other vessels at Blakeney quay about 1906.

which had to be amputated.

It was said that the tubs and packages of tobacco and brandy, 'upwards of 200 in number', were worth between £800 and £1200 'and will prove a rich harvest to the service of the district'.

Pigot's 1830 directory listed four merchants in Cley, Corbet Cooke, merchant and maltster, John Lee, miller and merchant, William Mash, and John Barber Jackson, who was the son of Thomas Jackson, also a merchant. When the Jackson family's properties were sold in 1835 they consisted of 'a convenient & substantial Dwelling House, in the centre of the Town & fronting the main street', a three-storey granary 187ft. long, a 'very substantial' coal house, extensive maltings and granaries on the quay, and 'an exclusive right to Clay Quay'. It was a little commercial empire built up over many years.

John Lee was the tenant miller of the big brick windmill on the quay that was described in an advertisement of 1819 as 'that capital new erected Tower Windmill'.[19] According to the advertisement 'A very extensive business is capable of being carried on here at a relatively trifling expense, as the flour may be sent out to sea without any land carriage'. Lee did carry on an extensive trade, for he was a corn merchant and maltster as well as a miller, and also a shipowner. Following his death in 1848 his malthouse, granaries and coal houses, together with 'a large yard for timber, bricks &c', two lighters and shares in five vessels that had been employed in his business were advertised for sale.[20]

The mill was sold in 1921 for a mere £350 and converted into a holiday home. Sixty years later it was put up for sale, offers being invited 'in excess of £100,000'; it did not sell at that time but has since become a popular venue.

At Blakeney the most prominent business was that operated by Robert and Randall Brereton, who have already been mentioned as working maltings at Wells, though for a time their enterprise was rivalled by the firm of Muskett, Smith and Co. which in 1839 was said to have purchased and built the schooners *Thetis*, *Pomona* and *Fanny* and the brig *Livorno* since the previous year. Muskett, Smith also acquired the teak-built full-rigged ship *Louisa* in the trade to India and Australia, an example of a ship that was far too big to visit her home port.[21] In the 1830s the Breretons were enterprising enough to acquire the paddle steamer *Premier* for use as a tug; as her name implies, she was almost certainly the first steam vessel to operate in the north Norfolk ports.

Not all the vessels registered at Cley were owned there or at Blakeney. The schooner *Newcastle Packet* was owned by William Cook, the Glandford miller and merchant, and the 168-ton brig *Elizabeth* belonged to William Allen, the Weybourne sub-postmaster, draper and grocer. Members of the Bolding family, who had what was described in Harrod's directory of 1863 as an extensive brewery and malting establishment at Weybourne, were also shipowners, and there is an interesting correspondence in the Bowden Smith papers in the Norfolk Record Office relating to the Bolding family and their vessels. Some of these letters are from Captain Augustine Spaul, who was master of one of William Bolding's ships; he had married Bolding's daughter Mary.

Captain Spaul's ship wandered afar and did not put in at Blakeney very often. In 1789 he was sailing between Sunderland and Rotterdam, and the following year he found himself in Bristol, where he loaded a cargo for Hull. He would be sailing along the Norfolk coast on the way, and promised to hoist an ensign and fire a gun when passing Weybourne; one can imagine the Boldings hearing the bang and running out to see their ship sailing by.[22] The ship is not named in the letters, but an item in the *Norwich Mercury* of 10th November 1798 reports that 'The Elizabeth of Blackney, Austin Spaul master, laden with coal for Rochester, was driven ashore at Horsy in Norfolk; the master was forced off the deck by the violence of the sea, and unfortunately drowned'; it might not be entirely coincidence that Captain Spaul and Mary had set up home in Rochester.

As an example of the wanderings of these vessels there is a report of the brig *Lively* of Cley clearing out at Liverpool on 27th July 1832 for Aberdeen with a cargo of cotton, brimstone, salt and sundries. She went round south, lying off her home port on 6th August. She reached Aberdeen three days later, spent eight days discharging, and then sailed in ballast to Newcastle, 'where she laid a turn of coals for this port' (Cley) of six days. She ultimately made her home port on the 28th, thirty-two days after leaving Liverpool. In the days when a vessel was entirely dependent on wind and tide that was considered a very good piece of work.[23]

The Glaven ports played a vital part in the trade between the North and places like Sheringham, Cromer and Mundesley, whose trade is described in later chapters. Quite often the vessels taking part in the trade on to the beaches came into Blakeney or Cley for shelter when bad weather or an onshore wind made their position uncomfortable. The Blakeney and Cley shipping list in the *Norwich Mercury* for a few weeks in the summer of 1832 contains many an echo of that trade. In the issue of 11th August we find the *Herring* from Cromer Beach in ballast, the *Upcher*, Captain West, from Sheringham Beach in ballast, the *Amos* from Newcastle with coal and the *Commerce*, Captain Rigden, from Seaham Harbour with coal; it is likely that the last two ships were bound for Cromer.

The following week the *Friends' Economy* and the *Hero* arrived from Mundesley with iron, having presumably found conditions too bad to land their cargoes; both subsequently sailed 'for Mundsley with iron and goods' when the weather moderated. At the beginning of October the *Amos* arrived from Cromer Beach in ballast and the *Robert & William* sailed for Sheringham with salt. Later in the same month the *Anna* arrived from Cromer Beach in ballast, along with the *Commerce*, 'from off Cromer Beach with part of her cargo of coals, wind being from the N.E. could not deliver'. And in June 1833 the *Dolphin* arrived from Seaham Harbour with coal and subsequently sailed for Sheringham Beach to deliver her cargo.

The wanderings of a small vessel in the coasting trade can be reconstructed from the crew records preserved in the Suffolk Record Office at Lowestoft. Those for the schooner *Palmers* of Lowestoft, owned in 1871 by her master, George Smith of Bacton, show that in that year she left Lowestoft, where she had laid up for the winter, on 20th March for Hartlepool, arriving two days later. At Hartlepool she loaded coal for Deal, which she unloaded on the beach after a four-day voyage, and she then made a further trip to Deal with coal at the end of April. Returning to Hartlepool, she left on 12th May with a cargo for Walcot, on the Norfolk coast between Happisburgh and Bacton;

on this passage it took her ten days to reach Walcot, which probably means that she was sheltering in the Humber or some other convenient anchorage for several days. Another two trips from Hartlepool to Walcot followed, and then she took two cargoes from Blyth to Walcot and another from Hartlepool to Walcot before sailing to Sunderland to load coal for Deal. Her next cargo was also to Deal, but this time from Hartlepool; then she returned in ballast to Hartlepool, taking a further cargo from there to Kingsdown, about two miles south of Deal. Her last trip that year was from Hartlepool to Hastings, from where she made a fast trip on 14th/15th November to Lowestoft to lay up for the winter.

The following year began badly for the *Palmers* and her crew of Bacton and Walcot men, for she was in trouble after leaving Lowestoft for Hartlepool on 1st April. She collected her cargo all right and was laid on Walcot beach to deliver the coal to James Palmer, the Walcot coal merchant, but then the wind changed to nor'westerly, bringing up a heavy sea. When the wind strengthened to a northerly gale she began to pound, and although she was a relatively new vessel, built at Hartlepool in 1862, fears were expressed for her survival.[24] Survive she did, however, but the damage she received took a whole month to repair once she had been refloated and taken to Yarmouth three weeks later. Only towards the end of May did she resume trading, making three round trips from Hartlepool to Walcot beach, then a voyage from Hartlepool to Blakeney and another to Deal. She got in another trip to Walcot in October and then one to Lowestoft, where she laid up for the winter at the beginning of November.

In 1873 she began by leaving Lowestoft on 17th March and arriving at Hartlepool eight days later, and then making voyages to Kingsdown, Deal, Cromer and Walmer. During this period she was acquired by William Starling, of Blakeney, who on 9th August made an agreement for a voyage from Newcastle to Gothenburg 'and if required to any other port or ports, place or places on the Cattegat, Baltic Sea, Gulfs of Finland and Bothnia, and in the Danish Islands, and back to any port or ports of Call and Discharge in the United Kingdom – probable length of voyage about three Months'. Robert Thurston of Cley was appointed master for this foreign-going voyage, which terminated at Blakeney on 13th September.

Besides knowing all about the navigation of the Baltic Robert Thurston would have required knowledge of the protocol for proceeding through the Sound past the castle of Elsinore, and much else. *The Seaman's Guide and New Coaster's Companion*, compiled by Trinity House pilot John Diston and published in London in 1792, contains the following *Ordinance respecting the Ceremony of Lowering in the Sound*:

> ALL ships sailing through Oresund, whether they come from the North or South, must lower their sails, and keep them lowered full five minutes, to pay proper respect to the castle. The salute is to be made whilst the northernmost church in Elsingoer enters or is concealed behind the castle, coming either from North or South. So that the lowering must not commence before the church goes in behind the castle, and must continue till the church opens itself without the castle again. Every person neglecting this duty

must expect to be compelled, by cannon-shot, to the same, and to be fined, besides, for his contumacy.

There were strict regulations as to which sails were to be lowered and under what circumstances vessels might be exempt from lowering. When they faced a contrary wind or the current was so strong against them that it would set them astern if they lowered their sails, the castle hoisted colours to make it known that no salute was required. Failure to observe the regulations would not only bring a shot from the castle but would involve the master in further trouble.

Tenders, skiffs, inflatables and fishers crowd today's harbour at Blakeney, where once coastal traders shipped goods to and from the quayside warehouses.

> When any vessel has been fired at, then the master or mate, with two of the ship's crew, must go on-shore, and make declaration, on oath, before the court of inquest, for that purpose established, why they have not lowered in the time ordained, or in the manner prescribed. If an oath be required that the lowering was performed in due time and manner, and it is deposed to by the master and his people, then will he be free from paying for the shot fired at him; on the contrary, should they not venture to take the oath, he must then pay, for each shot fired at him from the castle, 5 rix-dollars 20 stivers current; and one ducat for each shot from the guardship's boat, when in pursuit of the ship. – If the master of any vessel should sail away without acquitting himself, when it is proved who the master or ship was, the fine will be demanded of the person who clears him at the custom-house.

The channel at Blakeney snakes across the marshes.

In spite of the clause in the agreement referring to other ports 'on the Cattegat, Baltic Sea, Gulfs of Finland and Bothnia' the *Palmers* seems to have confined her five-week voyage to just the Swedish port of Gothenburg. Had she been going to St. Petersburg or any other Russian port the rigmarole to be undergone would have been many times worse: *The Seaman's Guide and New Coaster's Companion* contains no fewer than four pages of regulations and instructions for 'Masters of Ships and other Persons sailing and coming in Merchant-Men into any Ports or Harbours belonging to the EMPIRE OF RUSSIA, to know how they ought to behave themselves, and what they must observe'.

Having returned from the Baltic the *Palmers* shuttled back and forth between Newcastle and Blakeney, her third round voyage finishing with her arriving in Newcastle on Christmas Day. No longer did she lay up for the winter. Under Capt. R. Holmes, of Blakeney, she spent 1874 sailing mainly between Newcastle and Blakeney, with an occasional voyage to London and in August a trip with coal to Poole in Dorset. From there she went to Runcorn on the Mersey, presumably to pick up a cargo of salt with which she returned to Blakeney; the weather must have been either stormy or a succession of contrary winds, because she took six weeks getting from the Mersey to Norfolk. She made another trip to Runcorn in July-August 1876, and that time took five weeks to get home. The *Palmers* was still in the register at the end of the century, but by then was owned in Sunderland.[25]

As late as the 1860s there were around thirty vessels owned in the ports

A ketch, possibly the *Fiducia*, in Blakeney. Warehouses and granaries can be seen lining the street up from the quay.

The schooner *Minstrel*, owned by John Savory, the Burnham Overy miller, in Blakeney at low water. Lying on the shore is a Colchester smack which had undoubtedly been dredging oysters off the North Norfolk coast.

Coxswain George Long at the tiller, Second Coxswain William Starling alongside him, on the Blakeney lifeboat *Caroline*.

of Cley and Blakeney, several of them being of considerable size and engaged in world-wide trading. At Blakeney Charles Temple had a fleet of six vessels, the largest of them the 291-ton brig *Ann*, built in 1845, and the 182-ton brig *Mignonette*, built in Bristol in 1855. Another Blakeney merchant, John Starling, had three vessels, all of them apparently commanded by members of his family. The Starlings played a notable part in the history of the port of Blakeney, and in 1879 Robert Starling was recorded as being a shipbuilder there.

At Cley James William Porritt, who was a corn, coal and cake merchant and maltster, owned the brig *Tweedside*, which at 254 tons could never have entered her home port; built in Nova Scotia in 1854, she was typical of many vessels launched on the far side of the Atlantic for the British merchant fleet in the mid-nineteenth century. Porritt also had the 177-ton brig *Riga*, built at Dundee in 1846, and the 147-ton barque *Waterloo*, as well as three smaller craft, one a schooner and the other two sloops, engaged in the coasting trade.

A small vessel that sailed from Blakeney for most of her life was the billyboy ketch *Bluejacket*, which was built at Walsoken, a suburb of Wisbech on the Nene, in 1860 and was in her youth owned in Wisbech. She first appeared in Blakeney in 1864, when she paid 7s. 1d. harbour dues, and at some time thereafter she passed into Blakeney ownership. Although undoubtedly a billyboy with bluff bows and a rounded stern, she was carvel built and did not carry leeboards. She might have been slow and have had a reputation as a wet ship, but she was reliable: 'Gundy' Holman, a Blakeney man who had sailed in her, is reported to have said of her that 'She'll starve you but never drown you'.

The only accident known to have befallen her occurred in 1887 when a coal-laden truck dropped into her as she was loading at a coal staithe in Hartlepool, breaking the main beam and doing much other damage. Her master, Barty Pells, arranged for her to be towed back to Blakeney and the necessary repairs were carried out alongside the quay. She sailed on into the twentieth century, and then her masts were taken out and her owners, the Blakeney maltsters and merchants Page & Turner, employed her in the harbour as a lighter until 1911, when she became a houseboat in a mud berth on the west side of Morston Creek.[26]

Some of the larger vessels trading to Blakeney overcame their inability to reach the quay when fully laden by anchoring in the Pit and unloading their cargo into lighters such as the *Glaven*, which was built by Thomas Claxton at Blakeney in 1841. She set two lugsails, a fairly large one on a mast at the fore end of the hold and a smaller one on a short mizzen mast at the aft end, not a very efficient sailplan but sufficient to get her from the Pit up to the quay. Other lighters did not have sails but were pushed along using what would be known on the Broadland rivers as quants.

There was in the first half of the nineteenth century a useful oyster fishery off this part of the coast, but like other local fisheries elsewhere it was depleted when the men of the Colne descended upon it and cleaned up. Nothing much is known about the dredging smacks that worked out of Brancaster, Wells and Blakeney, but it is possible they developed along similar lines to those of the Colne.

The Colchester smacks used Blakeney when working on the north Norfolk oyster beds, and, as was the case at Lynn, local owners acquired some of their craft second hand from the Colne, while others were bought from Yarmouth.

Oyster dredging was certainly going on in 1821, for in that year it was reported that 'an extensive bed of oysters has been discovered off Happisburgh, on the coast of Norfolk, and some hundred tubs of them have already been brought on shore by the Wells fishing smacks'. There were oyster fattening pits at Blakeney and Brancaster, and in 1870 there were eighteen decked Blakeney-owned oyster smacks using Blakeney harbour, as well as fourteen herring luggers owned in Sheringham and Cromer. About that time the total number of fishing boats registered at Blakeney was 300, but this included boats working from the Sheringham-Cromer area.

The last of the Blakeney oyster smacks was the *Pelican*, a double-ended cutter with an overall length of about 25ft., a small cuddy forward and a large after cockpit. Owned by Ted Buck, she last dredged about 1935 using what is remembered as a most temperamental engine.

The shallow tidal harbours along the north Norfolk coast were eminently suitable for the cultivation of mussels, which were raked out of the sand on the mussel scaups and brought ashore to be boiled in coppers either close to the harbour or in the backyards of the fishermen's cottages. The mussel fishermen used a type of craft known in Wells as a flatbottom but in Morston and Blakeney as a canoe, pronounced by their users 'canew'. These were craft of about 15ft. in length and around 3ft. in beam used to carry loads of mussels from the scaups to the Carnser. The sides consisted of three, four or occasionally five planks a side, laid clinker fashion and meeting the almost flat bottom at a chine. The great peculiarity of these boats was the broad heel given to the transom stern, generally about eight or nine inches wide; it provided the necessary buoyancy aft to cope with heavy loads of mussels.

Normally rowed or poled in shallow water, they sometimes set a loose-footed standing lug. They were built all along the coast, and consequently both design and materials varied widely, but elm was preferred for the bottom, with deal for the topsides and oak knees. Frederick Whitaker in Wells built several with a broad heart-shaped transom which were very highly regarded, but the fashion did not catch on.

As late as about 1950 there were still plenty to be seen at Burnham Overy, Wells, Morston and Blakeney, but the type seems now to be extinct. Fortunately an example has been preserved at the Museum of East Anglian Life at Stowmarket, along with some of the tools used by the mussel fishermen.

At Weybourne, where the coastline changes to the cliffs of the Cromer-Holt ridge, the oft-quoted rhyme is:

> He who would old England win,
> Must at Weybourne Hope begin.

The reference is to the deeper water immediately off the beach, which remains a problem for the last of the beach launched fishing boats today. It was certainly considered a possible invasion point in Elizabethan times, when fortifications were planned – but never built – for this stretch of coast. During the Second World War, Weybourne was a base for anti–aircraft artillery training. Post-war there was a plan for a nuclear power station at this point but once again it did not come to fruition.

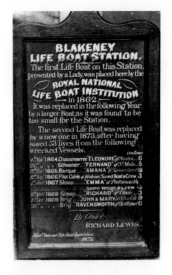

The honours board for the Blakeney lifeboat station. Today the lifeboat house provides an information point for the visitor.

The low-lying coastline of Blakeney and Cley begins to rise into cliffs at Weybourne. Two traditional shaped north Norfolk fishing boats operate from there, the last two of fibreglass construction. The beach remains a very difficult place to launch, with full caterpillar tracks necessary on the launching tractor used.

Sheringham 5

The original village of Sheringham (it used to be spelt Sherringham until about 1870) lay a mile or possibly more from the coast, but at some time a subsidiary settlement inhabited largely by fishermen and others connected with the sea sprang up on the cliff top. At the beginning of the nineteenth century the entire population of both Upper Sheringham, the original settlement, and Lower Sheringham was no more than 392, but growth was rapid and by mid-century there were nearly 1,400 inhabitants, though that total included the paupers in the Erpingham Union Workhouse, which was at Sheringham until replaced by a larger institution at West Beckham in 1849-50. That might not have been the full population, however, for when the 1841 Census was held fifty Sheringham fishermen were away from home, perhaps fishing off the Yorkshire coast.

On the map Lower Sheringham was a rather insignificant place, nowhere near as big as its neighbour Cromer, yet Francis White's directory of 1845 describes it as 'a considerable fishing station' with six curing houses run by Elmer Breeze, John Cooper, John Fox, Sarah Nightingale and Nathaniel Sheldon, and twenty-six fishing boats. It is surprising to read that in the 1840s considerable quantities of crabs and lobsters were being sent from Sheringham to London, possibly by light horse-drawn vans. The little rivulet that had dug out for itself a ravine in the cliffs powered a paper mill operated by Sarah Skipper, and among the inhabitants were two ropemakers and twine spinners who doubtless supplied the fishermen. Within ten years there were said to be twenty-six decked fishing boats and 150 smaller ones. Not only was the village growing into a small town but the fishing was obviously thriving.

There were problems, however. The sea was making inroads into the land even in 1800, for in that year a large inn was undermined and fell in ruins on to the beach; and on St. Thomas's day 1862 a large portion of the cliff was washed away. The process did not stop there, and the urban district council which came into existence in 1901 had to spend many thousands of pounds endeavouring to protect the cliffs from the waves. The population of the urban district at the time of its formation was 2,300, and the place was flourishing as a seaside resort served by the Midland & Great Northern Joint Railway, whose engineer William Marriott had a hand in the development of the growing town. Thirty years later the population had topped 4,000.

The shingle beach beneath the cliff could be a dangerous place for beaching open boats in an onshore wind. The double-ended boats used by the fishermen were rowed through a gap in the offlying bank and when close to the beach were laid broadside to the seas, which would knock them up

Opposite: Towards the end of an era. A line of the traditional double-ended crab boats at the east end, Sheringham, in 1980. Another generation would see this type of vessel retire to the Mo museum rather than be active from the beaches.

This photograph from the latter part of the 19th century gives some impression of the considerable number of boats that operated from the beach at Sheringham at that time.

the beach; the fishermen would then pass the oars through the arruck holes, as they called the oar ports cut in the washstrake, crook one arm round the loom of the oar and with the other arm reach over the washstrake to grasp the 'roosings' inside the boat. With the help of other fishermen they would then carry the relatively light boats up the shelving beach. After the introduction of motors and the increase in size and weight of the boats, winches at the top of the two slipways were used to haul the boats up.

The crab boats became generally known on the coast as Shannocks, taking their name from the nickname borne by the Sheringham fishermen. How the men came by this name is a mystery; some are unkind enough to say that it is derived from the word shanny, used to describe someone who is out of his mind; others say that this dialect word means unruly or venturesome. It is often said that these boats were a development from the basic Scandinavian double-ender, and they have certainly remained basically unchanged in design for a very long time. A map in the Hatfield papers of 1586 shows a double-ended boat like a crabber, and there are many illustrations of them from 1750 onwards. E.W. Cooke drew one which appears hardly to differ from those used 150 years later.

The basic design did not change with the introduction of motors, though motor boats tended to be a little longer, with flatter floors and higher sides than those built in the days of sail. Even when glass-reinforced plastic was introduced into boatbuilding a number of traditional crab boats were built of that material; nevertheless more recently fishermen have acquired craft which owe nothing to local tradition.

A typical crab boat had an overall length of 17-18ft., with a breadth of 7ft.

Fishermen baiting their lines on Sheringham beach, about 1907.

and a depth amidships of 2ft. 9in. The planking was of elm, oak, larch or pine, oak if possible for keel, stem and hog, and ash for timbers; the use of larch made it easier to repair damage caused during use. Grown knees were used wherever possible. There was no gunwale, but the washstrake was topped with a strip of iron to take the chafe of the fishing gear.

The normal rig was a dipping lug, high in the peak and with a very short luff. When close hauled the tack was made fast to a hook on the outside of the stemhead, but when running before the wind it was shifted to a hook inside the sheerstrake a few feet from the bow. The sail was dressed with a mixture that made it almost black. The mast and yard were of spruce or pine, although bamboo was sometimes used for the yard, particularly when racing at regattas. The bamboo was 'wapped' between every web with cotton snooding, which was a very time-consuming business and rough on the hands. The sheet was led through a hole in the top of the sternpost, taken along the boat's side and in through the aftermost arruck hole; it was held in the hand and not made fast, there being no provision for doing so.

With heavier boats, skeets with rollers were used to move the boats across the beach until the winch could be attached.

Before engines were fitted, boats would be carried up the beach.

Fishermen at Sheringham, earlier twentieth century.

Launching facilities at Sheringham have deteriorated over the years; the drop from the slip to the shingle is evident.

Heading off up Morris Street, maybe for winter attention.

The ballast was simply stones from the beach, carried in bags. It had to be trimmed to windward and shifted each time the boat was put about. When fishing, the sail was rolled round the yard and, with the mast, placed forward out of the way of the crew, who would be busy hauling and emptying the pots. The only floorboards fitted were in the stern where the crew stood to haul the pots, or the lines when fishing for ling.

The perils of landing on an open beach in rough seas brought up by an onshore wind were such that through the years there have been many accidents which have resulted in the loss of fishermen as well as boats. Too many times has a boat making for the gap in the offlying bank been overwhelmed by a breaking sea and the men, encumbered by seaboots and oilskins, been drowned within sight of those ashore, but it was not only in such circumstances that disaster struck. In 1807 two boats were dashed to pieces when caught in a sudden gale as they set off and the seven men in them were drowned within fifty yards of the beach they had just left, and a similar disaster occurred in 1836 when another seven people died. They were seventy-five-year-old William Little, forty-four-year-old Cutler Craske and his thirteen-year-old son Nat, twenty-three-year-old John Wilson, and three members of the Bishop family, sixteen-year-old Paul, fourteen-year-old Robert, and twenty-two-year-old James.

Two years later there occurred an accident that led to the Hon. Mrs. Upcher, widow of Abbot Upcher, of Sheringham Hall, providing a lifeboat for use by the town's fishermen. A number of Sheringham fishermen set off on the frosty morning of 14th November, 1838, to salve the rigging from a vessel wrecked on Sheringham Shoal, about five miles out. It was while the salvage work was proceeding that their boat, a large one known locally as a 'twenty-footer', was thrown against the wreck and so damaged that she quickly sank, throwing those on board her into the sea. One man named Cox was drowned, but the others swam to the wreck and took refuge on her mast, where they remained all that day and well into the following night until a Harwich smack came within hailing distance and the smacksmen, hearing their shouts, took them off.

There was great distress in Sheringham, where it was assumed that they had all been lost. It was only after a couple of days that the men were landed at Winterton, from where they set off to walk home. When they reached Sidestrand someone, most likely Miss Anna Gurney, provided a farm wagon for the rest of the journey and sent a horseman ahead to take the good news of their survival to Sheringham. Miss Gurney, who lived at Northrepps Cottage, was an early supporter of the lifesaving services, at one time operating her own team of fishermen-lifesavers whom she provided with equipment.

Mrs. Upcher paid Robert Sunman, the local wheelwright and boatbuilder, £150 for the building in 1838 of a pulling lifeboat on rather similar lines to the local crab boats. This boat was 33ft. 6in. long and 10ft. 2in. in breadth, with a depth of 4ft. 2in., and pulled sixteen oars; like the crab boats she set a dipping lugsail on a single mast. The *Augusta*, given the name of Mrs. Upcher's youngest child who had died two years earlier from tuberculosis, rendered great service to the local fishermen, who were sometimes brought ashore safely by the lifeboat through seas that would have swamped their own boats. No record was kept of her services over fifty-six years, but her first coxswain, Robert Long, has been quoted as saying that it was 'impossible to say how

many lives might have been saved, or how much loss prevented and good done' by Mrs. Upcher's boat.

The story of the wreck of the *Swan*, 26th February 1900, is recalled in this painting and in a series of photographs in the collection at Cromer Museum. The crew were saved – and salvage from the wreck would help through the winter.

Not only was the *Augusta* used to give assistance to the fishermen but she was taken out by her fisherman crew to many merchant vessels in distress on the north Norfolk coast. The first vessel from which she rescued the crew is said to have been a nearly new Russian barque which had been beating about the North Sea for more than two weeks and was so completely lost that when the captain sighted Blakeney church with its lofty tower and its turret above the nave he took it for Dover castle. The crew of this vessel were reported to have insisted that they were in no need of help, but after the lifeboat had followed the ship for some distance they thought better of it and the seventeen men were taken off safely.

Abbot Upcher had bought the Sheringham estate in 1812 and had begun the building of Sheringham Hall, which was incomplete when he died in 1819. His son Henry Ramey Upcher took a considerable interest in the welfare of the local seafarers, not only supporting the work of the *Augusta* but encouraging the fishermen to obtain larger decked craft in which to carry on their fishing activities.

It seems that he advanced the money for the purchase of these boats, the fishermen repaying him out of the profits of the fishing, and it may be that he was responsible for the Sheringham men acquiring the 'Great Boats', the fishermen's name for the big decked luggers that came into use in the 1830s and 1840s. Most of the great boats were built in the Yarmouth boatyards that turned out such fishing craft in great numbers for the North Sea fisheries,

One of the series of photos of the *Swan*, probably used by the artist to help with his painting.

A Sheringham fish auction, by Stanley Barwell.

though three of them, the *Admiral, Adriel* and *George*, were built at Sheringham between 1837 and 1842. In addition to those Arthur Purchas, who searched the Wells shipping registers then in the Customs House at King's Lynn, gives the names of a trio of three-masted luggers built at Sheringham in 1835; the *Anna Mary, Seagull* and *New Henry* were all 32ft. long and 11ft. in beam.

The majority of the great boats were owned in Sheringham, with a dozen or so being owned in Cromer and others in Runton, Overstrand and Northrepps. Some of them were bought second hand from their Yarmouth owners, and some were sold back to Yarmouth later in their lives. They were in fact very similar to the Yarmouth luggers used for the herring fishing, and were rigged with a large dipping lug mainsail and a small standing lug mizzen. Like the Yarmouth boats they were converted into dandies about the 1870s, setting a loose-footed fore-and-aft sail (with no boom) on the mainmast but retaining the standing lug on the mizzen. By the 1890s the fleet numbered only eleven, four luggers and seven dandies, one of them converted from a lugger and the rest of them built as dandies in the 1870s and 80s.

In these craft the Shannocks would sail off down the North Sea in summer long-lining for cod, working out of Grimsby. They used to take crab boats on deck for working the lines, which they baited with 'lamper eels' brought alive in tubs from Holland. They also went crabbing off the Yorkshire coast from the last week of March until June or July, using a crab boat to help work the pots. On many of those voyages the Shannocks brought back with them live crabs which were planted on the home grounds to replenish the local stock; light brown crabs caught by the Shannocks were always referred to as 'Yorkshiremen'. The Shannocks in their great boats also followed the herrings

A two master Yarmouth lugger c.1859, drawn by Martin Warren after E.J. March – one of the 'Great Boats'.

from Scarborough and then came south to take part in the autumn herring fishing alongside the Yarmouth driftermen and the Dutch fleets.

When I was first making inquiries about fishing in north Norfolk in the 1950s I called to see 'Teapot' West, who was then in his eighties and could remember the last of the great boats. He recalled for me the *Great Paragon*, built at Yarmouth in 1858 and sold to Norway for £75 complete with sails and gear when the fishing failed, and the *Endeavour*, which holed herself on her anchor when laid up for the winter in Blakeney. Then there was the *New Walter and Ann*, built as far back as 1840 and still owned by the West family at Sheringham more than thirty years later.

Others, too, passed on stories that they had heard from their elders years before. Life must have been far from comfortable when fishing away from home, but the Shannocks made light of the discomforts; one who had sailed in the great boats told of 'eating dogfish fried in tallow candles' almost as a joke, and enjoyed recounting the story of a cook aboard a lugger who boiled a suet dumpling in a piece of tanned sailcloth, to the detriment of the pudding.

The names of others of the great boats were still remembered fifty-odd years ago: the *Paragon* – not to be confused with the *Great Paragon* already mentioned – built at Yarmouth in 1844 and owned by the West family; the *Robert & Henry*, another belonging to the Wests, built at Cobholm in 1877 and blown ashore at Morston; the *Welcome Messenger*; the *Gratitude*; two boats named *Liberty*, one owned by a member of the Craske family at Sheringham and the other owned at Runton; and the Cromer luggers *Olive Branch*, *Providence* and *Sea Nymph*. Many other names are to be found in old registers.

The luggers and dandies were too big to be hauled up the beach like the crab boats, and they returned home only twice or three times a year, to land their gear before being laid up in Blakeney haven or Yarmouth harbour or to exchange long lines or crab pots for drift nets before taking part in the autumn herring fishing. At such times a fleet of great boats might be seen lying at anchor off Sheringham as crab boats brought pots or lines ashore and ferried out the drift nets which had been made ready in net stores in the town.

There were eight great boats lying off Sheringham when the 'October Gale' of 29th October 1880 broke over them. The crews made haste to get under way and make for the open sea, but as they did so one of the boats, the *Gleaner*, was struck by a huge wave that carried away mast and sail and overturned the boat. The *Gleaner* drifted ashore bottom-up beneath the cliff at Beeston; her skipper-owner, George 'Coaches' Craske, and the entire crew of ten or eleven men were lost. 'Teapot' West told me how an old man known as 'Claw' Fields was lowered from the cliff top to ascertain which of the boats had been wrecked.

In the same gale a 25-year-old fisherman, William Balls, was lost from the lugger *Egmere*. On his gravestone in Cromer old cemetery is the epitaph:

> My sails are split, my anchors gone,
> My soul hath fled the deck;
> And here beneath this cold damp stone
> My body lies a wreck.

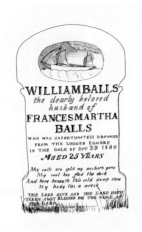

The gravestone of William Balls, drawn by Martin Warren.

Lenny West, young 'Teapot', continues to show the traditional way to make crab pots – though the materials have changed over time.

The last of the great boats to be owned in north Norfolk was the *Thalia*, built by S.C. Allerton at Lowestoft in 1886 and owned at the turn of the century by Walter Haylett, of Caister. She was bought by Philip Wells of Sheringham in 1905 or thereabouts and was employed by him in crab fishing and lining for cod for five or six years until being transferred to Hull registry in 1911. She passed to Lowestoft registry in 1917 and was wrecked on the Sunk Sand off the Essex coast in December 1918.

The Sheringham lifeboats

The fishermen's lifeboat *Augusta* did some excellent work, and it is unfortunate that no record was made of her services. She performed a useful if unspectacular service on 21st May 1845 when she picked up the crew of the *Alpha* of North Shields after they had abandoned their vessel on the Sheringham Shoal. The fishermen in the *Augusta* fortunately won a race to get to the boat before it reached the shore; it was heavily laden with eight men and boys and two female passengers who had scrambled out of their beds in their nightclothes, and the crew of the *Augusta* knew that it would almost certainly be swamped by the breakers brought up by a heavy NNE gale as it approached the beach.[1]

As it was, people ashore waved the lifeboat off from its usual landing place because the sea was breaking against the cliff, and the rescued people had to be landed at the east of the town. The Norfolk Association for Saving the Lives of Shipwrecked Mariners awarded the crew of the lifeboat £15 for this service.[2]

In 1866 the RNLI made up its mind to open a station at Sheringham and built a 'commodious and substantial boat house with a reading room above it for the use of the fishermen' at the east end of the town, and the following year a 36ft. self-righting lifeboat was placed on station. Built by Forrestt of Limehouse, the *Duncan* was brought by the Great Eastern Railway to Fakenham and from there was hauled on her carriage to Sheringham by road; the railway had not then reached Sheringham. It is significant that when it opened the station the RNLI expressed its indebtedness to Henry Ramey Upcher, who seems to have been prepared to support not only the *Augusta* but also the Institution boat. Possibly that is why there was at Sheringham none of the intense rivalry that existed at some other places where there was both a private lifeboat and a 'National' boat.

Both the *Duncan* and the *Augusta* seem to have been launched on 3rd December 1867, when the schooner *Hero* of Maldon was blown ashore at Beeston in a particularly severe gale that saw nine other lifeboats in Norfolk and Suffolk engaged in rescue work. The *Duncan* was credited with saving three men from the *Hero* and another man was brought ashore by the lifesaving apparatus, which was also used to save the master and his wife and crew from the billyboy schooner *Jane & Margaret* of Goole. A contemporary report of the wreck makes no mention of the fishermen's lifeboat, but an account of the *Augusta*'s services published to commemorate the launching of her successor credited her with saving seven from the *Hero*; that could have been a mere error of someone's memory.[2]

Between 1867 and 1886 the *Duncan* was launched a dozen times and saved eighteen lives, then she was replaced by a larger self-righting boat, the

The *Augsuta* was replaced by the *Henry Ramey Upcher*; still to be seen in her boathouse.

William Bennett, which like the *Duncan* was built by Forrestt at Limehouse. The *Duncan* served rather less than twenty years at Sheringham, but the *Augusta* remained in service for more than half a century, during which time she never lost a member of her crew. By the end of that time she was, however, showing signs of age; her planks had been fastened with iron nails and after so many years those nails had rusted badly so that she was suffering from nailsickness.

Hearing that the old *Augusta* was coming to the end of her active life, Mrs. Caroline Upcher, the daughter-in-law of her donor, let it be known that she would provide a new boat as a memorial to her husband, Henry Ramey Upcher, who had died in 1892. It was at Mrs. Upcher's invitation that a meeting of the fishermen was held on 3rd November 1893 to discuss the design of a new boat. There was general agreement that the new boat should be similar in design to the old one, but with more breadth – and with copper fastenings.

It is interesting that an account of the building of the new boat has survived, telling how Lewis Emery laid the keel in a temporary shed erected on the cliff to the north-west of the *Augusta*'s boathouse. That keel was cut from a perfect beam of American oak, purchased in Yarmouth, 'without chick, knot or worm throughout its entire length'.[3] For five months Lewis Emery and his son Robert, together with a workman named Harry Diver from Yarmouth, worked on the boat, helped from time to time by Lewis Emery's brother George and his other two sons, James and Ben, and a number of other local men. The work was, we are told, 'carried on without interruption or accident of any kind, and seldom for long without the faces of fishermen or other interested spectators looking in at the unglazed windows of the shed'. The building of

Society photographer Olive Edis took wonderful portraits of the fishermen of Sheringham. She sometimes used the early ambrotype colour process, as with this photograph of 'Belcher' Johnson.

A scouring tide will every now and again uncover the bones of the *Ispolen*; part of one of her sides remains.

the new lifeboat was clearly something of a labour of love, for towards the end
the men arrived in the shed at daybreak and worked until dark to ensure that
the boat was ready for launching on the appointed day.

The end of the temporary shed was removed to enable the boat to be
taken out for her launching on 4th September 1894, when she was named
Henry Ramey Upcher. Within little more than a month the new boat was out
on service, escorting the town's crab boats ashore. While she was doing so the
wind and sea rose suddenly; the coxswain, Barnes Cooper, described the sea
as being 'as high as he'd ever seen it'. Of the thirty-seven services recorded on
the boards in the Upcher boathouse, no fewer than twenty-five involved the
local fishing boats.

It was not only when they were afloat that Sheringham lifeboatmen were
in danger from storms, for in 1870 and again seven years later heavy seas
washed away the slipway down which the RNLI boat had to be launched. Then
in 1897 an onshore gale that is said to have carried spray fifty yards into the
town undermined the cliff and brought an extension to the Crown Hotel down
on to the beach, blocking the slipway. In that same gale a Norwegian brig was
in serious trouble off the town.

The captain of the *Ispolen* sought help from a steamer that was riding
uneasily somewhere off Sheringham, but the Norwegians could not make
themselves heard above the roar of the wind. It seems that what they wanted to
know was the whereabouts of the nearest lifeboat station, for the captain had
been wrecked twice before in the previous three years and, resigning himself
to the loss of his vessel, he was anxious to preserve the lives of his crew, and
his own, if he could. Seeing a town to leeward, he turned his ship towards it.

In Sheringham the fishermen threw open the doors of the boathouse and
brought out the *Henry Ramey Upcher*, getting her to the beach and afloat in a
very short time. In fact, the fishermen's lifeboat was taking the crew out of the
Ispolen before the launchers could get the RNLI boat into the water.

Faced with the difficulties of launching the boat the local RNLI committee placed the *William Bennett* 'temporarily' on the East Roadway. She remained there until in 1902 she was moved to the Old Hythe, to the west of the town, where she still stood out in the open. It was only when a new boat, the *J.C. Madge*, was sent to the station in 1904 that a boathouse of corrugated steel was put up and a timber slipway constructed at the Old Hythe.

Whereas both the *Duncan* and her successor had been self-righting boats the *J.C. Madge* was a non-self-righting boat of the Liverpool type, built by the Thames Iron Works at Blackwall at a cost of £1,436. She and the fishermen's lifeboat were kept busy not only aiding the local fishing boats but also assisting the big sailing barges that took over so much of the east coast trade from the brigs and schooners of the nineteenth century. In January 1906 the *J.C. Madge* saved three people from E.J. & W. Goldsmith's spritsail barge *Gothic*, one of a group of steel barges built for the Grays, Essex, firm in 1903-4, and the *Henry Ramey Upcher* rescued the crew of the same firm's *Teutonic*, whose sails had been carried away by the gale. The RNLI awarded seven shillings and sixpence to each of the crew of the fishermen's lifeboat for that rescue. Having landed the men of the *Gothic* the *J.C. Madge* went out again and salvaged the barge, and three years later she saved another Goldsmith barge, the sprittie *Lord Moreton*, and her crew of three; the *Henry Ramey Upcher* was also launched to the *Lord Moreton*.

One almost wonders if the Sheringham lifeboatmen had an informal contract with Goldsmiths, for in 1924 the *J.C. Madge* saved another of their Dutch-built barges, the *Oceanic*, and her three-man crew. In 1933, in the same gale in which the sprittie *Sepoy* was wrecked at Cromer, the *J.C. Madge* went to the help of the mulie barge *Fred Everard*, one of four big steel barges built for F.T. Everard & Sons by Fellows at Yarmouth, which had gone ashore near the entrance to Blakeney harbour. The crew of the barge ignored the lifeboatmen's signals, so the Sheringham men put the lifeboat ashore at Morston and returned home by bus.

It was not the only time the lifeboatmen were ignored in this way, for in November 1914, when the *J.C. Madge* went to the assistance of the *ss Vera*, aground on Cley beach in a heavy gale and a rough sea, the captain of the grounded ship refused to answer the lifeboatmen's signals. The lifeboatmen assumed that the crew had been taken ashore, so they returned to their station, having an extremely rough return journey.

In fact the crew were still on board and were brought ashore the next morning by the Cley lifesaving apparatus team, assisted by some fishermen from Sheringham. The captain later said that he felt it would have been impossible for the lifeboat to have reached the ship in the darkness and he feared it would have been knocked to pieces if an attempt had been made to bring it alongside, so he thought it better not to answer the lifeboatmen's signals.

During more than thirty years at Sheringham the *J.C. Madge* won not only the confidence but the affection of her crew, and it was with mixed feelings that the men heard that she was to be replaced by the town's first motor lifeboat in 1936. Appropriately enough, the old boat's last service on 2nd April 1936 was to a fishing boat called the *Little Madge*; she saved the boat and her two fishermen, bringing her tally of lives saved to fifty-eight.

All those with the slightest interest in maritime history will make their way to The Mo museum at Sheringham. There the restored lifeboats *Foresters Centenary* and *J.C.Madge* are just two of the exhibits amongst the fishing and lifeboat memorabilia.

Her replacement, built at Cowes in the Isle of Wight by Groves & Guttridge, was a 35ft. 6in. motor lifeboat of the Liverpool type subscribed for by members of the Ancient Order of Foresters friendly society and named *Foresters Centenary*. With a single screw and a petrol engine the new boat cost £3,569, more than ten times as much as the *Duncan* had cost in 1867. Another £7,616 was spent on a new boathouse and slipway on the promenade at the western side of the town, with a turntable so that the lifeboat on its carriage could be swung round to face the sea.

The day of the pulling and sailing lifeboat in which the Norfolk lifeboatmen had done such fine work was coming to an end: Wells and Sheringham both received motor boats in 1936, Cromer had had one since 1923, Great Yarmouth and Gorleston since 1924, and Caister would get a motor boat in 1941. The stations at Hunstanton, Brancaster, Blakeney, Mundesley, Bacton, Happisburgh and Palling had all closed by 1936. The motor lifeboats could

The Oddfellows friendly society has been very generous to the Sheringham lifeboat station. The last of the offshore boats bore the proud name *Manchester Unity of Oddfellows.*

both cover a wider area than the old pulling and sailing boats and accomplish rescues that would have been well-nigh impossible under sail and oar.

The outbreak of war in 1939 brought new challenges and additional dangers for the crew of the Sheringham lifeboat, who had been called out three times to search for missing airmen by the end of that year. One of the calls came when a German seaplane crashed into the sea, but no survivors were found. The third call resulted from a disastrous raid by Wellington bombers from East Anglian bases during which no fewer than fifteen of the aircraft were lost, one of them crashing into the sea in the area of the Cromer Knoll. In spite of a search in which the Sheringham boat was joined by lifeboats from Wells and Cromer and by an RAF air-sea rescue launch and a naval vessel, no trace could be found of the ditched airmen.

Lifeboats between Wells and Aldeburgh were called out more than a hundred and fifty times to aircraft down in the sea, airmen seen coming down by parachute, or sightings of rubber dinghies during those wartime years, yet no more than thirty-six airmen were saved, and almost half that number were picked up by the Sheringham men. Their first success came on 21st October 1940, when the crew of the *Foresters Centenary* found five men, soaked to the skin but otherwise uninjured, from a British bomber that had ditched near Blakeney. The airmen were treated to brandy and chocolate from the lifeboat's emergency rations as the boat returned to Sheringham, where they were able to have hot baths and a change of clothes before enjoying a meal at the home of lifeboat secretary Mr. H.R. Johnson as they awaited the arrival of a lorry from their station at Linton-on-Ouse in Yorkshire.

It was not only British airmen who owed their lives to the Sheringham lifeboat, for a year later it was five Polish flyers who were rescued. The landlord of the Crown Inn, Charlie Holsey, was wiping glasses behind his bar and held one up to the light to make sure that there were no smears on the glass; it was a matter of pride that glasses were never less than glistening when he handed one to a customer. It was as he held it up to the light that his keen eye picked out a tiny speck on the sea a couple of miles offshore. It had been a foggy morning, but as the landlord's eyes strayed to the window the sun broke through, lighting up that tiny speck. Putting the glass down, the landlord fetched his telescope and with its aid made out men on what he took to be a raft; in fact it was a rubber dinghy.

Just at that moment the second coxswain of the *Foresters Centenary*, John 'Sparrow' Hardingham, came in for his lunchtime glass of beer. Without waiting for his beer he ran off to call other members of the crew and to prepare the boat for launching. It took twenty minutes for the lifeboat to reach the dinghy with its five occupants, survivors of a crew of six. Seasick and soaked, they had been tossing in their dinghy for seventeen hours after their aircraft had ditched.[4] They were brought safely back to the lifeboat station at Sheringham

The lifeboatmen were ably backed up by a shore organisation that swung into operation on such occasions. The workings of that network of ordinary people can be illustrated by an account of the happenings of 30th October 1942, when the Coastguard rang the honorary secretary just before seven in the morning to report that a Handley-Page Halifax four-engined bomber

The rescue of her crew by the Sheringham lifeboat was just one amongst many adventures that befell the *Eaglescliffe Hall.*

had crashed into the sea off West Runton. Within minutes the Coastguard was back on the phone to say that he could see men on the sinking aircraft.[5]

Mr. Johnson had his telephone beside the bed. Without pausing to get out of bed he rang Coxswain Jimmy Dumble, and as soon as he had done that he called his daughter to run to the home of the winchman, another Johnson, to warn him to hasten to the boathouse and prepare to launch. Having done that he rang the two motor mechanics, the bicycle messengers who called the other members of the crew, and the officer in command of a company of locally based soldiers who acted as launchers; many of those local men who in peacetime had acted as launchers had gone into the Navy or into the other services, and the soldiers had stepped into the breach. Two minutes later he heard those soldiers going by at the double.

The soldiers did not have an easy task. The tide was low and the lifeboat had to be dragged on her carriage across a sandbank over which the sea was flowing before it was possible to launch her into deep water, yet the *Foresters Centenary* was on her way only twenty-one minutes after that first call from the Coastguard. By the time Coxswain Dumble gave the signal to haul the boat off her carriage the launchers were all in the sea up to their waists, and some of them up to their necks. It took the lifeboat a quarter of an hour to reach the sinking bomber and to pick up the six Polish airmen from their dinghy, and another quarter-hour to return to its station and land the rescued men.

In the meantime Mr. Johnson had been far too busy to get out of bed. As soon as he had arranged the despatch of the lifeboat he had telephoned two doctors asking them to go to the boathouse and had arranged for an ambulance to stand by on the cliff top above the boathouse in case any of the airmen were injured. That done, he made four calls to neighbours asking them to have hot baths ready for the rescued men. In twenty-six minutes he received or made twenty-one telephone calls.

Then he got up. In another ten minutes he was on the seafront with his telescope, just in time to see the lifeboat coming alongside the rubber dinghy. His work was by no means over. With the return of the lifeboat he rang the Coastguard to report that six airmen had been rescued, then he arranged breakfast for the rescued men. While they were eating their breakfast the boat went out again to tow in the aircraft, but found that it had already drifted ashore. Immediately she returned the lifeboat was hauled into the boathouse, the fuel tanks were replenished and the engines re-oiled, the plugs taken out to drain her and the ropes all coiled down. She was ready for her next service.

Because of the need for speed when dealing with crashed aircraft the *Foresters Centenary* was sometimes launched to stand by as the great bomber fleets returned from raids on Germany and Occupied Europe. Minutes, even seconds, counted when aircrew were thrown into the sea as their aircraft sank. On one occasion a four-engined Boeing B-17 of the 8th United States Army Air Force crashed into the sea off Sheringham and sank in about seven minutes. As the lifeboat crew assembled and the launchers were dragging the *Foresters Centenary* into the water six fishermen dragged one of their light motor crab boats down the beach and managed to pick up the ten members of the Fortress's crew, some from their inflatable dinghy and others from the water.

The efforts made by the lifeboat crew to rescue ditched airmen not unnaturally led to friendship between them and aircrew stationed at nearby bases. A wartime publicity photograph showed Coxswain Dumble, in oilskins and sou'wester, being assisted into an Avro Anson at Bircham Newton preparatory to a flight. Jimmy Dumble was awarded the RNLI Bronze Medal in 1941 for his part in the rescue of fifteen men from the Canadian ship *Eaglescliffe Hall* off Cley. When he retired in 1947 after twenty-two years as coxswain he was succeeded by John 'Sparrow' Hardingham, who must have been the only coxswain to retire from the post while at sea in the lifeboat.

The flat profile of the *Wimbledon* enabled her to pass under the bridges on the Thames as she made her way up with coal for the gasworks.

The *Foresters Centenary* had been called to the aid of a Dutch vessel late in the night of 31st December 1950, and was returning from the casualty when, at one minute past midnight, 'Sparrow' turned to his second coxswain, 'Downtide' West, and told him 'You're in charge now!'

'Downtide' was coxswain for twelve years and won the RNLI Silver Medal for a rescue carried out on 31st October 1956 in collaboration with the Wells lifeboat *Cecil Paine*, like the *Foresters Centenary* a Liverpool type boat but built nine years later with twin engines. The steamer *Wimbledon*, a 'flatiron' upriver collier used by the South-Eastern Gas Board to supply London's gasworks with coal, was on her way from Sunderland for London when she sent out a radio message saying that she was taking water and required assistance. A fresh nor'easterly gale was blowing and the vessel was rolling heavily with the seas sweeping right across her decks. Water was entering the gooseneck air pipe of no. 1 starboard tank, and waves washing across the foredeck thwarted the attempts of crew members to plug the pipe. Another collier, Stephenson Clarke's *Eleanor Brooke*, was standing by, but there was little she could do to help.

It was at 8.20am that the honorary secretary received a message from the Coastguard at Cromer telling him that a vessel was in serious trouble some thirteen miles off the coast. The maroons were fired to call the lifeboat crew, but several of the crew members were away helping to lift the sugar beet crop and other volunteers took their places. Heavy seas were breaking on the beach as the *Foresters Centenary* was launched just after nine.

Having been told of a message from the MV *Sydenham*, another 'flatiron' collier belonging to the South-Eastern Gas Board, saying that she was also standing by and the *Wimbledon* was making for the shore at Blakeney, Coxswain West set course for the Blakeney bell buoy, and in due course sighted the three ships. The *Wimbledon*'s problems were by no means over, though.

Realising that if the ship were to be saved the air pipe had to be plugged, the ship's master, Captain Arthur Hill, decided that he must tackle the job himself. It was an attempt that would cost him his life. As he made his way forward a huge wave carried him over the side. He was picked up by the *Eleanor Brooke*, but the crew's endeavours to resuscitate him proved fruitless. In desperation a call was made for a doctor to be flown out by helicopter, but it was all in vain. The RAF doctor who was lowered to the deck of the *Eleanor Brooke* by a search and rescue helicopter from RAF Coltishall, north of Norwich, could only confirm that the captain was dead.

Taking over command after the loss of the master, the chief officer of the *Wimbledon* decided to anchor in the lee of Blakeney overfalls rather than to beach the ship. When 'Downtide' brought the *Foresters Centenary* alongside eight men transferred to the lifeboat, the rest remaining on board in hopes of saving the vessel. Realising that he might have to return to the *Wimbledon* later, 'Downtide' considered it wise to put the rescued men aboard one of the ships that were standing by. And when a message came asking for the RAF doctor and Captain Hill's body to be taken ashore the coxswain felt it necessary to request the launching of the Wells lifeboat to perform that service and at the same time to bring out extra fuel for his own boat.

Coxswain West had made the right decision. By the time the *Cecil Paine* had transferred cans of petrol to the Sheringham boat and had taken the doctor and the captain's body off the *Eleanor Brooke* the chief officer of the *Wimbledon* had realised that the time had come to abandon ship, for the whole of the forepart of the vessel was awash and seas were breaking against the bridge structure. The *Wimbledon* was head to the seas and neither side offered anything of a lee; getting the men off would not be a simple operation.

'Downtide' brought the boat up the starboard side and two ropes were made fast, but only two men had jumped into the lifeboat before the lines parted. Each time the lifeboat was brought alongside fresh lines were made fast, and each time they parted. As he circled and brought the lifeboat alongside once more the coxswain realised that in those confused seas no ropes would hold the boat in position. The coxswain and the motor mechanic, Teddy Craske, had to work closely together to hold the boat in position by using the engine as the *Wimbledon* settled lower and lower in the water. Seas flooded the cockpit and the mechanic was at times up to his armpits in water, with the radio-telephone microphone held above his head to keep it clear of the water.

As the two men worked to hold the lifeboat alongside, a heavy sea lifted her almost on to the submerged deck of the *Wimbledon* and part of the lifeboat's fendering was torn away, but at last the job was completed and the tenth man was dragged into the boat. Four were transferred to the *Sydenham* before the *Foresters Centenary* made for Wells with the remaining six, one of whom had a severe head injury. As the *Cecil Paine* put out to escort the Sheringham boat into harbour the *Wimbledon* slipped beneath the waves.

Photographer Reuben Saidmen was dispatched from London to take this wartime photo of the crew of the *Foresters Centenary*.

Not only did 'Downtide' earn the Silver Medal that day but 'Teddy' Craske gained the Bronze Medal; the other members of the crew all received the Institution's thanks on vellum.

Coxswain West and other members of the lifeboat crew were members of the Independent Order of Odd Fellows, Manchester Unity, and they were very keen that when the *Foresters Centenary* came to the end of her service she should be replaced by a boat bearing the name of their organisation. 'Downtide' worked very hard to encourage his fellow members to raise the money to buy the new boat, and when in 1961 the old boat reached retirement her place was taken by a boat bearing the name *The Manchester Unity of Odd Fellows*. A large part of the £28,500 that she cost to build was subscribed by members.

Built by W. Osborne at Littlehampton, the new boat was one of a new generation designed by Mr. R.A. Oakley, who had joined the RNLI in 1928 and had become its Surveyor of Lifeboats in 1940. When the first of the Oakley type entered service in 1958 at Scarborough it introduced a new concept to the lifeboat service: unlike the Liverpool type it would right itself if capsized, and at the same time it avoided the disadvantages of the 35ft. 6in. self-righters, of which there were still five in service at that time.

The self-righting capacity was gained through an ingenious system of shifting water ballast, a ton and a half of seawater being automatically taken into a bottom tank as the boat entered the water. Should the boat turn over the water ballast was transferred through non-return valves to a righting tank on the port side, and the weight of water in the righting tank brought the boat upright in seconds. As she came upright the righting tank emptied and fresh ballast was taken into the bottom tank. In tests it was found that the Oakley boats had greater initial stability than the Liverpool boats they replaced.

Boats under construction at Emery's shed – one above the other. The Emery collection of tools and a reconstruction of the workshop can be seen at The Mo museum in Sheringham.

Boatbuilders and migrants

History does not record the name of the builder of the great boats launched at Sheringham, but the only boatbuilder to appear in local directories at that time is Robert Sunman, who combined the trades of boatbuilder and wheelwright. Some time in the 1850s his place was taken by Leonard Lown, who was both carpenter and boatbuilder, and about the same time Lewis 'Buffalo' Emery began a boatbuilding business on Lifeboat Plain in a shed that had begun life as a fishing store in the days of the great boats. Lewis Emery was followed by three further generations of his family: Robert Emery continued to build boats in the two-storey building until the 1950s.[6]

Leonard Lown was succeeded by Henry Lown, presumably his son, who remained in the business until 1906 when the Cremer Street premises were taken over by 'Johnny' Johnson, who had learnt his boatbuilding skills from the Lowns. He retired in 1950 and died ten years later at the age of seventy-five.

A surprising number of boats were turned out by these men: 'Johnny' Johnson was credited with having built about 130 in a career of forty-four years. The largest boat built by Johnson was a 33ft. half-decked fishing yacht, the *Three Sisters*, for Raymond Quilter, of Bawdsey. It is said that 'Caller' Emery, so called because of his curly hair, would sometimes have a whelker

Boat-builder 'Johnny' Johnson.

under construction on the lower floor of the Lifeboat Plain shed and two crab boats building on the upper floor. The crab boats would be 'launched' out of the big doors at the end of the first floor and taken down to the gangway on a trolley. The boats went to owners at Cromer and Wells as well as to more local fishermen.

Robert Emery's son, who took over the business on his father's death in 1959, continued for some years to repair the local boats but no further boats were built at Sheringham. In the mid-twentieth century a number of crab boats were built to the traditional design by the Worfolk brothers at King's Lynn, and others were built on the Broads at Potter Heigham.

Besides crab boats the Sheringham builders produced a rather larger but similar boat known as a hubbler or hoveller, with a length of about 15ft. on the keel. The name suggests that originally these might have been employed in attending on shipping and in salvage work in much the same way as the yawls of the beach companies further along the coast, though there is no record of such an organisation in Sheringham, nor is there any oral evidence of them having been employed in this way. They are known only to have been used for herring and mackerel fishing and for lining.

Old men at Sheringham used to recall cod being laid out on the beach for auction when the hovellers returned from a fishing trip. Each boat's catch was laid out close to the boat and the fisherman would act as his own auctioneer; when he failed to get another bid he would bang two beach cobbles together to indicate a sale. Peter Catling told me that this type of sale took place on Cley beach in the early 1930s when a crab boat had been long-lining.[7]

The hovellers had a removable cuddy forward in which the crew could sleep when working from Yarmouth in the herring fishery. When this was shipped for the herring fishing the forward arruck holes would be blocked with plugs cut from the flat corks used on herring nets and crab-pot tows; this was considered more reliable than a wooden plug, being more elastic and more waterproof.

The last of the hovellers were fitted with motors in the 1920s, and by the middle of the twentieth century the type had disappeared from Sheringham beach, but from them were developed the big clinker-built whelkers employed at Wells for the flourishing whelk fishery, said to have been introduced to Wells by fishermen who moved to that port from Sheringham. In the days of motors the whelkers were as much as 30ft. long with a beam of some 10ft. 9in.

Perhaps because of their experience in the great boats the Shannocks proved great travellers, settling with their boats in places as far apart as Whitstable and Grimsby. There were in the early twentieth century seventeen of the little crab boats to be seen moored in the lock pit at the entrance to the fish docks at Grimsby,[8] and the crew of the Grimsby lifeboat was composed entirely of Sheringham men up to the time the station was closed in 1927. It is said that there was something of a reunion at Grimsby in 1916 when the Sheringham lifeboat *J.C. Madge* escorted the ss *Uller* into the Humber. Shannocks also settled at Spurn and Withernsea in the Holderness area of Yorkshire and at Hornsea in Lincolnshire: around 1900 there were at least half a dozen crab boats at each of these places.

A Sheringham fisherman who sailed for some years with the Grimsby fishing fleet, eventually gaining his skipper's ticket, was Walter Little. After his deep-sea experience he returned to his home town and became a member of the Sheringham lifeboat crew, but in 1920 he moved with his crab boats to the Suffolk resort of Felixstowe. When in the 1930s W.M. Blake was making plans of fishing and coastal craft for the Society for Nautical Research it was one of Walter Little's boats, the *Star of Peace*, built by Robert Emery in 1912 for the sum of £19 2s. 6d., that he chose as an example of a north Norfolk crab boat.

Around 1904 a group of fishermen moved from Sheringham with their families and their boats to Whitstable, on the southern shore of the Thames Estuary, where they engaged in whelk fishing, working their boats off the beach. According to Derrick West, grandson of one of the migrating fishermen, five families settled in the Kent port, which was known for its oyster fishery.[9] The whelks, caught in pots off Whitstable and Herne Bay, used to be boiled ashore and then sent to Billingsgate market by rail. The Whitstable boatbuilding firm of Anderson, Rigden & Perkins produced a number of boats on the lines of the traditional crab boats for members of the Sheringham families, the last one being the *Floreat* (F91) in 1959.

In 2012 there are about 50 commercial fisherman working from the north Norfolk beaches in the crab and lobster fisheries. Within a generation a long line of family tradition has been broken as the next generation has moved away from this hazardous and difficult way of earning a living. Sheringham itself is no longer the favoured location for the full-time fisherman; in general the Runton, Sheringham and Overstrand boats have moved to Cromer where the beach is much easier to work.

Even more startling has been the change in the type of boat used. The traditional double-ender, once rowed or sailed on and off the beach and in the 20th century provided with an inboard engine, has nearly gone. The coming of powerful outboard engines and the economics of needing to pay a crew has resulted in the change of most of the commercial boats to single handed skiffs, with the efficiency of the engines enabling the fisherman to make the beach in greater safety. The balance has been the danger of single handed working, with no assistance to call for aid in the event of a mishap at sea.

The construction of the Sheringham Shoal wind farm has seen a wide variety of specialist vessels working off the town.

Cromer   6

In spite of not having enjoyed the advantage of a conventional harbour for some hundreds of years, Cromer had a long history as a fishing and trading port. Whether it ever had 'a real harbour with a heavy-timbered pierhead ... with rough stone walls clumsily contrived and repaired again and again in our obstinate English fashion', as described by Walter Rye in the introduction to his *Cromer, Past and Present* (1889), is open to question, but the town certainly has not had what we would understand as a sheltered harbour since the town of Shipden was overcome by the sea in, perhaps, the fourteenth century.

Shipden is commonly supposed to be a lost town somewhere to the north of Cromer, and the rock on which the Yarmouth paddle tug *Victoria* was wrecked in 1888 is reputed to be the tower of Shipden church, whose churchyard was 'wasted' by the sea about 1300. There is nothing in Domesday Book to suggest that this predecessor of Cromer was a large port like Dunwich. We are told only that the land was held by the great Roger Bigot, Sheriff of Norfolk and Suffolk, by the Bishop of Thetford and by the abbey of St. Benet at Holm. By 1417 Cromer was having ships taken for the king's use, a document relating to this business naming the farecosts *Blithe* and *Trinity*, the navis *La Trinite*, the doggers *James*, *Mighel* and *Garland*, and the lodeships *Nicholas*, *Petre*, *Mighell* and *Marie*, and the collet *Katerine*, all of Cromer.

Some kind of pier was constructed to shelter ships, but it cannot have been much of a harbour at the best of times, and the town was put to repeated expense to repair the structure. By the nineteenth century vessels were landing on the beach to unload their cargoes, sheltered only by the Jetty, which had to be replaced after a storm washed it away in 1845. Yet in that year Cromer remained a minor shipowning centre, with a number of master mariners and shipowners among its population, though by that time many of its inhabitants were turning their attention to attracting visitors. Besides the little schooners unloading coal the beach was occupied by nine or ten bathing machines, and in Jetty Street were Mr. Randell's warm baths; he had moved the baths there after the original premises on the beach had been 'shattered' by the sea.

The town 'was first frequented as a watering place about the year 1785, by two or three families of retired habits, whose favourable reports of the beautiful scenery and pleasant walks in the neighbourhood, the excellence of the beach at low water, and the simple manners of the inhabitants, soon attracted others here to share these enjoyments,' William White tells us in 1845. 'The number

Opposite: Whilst in recent years the commercial fishing at Cromer has moved entirely to the east beach, in the latter years of the 19th century it used both beaches. Over the years there had been many jetties, few lasting an extended period of time. A millennium ago the village of Shipden lay towards the top left of the picture, perhaps a hundred yards beyond the end of the jetty.

of visitors continued to increase yearly; and for the accommodation of this growing influx of company, many neat houses have been erected during the last forty years, and the town so considerably improved, that it now ranks as one of the most fashionable sea-bathing places in the kingdom.'[1]

That date of 1785 might be a little late, for an advertisement of 1779 announced that 'For the Convenience of Gentlemen, Ladies, and others, there is now erected at Cromer, by Messrs. Terry and Pearson, a Bathing Machine entirely upon a new Construction, by which the Ladies, &c. are conveyed into and out of the Water with the greatest Ease, Safety and Expedition.'[2] Such machines are said to have originated at Deal, and they had come into use at Lowestoft some ten years before that advertisement was published.

Even though the ships engaged in trade to places like Cromer were laid up for the worst of the winter months, landing cargoes on an open beach was certainly a risky business, and insurers looked askance at such dangerous practices. Casualties were not all due to the practice of beaching these vessels, however, for in 1846 the schooner *Frank* of Cromer, owned by her master, Captain William Jarvis, whose home was in Pump Street, Cromer, foundered off the Isle of Wight when bound from Caen in Normandy to Portsmouth with a cargo of stone. The crew were picked up by an Antwerp galliott, the *Wilmina*, and landed at Folkestone.[3] The same year the Sheringham schooner *Industry* was in collision with another vessel off the Yorkshire coast and was taken into Bridlington dismasted after having been abandoned by her crew, and in 1859 the ketch *Jane and Ellen* was towed into Lowestoft Roads by a steamer which had run foul of her off Flamborough Head when she was on her way from Seaham to Mundesley. It is difficult to identify her positively, but she was probably the *Jane and Ellen* of Whitby, a 40-tonner built at Sunderland in 1839.

Among the documents deposited by the Registrar of Shipping in Swansea with the Suffolk Record Office were several items relating to trading vessels regularly landing cargoes at Cromer, Bacton and Mundesley which throw a valuable light on the operations of these vessels. They confirm, for instance,

A team of horses waits on the beach to take another cartload of coal up the Gangway and to Nathaniel Field's coal yard in Church Street. With her flat bottom the *Ellis* sits upright on the beach, unlike the other beach traders.

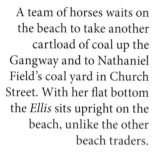

This rather crude picture of Cromer Jetty shows a sloop about to unload on the beach. This Jetty was constructed in 1821-22, the ironwork being supplied by Thomas Hase from his foundry at Saxthorpe, some ten miles from Cromer. It was damaged by a storm in 1836 and completely destroyed by another storm in 1845, being replaced in the same year by a wooden jetty.

the evidence given by the shipping lists in local newspapers that these beach traders normally laid up for the winter months either in Lowestoft or in one of the north Norfolk harbours. The crew lists reveal that the crews consisted almost entirely of local men.

In 1863 the *Commerce*, 61 tons, said to be owned by her master, William Rigden, made thirteen voyages from Middlesbrough to Cromer between 7th April and 4th December, and then left Middlesbrough on 6th December for Lowestoft, where she arrived on the 11th. Rigden had been born at Weybourne in 1802; his crew were all Cromer men. William or another of his family had been master of an earlier *Commerce* back in 1832, when she was recorded as sailing 'from Stockton to Cromer Main with coals'.[4]

The ownership of the *Commerce* is puzzling, since we know from other sources that she had been built in 1846 at South Stockton, on the Tees, for Henry Sandford, a Cromer coal merchant who was a member of the local lifeboat committee in the pioneer days of the Norfolk Shipwreck Association. She replaced an earlier vessel of the same name, possibly a brig built at Whitby in 1806, which was damaged as she came ashore with a cargo of coal at Cromer in 1845. Henry Sandford and then William George Sandford continued to own her up to the time of her loss in 1876, but it seems that a succession of

The schooners *Wensleydale*, *Commerce* and *Ellis* unloading coal on Cromer beach; the chutes down which the coal is tipped into carts can be seen rigged on the starboard side of all three ships. In the left background, nearly hidden by the yards of the *Wensleydale*, is another vessel which is probably waiting to come on shore at high water. In the left foreground in the lifeboat house at the bottom of the gangway.

A faded photo taken in 1867 showing a schooner, thought to be the *Wensleydale*, ashore at high water. In the background can just be seen a fleet of fishing luggers at anchor and also a two-funnelled paddle tug; unfortunately they do not appear at all clear in reproduction.

A drawing by Martin Warren of the *John and Thomas*, a dandy rigged lugger owned in Cromer and renowned for her turn of speed. The drawing is based on a contemporary watercolour.

masters owned shares in her and were sometimes recorded as owner.

The system of dividing the ownership of a vessel into sixty-four shares can provide a trap for the unwary researcher. Although often enough a single owner was named in a document, the ownership was sometimes divided between a number of shareholders, each of whom might have 16/64 or even just 8/64, a one-eighth share. In 1810 it was announced that 'One Fourth Part or Share of the new brig *Thomas & Martha*, of Cromer, burthen by register 96 tons; also Two-ninths of the Good Brig *Yare* of Cromer, by register 82 tons' were to be sold by auction at the Red Lion Inn, Cromer.[5] The *Thomas & Martha* was in trouble in 1815 when she was driven ashore near the South Battery at Yarmouth while on her way in ballast from London to Cromer;[6] it was expected she would be got off without material damage—after all, she spent her life going on the beach.

Matthew Brooks, of Cromer, who aged three years between January and July 1872 (if the records are to be believed!), was master of the *Commerce* in the early 1870s, when she made an average of fifteen or sixteen voyages a year between Hartlepool and Cromer, laying up between December and February each year in Lowestoft. Always the crew were predominantly Cromer born, though for several years the 'Boy' was a lad from Derby.

The *Commerce* was lost with all hands off the north Norfolk coast on 13th April 1876. That left only two vessels owned by other Cromer coal merchants still working to the town. These were the *Wensleydale*, a topsail schooner built at Paull on the Humber in 1813, owned by Jeremiah Cross and sold away from

Something of a contrast in hull design, the schooner *Wensleydale* is seen unloading coal close to the foot of the Gangway. Built at Paull on the Humber in 1813 and owned in Cromer by corn and coal merchant Jeremiah Cross, she was a regular trader to Cromer until sold away from the town in 1879.

the town in 1879, and the schooner *Ellis*, which had been owned by Nathaniel Newstead Field since her building at Hartlepool in 1858.

The *Ellis*, nicknamed by Cromer people the *Plumper* (plump, a Norfolk dialect word meaning to plunge heavily, to flop, to sink),[7] was a dumpy, almost flat-bottomed vessel particularly well adapted for lying on a sandy beach to unload. One suspects that she might have been named after the owner's father or some other relative; in White's directory for 1854 Ellis N. Field and Sarah Ann Field were listed as lighthouse keepers at Cromer.

Under a Cromer master, William Bloom Payne, she led an apparently humdrum life running between Hartlepool and Cromer. In 1871 she laid up at Lowestoft until 6th February, made fourteen round trips to Hartlepool for coal and then was laid up at Lowestoft again in December. The shortest return voyage took a week, the average was about sixteen days, and the two longest four weeks, with anything from two days to nine for unloading at Cromer. The following year she seems to have made fifteen voyages, the last ending at Cromer on 16th December, before being 'laid up at Cromer remainder of year'. Assuming this is not a clerical error, that is almost certainly the year the *Ellis* was washed up the beach in a storm and had to spend the winter there. Legend has it that the following spring she was jacked up, ways were laid under the hull and she was launched down the beach as though on a shipyard.[8]

Having given up her regular run from Hartlepool with coal, the *Ellis* passed into the possession of W.S. Juniper and Austin Blythe in 1888 and eight years later was sold into Hartlepool ownership; she survived until 1920.

Another view of the *Commerce*, on Cromer or possibly on Overstrand beach about 1850.

William Bloom Payne had by 1874 become a shipowner as well as a master mariner, for the *Mercantile Navy List* for that year shows him as owner of the 70-ton schooner *Julia* of Wells, built at that port in 1843.

The trade on to the beaches was killed off by the railways, which reached Cromer in 1877 and Mundesley in 1898. The last cargo of coal was landed on Cromer beach by the *Ellis* in March 1887.[9]

Lighthouses and lightships

The high cliffs of boulder clay, gravel and sand to the east of Cromer provided a prominent seamark that was commonly used by seamen as a point of arrival and departure when bound into the Wash or for the north. As Sir Walter Runciman said when writing about the Geordie collier brigs that carried coal from the North to London, the real excitement of a passage to London commenced when Cromer was reached, if a head wind were blowing. It was not unusual, he said, for the colliers from all the north-east coast coal-ports to congregate in the Cromer vicinity, and have to beat against a head wind along the coast of Orfordness, then up the Swin and London River, having to let go and weigh the anchor at every turn of the tide.[10]

Sir Walter, who went to sea first in the middle of the nineteenth century, paints a vivid picture of the east coast sea routes at that time. 'Beating of a large fleet of competing vessels up and through Yarmouth Roads and the Cockle Gat (if the tide was with them), and the occasional collisions through one vessel not giving way to another if she was on the wrong tack, led to a shower of abuse at the offender. Many accidents were avoided by courteous captains relaxing their rights and merely cautioning the culprits not to repeat

The old and new lighthouses at Cromer just before Edward Bowell's tower on the right went down the cliff. The earlier light in the town had been in the church tower, in the centre of this picture.

the impertinence of acting as though the sea belonged to them again, or they would have to take the risk of being sunk. Nothing more thrilling will ever be known on the face of the waters than the sight of a fleet of sailing vessels beating through narrow channels and having to anchor in the open sea when the tide made against them.'

All too often the collisions that occurred because a proper lookout was not being kept and the rules for the avoidance of collision were not obeyed led to rather more than a shower of abuse. Many ships were sunk and many seamen drowned, and many lawyers made a good living sorting out the consequences. In 1856, for instance, the little billyboy sloop *Ocean* of Boston, on her way from Sunderland for Maidstone with a cargo of coal, was making her slow way through the Cockle Gat when she was run down by the Lowestoft lugger *Anchor*. The case came up at Norfolk Assizes the following year, and the lugger was held exclusively to blame.

When the masters and owners of ships engaged in the coal trade called for lighthouses to enable them to navigate the coast more safely this was one of the places they thought should be lit, and it was one of four places where Sir John Clayton, a seventeenth-century speculator, proposed in 1669 to erect lighthouses. When Captain Greenville Collins produced *Great Britain's Coasting Pilot* in 1684 his chart of the Norfolk coast contained the note 'Foulness which is high land on which standeth a Lighthouse, but no Fire kept in as yet'. Alas, it never was lit, thanks to the opposition of Trinity House. Nor was the tower that Clayton built at Flamborough Head; that one at least survives, while the Foulness tower disappeared in a cliff fall some three centuries ago.

A photograph of Cromer lighthouse and the adjacent keeper's residence taken by H.C.Jennings in 1895. The light at that time was burning oil, consuming about 970 gallons of best colza oil every year. The building remains today but with a number of changes; the lamp house was reduced in size with the introduction of electricity.

It was not until 1719 that Edward Bowell of Ipswich was granted Letters Patent by George I and a lease by Trinity House – at a rent of £100 a year! – enabling him to exhibit a light from the Cromer tower. The light came from a coal fire burning in a glazed lantern atop the tower. When Bowell, who had been Bailiff of Ipswich in 1723 and 1729, died in 1737 he was buried in the graveyard of St. Clement's Church in Ipswich; his gravestone, now long gone, recorded that 'He erected the Light at Foulness in Norfolk. Anno 1719.'[11]

One of the objections raised to Clayton's proposal to erect lighthouses was that they would be dangerous 'because ships might be lost by mistaking the lights'. When Cromer lighthouse was improved and the illumination changed from a coal fire to oil lamps in 1792 it was given one of the first rotating lanterns which gave a single flash every minute, thus clearly identifying that light from others.

The reason men such as Clayton and Bowell sought to obtain leave to build lighthouses was that these produced income from the dues paid by shipping passing the lights. In the last three years of the lease, 1818-20, Bowell's descendants and the owner of the land on which the lighthouse stood gained between them profits averaging £2,461 a year. As the end of the lease approached Trinity House declined to renew it, and in 1822 the Corporation of Trinity House bought the lighthouse for £3,892.

The cliffs on which the lighthouse stood had been eroding for centuries. The sea bit away at the cliff foot, but even more damaging was the build-up of ground water behind the cliff face, which sometimes created such pressure that a whole section of the cliff burst out and fell to the beach below. No less than twelve acres was lost in this way in 1825, and a similar huge fall in 1832 posed an obvious threat to the lighthouse.

The answer to the threat was to build a new lighthouse further inland, which came into service in 1833, and to abandon the old one. The new tower, which had a light far more powerful than the old one, was completed in less than a year, but the old lighthouse survived until 1866, when a long period of heavy rain resulted in a massive fall of cliff that carried the building with it. Much has changed, new forms of lighting have been introduced and such things as radio beacons have taken over much of the work of the lighthouses, but Cromer light still shines out night after night to guide mariners on their way.

Look out to sea from near the lighthouse and one might see the waves breaking on the Haisborough Sand, the grave of so many ships and of one whole convoy during the Second World War. The northern end of the sand used to be marked by a lightship, one of many which were moored in the waters off the east coast both to mark known dangers and to serve as signposts for vessels navigating the narrow seas. Its arrival on station in 1832 was recorded in one of the local newspapers: 'The equipment of the floating light . . . near the North end of Happisburgh sands, having been completed, the vessel has taken her station, and two lights, raised on separate masts, are burning every night . . .'.[12] In the early part of the twentieth century the lightship carried a red ball at the masthead and showed a group of four white flashes every half-minute; later it was a modern lightvessel with the light carried on a short tower amidships.

One of the lightships which once served off Cromer is now to be found at the Haven Ports Yacht Club at Levington, near Ipswich, where she acts as a club house.

The story of lightships is an interesting one, for like the early lighthouses the first lightships were the result of private enterprise and, if some accounts are accurate, of remarkable subterfuge. The idea of floating lights, as they

The Smith's Knoll light vessel alongside the Trinity House base at Great Yarmouth in the 1970s.

Robert Marten drew this splendid sketch of the then Cromer lighthouse in 1825.

were known in the early days, had been suggested in the seventeenth century, and in 1724 Captain John Waggett, a Yarmouth collier master, sought the establishment of a floating light in the Cockle Gat, the northern entrance to Yarmouth Roads. Trinity House would not countenance such a wild notion, pointing out the danger of the vessels parting from their anchors in stormy weather, an ever-present danger before the introduction of chain cable in the early nineteenth century. Not only would the light-vessel be in danger of destruction on the sandbank it marked but it was said that a floating light off station was a greater danger to navigation than an unmarked shoal.

Then in 1730 two men, Captain Robert Hamblin, said to be master of a Lynn collier, and David Avery, obtained Letters Patent under which they stationed a 'fireship' at the Nore, in the approaches to the Thames, two years later. It seems to have been nothing more than a small vessel with a pair of candle lanterns hoisted on a yard on its single mast, but it proved valuable to those trading into the port of London. Although Trinity House succeeded after some difficulty in gaining the revocation of the patent, the new floating light found so much favour with seamen that it was suffered to remain. Avery was granted a lease at £100 a year for sixty-one years, the same as the charge on Bowell for the Cromer lighthouse, and in 1736 he in alliance with two 'gentlemen of known worth and character' obtained a patent under which a second lightship was established at the Dudgeon, a dangerous bank lying almost in the direct path of vessels steering from Flamborough Head towards Cromer.

Disappointingly, we know little or nothing of these two entrepreneurs, Hamblin and Avery, other than what the then clerk of Trinity House, John Whormby, tells us in his account of sea marks, written in 1746 but published only in 1861.[13] Quite clearly Whormby set out to denigrate the men, whom he regarded as usurpers of the Trinity House function, and what he says of them is almost certainly misleading in certain essential particulars, if not totally inaccurate.

'This Hamblin was a barber at Lynn, and marrying the daughter of a master of a ship there, he became master of a collier himself, and some say of a smuggler also, but never in any other command; nor was he bred to the sea; neither was he able to give any account of our coast to the westward, or judged to have been farther than the Downs, when questioned at the Trinity House Board: at least, he then owned that he had never been as far as Scilly, nor could he tell anything of Portland,' says Whormby scathingly. The fact that a collier master trading between the Tyne and an east coast port might have neither the need nor the opportunity to navigate beyond the Foreland was conveniently ignored.

Having made so good a start on the path of character assassination, the clerk of Trinity House warmed to his task. 'This poor man, after ill success in other undertakings, and being reduced to poverty, happened to take it into his head to form one project (amongst many) for distinguishing lights from one another, or rather (as the sequel showed) to introduce floating lights under that strange and ill-suited disguise. Then falling in with Mr. David Avery, (a gentleman of infinite projects, who rises every morning with 100 estates in his head, though most of them slip his pocket,) they moulded this project into the shape of a new invention, for which a patent for fourteen

The East Dudgeon lightship, attacked from the air early in the Second World War and the subject of a continuing mystery, when the Sheringham lifeboat arrived to search for the crew.

years was to be obtained, as is usual and legal in cases of new inventions ...'.

Whormby's spiteful and partisan assessment of Captain Hamblin's proficiency as a seaman has generally been accepted by historians, and the Lynn shipmaster has been given scant credit for his achievement in setting up the first lightships on the east coast. His name does not appear in *The Dictionary of National Biography* or *The Oxford Companion to Ships and the Sea*, and nothing seems to be known of him other than Whormby's scurrilous words. There was a barber named Robert Hamblin who became a freeman of Lynn, but is he really our man? There were Hamblins at Ipswich who went to sea, and there is a tradition in the family that one of their ancestors was the one implicated in the establishment of the first lightship. Nearly three hundred years after the event, who can tell?

Eventually Trinity House came to realise the utility of the floating light and established its own stations around the British coasts, while remaining unenthusiastic about this type of light. One of the earlier lightships was the *Haisbro'*, first placed on station in 1791. In 1825 the Corporation of Trinity House announced that it was improving the light at the Nore, substituting a single more powerful lantern for the two small lights that had been shown up to then, and others were similarly improved over the course of time.

Little as they were liked by the Brethren of Trinity House, the new floating lights were popular with those who traded along the east coast. Anything that helped them to avoid the many dangers and to find their way safely through narrow and ill-defined channels was appreciated by the men who sailed in these congested and treacherous waters. All too often ships were cast up on the beaches or wrecked on the sands that in some cases lie far out in the North Sea, out of sight of watchers ashore. To give just one instance, a storm on 30th October 1789 caused the loss of about eighty ships and fishing boats between Cromer and Yarmouth, and 120 dead bodies were washed up on the beaches.

That storm led to an inquiry being undertaken by Trinity House into the lights on the Norfolk coast. The Elder Brethren came to the conclusion that the lighthouses they had established at Caister about 1600 were misleading and decided to abandon them, in their place establishing a lightvessel at the Newarp sand off Winterton and two lighthouses at Happisburgh at a total cost of some £10,000. All three lights shone out for the first time on the first day of 1791.

Wrecks were by no means infrequent, and when vessels came ashore on the beach and were too severely damaged to be refloated the materials were often sold by auction for the benefit of the underwriters or, if the ship was uninsured, the owners. In 1834 the wreck of the brig *Traveller* was advertised for sale at Mundesley, where she had stranded on her voyage from Shields to France: it was stated that 'the hull is broken up and divided into lots of excellent oaks and other plank, floors, futtocks, beams, kelson, rider, stem and stern post, which are well calculated for shed, gate and other posts, with good scantlings for building . . .'.[14] Daniel Defoe, who published the description of his tour of the country in 1723, recorded that in this part of the coast he found that almost every barn and shed, and even the paled fences of the countrymen's yards and gardens, contained old planks and timbers from wrecked ships.

The Foulness buoy, with radar reflector and single light, used to be positioned some one nautical mile north–east of Cromer.

The buoyage system is now standardised throughout the world. Navigation by GPS has reduced the need for lighthouses and manned lightships have long gone but the ever shifting sands of the Norfolk and Suffolk coasts require constant attention by the vessels of Trinity House

In the 1970s all commercial fishing boats operating from the Cromer and Sheringham beaches were of the same basic design, though glass fibre had been used to make at least one boat using a mould from a wooden boat. A catamaran was then introduced by Richard Davies and subsequently a larger catamaran for work further offshore. The boats for the inshore grounds gradually became single handers, using outboard engines, sufficiently powerful to beat the breakers when returning to shore. These smaller vessels could be worked without so much co-operation required to manhandle them on the beach.

The Cromer lifeboats

Not surprisingly the first move to station a lifeboat on the Norfolk coast was made at Cromer in 1804, when an advertisement was placed in the *Norwich Mercury* of 20th October requesting 'Those Gentlemen, Visitants and Inhabitants of Cromer and the neighbourhood, who wish to encourage the establishment of a Life Boat' to meet at the hotel in Cromer at midday on the last day of the month. At that meeting the need was expressed for more than one boat to cover the coast from Sheringham to Yarmouth, but the resulting subscription brought in only sufficient money to obtain a single boat for Cromer. A rowing lifeboat built by Henry Greathead of South Shields similar to those that had been stationed on the Suffolk coast at Lowestoft and Bawdsey three years earlier was acquired. Possibly it was reports of the success of the Bawdsey boat in saving eight people,

Whereas at Sheringham winches were employed to haul boats up the beaches, at Cromer agricultural tractors have been called into use to handle boats up the beach.

Opposite: The *Mary Ann*, last of a lengthy era. The double-ended crab boats of Cromer and Sheringham have been replaced by skiffs.

The model made for the Great Exhibition of 1851 of the first Cromer lifeboat.

The second *Benjamin Bond Cabbell*, a reversion to the North Country type of lifeboat introduced by Henry Greathead.

one of them a woman, from the London brig *Pallas* in February 1804 that prompted the calling of that meeting in the following October at Cromer, for a letter from Dr. Frank of Alderton, who had initiated the purchase of the Bawdsey boat and had been an eye-witness of the rescue, was read at the meeting.[15]

Very little is known of the early operations of this first Cromer lifeboat. She was launched by the local fishermen during a nor'-easterly gale in November 1810 when the Sunderland brig *Anna* came ashore to the west of the town, saving fourteen men and a woman passenger. During the same gale another brig also

named *Anna*, from North Shields, was flung ashore at Mundesley, and the crew of ten were all drowned before the lifesaving mortar could be brought the six miles from Happisburgh.

The contrasting circumstances of the two wrecks persuaded the Cromer lifeboat committee to station a lifeboat at Mundesley just as soon as enough money could be raised. A beach boat was fitted up as a temporary lifeboat for the village, and in due course a small lifeboat costing £130 was built at Sunderland and stationed at Mundesley.

The second *Benjamin Bond Cabbell* was built by Beeching at Great Yarmouth and served at Cromer for 18 years.

The lifeboat *Louisa Heartwell* stands by to launch.

The lifeboat lines on the pier forecourt at Cromer point to services which go back to the earliest years of Cromer lifeboat station. The compass is based on the compass of the *H.F. Bailey* in the Henry Blogg Lifeboat Museum, further east on the promenade.

In 1819 the Mundesley lifeboat was launched from the beach to the aid of the *Endeavour* of Sunderland and a number of other vessels that were in trouble close inshore, using a line fired from a lifesaving mortar to haul the boat off through the surf. It was commented at the time that the Cromer boat had not been used for several years, and there was a suggestion that she should be moved to a station where she was likely to be more useful. One wonders just why she had been 'unemployed for years'. It was as well that the proposal to move the boat elsewhere was not implemented because on 13th October 1824 she saved the crew of seven men from the Scarborough brig *Equity* which had been run ashore near the lighthouse in a nor'easterly gale while on passage from Cardiff to Newcastle with a cargo of 182 tons of iron bars and rods.

On that occasion three of the local gentry seem to have given a lead to the fishermen in getting the lifeboat afloat, just as they had taken a prominent part in the foundation of the Norfolk Association for Saving the Lives of Shipwrecked Mariners a year or so earlier. Lord Suffield of Gunton Park had been to the fore in setting up that organisation, having seen the horrors of shipwreck at first hand while helping to save the crew of a ship ashore off Bacton. It is said that the very next morning after the wreck he sent his servants to the Lord Lieutenant of the county, to Mr. Thomas Coke at Holkham and Mr. Edmond Wodehouse, the Vice-Admiral of the Coast, with a proposal for the institution of 'an association for preserving the lives of shipwrecked mariners on the whole line of coast of Norfolk'.

When that association was founded at a meeting in Norwich in November 1823 it was the first county lifesaving association in Britain. It not only established lifeboat stations at Yarmouth, Caister, Winterton, Bacton, Blakeney, Wells, Brancaster and Hunstanton but continued to operate the county's lifeboat service until 1858, when it handed over to the Royal National Lifeboat Institution.

Just a year after the service to the *Equity* the Cromer lifeboat was in action again, rescuing the crew of three of the *Liberty* of Boston, laden with a cargo of oats for London. The lifeboat was quickly brought into action when the little *Liberty* came ashore in heavy seas on 21st October 1825 and, manned by a crew of local fishermen, brought John Hargave, the master, and his two crewmen safely ashore.[16]

The Norfolk Shipwreck Association, as it was called for short, had a new lifeboat built for Cromer in 1830 to replace the original Greathead boat, which was transferred to Wells. It gave another 21 years' service at that station. A larger boat than the first one, 32ft. 3in. as against 25ft. and rowing twelve oars instead of ten, the new boat was built by a Shields boatbuilder named Robson and was of the same basic design, though with improvements that included relieving tubes to clear the boat of water.[17] A contemporary model of this boat that used to be in the maritime museum at Yarmouth is now on display in the Henry Blogg RNLI museum at Cromer.

In the early years of the station the record was unimpressive, for there was no regular crew and apparently little organisation. By 1839 it would seem that the foundations of Cromer's strong lifesaving tradition were already being laid, if we are to judge from reports of the services carried out in the course of a single week that year. At daybreak on Monday 28th October a vessel was seen some seven miles from the town exhibiting signals of distress and the lifeboat

The 1863 lifeboat house from a magic lantern slide.

In 2004 thousands gathered on the seafront for the visit of a rowing lifeboat of the type once kept in this boathouse.

The silver medal of the Norfolk Shipwreck Association, awarded to Captain Pank for the *Achilles* service.

was launched with Captain Francis Pank, a master mariner and shipowner who had his home in Church Street, and Simeon Simons, proprietor of the Bath House on the cliff, heading a crew of fishermen.

It took the men two hours of hard rowing to reach the casualty, the brig *Achilles* of South Shields, which was bound to London with a cargo of coal and had carried away her mainmast and fore topmast and was being driven towards the shore. The lifeboatmen aided the crew in bringing her into the roadstead and anchored her off Cromer, and then took the eight men out of her. They went back at first light next morning and attempted to pump the vessel out, but the sea was 'making a passage over her' and they found it impossible to slip the anchor cables. The salvage operation had to be abandoned, and the *Achilles* sank about noon.

It had not been an easy service by any means. One of the fishermen, Henry Nockels, was washed overboard, but by grabbing a rope he managed to get back into the boat, and Captain Pank injured his leg when he fell between the lifeboat and the brig. In 1840 Captain Pank was awarded a silver medal by the Norfolk Association.

On the following Friday, 1st November, the lifeboat was again quickly manned when another vessel was seen showing signals of distress. It turned out to be a Dutch galliot, the *Elizabeth Jacoba Tromp*, which had left Memel with a cargo of oak boards nearly three weeks earlier and had been caught by a storm as she approached her home port of Harlingen, on the Zuyder Zee. Winds said to have increased to a hurricane blew her across the North Sea, and by the time she arrived off Cromer she was in a sinking state. Although her crew were forced to run her ashore, the lifeboat reached her and took out the seven men just as she hit the beach. The coastguards threw two rocket lines over the vessel, but it was the lifeboat that brought the Dutch crew ashore. They 'testified their joy on landing by kissing each other and the spectators indiscriminately,' to the amusement of the crowd that had assembled on the beach to watch the rescue.[18]

The galliot quickly went to pieces, but much of her cargo was salvaged and taken to Henry Sandford's coalyard in Church Street, where it was sold by auction later in the month together with parts of the wreckage of the *Elizabeth Jacoba Tromp.*

The Cromer lifeboat and the *Augusta* from Sheringham shared the first prize for pulling boats in the trial of lifeboats held at the Yarmouth North Roads Regatta in 1845, but no record has been found of any services performed by the boat during the 1840s and 1850s. One would have expected that the boat would have been well used, but such evidence as there is suggests that it was not. Correspondence in one of the local newspapers in 1857 revealed that the boat 'had not been out of its house for three and a half years up to last August, and it was then only taken out at the earnest wish of some of the visitors staying here, and the expense subscribed by them.'[19]

In the autumn of 1857 the fishermen were unwilling to go out in the lifeboat when a vessel was seen to have hoisted signals of distress. Eventually when a sum of money was offered by some of the local residents the men were persuaded to man the boat, but the vessel hauled down the distress signal 'and refused their tardy aid,' as a correspondent put it. 'The lifeboat has not been used for a considerable time, so long, I am told, that it might be a question whether she were seaworthy,' he added.[20]

It is odd that the Cromer men and others in north Norfolk favoured the North Country type that was so disliked by crews elsewhere in the region. On taking over the Norfolk stations the RNLI sent a self-righting lifeboat to Cromer, but when in 1884 the second of the self-righters came to the end of its life the Cromer crew asked for it to be replaced by a boat of the kind they had had in the past, a North Country boat. Built by Beeching Brothers at Yarmouth, the *Benjamin Bond Cabbell* was the first of three boats of what the RNLI termed the Cromer type, the others going to Blakeney in 1891 and to Wells in 1895.

The *Benjamin Bond Cabbell* with her fourteen oars and no sails was still in service when a young fisherman named Henry Blogg became a member of the crew in 1892, but she had been superseded by the Liverpool-type pulling and sailing boat *Louisa Heartwell* by the time he was chosen as coxswain in 1909. It was in the *Louisa Heartwell* that Blogg carried out an all but impossible rescue in 1917 that earned him his first RNLI Gold Medal.

The weather was atrocious, with a strong nor'easterly gale blowing straight on shore and frequent showers of sleet and hail, when in the middle of the morning of 9th January the Greek steamer *Pyrin* hoisted the International Code signal CM, a white pennant with a red ball over a blue flag with a white diagonal cross, indicating that she was drifting and required assistance. The lifeboatmen who ran pell-mell down the streets to the lifeboathouse were not young men in the prime of life, because after nearly three years of war most of the younger men were away in the services; the average age of the crew that manned the boat that day was not far short of fifty, and the oldest were nearing seventy.

The *Pyrin* had been riding at anchor some two miles out, but with the anchor dragging it was inevitable that she would be blown ashore before too long. The chairman of the local lifeboat committee asked Blogg if he thought it possible to launch the lifeboat into such a terrible sea. 'I doubt if we shall, but we shall have a rare good try,' the coxswain replied.

The *Louisa Heartwell* was launched from a carriage, but that carriage was hauled across the beach not by a team of horses but by a launching party of men headed by Tom 'Bussey' Allen. Among those who tallied on the drag-ropes were soldiers stationed in the area. They had to wade into the breakers and haul the carriage across a shallow 'low' and over a sandbank to get the boat into water deep enough for launching. Three times the boat was thrown back by huge waves that washed the launchers off their feet, but eventually she was successfully launched, though even then the wind and tide threatened to cast her into the pier, which she cleared by the narrowest of margins thanks to the efforts of the men on the fourteen oars and the skill of the coxswain.

Once clear of the pier the crew hoisted sail and the boat beat against the wind towards the *Pyrin*. It was painfully slow work, and more than two hours had passed by the time Blogg was in a position to bring the boat alongside the Greek ship and take off the sixteen men of her crew. It took no more than an hour to bring them to land. With the boat running before the wind, the crew found it necessary to tow a drogue astern to steady the boat.

While this rescue was taking place the Swedish steamship *Fernebo* with a cargo of timber was in dire trouble some four miles from the shore. The chief engineer, Johan Anderson, had been injured in an accident in the engine-room, and while he was being helped by other members of the crew there came a devastating explosion that blew the ship in half. It seems likely that she had struck a mine, possibly an early example of the magnetic mine that proved so troublesome a weapon in the Second World War.[21] The cargo of timber kept both halves of the *Fernebo* afloat, but the vessel was doomed, for the gale was blowing towards the coast and it was likely to be only a matter of time before both sections came ashore.

The lifeboat crew were near exhaustion from their struggle to reach the *Pyrin*, and though the launching party had recovered the *Louisa Heartwell* and got her back on to her carriage in preparation for another launching it seemed unlikely she could go to the aid of the stricken Swedish ship. When messages came from the flanking stations that neither the Sheringham lifeboat *J.C. Madge* nor the Palling boat could be launched because of the sea conditions, however, the Cromer men decided to attempt another launch. Three fresh men joined those who had taken part in the earlier rescue, and for a whole half-hour crew and launchers tried to get the *Louisa Heartwell* afloat in spite of mountainous seas rolling in before the gale. Eventually the boat was cast on to the beach, and the lifeboatmen had to give up.

It was while the Cromer men were vainly attempting to row the heavy lifeboat through the breakers, watched by scores of townspeople from vantage points on the cliff, that six men decided to take the risk of setting off in a small boat from the *Fernebo*. Even if the boat could live in those seas and reached

The reserve lifeboat William Gammon hits the water for a service in December 1978. She was a reversion to an open boat design.

Norfolk has several Inshore Lifeboats provided by the RNLI or independently.

the beach there was little hope of the men getting ashore alive, for it was clear that the great waves breaking near the beach would upset the boat and throw them into the water before they could reach the land. Over the years many local fishermen had lost their lives in conditions far less severe when their crab boats were overwhelmed as they approached the shore.

It seemed a miracle that the boat remained afloat in such seas, yet it did. Then, just as it seemed they might make the beach in safety, a great wave turned the boat over and threw the six men into the water. A dozen rescuers

linked arms and waded into the surf. Stewart Holmes, a private of the Seaforth Highlanders, managed to grab one of the struggling men. A second chain of rescuers got that man ashore, and then Holmes reached another drowning man, helping to drag him ashore. All six men were brought out of the sea that way, though Holmes was himself almost drowned when one of the men, struggling for life, seized him and pulled him under water.

About five o'clock in the afternoon the two parts of the *Fernebo* washed on to the shore, some hundred and fifty yards apart and with many yards of

The loss of Walter Allen on the *English Trader* service is remembered.

English Trader survivor Charles Rogers on the *H.F.Bailey* lifeboat in December 2011

turbulent water separating them from would-be rescuers on the beach. The remaining crew were all on the afterpart, though those ashore could not have known this at the time. The Cromer lifesaving apparatus company, volunteers working under the control of the Coastguard, fired rocket after rocket in attempts to get a line to the bow section of the broken ship, but time after time the rockets were thrown back by the strength of the wind or the line was blown aside. The Sheringham LSA company had no better success in their attempts to get a line to the men on the afterpart of the *Fernebo*.

As darkness fell the men of a nearby anti-aircraft battery brought two searchlights to the top of the cliff and used them to light up the beach and the wreck. Working by their light the men of the two lifesaving companies still sought to make a communication with the men on the afterpart, but by nine o'clock they had fired twelve rockets, and not one had been effective

In charge of the combined operation was Commander Basil Hall, RN, an inspector of lifeboats. Henry Blogg went to him and proposed that a further attempt be made to launch the lifeboat. It was at this point particularly that Coxswain Blogg showed the strength of character and the quite remarkable qualities of leadership that made him one of the greatest lifeboatmen of all time. Although Commander Hall pointed out that the lifeboatmen were already exhausted by their earlier exertions, that they were not resilient young men but ageing veterans, and that the conditions were such that it was unlikely the boat could be launched, Blogg persuaded him to sanction a further attempt.

The *Louisa Heartwell* was launched again about 9.30pm into a tremendous sea. The oarsmen could make no headway against the waves, and time after time the boat was at risk of being driven on to the beach, yet each time they fought back and forced the heavy boat a little way towards the wreck. They had got half way to the ship when a succession of heavy seas struck the boat, breaking several oars and threatening to drive her into a breakwater against which she would have been battered to pieces.

The author of *The History of the Cromer Lifeboats* describes how 'Again and again the furious waves, foaming with rage, beat on her, oars were broken, and the boat rendered almost unmanageable. Bathed in the brilliant beam of the searchlight, which cut into the darkness like a gleaming sword, the lifeboat was seen one moment standing on end, at another buried in the foam as the seas broke over her, or lost to sight as she sank in the trough of the waves.'

It might sound melodramatic, but those who watched from the cliff that night would say that it was nothing more than an entirely factual account of what happened. After five oars had been broken and three others lost, to be washed ashore, the crew were driven back and the boat was thrown on to the beach. Yet even then they would not give up. About eleven o'clock that night they decided to make another attempt to reach the men on the shattered *Fernebo*.

The boat was again launched, not without great difficulty. Time after time she was hurled back by great waves, but after more than half an hour of heavy labour at the oars the lifeboatmen had the satisfaction of reaching the wreck and taking off the eleven men they found there. It is said that there was thunderous cheering from the crowds still massed on the beach and on the cliffs as the lifeboat was beached with the rescued men on board.

Henry Blogg was then a man of forty and had been coxswain for seven years, having taken over from James 'Buttons' Harrison in 1909. He was not yet known beyond his own town, but that day in 1917 he had shown clearly the stuff he was made of. He had learned a great deal from his stepfather, John James Davies, who had served as second coxswain in the *Benjamin Bond Cabbell* under his own father, James Davies, and he used that acquired knowledge to hone his undoubted skill as a seaman.

'Without for a moment detracting from the part played by the rest of the crew, I feel bound to say that I believe, and I know that the hon. secretary believes, that without him a crew could not have been got to take the boat off during the afternoon and evening of the day in question,' Commander Hall said in his subsequent report to the RNLI. 'It was his own remarkable personality and really great qualities of leadership which magnetised tired and somewhat dispirited men into launching, and when the boat was launched it was the consummate skill with which he managed her and the encouragement he gave his crew which brought their efforts to such a successful conclusion.'

Not only did the coxswain gain the Gold Medal but William Davies, his acting second coxswain, was awarded the Silver Medal, as was Stewart Holmes, the soldier who played a leading part in pulling six of the *Fernebo* crew from the sea after their boat had swamped. Those members of the crew who had borne the brunt of that long and arduous service were awarded the Bronze Medal, which had just been introduced. They were in fact the first recipients of the new award.

All those who had gone out three times in the boat, including coxswain and second coxswain, were awarded an additional £2, not as insignificant a sum as it might appear today. Five lifeboatmen who went out twice received an additional £1 1s. and two who went out once an additional £1; Private Holmes was also granted £2.

The *Louisa Heartwell* was almost wrecked on the remains of the *Fernebo* when in January 1921 she was launched to the aid of a small Belgian steamer flying signals of distress off the town. Wind and tide set her down towards the wreckage, but Coxswain Blogg somehow got her clear. The remains slowly sank into the sand and shingle, yet they still emerge from time to time when the beach is scoured by storms.

Cromer received its first motor lifeboat, a 46ft. 6in. Norfolk and Suffolk type boat built by J.S. White at Cowes, in 1923. The *Louisa Heartwell* remained in the boathouse at the bottom of the Gangway as the No. 2 boat and a new boathouse with a slipway costing a total of £32,000 was built at the seaward end of the pier for the new motor boat, which was named *H.F. Bailey* after Mr. Henry Francis Bailey, of Brockenhurst in Hampshire, whose legacy had paid the cost of the building of the boat, almost £11,000. The Cromer men, who had never had a Norfolk and Suffolk type boat in sailing days, found her unsuitable for the conditions of their area, and she made only three service launches, saving twelve lives, before being transferred to Gorleston as the *John and Mary Meiklam of Gladswood* in 1924.

In her place the Cromer station received a 45ft. Watson type boat, also built at Cowes by J.S. White, which took the same name as her predecessor. She cost £7,580. It was this boat that took part in another famous rescue, that from the Dutch oil tanker *Georgia* on 21st November 1927. The *Georgia*, a 5,111-gross-

The half of the *Fernebo* on the beach at Cromer would stay there until the Second World War, when most of it was removed in the drive for scrap metal. A scouring tide will still reveal some of her keel.

ton tanker built at Newport News in the USA in 1908, was on her way from Abadan in the Persian Gulf to a refinery at Grangemouth on the Firth of Forth with oil when she broke in two after being driven on to the Haisborough Sand when her steering gear broke down during a fierce gale in the North Sea.

So quickly did disaster strike that the radio operator had no time to send a distress call before the aerials were carried away. The stern section with sixteen of the crew on board was carried north-westwards by the gale with the seas constantly sweeping over the deck. They were taken off the following morning by the Dutch steamer *Trent*, which then turned towards the Haisborough Sand with the intention of rescuing the fifteen men on the bow section, still held fast on the sand. As she turned south her radio operator sent a message stating that help was urgently needed to rescue the men still on the forepart of the ship. That call was answered by a number of other ships in the area, and by the Gorleston lifeboat *John and Mary Meiklam of Gladswood*, formerly the first *H.F. Bailey*.

Those on the after section had already been taken off when watchers at Cromer espied what they thought to be a vessel down by the head. The *H.F. Bailey* was promptly launched from the pier boathouse and went to investigate, but Coxswain Blogg found no signs of life on board. Nonetheless he decided to stand by the wreck all night since it was a danger to other shipping.

Next morning the *H.F. Bailey* returned to her station and came alongside the slipway so that food could be passed to the crew, who had been out all night in the bitter cold and rain without any sustenance. While this was being done a message came from the Coastguard at Mundesley that a ship's boat was drifting north from Bacton, and it was thought there was somebody aboard it. Blogg took the *H.F. Bailey* to investigate and the *Louisa Heartwell* was launched to stand by the drifting wreck. The crew of the motor lifeboat soon discovered that the drifting boat was unoccupied and returned to Cromer, but then as they worked to get the boat up the slipway there came a further message telling them that the forepart of the *Georgia* was on the Haisborough with fifteen men awaiting rescue. Because of the heavy seas the Gorleston boat had been unable to get alongside the *Georgia*; a line had been fired to her and a two-inch rope had been secured, but that broke when a huge wave caught the lifeboat and swept the line to leeward.

The *H.F. Bailey* arrived on the scene just after four in the afternoon. The seas were still battering the broken ship, and by chance just as the lifeboat approached one of the oil tanks ruptured, releasing thousands of gallons of oil into the sea. This had the effect of flattening out the waves, giving Blogg the chance he needed to take the lifeboat alongside. 'The job had to be done before dark, so I went straight at her,' he said later. 'We threw lines aboard and made fast and got alongside of her and the men jumped in one by one from the bridge.'

In the coxswain's words it sounded easy, but it was not. As he was bringing the boat alongside a heavy sea caught her and threw her against the ship's side, badly damaging her sternpost and rudder. Nevertheless, obeying the coxswain's orders to 'take your time, be steady, and jump one at a time,' the fifteen men leapt into the lifeboat. Captain Harry Kissing was the last to jump.

Then, as the lifeboat endeavoured to get clear, she was caught by another sea and driven right on to the bulwarks of the *Georgia*. Without waiting for orders

Opposite: The technology may have changed since that first decision to place a lifeboat at Cromer in 1804, but the commitment required of the crew remains the same. The *Lester* enters the water from her slipway, one of the very few open water slipways in the British Isles.

from the coxswain, motor mechanic Robert Davies put the engine astern, and as another wave lifted the lifeboat she drew clear. There was a jagged hole on the starboard bow, and the forepeak was flooded, but the *H.F. Bailey* reached Gorleston safely that night after a twenty-eight-hour service.

For that rescue the coxswain received a second service clasp to his Gold Medal, and the rest of the crew all received either the Bronze Medal or a second service clasp to the Bronze Medal they had won in 1917. When the Prince of Wales, later King Edward VIII and Duke of Windsor, presented Blogg with his award at the RNLI annual meeting the following March he joked that 'there is one little habit which I think Coxswain Blogg ought really to break himself of . . . he seems to regard it as an indispensable condition of the highest exercise of his seamanship, at any rate in Gold Medal cases, that the vessel must break in two.'

It is easy to get the idea that every time Henry Blogg went out in the lifeboat he performed some amazing rescue, but there were many abortive launchings. One of them, just a month after the service to the *Georgia*, did not result in any lives being saved but it proved one of the worst trips that Blogg ever made in the *H.F. Bailey*. The Union Castle liner *Crawford Castle* collided with the Haisbro' lightvessel on the evening of Christmas Day in a violent north-easterly gale and when reports of the collision reached Cromer the lifeboat crew mustered in the boathouse awaiting the call that they considered almost inevitable. It was, however, not until the morning of Boxing Day when the *Crawford Castle* was in the vicinity of the East Dudgeon lightship that the vessel called for assistance from lifeboat and tug. The *H.F. Bailey* was launched into a raging sea and set off towards the position given. So appalling were the conditions that Second Coxswain George Balls joined Blogg on the wheel to help control the boat as she was lifted by the seas and then dropped dizzily into the trough time after time. Every man had to hang on grimly as the boat took sea after sea on board, sweeping the deck and filling the cockpit.

When eventually they learnt from the lightshipmen that the *Crawford Castle* had apparently been able to proceed under her own steam Blogg knew that it would be impossible to rehouse the boat at Cromer in such conditions and decided to make for the Humber. From Grimsby he tried to telephone his wife Ann and the Coastguard at Cromer, but the lines were down. In Cromer it was known only that the *H.F. Bailey* was missing, and fears grew that she had met with disaster as the hours went by without news of her and her crew. It was only when the train on which they were returning home the next day reached King's Lynn that Henry Blogg was able to get through on the telephone to tell Ann that all was well.

In 1928 the *H.F. Bailey* had to go to a boatyard for permanent repairs to the damage she had sustained in the service to the *Georgia*. Her place was taken by one of the first twin-screw 45ft. 6in. Watson boats built by S.E. Saunders at East Cowes and named *H.F. Bailey II*. It is said that when Coxswain Blogg went to the Isle of Wight to collect the new boat he found plenty to complain about to the lifeboat inspector who took passage with them back to Cromer. Though he had made no complaint about spending twenty-eight bitter hours at sea on the *Georgia* service he found plenty to say about the new boat, and little of it was complimentary. As they neared Cromer he finished up by saying, 'Of course, you know she won't fit in the boathouse!' As she was being hauled up the slipway it was found that he knew exactly what he was talking about; the funnel had to be removed to allow the boat to be housed.

When the repairs were completed the following year the *H.F. Bailey* was returned to her original station and the *H.F. Bailey II* was transferred to Selsey and renamed *Canadian Pacific*. She served at the Sussex station until she was destroyed in a fire at a Cowes boatyard in 1937 while undergoing a refit.

The *Louisa Heartwell*, which had been built by Thames Iron Works in 1902, came to the end of her service in 1931, the slightly smaller Liverpool pulling and sailing lifeboat *Alexandra* being transferred from Hope Cove, near Salcombe in Devon, to take her place; she had come from the same yard at Blackwall the year after the *Louisa Heartwell*.

The problems faced in launching a pulling and sailing lifeboat from the beach were underlined when it proved impossible to get the *Alexandra* off to the assistance of a sailing barge one December day in 1933. The *H.F Bailey* had been launched at 4.30am on 13th December to the assistance of the spritsail barge *Glenway*, one of several vessels in trouble off the Norfolk coast in a severe easterly gale. Built at Rochester in 1913 and owned in London by Samuel West Ltd, the *Glenway* had gone ashore near the Cart Gap at Happisburgh while on her way from Keadby to Rye with 170 tons of coal. When the lifeboat arrived it was found that the barge had been driven into shallow water, making it impossible for the boat to be brought alongside. With the tide ebbing, at 8.30am the crew of the barge were able to walk ashore, and neither the lifeboat nor the Happisburgh lifesaving apparatus company, who were standing by, were needed. Blogg knew that in such a gale it would prove impossible to haul the lifeboat up the slipway, so he turned the boat south with the intention of putting into Gorleston. He took care to signal to the Coastguard station at Palling asking if they were needed elsewhere, but in the very bad weather the signals could not be understood.

Back at Cromer another spritsail barge, the *Sepoy* of Dover, was in trouble. Built at Rye in 1901, the *Sepoy* had been fitted with an auxiliary motor, but on this trip the motor had let her down; a gasket blew out when she was off the Humber. The skipper-owner, Captain Joseph Hempstead, and his twenty-year-old mate, John Stevenson, let go both anchors off Overstrand and slacked away on both chains as the barge drifted before the gale. The anchors failed to hold her, however, and slowly but surely she dragged towards the shore.

The *Alexandra* was brought out of her boathouse and manned by a crew under Bob Davies, the former mechanic of the No. 1 boat who had had to retire because of failing eyesight. Just as soon as she was launched the boat was thrown broadside back on to the beach, and it took an hour's hard work to get her back on to her carriage in preparation for a second attempt. Again she was launched, but the rowers could make no headway against the heavy seas and once more she was thrown back on to the beach. The strength of men's arms was as nothing against the power of the seas sweeping in to break with stunning force on the shingle.

Minute after minute the oars dipped into the sea, urging the boat on, but the lifeboat still made no progress towards the barge, which was drifting nearer and nearer the breakers. After a twenty-minute struggle the lifeboat was again thrown back on to the beach. The work of dragging the boat clear of the water and remounting her on her carriage had to begin all over again.

This time a hundred men and women tallied on the lifeboat carriage's drag-ropes to haul the *Alexandra* half a mile along the beach to bring her to windward of the *Sepoy*, which was by then in shallow water near the shore. Their faces stung by gale-driven sand and with the icy wind freezing the spray on their clothing, the launching party and their helpers were determined that this time the lifeboat should succeed. But what if she could not reach the barge, whose master and mate had now taken to the rigging?

The hon. secretary, Mr. F.H. Barclay, telephoned to his counterpart at Gorleston asking that a message should be given to Henry Blogg telling him to return with all speed. Knowing that minutes counted if the men on the barge were to be snatched from the rigging, the Gorleston secretary ordered his own boat, the *John and Mary Meiklam of Gladswood*, to go out to meet the Cromer boat in the roads, and if necessary to go on to Cromer to rescue the two bargemen.

The two lifeboats did meet, and the message was passed. As soon as he received it Henry Blogg reversed the lifeboat's course and steered for Cromer.

With the barge aground within a fairly short distance of the beach the Cromer lifesaving apparatus company got to work. Three times the wind caught their rockets and flung them aside. Then the fourth shot fell right across the barge's deck.

Young Stevenson saw his chance, climbed down the rigging and crawled along the barge's deck towards that precious lifeline. The seas were lifting the barge and dropping her heavily on to the shingle, and each time she lifted the barge rolled giddily, but he succeeded in grabbing the line. As he began to make his way back with it Skipper Hempstead saw a big sea rising up. He knew that it would sweep right across the barge's open deck, and yelled a warning to his mate: 'Look out, Jack! Hold tight!'

Heeding the skipper's shouted warning, the mate threw himself down and clawed at the nearest handhold as the freezing water engulfed him. As soon as the wave had passed he scrambled up and climbed back into the rigging, helped by his skipper. Together they prepared to haul in the warp on which they might be carried ashore.

The barge was still drifting to the westward, but the battering she was taking as she lifted on each succeeding wave and was then dropped heavily on to the shingle was proving too much, and she was probably holed as she crossed one of the groynes. Each wave that swept across the deck did further damage. The main hatch cloth was washing out of the battens and the barge was filling with water. As the LSA company tramped along the beach with their line, keeping pace with the drifting barge, preparations were made to launch the *Alexandra* once more.

This time the lifeboat was successfully got afloat. The crew pulled at their oars with a will, knowing that two men's lives depended on their efforts. They got the Alexandra to windward of the barge and tried to get alongside. But it was all in vain, for the gale and the heavy seas swept the boat down past the barge's stern, and as she was driven between the barge and the shore the lifeboat fouled the rocket line, which parted as the lifeboat was thrown back on the beach yet again.

The *Sepoy* continued to drift along the beach until, rapidly filling with water, she stuck fast about 200 yards from the shore. Wearily the lifesaving

The moment of near success as Henry 'Shrimp' Davies in the bow of the *Alexandra* cocks up his oar and attempts to grab the rocket line that has crossed the *Sepoy*. Photographer Philip Vicary had found a niche in the cliffs in which to protect himself in the howling wind. Using his glass plate camera, these two pictures are amongst the dramatic images he captured.

apparatus company set up their gear ready for another attempt to fire a line to the barge, only abandoning their efforts when the *H.F. Bailey* came in sight a little before three in the afternoon. The tide was making and the waves were breaking over the barge's deck, but above the roar of the waves and the howl of the gale the men in the rigging heard the shouts of the crowd on the shore and knew that rescue was near.

Their ordeal was not yet over, nor was the work of the lifeboatmen, who had already spent more than ten hours at sea in the *H.F. Bailey*. Quickly assessing the situation, Coxswain Blogg realised that he could not anchor and approach her from windward because of the barge's anchors and cables. Instead he took

The moment of actual success as Henry Blogg, returning from Gorleston with the *H.F.Bailey* motor lifeboat drives her onto the deck of the *Sepoy* and crewman 'Pimpo' Davies seizes the rigging to help the two men onto the lifeboat.

the lifeboat round the barge's stern, passing between her and the shore, and endeavoured to bring her alongside the *Sepoy*.

Twice the lifeboat was swept away by the seas and the strong flood tide. He made a third approach, and Jack Davies flung a grapnel into the rigging. This time a big sea drove the lifeboat against the wreck, and the grapnel line broke. If orthodox methods would not avail, something more drastic would have to be tried, Blogg decided.

On his next run-in he thrust the bows of the *H.F. Bailey* right on to the barge's bulwarks. John Stevenson simply did not have the strength to obey his skipper's shouted injunction to 'jump!' He clung to the backstay with one hand and reached out with the other arm, which was grabbed by one of the lifeboatmen, who hauled him on board the lifeboat. Then a sea lifted the lifeboat and carried her clear of the barge before lifeboatmen could drag the skipper aboard.

Watching for his chance, Blogg brought the lifeboat's bows up to the barge a second time, forcing the forefoot right up on to the deck. Skipper Hempstead jumped, grabbing one of the lifeboat's stanchions with his left hand; a lifeboatman grasped his right arm and lifted him into the boat.

There was no hope of bringing the lifeboat alongside the slipway in the prevailing conditions, but it would take four hours to reach Gorleston. Blogg looked at the two rescued men, who had been exposed to driving spray and biting wind for several hours; they were in bad shape and needed medical attention. The lifeboat crew were chilled to the marrow, wet through, and worn out by their exertions. Blogg had to make a quick decision.

He opted to drive the boat ashore on Cromer beach. That way the rescued men could be taken to hospital with the minimum of delay. As the sturdy but damaged lifeboat ran on to the beach the shore helpers were ready, wading out into the surf to steady her and to lift the two bargemen ashore. The skipper walked up the beach, the younger man was carried off on a stretcher.

The lifeboat's stem had been broken away when she was driven on to the barge's rail and there were two holes in her side. Temporary repairs were made as she lay on the beach, and later she was taken to Lowestoft for permanent repairs at a boatyard, the stem being made good and chocks being fitted inside the holes and brass plates fastened on outside. First the heavy boat had to be refloated, and that proved to be no easy task. It was not until the afternoon of 16th December that she could be freed from the beach, and by then her crew and helpers had been at work almost continuously for nearly seventy hours. Four days later she was back on station after being repaired at Lowestoft.

Coxswain Blogg, who had received the Silver Medal the previous year for the rescue of thirty men and a St. Bernard dog from the Italian steamer *Monte Nevoso*, won a second service clasp to that medal for the *Sepoy* rescue, while every member of the crew received the thanks of the Institution inscribed on vellum. Similar thanks went to Bob Davies, who had taken charge of the *Alexandra*.

A wooden barge, the *Sepoy* was over thirty years old and could not stand the hammering of the seas as she lay on the unyielding sand. She broke up even as the lifeboatmen were working to refloat the *H.F Bailey*, and her cargo of 144 tons of tiles was carried ashore when the tide was low and stacked for sale.

More fortunate was the big steel mulie barge *Fred Everard*, built at Fellow's yard in Yarmouth in 1926, which had been in trouble a little to the westward of Cromer at the same time as the *Sepoy*. She drifted ashore near the entrance to Blakeney harbour, and was refloated some days later to continue her voyage to Wells with a cargo of sugar beet.

In 1935 the *H.F. Bailey* came to the end of her service at Cromer, being transferred to the RNLI reserve fleet and given the new name *J.B. Proudfoot*, under which she continued to serve until 1953; from 1941 to 1945 she was stationed at Southend, where she had an extremely busy wartime life. Her place at Cromer was taken by a 46ft. Watson cabin boat built by Groves & Guttridge at Cowes, also named *H.F. Bailey*.

The redoubtable Henry Blogg served as coxswain for thirty-eight years, including the busy years of the Second World War, and became one of the best-known lifeboatmen of all time, gaining the Gold Medal three times and the Silver Medal four times, and also being awarded the George Cross and the British Empire Medal. One of his more spectacular and most difficult rescues resulted from a navigational error that set six vessels aground on the Haisborough Sand one August night in 1941.

Rain squalls limited visibility severely as a convoy of merchant ships escorted by two V & W class destroyers, *Vimiera* and *Wolsey*, and a handful of armed trawlers made its way along the coast in a nor'westerly gale. Buoys had been removed and the coastal lights were unlit because of wartime conditions, and the convoy's navigating officers were unaware that the tide and the gale were together setting the convoy on to the dangerous sands. One after the other the six ships ran aground; engine room telegraphs were swung to 'full astern' but the ships remained fast, battered by heavy seas and being pounded on the hard, unyielding sand.

The Cromer lifeboat *H.F. Bailey* was launched from her boathouse on the outer end of Cromer pier under Coxswain Henry Blogg, who took the boat over the submerged deck of the steamer *Oxshott* and drove her bows into an opening in the ship's superstructure to rescue sixteen of the steamer's crew. He then took the boat to the French steamer *Gallois* and took off thirty-one men from her. The rescued men were taken to a destroyer, and while they were clambering on to the naval vessel the lifeboat's crew were handed a tot of rum each, though the coxswain, a lifetime teetotaller, refused his.

The Cromer No. 2 boat *Harriot Dixon* then arrived, and Blogg transferred his second coxswain, 'Jack' Davies, to her; having already taken part in the rescue work he knew the state of the seas on the sands. While the *Harriot Dixon* took eight survivors from the Estonian ship *Taara* Blogg turned his attention to the France, Fenwick steamer *Deerwood*, whose crew were huddled on the bridge, the only part of the vessel still above water. Again he drove the lifeboat right in over the steamer's submerged deck and used the engines to hold her against the bridge structure while the nineteen surviving men of the *Deerwood*'s crew scrambled on board. He next made for the Scottish steamer *Aberhill*, but finding the Gorleston lifeboat *Louise Stephens* secured alongside and the steamer's men jumping into her as she rose and fell in the heavy seas he went to the *Taara*. 'Jack' Davies in the *Harriot Dixon* was taking the men out of her, so Blogg turned to the sixth ship, the *Paddy Hendly*,[22] a new vessel on her maiden voyage. With superb seamanship he held the lifeboat alongside her while twenty-two men leapt down into her.

The *H.F.Bailey* brings ashore the crew of the *Realf*, early in the war years.

The *H.F. Bailey* was heavily laden, with forty-one survivors on board, and as she made for deep water she went hard aground. Providentially the next wave lifted her off, and she made for Yarmouth, as did the Gorleston lifeboat with the twenty-three men she had rescued. The Lowestoft lifeboat *Michael Stephens* and the Sheringham boat *Foresters Centenary* were also called out, but they arrived at the sands to find the rescue accomplished.

As a result of their work that day Blogg was awarded the third service clasp to his RNLI Gold Medal, as well as the British Empire Medal, while 'Jack' Davies and Coxwain Charles Johnson of Gorleston both received the Silver Medal. Lewis Harrison of the *Harriot Dixon* and motor mechanic 'Swank' Davies both won a second clasp to the Bronze Medal and the motor mechanics of the *Harriot Dixon* and the *Louise Stephens* were awarded the Bronze Medal, while the other members of the three crews were voted the thanks of the Institution on vellum. And a signal from the flag officer in charge at Yarmouth conveyed to the lifeboatmen the congratulations of the Commander-in-Chief, Nore, on their superb seamanship.

The risks faced by the lifeboat crews were starkly highlighted when the Cromer men were called by the naval authorities at Yarmouth some ten weeks after the service to the ships of Convoy FS59.[23] The *H.F. Bailey* was launched at 8.15 on the morning of Sunday 26th October 1941 and set course for Hammonds Knoll, the bank on which the *Invincible* had been wrecked. This time it was a 3,953 gross ton steamer, the *English Trader*, built on the Tees in 1934, which had been sailing in convoy from the Thames. Perhaps because of the inexperience of the firemen in the stokehold the ship was unable to maintain the speed of the convoy and fell behind, and then the strong ebb tide set her on to the bank. It took the lifeboat more than three hours to reach Hammonds Knoll, and by the time she arrived the steamer was almost under water with waves crashing down on her decks and bursting almost mast-high; they had swept five men overboard, and the remaining forty-four had sought refuge on the lower bridge and in the wheelhouse.[24]

The sight that met Coxswain Blogg's eyes as the lifeboat approached was a daunting one. The seas on the bank were not only heavy, they were also confused. One huge wave would run along the weather side of the *English*

Trader from ahead, another would rear up from astern, and when they collided an immense fountain of almost solid water would erupt almost to the height of the ship's masts before crashing down on to the decks. The weight of water falling on to the ship smashed the hatch covers and washed the cargo from the holds, adding to the risks the lifeboatmen ran when they attempted to approach the wreck from the lee side.

Blogg was to say afterwards that those confused seas presented him with the most appalling problem he had ever had to face in his years as coxswain. He had been elected to that position in 1909 and was to serve until 1947.

Five hours had passed since the *H.F. Bailey* had left Cromer when Blogg took the boat towards the wreck in an attempt to fire a line to the men on the ship's bridge with the Schermuly line-throwing pistol. Signalman 'Boy Primo' Allen stood on the lifeboat's deck with the pistol as Blogg sought to position the boat close to the ship, using his engines to steady the boat in the swirl of seas. He fired at just the right moment, and the men on the bridge readied themselves to seize the line, but it never reached them. The wind caught the line and flung it back, to drop into the sea within yards of the waiting seamen. Blogg took the boat round in a wide arc and returned for a second attempt, but again the line fell short.

With the situation as it was there was nothing to be done except take the lifeboat into deeper water and wait for slack water, at about 4pm. Even there conditions were appalling, with the lifeboat lifted one moment on a wave and the next moment plunging into the trough in a welter of spray, the water pouring on to the deck and soaking the already soaked lifeboatmen again and again. For an hour or more the boat was kept head to sea, the coxswain and the motor mechanics working hard to ensure the safety of the boat. For the other members of the crew it was a time of boredom, but Blogg resisted the urging of some of the younger lifeboatmen to make another attempt to get a line on board.

Eventually the coxswain thought that the seas were becoming a little less heavy, and at 2.15pm he gave the word for another attempt to be made. In order to approach the ship the boat had to be taken over the bank and turned towards the lee side of the wreck. It was as she turned broadside to the seas that a huge wall of water rose up on the port side. There was a shout of 'Look out!' and moments later the boat was overwhelmed by the sheer weight of water. Blogg himself was lifted out of the boat 'just as though I'd been a bit of cork,' as he said later.

The waiting men on the *English Trader* watched in horror as the lifeboat was thrown over to starboard until her keel came right out of the water. They expected her

Huddled in the chart room of the *English Trader*, you've survived a night which you perhaps thought was an impossibility. Crew member Robert Aldwin, a trainee journalist, still had the presence of mind to take a photo of the lifeboat *H.F.Bailey* as she approached to complete the rescue.

to turn right over, but miraculously she righted herself. As she did so William Davies, the son of second coxswain 'Jack' Davies, sprang to the wheel and brought the boat under control. Seven men had been washed out of the boat, but two of them had managed to grab the handrails as they went overboard and had hauled themselves back on board. Those who had remained on board were thrown down by the weight of water hitting the boat and were knocked about and winded.

Looking around him, young John Davies saw his father and Henry Blogg in the water. He took the lifeboat over to where they were and other crew members hauled them back on board, not without considerable difficulty. Blogg, a man of sixty-five at the time, hung on to the canopy for a few moments to recover his breath, and then resumed command, taking the boat over to where other men were floating, mercifully held up by their kapok lifejackets. One by one they were rescued, but getting them on board proved an awsome task; their waterlogged clothes made them extremely heavy to lift, and there was little those in the water could do to assist their rescuers. It took a good five minutes to haul each man over the gunwale into the boat.

By the time they got to the last man, signalman 'Boy Primo' Allen, he had been twenty-five minutes in the icy water and was unconscious. His colleagues rubbed his limbs to try to restore his circulation, and it seemed they were succeeding. At last he sat up, spoke a few words, then suddenly collapsed and died.

It was remarkable that in those seas all five men had been picked up from the water. There was nothing now that they could do for the men of the *English Trader*, and Blogg decided to make for Yarmouth. As they headed south the Gorleston lifeboat *Louise Stephens* was on her way out to Hammonds Knoll, having been launched at noon at the request of the naval authorities. The two boats did not pass within sight of each other, but the Gorleston men picked up a radio message from the *H.F. Bailey* asking for a doctor and ambulance to be waiting when they arrived, and they passed this on to the Yarmouth naval base, who for some reason had been unable to receive the message direct.

It took the *Louise Stephens* three and a half hours to travel the nineteen miles to Hammonds Knoll against the gale and the flood tide, and it was almost slack water as Coxswain Charles Johnson took her towards the *English Trader*. Like the Cromer boat before her, the *Louise Stephens* suffered a fearful battering from the confused seas which poured over the deck and flooded into the cockpit. Time after time the lifeboat was brought towards the *English Trader*, and on one occasion a line was fired to the wreck and a rope hauled across, but the lifeboat was caught by a wave and the rope snapped. Another time a line was successfully fired to the men on the steamer's bridge, but the line was snatched away by the sea. The coxswain endeavoured to retrieve the line, but Captain Grimstone on the bridge blew a whistle to attract the lifeboatmen's attention and waved them away. He realised that it was far too dangerous for the lifeboat to approach close to the wreck in those conditions and was fearful of another such accident as had occurred to the Cromer boat.

The naval authorities ordered the Gorleston lifeboat to return to her station, although Coxswain Johnson was all for standing by through the night. As she turned for home the men of the *H.F. Bailey* were refuelling their boat and preparing for another rescue attempt before going to the Shipwrecked Sailors'

Home on Yarmouth's Marine Parade for hot baths, dry clothes and a good meal.

News of 'Boy Primo' Allen's death was telephoned to Cromer, together with a request for another man to come to Yarmouth to take his place in the crew. And when at 10.30 that night Henry Blogg heard that the Gorleston boat had reached home he telephoned Coxswain Johnson to discuss arrangements for the next morning.

Blogg did not get much rest that night. Between 3.30 and 4am he was telephoning the Yarmouth naval base and the coastguard at Cromer seeking weather reports. The wind and sea had dropped just a little, but conditions were much as they had been the day before, he was told. By 4.15am he was at the naval base, requesting that the boom at the harbour mouth be opened for the lifeboat to go out, and twenty-five minutes later the *H.F. Bailey* was on her way out to Hammonds Knoll.

Daylight came shortly before the lifeboat arrived, and with the dawn the wind had backed to the nor'west and had eased, and the sea had gone down. The destroyer HMS *Vesper*, having kept watch over the *English Trader* ever since she had gone aground, was still lying off in the vicinity. The *English Trader* had sunk deeper into the sand during the night and the whole forepart of the ship was under water; as the lifeboat was brought alongside the lifeboatmen found the steamer's rail no more than two feet above the lifeboat's deck. The lifeboat was moored fore and aft, members of the crew standing by with boathooks to fend her off from the steamer's torn steel plating; she had broken in two just ahead of the bridge under the pounding of the waves.

It took no more than half an hour for the forty-four survivors to be embarked in the *H.F. Bailey*; Captain Grimstone was the last to drop into the lifeboat. The *H.F. Bailey* was already on its way to Yarmouth with the survivors when the *Louise Stephens* reached Hammonds Knoll to find the *English Trader* deserted. Coxswain Johnson turned her about and followed the *H.F. Bailey* back to Yarmouth harbour.

For that service Henry Blogg received a fourth service clasp to his Silver Medal, each of the other crew members including 'Boy Primo' Allen being awarded either the Bronze Medal or a clasp to the Bronze Medal already held. The Institution granted to Allen's widow a pension on the same scale as if her husband had been a seaman of the Royal Navy who had died in action. The Gorleston coxswain was awarded a third clasp to his Bronze Medal, and each of the other six members of his crew was given the thanks of the Institution inscribed on vellum.

In those dramatic wartime years, Coxswain Blogg had succeeded in having his nephew Henry 'Shrimp' Davies released from wartime service with the Royal Navy in order to have the younger man beside him in such a challenging period. When Blogg finally stood down it was to 'Shrimp' that he handed the reins, and it was not long before the new coxswain was to take the lead in a particularly dramatic service.

In 1948 the French collier *François Tixier* was in trouble in a storm when her cargo shifted. The new lifeboat Henry Blogg, named after the illustrious coxswain, put to sea and the successful rescue of the crew of the *François Tixier* led to the award of a French maritime medal to Coxswain Davies. A further surprise came in 1976 on his own retirement when he was the subject of

Seventy years on, Walter 'Boy Primo' Allen's stone in Cromer cemetery was restored as part of the recollection of the service and his sacrifice.

Allen had a remarkable career. In the First World War he had served in the navy – but in an armoured car squadron on the Russian front. His ability to receive and send semaphore led him to be signaller on the lifeboat.

television's 'This is Your Life' programme and met the French skipper again, this time in the television studio.

In turn 'Shrimp's' nephew Richard Davies became coxswain. He won a bronze medal for the rescue of a swimmer off Cromer beach, and he was with lifeboat doctor Paul Barclay when the doctor jumped from the rolling lifeboat to the Lowestoft trawler *Boston Jaguar* in 1973. The fishing vessel had suffered an explosion in which one man had been killed and another injured; the doctor's courage led to his being awarded the RNLI bronze medal.

Richard Davies continued to lead the lifeboat crew as the new generation of higher-speed lifeboats was introduced, handing over in 1999 to his cousin Billy Davies, who was in turn followed by Richard's son John.

Henry Blogg's story is now told in a purpose-built lifeboat museum at Cromer that houses his famous *H.F. Bailey*. Her pier-end boathouse has made way for a new and larger building to accommodate the Tamar-class lifeboat *Lester*, which entered service in 2008. The old boathouse lives on, however, providing a home for the restored pulling and sailing lifeboat *Alfred Corry* at Southwold.

Tragedy on the beach

The constant danger involved in earning a living from the sea has already been referred to. Looking back into the records, all along the coast there are accounts of inshore fishermen losing their lives, often within almost grounding distance of the beach. The decision to launch could be be made based on the state of the weather and the sea at the time, but the necessity of landing when caught at sea by increasing wind and swell could not be avoided.

Just such a tragedy occurred at Cromer on 2nd May 1907. Young fishermen Robert Rix and James Harrison jnr. were caught in a squall which led to the capsize of their rowing and sailing crab boat as they attempted to regain the land.

June 1953 brought perhaps an even more poignant loss. The town had been decorated for the new Queen's coronation, but a mood of celebration was turned to sadness for the whole community and the decorations were removed when on a Friday morning the crab boat *Boy Jimmy* was overwhelmed just a few yards from the shore. James Davies, both coxswain of the No. 2 lifeboat and member of the town council, was one of the three who lost their lives. With him were his brother Frank Davies and the 21-year-old Edward Bussey.

Among those who sought to rescue the men was the elderly Henry Blogg. The exertion proved too much for him; he collapsed at the water's edge, and never fully recovered his health after the tragedy. The *Boy Jimmy* was washed ashore some 300 yards from where the boat had been swamped.

The parish church was filled to overflowing for the funeral of the three men, the townsfolk being joined by representatives of the fishing, lifeboat and coastguard community from all along the Norfolk coast. At the inquest a straightforward Henry 'Shrimp' Davies said that short of not going to sea, there was nothing that could be done to provide absolute safety against such accidents.

At that time there was local coastguard provision, watching the sea, at every appropriate point along the Norfolk coast. At the time of writing the closure of the regional coastguard centre at Great Yarmouth is pending, and while there are local retained teams at various points on the coast that can be called out, the service is not at all what it once was. In response to accidents at sea, the Maritime and Coastguard Agency has over the years increased its service in respect of maintenance of standards of commercial vessels; the smaller fishing boats now require inspection and a balance of advice and formal requirement is applied through the MCA, with Certificates of Competence being required by fishermen where appropriate.

In the event of the report of an incident at sea, it is the Coastguard service which co-ordinates the rescue effort. The team currently based at Great Yarmouth provides a 24-hour listening service on the marine frequencies and also responds to 999 calls from members of the public. They assess the kind of help needed, and while they will not have direct visual contact any longer, they have an array of computer-based facilities available to call up tidal and meteorological information. The sailor of old would gain assistance from his charts, almanacs and tidal data; today electronic chart and satellite information and communications can all come into play. Having said that, there remains an important role for local knowledge!

Legislation on fishing is the responsibility of the Eastern Inshore Fisheries and Conservation Authority, which took over from Eastern Sea Fisheries in 2011. The authority's responsibility is 'to lead, champion and manage a sustainable marine environment'. To that end, its research vessel *Three Counties* and its inspection vessel *Pisces III* are common sights around the East Anglian coast as they carry out their duties; the patrol vessel *ESF Protector III* was retired from service in 2012.

The gas industry, with its nearest platforms being seen in good visibility from the Norfolk coast, has stringent safety precautions and a safety fleet always at sea. The orange hulls of the Putford rig standby vessels are another familiar site. Since the 1950s, safety at sea has also been a responsibility undertaken by the Royal Air Force search and rescue organisation with its Westland Whirlwind, Westland Wessex and more recently Westland Sea King helicopters.

Initially No. 22 Squadron based a detachment at Martlesham Heath in Suffolk, moving from there to RAF Felixstowe in May 1956. When that station closed down they moved first to Horsham St Faiths and then in 1963 to Coltishall, where they were within a few minutes flying time of the north Norfolk coast; in more recent years the Sea Kings have been based at Wattisham in Suffolk. Right from the early years helicopter aircrews have collaborated closely with the lifeboatmen; today they undertake regular exercises with lifeboat crews, ensuring that the two services integrate well and that all are familiar with the process of transferring casualties from one to the other.

The *Putford Achilles*, here seen leaving Great Yarmouth harbour, and the Cromer Lifeboat *Ruby and Arthur Reed II* had worked together in the search for survivors of a rig helicopter crash in 2002, but tragically 11 lives were lost.

East Norfolk   7

That part of the Norfolk coast between Cromer and Yarmouth has been eroding for centuries. In places where there are lofty cliffs these have been eaten away by the waves; where the coast is low the only protection is provided by sand dunes that form no more than a frail and easily breached barrier, and here the land behind the coast has from time to time been flooded by the sea. As long ago as the thirteenth century a monk of St. Benet's Abbey in Horning, one John of Oxnead, described how 'the sea flowing and swelling dreadfully, crossed its usual boundaries by claiming further shores' in 1251. Thirty-six years later the sea broke in again between Waxham and Winterton, inundating places which nobody remembered having been flooded by the sea before.

Brother John tells us how 'about midnight, climbing up in its approach, it suffocated or drowned men and women sleeping in their beds and babies in their cots, all kinds of draught animals and fresh water fishes; houses with their contents were ripped entirely from their foundations and carried away and with irrecoverable loss hurled into the sea.' Those who could climbed into trees to get above the water, but he describes how they were overcome by the cold and fell into the water, drowning with the rest. No fewer than 180 men and women died in the village of Hickling alone.

That was by no means the last time the sea took its toll. Brother John relates how there was further flooding in the same area in 1292, and more than three hundred years later the sea broke in twice within a decade. When William Faden published his map of Norfolk in 1797 he showed at Waxham and Horsey a number of 'Gaps or Breaches made by the Sea in the Marum Hills prior to Summer 1790', the two worst of which were 120 yards wide.

And all the while the sea was eating into the cliffs and washing the soil down the coast to replenish beaches further south. The parish of Eccles, 'once a noted fishing town',[1] had almost disappeared by 1797; Faden marks it as 'Eccles in Ruins'. In 1605 the inhabitants appealed for a reduction in their taxes because there were then only fourteen houses and three hundred acres of land, 'the rest being all destroyed by the sea, together with the church'. The church of St. Mary had gone but its round tower survived, standing alone on the beach until it was felled by a storm in 1895. By 1845 the parish had only fifty-three inhabitants, and in 1901 the population was no more than seventeen.

Further south Happisburgh was said in 1854 to be facing the same fate.[2] 'The continual encroachments of the sea during the last 70 years has wasted

Opposite: James Haylett wearing the RNLI Gold Medal that he was awarded for his part in rescuing survivors from the *Beauchamp* disaster.

Happisburgh, despite many attempts at defending against the sea, remains one of the most critical sites on the east coast.

upwards of 250 yards, and it is calculated that a great part of Happisburgh will be engulfed in the ocean, if the same wasting process continues during the ensuing century,' we read in White's directory. The sea has not yet brought Happisburgh church with its 112ft. seamark tower down the cliff, as the directory predicted, but it has been claiming houses one by one, and if the government sticks to its policy of managed retreat and refusal to fund defences who can tell how long it will be before church and village disappear?

Those who had the money attempted to protect their properties, but piecemeal projects did little good. At Trimingham, where the sea washed away two farmhouses in the 1820s, local landowner Sir Thomas Fowell Buxton built a sea wall, and at Mundesley a well-to-do resident sought to protect the little town with two massive walls which were destroyed by high tides in 1836 within a few years of their erection. The walls, which formed terraces in the cliff face, were replaced, but by 1880 they were again in ruins.

Mundesley, which in 1845 was said to have four large herring boats and seven smaller craft engaged in crab and lobster fishing, possessed one of the few watermills in Norfolk powered by an overshot wheel in which the water was directed on to the upper part of the wheel. After turning the wheel the stream tumbled down the cliff through what the 1845 directory described as 'a deep ravine'. The mill fell victim to fire about 1960.

Mundesley lifeboats

As early as 1810 the Cromer lifeboat committee fitted up a fishing boat as a temporary lifeboat for Mundesley, and as related in the previous chapter a small lifeboat built at Sunderland at a cost of £130 was stationed there a few years later. This ten-oared boat was 26ft. 10in. long, with a beam of 9ft. 4in. and a depth of 3ft. 10in., and was presumably a pulling boat of the North Country type.

A contemporary description of the boat reveals that the bottom was 'so contrived that if a sea breaks over it the water instantly runs away. This boat is completely decked 18 inches from the keel and 4 inches above water level, and there are pipes leading from this deck through the bottom of the boat to carry off the water. If filled, it will thus empty itself in two minutes. This has no cork, but is fitted with airtight copper tubes (in distinct compartment) under the seats.'[3]

A prominent Mundesley resident, Captain Francis Wheatley, took charge of her. Captain Wheatley had gained such a reputation for lifesaving that it is said that seamen who could not escape shipwreck on the dangerous Norfolk coast would, if possible, drive their vessels ashore in the vicinity of Mundesley, knowing that the chances of rescue there were higher than on other parts of the coast. It was also said that he had been in the practice of giving a guinea to the first person bringing him tidings of a ship in distress. Wheatley had settled at Mundesley in the first decade of the century after experience as a shipmaster in the coasting trade – it is said he was himself shipwrecked three times during his career at sea. He became a shipowner and merchant importing coal for distribution in the neighbourhood, and was appointed a Deputy Vice-Admiral of Norfolk, a position that he took most seriously.

The lifeboat was in action on 26th October 1819, when it seems that a mortar line fired from the shore was used to haul her off through the surf to assist several vessels in trouble, including the *Endeavour* of Sunderland, but little has been recorded of her services. It seems likely that many of her exploits found no echo in the local newspapers, though the rescue of three men from the billyboy sloop *Union* of Hull on 19th February 1832 was well reported. Laden with a cargo of timber and deals for Yarmouth, the little craft was put ashore on Mundesley beach after springing a leak and becoming waterlogged. Captain Wheatley's horses were employed to haul the lifeboat to the spot and Lieutenant Wyld and some of the coastguardsmen, together with some local fishermen, manned the boat and saved the billyboy's crew.[4]

It seems likely that in January 1834 the Mundesley lifeboat was employed to rescue the crew of the brig *Traveller*, which ran on a sand about half a mile from the shore while on her way from the Tyne with a cargo of small coal for the French manufacturing town of Charente.[5] Attempts to get the *Traveller* off the sandbank failed, and her wreckage later drifted up on the beach, where it was sold a few weeks later.[6] Newspaper reports do not mention the lifeboat, merely saying that boats were sent out by Captain Wheatley, but it is probably safe to assume that the lifeboat was involved.

In 1823 a retired naval officer, Lieutenant Robert Rust, was given the care of the lifeboat by the Norfolk Shipwreck Association and paid £3 a year until his death in 1845, when a member of the general committee expressed a wish 'that the annuity had died with him.' It was the opinion of the committee that while money might be paid to superannuated seamen to look after the boats, gentlemen should do it for nothing.[7] The following year a dispute arose between Captain Wheatley and his fellow Shipwreck Association committee members.[8] Both the lifeboat and the line-throwing gun were kept at Mr. Wheatley's premises for six guineas a year, but it might well be that the dispute resulted in them being removed elsewhere.

The general committee of the Norfolk Association for Saving the Lives of Shipwrecked Mariners decided in April 1846 that the 'old Caister boat should be removed to Mundesley'.[9] Not only is it unclear what boat is referred to but it is by no means certain that any such transfer took place, since the committee seemed to be more than a little unsure what to do with the boat then at Caister, which the local beachmen were refusing to use.

In January 1849 the Mundesley lifeboat assisted the brig *London* into Yarmouth and the crew was awarded £250 salvage. The central committee of the Shipwreck Association was told that the salvors had to pay heavy costs out of the salvage award, but nevertheless insisted that the usual two shares be paid for the use of the lifeboat.[11] That decision did not please the crew, who had doled out £12 a man and had paid that amount to the association.

The Northumberland report stated in 1851 that the boat was in good repair, but with the RNLI takeover in 1858 she was replaced by a 30ft. self-righting boat pulling ten oars double banked, that is with two oarsmen to each thwart. While there is no reliable record of services carried out by the original boat it is recorded that the RNLI boat, built by Forrestt at Limehouse, went out six times on service and saved twenty-two lives. This boat, which was never given a name, had a somewhat short life as by 1867 she was said to be 'becoming rapidly unserviceable' and was replaced by a 33ft. self-righter built by Woolfe at Shadwell. A new boathouse was built for her on the north

Exceptional storms affect the Norfolk coast perhaps every 50 years - when wind and tide combine to create devastation.

side of the score leading down to the beach. Having been subscribed for by the grocers of England, the new boat was named the *Grocers*.

The *Grocers* was launched into a heavy sea brought up by a strong gale from SSE on 17th November 1868 to the aid of the Sunderland brig *George*, which was on her way from the Wear with a cargo of coal for Rouen, on the Seine. The master of the brig decided to beach her, but unfortunately she struck the outer bank and remained fast, full of water, and out of range of the coastguards' rocket apparatus.

The lifeboatmen had a long fight to reach the wreck, and while they were struggling to make headway they saw the mainmast, with six men clinging to it, go overboard as the vessel broke up. Only one man survived, clinging to a small piece of plank, and he owed his life to one of the lifeboatmen, William Juniper, who leapt overboard with a line and grabbed him as he drifted past. Both of them were hauled into the boat by other members of the crew. Juniper's gallantry won him the RNLI Silver Medal, the only award known to have been won by a member of the Mundesley crew.

There was still a heavy sea running the following day when the *Grocers* put off to bring ashore the crew of six from the Peterhead schooner *Restless*, which had been wrecked on the Haisborough Sand. The shipwrecked men had managed to reach the Haisbro' lightship, from which they were taken by the lifeboat.

During her fifteen years on station the *Grocers* was launched seven times and saved nineteen lives. She was replaced in 1882 by a 34ft. 4in. self-righter also built at Shadwell by Woolfe & Son. This boat, the *J.H. Elliott*, remained at Mundesley until the station was closed in 1895 because of continual encroachment of the sea, which was threatening to wash the boathouse away. The *J.H. Elliott* was launched on service only twice and saved ten lives, bringing to fifty-one the total of lives saved since the RNLI took over.

The beach traders

In spite of the unstable nature of this coast there was until the nineteenth century a considerable trade passing over the beaches, particularly at Mundesley, Bacton and Sea Palling where passable roads ran close to the shore. A visitor to Walcot Gap, a lonely spot between Bacton and Happisburgh, described how coal was landed on the beach in the middle of the nineteenth century.[12] 'A vessel arrives during the summer months, and rides off at anchor until the weather be propitious, then comes on shore on the top of high water, and is hauled as far up as possible by the strong capstan fixed at the head of the Gap. Then on sight of the usual signal, the neighbouring farmers send teams and broad-wheeled tumbrils, which set to work as the tide falls, and if the sand be not too soft and they work with a will, the whole cargo will be carried from the vessel to the storehouse by the Gap in a single tide.'

A kedge anchor was laid out astern to enable the vessel to be hauled off when unloading was completed. It could also prevent the vessel broaching to if bad weather blew up while she was on the beach. Even with such precautions, an unexpected storm during unloading could bring sudden disaster, as occurred in 1816 when the brig *Norfolk*, which was owned by Captain Wheatley, was on Mundesley beach with a cargo of coal.[13]

Without any warning the wind changed from a south-westerly breeze, off the land, to a west-nor'-westerly gale which piled up mountainous seas and caused a higher and earlier tide than predicted. The little brig was swung broadside to the seas as the water rose under the stern, and the crew and the workmen who had boarded her to help in the unloading gave themselves up for lost.

Helped by the inhabitants, who flocked to the shore to do what they could, Wheatley managed to haul a boat off the beach and rescued all on board except one unfortunate man who became entangled in a rope and drowned. Something rather similar happened in the first week of 1830 as the brig *Ocean* was delivering her cargo of coal from Newcastle on 'Mundesley Main'. Before unloading could be completed a nor'easterly gale sprang up and she was forced to leave the beach. Unable to work her way offshore against the gale, she went ashore on Bacton beach, the crew being saved 'by a communication from the shore'.[14] The *Ocean* was refloated on that occasion, but her end came when she went missing with all hands in October 1833 as she sailed in ballast from Mundesley to Christiansand in Norway to collect a cargo of timber; it was assumed that she had been run down by another vessel on her outward passage.[15]

It was not only really severe weather that caused casualties, for a nor'easterly wind of well below gale strength could bring up a sea on the shore that would cause a beached vessel to pound quite enough to cause damage. In 1831 two ships belonging to Cley put in at their home port after delivering coal 'in consequence of having sprung a leak previous to their coming off the Beach, wind blowing strong from N.E. to E'. One of them, the *Experience*, Robert Pank, master, had delivered its cargo on Bacton beach and the other, the *Dolphin*, Robert Claxton, master, had been on Sheringham beach.[16] The following year the *Commerce* arrived at Cley with part of her coal cargo still aboard because a nor'easterly wind had made it impossible to 'deliver',[17] and there were many similar records in the Blakeney and Cley ship lists in the local papers.

When an old vessel was involved even 'a stiffish breeze from the northward' could create havoc. In 1850 the brigantine *Chance* was lying on Mundesley beach unloading coal when such a breeze sprang up, 'and the vessel being very old, she soon became a total wreck, and part of her cargo was lost', as a local newspaper reported.[18] The same paper that recorded her loss also contained an advertisement of the sale of her wreck.

Identification of craft mentioned in newspaper reports can be impossible at times. The little *Mary Ann* arrived at Lowestoft from Mundesley at the beginning of December 1852 'to lay up for the winter', although the previous year she had continued trading to Mundesley until rather later, since we read of her putting in at Lowestoft, presumably for shelter, just after Christmas while on her way from Hartlepool to Mundesley. One has little or no hope of making a positive identification; there were no fewer than eighty vessels with this name in the *Mercantile Navy List* at about this time. It seems likely, however, that this Mundesley trader was the 47-ton *Mary Ann* of King's Lynn, a ketch built at Whitstable in 1832 and owned at Blakeney at this period; or she might have been the 49-ton Sunderland-built vessel registered at Wells from 1852 to 1864 and at Lowestoft for the last three years of her life, which

The *Elizabeths* was stranded on Walcot beach on February 22nd 1908. Her crew managed to get ashore in the ship's boat; it seems to have been the tradition that photographs were taken if you spent the night at the Shipwrecked Sailor's Home at Great Yarmouth.

was wrecked on Lowestoft South Beach in December 1867.

Among the several vessels owned at Mundesley was the *Diligence*, a schooner of 73 tons built at Southtown in 1820 and owned in the 1870s by Robert Juniper, maltster, coal merchant and victualler at *The Ship* in Mundesley. Juniper also owned the *Eleanor*, of West Hartlepool, a schooner of 72 tons built at Hull in 1847. The *Diligence* shuttled back and forth mainly between Hartlepool and Mundesley until she was lost on 25th November 1874 as a result of stranding; the crew, all but one of whom came from Mundesley, were saved.

Although the construction of the North Walsham and Dilham Canal in the 1820s enabled wherries to bring cargoes up the Ant to within a mile of the town of North Walsham it had very little impact on the trade of Mundesley. The market town's merchants seem to have preferred to have their goods landed on the beach and carried four or five miles overland rather than pay the canal dues. Possibly the inconvenience of having to transfer the cargo from ship to wherry at Yarmouth, with both the attendant cost and the risk of pilferage, influenced their decision to continue landing cargoes on the beach in spite of the obvious hazards inherent in that operation.

Cargoes were also landed at Bacton Gap, also known significantly as Coal Gap, some two miles from Mundesley. Focusing on that gap, known today as Cable Gap, is the hamlet of Bacton Green, which is credited in White's 1845 directory with having two fish curing houses and four large and a number of small fishing boats. Among a number of documents deposited by the Registrar of Shipping with the Suffolk Record Office is one of 1863 relating to the *Two Brothers*, 34 tons, registered at Lowestoft in 1861 and owned by her master, John Smith, of Bacton. She is recorded as making fifteen voyages in the coal trade between Hartlepool and Bacton beach during the period from early March to the end of October, when she was laid up in Lowestoft. She was by no means the only vessel owned at Bacton and crewed by local men, another being the schooner *Palmers*, mentioned in the chapter on north Norfolk.

Bacton

The Cubitt family were much involved in the trade to Bacton beach.[19] Towards the end of the eighteenth century Robert Cubitt established a coal business there which was taken over by his son Thomas Colk Cubitt on his death in 1814. In due course TC handed over the business to his cousin William Partridge Cubitt, who besides being a shipowner and coal merchant was well known as a farmer and cattle breeder. Not content with that, William Partridge Cubitt took over Ebridge Mill on the River Ant in 1856, and in 1867 bought the Bacton Grange estate. He was a partner with George Walker in the little schooner *Shepherdess*, built at Yarmouth by Henry Fellows, supposedly out of timber left over from the building of a larger vessel. As the firm of Cubitt & Walker expanded it took over other mills on the Ant and gathered together a small fleet of wherries working on the rivers.

Several members of the Cubitt family were associated with the Bacton lifeboat, which had been established in 1822 and taken over by the Norfolk Association for Saving the Lives of Shipwrecked Mariners on its formation a year later. The first boat was a 29ft. 6in. North Country type boat pulling ten oars whose history is somewhat unclear.

In the 1840s Robert Cubitt was described as 'superintendent of life boats,' which suggests that he had responsibility for more than the Bacton boat. In 1845 he attracted the censure of the Norfolk Association's general committee for having expended £95 5s. on lengthening the Bacton boat. He and William

The Coastguards at Bacton with their rocket lifesaving apparatus cart in the early years of the twentieth century. At that time there was a chief officer and four men at that station.

Partridge Cubitt, along with other members of the Bacton crew, were awarded medals by the Norfolk Association for their 'gallant and effective assistance' when the lifeboat rescued three men, a woman and two children from the *Emperor* of Boston, wrecked off Bacton on 17th October 1843.

The Norfolk Association is reported to have sent the Bacton boat to Caister about 1844. The Bacton lifeboat that took part in lifeboat trials at Yarmouth Regatta in 1845 is described in a contemporary report as a sailing boat,[20] so it is possible that the original lifeboat was replaced at that period, though the Northumberland report of 1851 lists the 1822 boat as still in use at Bacton. Whatever boat was on station when the RNLI took over in 1858 was superseded by a 32ft. self-righter built by Forrestt at Limehouse on the Thames.

For a time William Partridge Cubitt served as coxswain and was twice awarded the RNLI silver medal, the first time in 1864 when the lifeboat saved twenty-two men from the barque *Ina*; he gained the second service clasp three years later when he swam his horse out to a wreck and brought the shipwrecked men ashore clinging to his stirrups.

The Forrestt self-righter, which seems never to have been given a name, spent only seven years at Bacton before being replaced by the *Recompense*, a 33ft. self-righter built by Woolfe in 1865. W.P. Cubitt's son of the same name won the RNLI gold medal in 1880 when the lifeboat *Recompense* overturned with the loss of two crew members while alongside the Fleetwood schooner *Richard Warbrick*; Cubitt threw himself into the sea and cut a rope which had entangled the rudder when the boat capsized, releasing the boat from a very perilous situation.

The elder William Partridge Cubitt made as great a name for himself on the land as on the sea, for he is said to have been the first Norfolk farmer to pay his workers a weekly wage of ten shillings and to have allowed the use of his barn for the first meeting of the Agricultural Labourers' Union to have been held in the district. Clearly a man with views that would have seemed extreme to some of his neighbours, he started a school for small children in the village and built four cottages to house his retired workers and other old people, charging them only a token rent. He went to Canada in 1880 to investigate farming prospects there on behalf of Norfolk tenant farmers, but it is said that he did not favour the Canadian farming methods.

The Bacton lifeboat station was closed in 1882. The Bacton boats had saved fifty-one lives since the RNLI took over; the number of lives saved during the years the station was run by the Norfolk Shipwreck Association seems not to have been recorded.

Bacton did at one time have a small company of beachmen, but it would seem that for a period the company was operated jointly with men from Happisburgh more than two miles away. David Higgins records that the yawl *Nautilus*, built in 1835, was in 1839 registered as being owned by Joseph Steward, fisherman, and John Thompson, blacksmith, of Happisburgh, and John Marshall, fisherman, of Bacton, though in later days she was owned entirely by Bacton men.[21]

Little is known about the operations of the early Bacton company, though in 1842 William Wright and a company of fifteen men were awarded £85 for assisting the brig *John* off Bacton beach and into Yarmouth.[22] Wright is described in the 1845 directory as a farmer at Bacton, but clearly his activities, like those of so many who lived on that coast, were not confined to the land.

The free traders

Smuggling was rife all along the coast of north and east Norfolk in the early part of the nineteenth century, and it is impossible to know just what the value of the 'free trade' might have been at any particular time. Every so often a paragraph appeared in the local papers chronicling the success of the forces ranged against the smugglers, but only on very rare occasions, if ever, does a successful run find its way into the news columns. The old East Anglian dictum 'nivver yew know nothin', they can't git uvver that' ensured that the regular delivery of tobacco, spirits, tea and fine lace was not advertised in places where the Customs men might read of it. We do know that Parson Woodford, the incumbent of Weston Longville, in the Wensum valley a few miles west of Norwich, was happy to avoid paying duty on the gin and rum that was from time to time deposited on his doorstep by a smuggler, and there were many other very respectable people who were prepared to patronise the free traders.

The very fact that the papers contained so many references to captures of illegal imports may be taken as an indication of the scale of the operation, for the amounts of goods seized must have been quite small in proportion to the total imports. The Customs were happy to publicise their successes, and the staff of the Custom House at Cley regularly provided the *Norfolk Chronicle* in the 1820s with handouts detailing their latest seizures of brandy, gin and tobacco, their press releases almost invariably ending with the phrase 'which have been lodged in his Majesty's custom-house warehouse here'.

In the issue of 2nd November 1822 it is recorded that thirty-nine half-ankers of Geneva had been seized by the crew of the preventive station at

Weybourne and that an open boat, three carts, eighty-six half-ankers of Geneva, nine of brandy and three casks of tobacco had been seized by the Bacton crew. On 20th November an open eight-oared galley with eighty-six half-ankers of Geneva had been seized at sea by the Morston crew, and a few weeks later the crew of the Morston preventive boat seized 101 half-ankers of Geneva, 'which were safely lodged in his Majesty's custom-house warehouse' at Cley.

A typical news item appeared in the *Norfolk Chronicle* of 14th December 1822:

> *CLEY, Dec. 12.*
> Tuesday se'nnight were seized on the beach near Smith's gap, by the crew of the Preventive station at Bacton, 37 half-ankers of brandy and 10 half-ankers of over-proof Geneva. – On the same day, were seized by the crew of the Preventive station at Mundesley, 21 casks of manufactured tobacco, 18 half-ankers of brandy, four half-ankers of over-proof Geneva, and one half-anker of Geneva, concealed in a vault in a field in the parish of Witton; all of which have been lodged in his Majesty's custom-house warehouse here.

Those who are curious to know what a half-anker was are unlikely to find enlightenment in a modern dictionary, but Dr. Johnson in his *Dictionary of the English Language* is more forthcoming. An anker was, he tells us, a liquid measure chiefly used at Amsterdam. 'It is a fourth part of the awme, and contains two stekans: each stekan consists of sixteen mengles; the mengle being equal to two of our wine quarts.' It would seem that half an anker was to the Dutch a stekan, but one is left to assume that the customs men were referring to a wooden cask containing that amount.

The efforts of the shore-based personnel were complemented by the work of the revenue cutters based at Yarmouth and elsewhere which spent their time cruising off the coast looking out for suspect craft that might be running illicit cargoes. Many of the smuggling vessels were specially built for the trade, fast luggers that in some conditions showed the cutters a clean pair of heels. Others were innocent-looking fishing boats that loaded contraband at sea from vessels that had brought it from continental ports and hid it under the catch in the fish hold, hoping to be able to land it undetected on their return home.

Towards the end of the eighteenth century the cutter *Hunter*, commanded by Captain Thomas Jay, who had married a daughter of one of the Palmer family, was based on Yarmouth. In 1791 Captain Jay and the *Hunter* had a notable success when, aided by a detachment of the 15th Light Dragoons operating on shore, they seized twenty-one half-ankers of Geneva on Scratby beach and another 123 ankers of spirits and two bags of tobacco on Hemsby beach.

Captain Jay and his crew lost their lives when the *Hunter* was wrecked on the Haisborough Sand in a severe gale on 18th February 1807; the vessel knocked over the sand and drifted into shallow water near the shore about a mile to the north of the old Happisburgh east gap. Lying with her stern towards the cliff, the wreck of the *Hunter* acted like a groyne and caused a build-up of sand and shingle that in time grew into a substantial extension of the beach that was only swept away about twenty years later when the sea eroded the cliffs to the northward and took it in the rear.[23]

The revenue cutters not only cruised the coast themselves but their boats were employed inshore looking out for smuggling activity. When the Yarmouth-based cutter *Ranger* was lost in an October gale in 1822 the only survivors were seven men who were on detached duty in one of the cutter's boats watching out for a suspected smuggler; they managed to beach the boat at Cromer. A second boat's crew was also out engaged in a similar task, but it was thought they had either returned to the cutter when bad weather blew up or had been overcome by the seas; they perished with the rest as the *Ranger* was driven on to the Haisborough Sand.

The account in the *Norfolk Chronicle* the following week told how rumours of the loss of the *Ranger* had spread through Yarmouth on the Monday morning and the wives and relatives of the crew 'were running about with tears in their eyes, in the deepest despair, seeking for information, but nothing satisfactory could be learnt'. All doubts of her loss were resolved next morning when the wreck of the cutter came ashore at Happisburgh bottom up, within 150 yards of the spot where the *Hunter* had finished up. Thirty of the crew of thirty-eight died in the disaster; the seven men of the boat's crew who landed at Cromer survived, along with one man who was sick at home in Yarmouth. Captain John Sayers, who was among those lost, had been appointed to the *Ranger* in 1809 after two years in command of the cutter *Lapwing*, which had replaced the wrecked *Hunter*. A single man, he lived in Yarmouth with his sisters in a house on the quay.[24]

The men of the *Ranger* were by no means the only seamen to die that October night. 'The beach, for many miles, was literally covered with pieces

The Happisburgh lifeboat *Huddersfield*, second of that name to serve there, being launched with the aid of a team of horses on an August bank holiday about 1903. A 34ft. self-righter, she had been built by Forrestt at Poplar in 1887.

of wreck, and from the bodies washed on shore, no doubt remained but that several vessels had been wrecked on the beach, with the loss of all hands,' the newspaper reported from Yarmouth. 'About thirty sail cut from their anchors in our roads, and during Monday, many were seen running through for shelter, and others in a very distressed state.'

At the time the *Ranger* was aground on the Haisborough Sand the people of Happisburgh and neighbouring villages were active in assisting fishermen from Cromer and Sheringham whose boats had been caught out when the wind flew round from the south-west to the north-east and rose to gale force. They had left their home beaches in fine weather with a gentle breeze off the land to take part in the herring fishery, but during the night the change of wind put them on a lee shore and more than twenty boats were forced ashore between Mundesley and Winterton. Ten Cromer fishermen, as well as three from Overstrand and another three from Sheringham, were lost that night, while four men from Cley were lost when the local fishing boat *Prosperous* sank in the storm.

The men of the preventive service were to the fore in the rescue work, in which many of the inhabitants joined with great energy, but as so often happens in such circumstances it seems there were those who were more interested in plunder than in helping the fishermen save their boats, if a report from Cromer is to be believed.[25] There were also allegations made by no less a person than Francis Wheatley of shameful neglect on the part of the Happisburgh people to make any attempt to save the men of the *Ranger*, the suggestion being that the smuggling fraternity were only too glad to see their enemies perish. Those allegations were disputed strongly by a gentleman from Happisburgh who pointed out that the revenue cutter had been wrecked on the Haisborough Sand a mile and a quarter from the shore, and thus far beyond the range of any lifesaving mortar.[26] It does seem highly improbable that any of the crew remained alive when the wreck came to the beach.

About a month after the disaster the wreck of the cutter *Ranger* was advertised for sale in a field near the Old Cart Gap at Happisburgh, 'broken up and divided into lots, comprising oak and fir planks of various lengths and thickness, several large scantlings of oak timber for beams &c . . .'.

The unequal struggle against the smugglers went on in spite of the loss of two cutters in fifteen years, and in 1838 the cutter *Badger* brought the sloop *Volharde* (Perseverance) of Flushing into Yarmouth Roads, having captured her after a six-hour chase in a fresh breeze from off Sheringham. By the time Lieutenant Richard Percival of the *Badger* boarded the suspected smuggler in the South Ham at Gorleston there remained no evidence of her clandestine activities other than a strong smell of spirits; once the smugglers knew they could not avoid capture they threw the cargo overboard. 'For the last mile and a half we sailed through staves and hoops of small kegs such as are used for bringing over contraband spirits, and these were directly in her wake . . . when I boarded her she stunk strongly of spirits,' Lieutenant Percival told the magistrates when three British members of the crew of the *Volharde* appeared accused of 'having been found on board a foreign vessel within eight leagues of the coast, and having been engaged in destroying spirits for the purpose of preventing seizure'.[27] A league was, in this instance, three nautical miles.

Happisburgh

Happisburgh, two or three miles south-east of Bacton, was said in 1845 to have two herring boats and several smaller fishing boats, and ten years later it was said that there were 'two yawls stationed to render assistance'. David Higgins casts doubt on this latter statement, since when a Happisburgh yawl was launched in September 1868 with a crew of sixteen to assist a vessel on the Haisborough Sand and was struck by a heavy sea and severely damaged it was said that 'the yawl was the only boat belonging to the Happisburgh beachmen and her loss is a severe calamity'. [28]

Note the spelling of the sandbank, sometimes abbreviated to Haisbro', and much simpler than the spelling given to the village of Happisburgh, which has led many visitors to mispronounce the name. Simplest of all, perhaps, was the spelling given by a local farmer when he painted his name and place of residence on his waggon: HAZEBRO. Whatever the spelling, the name is derived from a fellow named Hæp, whose burgh this was. He also gave his name to the hundred of Happing, which Professor Eilert Ekwall tells us means Hæp's people.[29]

The notorious Haisborough Sand, a few miles offshore, would, over the years, be the cause of disaster for many vessels. And if not the sands, storms in general would wreak havoc. In December of 1770 the naval vessels *Little Dick* and the *Peggy* were anchored off Cromer before continuing their eastward journey. As a storm picked up they were separated and early on the morning of 18th, the *Peggy* drove ashore on Happisburgh beach. 59 survivors were helped from the wreck by townsfolk but another 32 lie buried in Happisburgh churchyard. Thankfully the *Little Dick*, though with her foretopsail and her staysail carried away in the storm, was able to make her way to Great Yarmouth.

The motor barge *River Witham*, driven ashore 19th November 1939.

Also in Happisburgh churchyard is a memorial to the men of HMS *Invincible* who were buried there after their ship had gone to pieces on Hammonds Knoll, to seaward of the Haisborough Sand, in 1801 as she left Yarmouth Roads on her way to join the fleet under Admiral Sir Hyde Parker and Nelson that had sailed four days earlier. A 74-gun line-of-battle ship built at Deptford between 1761 and 1765, she carried a crew of 550 men, a great many of whom were lost. According to a contemporary report the mizzen mast went overboard as soon as she struck, killing about thirty men in its fall. As the tide flowed the vessel floated off the sand and was anchored in deep water, and men were put to the pumps. All through the night they worked to save the ship, which seems to have grounded again after the initial refloating, but it was all in vain.

The end of the *Invincible* came early next morning, before the boats which had been sent to her assistance from Yarmouth arrived on the scene. As the ship sank Captain Rennie tried to swim to the launch, which had been hove out when it became obvious that the ship was doomed. He nearly made it, but as he came almost within grasp of the boat's oars he was seen to lift his arms 'as if to implore the blessing of Heaven, and then placing them upon his face, he sank without any further struggle'. Beach boats from Winterton picked up a number of survivors, and the cod smack *Nancy* made a name for herself and her master, Daniel Grigson, by saving some 120 men, including Rear Admiral

Thomas Totty; altogether about 190 men were saved, but it was estimated that some four hundred were lost. Rear Admiral Totty later sailed from Yarmouth in HMS *Zealous*, joining the fleet after the action at Copenhagen. Having been one of the comparatively few men saved from the *Invincible*, he died the following year in the West Indies from yellow fever.

The men of the *Invincible* whose bodies drifted ashore, one hundred and nineteen of them, were buried in a large common grave dug in a piece of glebe land to the north of the Happisburgh churchyard. There is no record in the parish register of any burial service having taken place. Six other bodies from the *Invincible* were buried in Winterton churchyard. The Happisburgh grave has since been taken into the churchyard, but no memorial of any kind marked their burial place until 1988, when a simple stone slab bearing the ship's badge of the most recent HMS *Invincible*, an aircraft carrier, was dedicated to their memory. The ship's company joined with the parochial church council in providing the stone.[30]

The lofty church tower and the white-and-red-banded tower of the lighthouse half a mile to the south-east are the two most prominent landmarks of the village. Until 1921 there was also a postmill at Whimpwell Green, south of the lighthouse, that was unusual in being turned into wind by a fantail with twin fans. Harry Apling recorded that the mill had been built in 1773 to replace an earlier postmill wrecked in a storm on 19th December 1770.[31]

There were originally two lighthouses at Happisburgh which when brought into line led vessels safely clear of the southern end of the Haisborough Sand. The low light was discontinued in 1883 when threatened by erosion, but the high light still exists, though in 1987 Trinity House decided that it was no longer required and proposed its closure. Local people and fishermen protested, and an Act of Parliament was obtained to enable a special trust to take over the lighthouse and ensure that the light continued to shine out over the Would, the passage between the shore and the Haisborough Sand. Queen

The stone remembering the *Invincible* is one amongst several stones in Happisburgh churchyard that remember tragedy at sea.

The tradition of support from Friendly Societies is maintained through *The Oddfellows* at Sheringham and the current Atlantic 75 lifeboat at Happisburgh, *Friendly Forester II*.

The Happisburgh beach company's yawl *Friendship* at the top of the Gap.

Happisburgh lighthouse in the Trinity House era.

Elizabeth the Queen Mother was present in June 1990 when the lighthouse was formally handed over to local trustees.

The RNLI opened a lifeboat station at Happisburgh in 1866 when a self-righting boat provided by the people of the Yorkshire town of Huddersfield and built by Woolfe at Shadwell was supplied. Both she and her successor, a self-righter built by Forrestt in 1887, were named *Huddersfield*. Like most lifeboats on the Norfolk coast the Happisburgh boats depended on horses for hauling the launching carriage, and William Wilkins and his team of horses proved remarkably reliable. He was in charge of the horses at every launching, both on service and on exercise, from the opening of the station until his death in 1890. The Institution recognised his services by granting a gratuity of £5 to his widow.

After having a reserve boat for a year the station received a new self-righter, the *Jacob and Rachel Vallentine*, from Thames Iron Works in 1907. On the closure of the station in 1926 following the entry into service of motor lifeboats at Cromer and Gorleston the *Jacob and Rachel Vallentine* was transferred to neighbouring Palling, where she remained until that station was also closed in 1930, after which she went to Whitby. During the sixty years the Happisburgh station was operating its boats saved sixty-nine lives.

The lifeboat station was reopened in the summer of 1965 when an inflatable inshore boat was provided by the RNLI. Initially, the smaller D-class ILB, the boat is now the larger Alantic 75 class. In the winter of 2002 severe erosion by the sea removed the lifeboat launching ramp and made it impossible to launch the boat; a new station was established at Cart Gap, some two miles south of the village, a new boathouse being provided there.

Happisburgh beach has sprng to prominence in the last few years through the excavations undertaken there by the Ancient Human Occupation of Britain project, AHOB. The alert to the potential of this site came from research at Norwich Castle Museum and from 2005 a series of trenches was excavated on the beach. As a result, it is concluded that human ancestors were occupying the Happisburgh area between 780,000 and 900,000 years ago. It means that the beach is providing the earliest evidence for human occupation so far discovered in northern Europe. It was not then a beach but part of the flood plain of a great river; the site supplies a great deal of evidence on the environment in which our very ancient relatives lived!

Palling

The village of Palling, or Sea Palling as it is often called today, was given its first lifeboat by the Norfolk Shipwreck Association in 1852, but on the takeover by the RNLI in 1858 this was replaced by a self-righter from the Forrestt yard at Limehouse which served there for only six years. A succession of self-righters followed, the longest-serving boat being the *54th West Norfolk Regiment* which came from the Thames Iron Works in 1901 and was on station for a quarter of a century. A No. 2 station which operated from 1870 to 1929, on the other hand, had four Norfolk and Suffolk type boats in succession, the first of them being the *British Workman* built by the Yarmouth firm of Beeching. Between them the No. 1 and No. 2 boats had saved a total of 782 lives, an impressive record, by the time the No. 1 station closed in 1930.

While the village of Palling lies almost half a mile from the sea there grew up at the back of the beach a community of fishermen that might well have been founded by migrants from Winterton, six miles up the coast nearer to Yarmouth. There seems to be no record of when a beach company was formed, but one was certainly in existence in 1830 when Robert Rising, the owner of the Horsey estate just to the south of Palling, sent a letter to the *Norwich Mercury* regarding the bad relations between the officer in charge of the local Coastguard and the beachmen.[32]

One of the regulations made to counter smuggling was that no boat should put off with more than eight men, but it was generally appreciated that this rule was impracticable when it came to craft such as yawls putting off on salvaging or lifesaving missions, and that for such work a yawl required a crew of fifteen or twenty men. That is to say, it was appreciated by everyone except a Lieutenant Samuel Richardson who was in charge of the Coastguard station at Palling and had on one occasion seized the boats used by the local beach company because of an infringement of this nonsensical rule. Worse still, Lieutenant Richardson seems to have refused to collaborate with the beachmen in any way when they were engaged on rescue operations.

Launching the Palling lifeboat *54th West Norfolk Regiment* on August Bank Holiday, 1903. A practice on a bank holiday was not only convenient for those who had to take time off from work on any other day but it was also good publicity for the lifeboat service. No doubt collecting boxes were brought out.

The lifeboat house at Palling, with a meeting room and lookout on the upper floor.

One bleak January daybreak in 1830 the Palling beachmen who were on watch on the Lookout Hill saw a brig on the outer bank and launched their large boat with a crew of fifteen men to go to her assistance. The easterly wind was driving snow before it and the temperature was well below freezing. A heavy surf was breaking around the ship, but the beachmen succeeded in getting grapnels to the ship's stern and began taking the crew off. Heedless of the rescue taking place, the lieutenant began firing the lifesaving mortar regardless of the chance of hitting the boat. Indeed, after the beachmen had got the first man into their boat a shot fell so near the boat that the crew were afraid it would be sunk. One man fell overboard as the crew transferred to the yawl, but he was pulled from the water and in spite of the bombardment the beachmen got the whole of the crew off the brig, the *Oak* of Yarmouth.

'We landed all safe, as it so happened, with the ship's company, and hastened the captain and his crew up to prevent them being perished any more than we could help,' the beachmen said in a letter they sent both to Robert Rising and to Francis Wheatley at Mundesley. 'We well understand that our duty to men in such distress is to get them up as fast as we can to some place of comfort, but as we were taking the captain and crew up Lieutenant Richardson called out "Stop, captain." The captain replied "I cannot stop, I am so wet and cold." Lieutenant Richardson said to our people who were supporting the captain and his crew in getting them to a place of refreshment, "You ignorant men, clear away," with his pistol cocked and his thumb on the cock; but what his intentions were we cannot tell,' they said with admirable restraint.

The outcome of this matter is unknown, but the *Navy List* of 1839 shows that by then Lieutenant Richardson was no longer serving either with the Coastguard or afloat.

It was an unwritten rule of the beachmen that the first boat's crew to get aboard a casualty should have the job of salvaging the vessel, and it was their prerogative if they needed to do so to employ any subsequent arrivals, but only if they wished to employ them. This led to some hard-fought races between yawls belonging to rival companies, and also to severe criticism of the beachmen on some occasions. A ship was not derelict until all the crew had left her, and this rule could lead to a yawl's crew ignoring a ship's crew who had earlier abandoned their vessel, as happened in March 1833 when the barque *Crawford* went on to the Haisborough Sand, beat over the bank and began to sink in deep water.

The crew left the ship in three boats, in one of which was the captain's wife, his niece, and ten of the crew. They endeavoured to attract the attention of Palling beachmen who passed them in a yawl under sail on their way to the wreck, but the beachmen took no notice. When the master, Captain Davison Sandford, returned to his ship and offered them twenty guineas to run to leeward and pick up his wife and the others from their leaky boat they ignored his pleas.

'The wretched thirst of gain or plunder overcame the splendid feelings of humanity,' said a report of the incident in the local paper. 'They were left to the mercy of the sea in a sinking boat.' Fortunately, however, the Caister beachmen picked the women up and landed them safely, and the rest of the crew were landed by the Palling and Winterton lifeboats. Perhaps it was justice that when the *Crawford* went to pieces the Palling boatmen who had ignored the plight of the survivors had themselves to be picked up by the Winterton lifeboat.[33]

For a time there were two competing beach companies, traditionally said to have been known as the 'blues' and the 'whites' from the colour of the oars they used, but in 1842-43 two tragedies seem to have resulted in the amalgamation of the rival companies. The first accident occurred on 16th December 1842 when a yawl capsized some two miles out while making for a sloop that was in distress; five men were lost, two survived. The second followed hard on the heels of the first on 16th January 1843 when all seven men of a boat belonging to the rival company were lost after launching to retrieve a piece of drifting timber.

David Higgins records that the Palling company seems to have been reasonably successful even if some of the Winterton immigrants subsequently moved southward (the 1851 Census contains the names of seven Winterton-born men who had been in Palling for a time and had then moved to Yarmouth).[34] In the nineteenth century the company was organised in forty-eight shares, the rules stating that no member should hold more than three, though later the rules changed so that each member had just one share.

The Palling beachmen received a severe setback in 1897 when a particularly stormy period at the end of November not only caused many wrecks and heavy loss of life at sea and along the coast but created havoc ashore. While the Palling men were endeavouring to launch their No. 1 lifeboat *Good Hope* to the aid of those who were drowning within sight of the shore the waves were smashing at the beach company's watchhouse and at the three yawls drawn up on the beach. Two of the yawls, the *Aid* and the *New Dart*, were said at the time to have been destroyed and the third, the *Surprise*, built only three years earlier at a cost of £180, to have been damaged beyond repair. The *New Dart* was in fact destroyed, but the *Aid* was rebuilt and survived until 1921; the *Surprise* was also repaired and was bought in 1923 to become a houseboat on the Broads.[35] The lifeboat *Edward Birkbeck* at Winterton had been drawn up into the marram hills for safety, but even there she was washed about by the tremendous seas that swept right across the beach and into the marrams, and in the course of the battering she was stove in by a heavy piece of floating wreckage.

The RNLI gave £150 towards a fund raised for the Palling beachmen, who faced ruin through the loss of their three yawls, and also gave £10 to the beachmen at Winterton, whose yawl suffered damage from the storm while they were engaged in rescue work. A £5 donation for the Palling men came from their compatriots of the Caister Beach Company, and eventually there was enough to reimburse the beachmen in full. David Cook, a well-known boatman and bathing machine proprietor at Lowestoft, lent the Palling beachmen his yawl *Star of the East* as a temporary replacement for their three boats.

Vessel after vessel came ashore on the Norfolk and Suffolk coasts, and many of them went to pieces before the crews could be taken off. The brigantine *Olivia* of Portsmouth drove ashore at Palling and turned over, drowning her whole crew of ten men, and the brig *Pennine* of Newhaven was driven ashore between Palling Cart Gap and Eccles Point after breaking from her anchors, and only one of the seven men on board reached the beach alive. At Bacton the brig *Vedra* of Sunderland came ashore, and though three of her crew were washed ashore and saved, four others were drowned. The schooner *Vigo* of

Goole was wrecked at Hemsby, just south of Winterton, and all her crew were lost except the skipper's wife, who was brought ashore by the lifesaving company as the vessel broke up, only to die from exposure within minutes of being hauled to the beach. Another schooner from Goole, the *Ruby*, was lost further north.

The Happisburgh lifeboat *Huddersfield*, the second of that name to be stationed there, was taken on her carriage by road to Bacton with the idea of launching to the *Vedra*, but that vessel broke up before the lifeboat's arrival. Back trudged the lifeboatmen to Happisburgh, where they were told of other ships ashore some distance to the south, so they set off for Eccles. The roadway at the back of the beach, an unmade track at the best of times, was flooded by the high tide pouring across it and the horses pulling the lifeboat carriage had great difficulty in getting along; at times the water was up to the axle trees of the carriage. The procession of lifeboatmen, horses and lifeboat had not reached the scene of disaster when it was met by the Coastguards on their way back to their station with the news that both the vessels they were intending to aid had broken up.

A lucky escape came the way of the men of the Woodbridge ketch *Percy*, a little coaster built at Snape on the River Alde in 1860 and owned at one time by Newson Garrett, owner of the Snape maltings. She had sailed in ballast from Aldeburgh to load at the coal staithes at Sunderland, but after spending the night in Yarmouth Roads she had got no further than Cromer before the nor'westerly burst upon her. The crew wore the vessel round and tried to run before the wind back to Yarmouth, but in those conditions they could not get through the Cockle Gat. As the little vessel went scudding along before the wind the crew pinned their hopes on getting into Lowestoft harbour, but they

Palling Beachmen, circa 1900. From the left: Tom 'Duffle' Larter, Lou Pestell, Jimmy 'Cuckoo' Deane, Bob 'Fido' Bargewell, Frank 'Cuton' Kerrison, Frank 'Rucky' Pestell, Tom 'Crow' Nicholls, Ashe 'Dodd' Wolstone, Sam 'Crammo' Kerrison, Randall Johnson, Tom 'Odle' Brown, Fred Feather, John Pestell, Tom 'Fop' Grapes, John Brown, Jimmy 'Saul' Pestell, John 'Puddy' Amis, Dick Jones, William 'Wiking' Postle, George 'Sugar' Larter, Tom 'Dilsher' Bishop, Bob 'Fake' Kerrison, John 'Smoker' Nudd.

A drawing dated 1895 with the Palling beach company lookout, RNLI watchtower and beachman's pier.

54th West Norfolk Regiment returning from service, September 1923.

could not make it, so they put her head to wind and again tried to reach Yarmouth Roads.

The sea was breaking over the deck and the crew found it difficult to keep control of her. The weather was so thick that they lost sight of the coast, and they did not even know where they were when they felt the vessel strike. They were in fact well north of Yarmouth, for they had come ashore at Horsey. Being in ballast the *Percy* was carried right up the beach so that her bowsprit

stuck out over the sandhills. Two of the crew crept along the bowsprit and dropped into the sanctuary of the sandhills, and the captain followed them off the end of the bowsprit. The mate, however, was lame and could not get out along that spar; he was hauled ashore by means of a line, helped by a Horsey man who waded into the sea to his aid.

Also saved were the crew of the schooner *Martha and Ellen* of Goole, a billyboy built at Knottingley in 1862, which stranded on Blakeney beach while

The Palling yawl *New Dart*; the old boathouses in the background.

By the time of this photo in 2005, the artificial reefs at Palling were well established.

on her way from Sunderland with a cargo of coal for Ipswich. Another coal-laden schooner, the *Chase*, was run ashore at Weybourne during the afternoon after sustaining damage and losing her skipper overboard earlier in the day; three men were washed away before the eyes of spectators on the beach but a fourth, Tom Forster, was rescued by a party of fishermen from Sheringham who managed to get a rope to him and haul him ashore.

During those two days of 28th-29th November no fewer than twenty-nine RNLI lifeboats were launched on service and the lives of 108 people, including two women, were saved as a result; the majority of these services were carried out on the East Coast.

The Palling No. 2 station closed in 1929 and the No. 1 station followed in 1930; between 1860 and the closure the boats had saved 782 lives. For 44 years Palling was without a lifeboat, and then in 1972 a number of village residents got together to raise money and form the Palling Volunteer Rescue Service; two years later an inflatable inshore lifeboat was put into service and given the name *Hearts of Oak*, the name borne by the boat built at Lowestoft for the No. 2 station in 1893.

After seven years in service the *Hearts of Oak* was replaced by a rigid inflatable given the name *Leo*; the Norwich Leo Club was among the many organisations contributing towards the cost of the boat. The *Leo* remained in service for more than twenty years and carried out many rescues before being replaced by a new boat named *Lion's Roar* in recognition of the continuing support of the Hoveton and Wroxham Lions Club.

Unfortunately the *Lion's Roar* was seriously damaged when on 1st September 2011 it struck a then unidentified object while on a night training exercise. For some months the village was without its lifeboat; then in May 2012 a new rigid inflatable boat or RIB named *Lion Heart* came into service; the Palling Volunteer Rescue Service proudly claimed that it was the most technologically advanced inshore lifeboat on the east coast. The provision of the independent lifeboat has certainly proved beneficial now that the reefs at Palling are firmly established.

The Winterton coastguard team with the cart carrying their rocket line equipment.

Palling, like other villages on the Norfolk coast, has suffered from erosion and from flooding by the sea many times in the past; in 1953 seven villagers lost their lives when a tidal surge overwhelmed much of the east coast. Then in 1995 the Environment Agency undertook a project costing several million pounds and involving the erection of nine stone reefs which had the desired effect of halting erosion and causing a build-up of sand on the beach. Although the scheme appeared to have been a success it was subsequently announced that no further similar projects involving the importation of rock from Scandinavia would be introduced.

A relatively modern form of maritime vessel has found a home at Palling. The jet ski, of which the steady whine can often be heard along the coast on a weekend afternoon, is not popular with all. The necessity to access the beach with the jet ski on a trailer, often involving towing behind a four wheel drove vehicle, can lead to conflict even before the water's edge has been reached. Nevertheless, informal arrangements at Palling have made it a popular place for the launching of these vessels.

Winterton

The large village of Winterton, just to the south of where the River Thurne entered the sea in ancient times before the direction of its flow was reversed, was perhaps the most important fishing centre on the eastern section of the Norfolk coast apart from Yarmouth, with which it had many links. At various times throughout the nineteenth century Winterton men migrated to Palling, Caister and most importantly to Yarmouth, where they played a vital part in the herring fishery as skippers, boatowners and merchants; no fewer than 38 per cent of the beachmen, fishermen and fish merchants resident in Yarmouth at the time of the 1851 Census originated from Winterton, which enjoyed a satellite status in relation to Yarmouth similar to that occupied by Kessingland relative to Lowestoft. The population of Winterton remained fairly stable at around seven hundred throughout the century, with the migrants contributing

And a photo, doubtless taken on the same day, illustrating the rocket tripod and line.

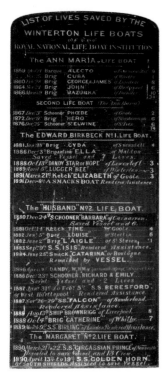

The service boards for the Winterton lifeboats are kept in the parish church.

to the growth of other villages such as Caister whose population grew from 909 in 1841 to 1,648 at the beginning of the twentieth century.

Winterton acquired its first lifeboat, a 32ft. North Country type pulling twelve oars, in 1822 and this was taken over by the Norfolk Association for Saving the Lives of Shipwrecked Mariners on its formation the following year. It was in this boat that Lieutenant Thomas Leigh, a Trafalgar veteran who was chief officer of the Coastguard at Winterton, carried out some remarkable rescues which earned him both the RNLI Gold Medal and the Gold Boat, an award since replaced by the Gold Medal second service clasp.

Lieutenant Leigh had been at Winterton only a few months when he performed his first service on 26th November 1830. The Whitby collier *Annabella* had struck on the south end of the Haisborough Sand and had been successfully extricated from the grip of the sand, but she was by then so leaky that Captain Thomas Bodlington decided that the only way to save his life and those of his seven crew was to run her ashore on Horsey beach. Unfortunately the outer bank on which she struck about eight in the morning was at that time more than 300 yards from the shore, and being already half full of water the brig did not wash over the bank but stuck there. Messengers were immediately sent to Winterton and Lieutenant Leigh and his men arrived within the hour with their lifesaving mortar, which was later supplemented by a larger mortar from the coastguard station at Palling.[36]

Although Lieutenant Leigh and his men made every effort to throw a line over the vessel they failed each time. When the mortar was fired with a full charge of powder the shock of discharge broke the line, and when the charge was reduced the projectile fell short, although as Robert Rising said in a letter to the *Norwich Mercury*, 'both the mortars were properly elevated and pointed with greater precision than I ever saw them before.' Thoughts turned to the Winterton lifeboat three and a half miles away, but it was pointed out that to bring her that distance by dragging her over skeets would have taken far too long; she had no carriage.

The only available boat seems to have been an elderly coble,[37] and this was taken out by the lieutenant and six men, four of them Horsey fishermen. It took them three-quarters of an hour to reach the vessel, but they succeeded in taking off the crew and bringing them safely ashore just before the brig began to break up.

Robert Rising had seen the mettle of the man. 'I never saw a man more anxious than was Lieutenant Leigh to save the men, or more gratified at its being effected,' he wrote.

Within a month Lieutenant Leigh had performed a second rescue which prompted the secretary of the Norfolk Association for Saving the Lives of Shipwrecked Mariners to state that 'the exertions of Lieutenant Leigh and his gallant crew upon this distressing occasion were such as have never been surpassed and seldom equalled.'[38]

It was in the early afternoon of Christmas Eve that the Hull brig *Henry*, bound to London with paving stones and potatoes, was seen on Winterton Ness shoal, nearly two cables' length (400 yards) from the shore with her crew lashed in the main rigging. Lieutenant Leigh and his crew were waist deep in snow as they struggled to the Ness with their lifesaving apparatus. They were successful this time in throwing a line right across the wreck, but the men in the rigging seemed incapable of hauling it in, so Lieutenant Leigh and twenty Winterton beachmen took out the lifeboat and endeavoured to reach the vessel. 'We went off at 3.30pm and exerted ourselves to the utmost to near the wreck, but a strong flood tide which swept us to leeward, and a heavy surf which broke over us, compelled us to put back with, however, a determination on my part, if supported, to make another attempt as soon as the boatmen had procured dry clothing and refreshment, which I recommended all willing to assist to hasten home for,' the lieutenant later said.

When the men reassembled in the evening the more experienced of them expressed the view that the crew of the brig were by then dead, no cries having been heard for some time, and that a further attempt to reach the wreck would be foolhardy. Lieutenant Leigh, however, argued that some of them might be still living but too feeble to make themselves heard. Eventually fifteen Winterton beachmen and three of his own men manned the lifeboat, which was by then covered in ice, and with great difficulty the boat was launched at nine at night. After great exertions they crossed the bank, on which the boat struck several times, and reached the wreck to find the master hanging head downwards from the rigging, having bled to death from an injury sustained when the ship grounded, and a lad frozen to death. Another member of the crew had been washed overboard and drowned. To get to the remaining men it was necessary to take the boat into very shallow water, with surf breaking over them all the time. Two of the Winterton men boarded the brig and helped the survivors into the lifeboat. 'By all hands redoubling their exertions we got safely over the shoal and bank, and had the unspeakable satisfaction of landing the whole crew, with the exceptions stated, amidst the cheers of hundreds of spectators,' Lieutenant Leigh reported.[39]

Those two services very deservedly earned Lieutenant Leigh the lifeboat institution's Gold Medal, and in 1833 he was awarded the Gold Boat for the

The hazardous life of the fisherman is remembered in a memorial in Winterton church.

rescue of the crew of the barque *Crawford* and a number of beachmen, already mentioned under Palling. He described that service in a letter that was quoted when his medals came up for auction at Christie's in 1990:[40]

> The barque had struck on the outer bank, in such a surf as to prevent the possibility of her holding long together, or for any ordinary boat to assist her. We put off in a lifeboat manned by twenty-five volunteers, the surf frequently breaking over us, on account of our being obliged to keep broadside on until well to the northward, to make certain of fetching the wreck.
>
> By the manly exertions of the volunteers we succeeded in getting alongside her in less than an hour, and had the happiness to rescue sixteen men, whom we safely landed.

Leigh, who had entered the Royal Navy as a volunteer in 1803 and was a midshipman in HMS *Conqueror* during Nelson's pursuit of Villeneuve's French and Spanish fleet in 1805, was promoted to the rank of commander in 1835. No doubt his exploits in the lifeboat had helped to bring him to the attention of his superiors. In that same year that he was promoted he won the lifeboat institution's Silver Medal for saving three men from the collier brig *Blackbird* which, like the *Henry*, had grounded on the Ness shoal. The *Blackbird* went aground in a heavy easterly gale in the early hours of 30th April, and it was about half past six that morning when the lifeboat was launched with a crew of twenty-five beachmen and Leigh in command. It was not an easy launch, with the surf crashing on to the beach, and the brig was already breaking up as the lifeboat headed towards her.

The mainmast went by the board as the lifeboat was being launched, and the boat was only half way to the wreck when the foremast also fell. Leigh

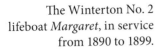

The Winterton No. 2 lifeboat *Margaret*, in service from 1890 to 1899.

A rather distant view of
Winterton lighthouse in
about 1905 showing the
extensive dune that had built
up in advance of the cliff.

saw a terrific surf roll clean over the collier, sweeping everything off the deck
and taking with it the master, mate and two seamen. Three men clung to
the sternpost as the vessel broke up, and the lifeboatmen concentrated their
efforts on reaching them before they too were swept away. As the ship broke
up great lumps of wreckage were thrown around by the waves, threatening to
smash in the lifeboat's planking, but in spite of the danger Leigh took the boat
in close and the three men were plucked to safety.

Commander Leigh, who died in 1846, had shown that the North Country
or Greathead type of boat could be a valuable asset in the hands of brave
and determined seamen, yet there was a time when it was said that none
of the local fishermen would trust themselves afloat in the Winterton boat.
With the takeover by the national institution in 1858 she was replaced by
a 30ft. self-righter built in that year by Forrestt at Limehouse, but that boat
was probably no more favoured by the local men than her predecessor. After
only three years the self-righter was replaced by a 32ft. Norfolk and Suffolk
type boat from the Beeching yard at Yarmouth which does not seem to have
been named at the time of her coming into service; six years later she was
given the name *Ann Maria*. In 1878 she was given the official number 15 and
renamed *Edward Birkbeck*, and in the following year a larger Norfolk and
Suffolk type boat, the *Husband*, ON16, was transferred from Corton to open
a No. 2 station. A 36ft. boat pulling fourteen oars, the *Husband* had been built
by Beeching in 1869 for the Suffolk station, where she saved three lives during
her ten-year stay there.

The *Husband* remained on the Winterton No. 2 station until 1890, when
her place was taken by a 44ft. Norfolk and Suffolk type boat, the *Margaret*,
ON270, built by Beeching a year earlier. The *Margaret* remained at Winterton
for nine years before being transferred to the reserve fleet as *Reserve No. 1*,
taking the place of the ill-fated Aldeburgh lifeboat *Aldeburgh* for three years
after a disaster which cost the lives of seven lifeboatmen. She was replaced at
Winterton by the *Mark Lane*, ON233, a 44ft. Norfolk and Suffolk type boat
that had been built by Beeching in 1889 for Gorleston and had then spent

some time at Lowestoft before being transferred to reserve. On being sent to Winterton the *Mark Lane* was renamed *Margaret*.

The second *Margaret* was one of no fewer than seven lifeboats called to the 3,554-ton steamer *Newburn*, which ran on to the southern end of the Haisborough Sand when outward bound from the Tyne with 4,700 tons of coal in January 1906. She and the Palling No. 2 boat *Hearts of Oak* were launched to the collier on 29th January, their crews spending the night helping to jettison cargo from the stranded vessel. The following morning the *Edward Birkbeck* took out more men to assist in the work and the steam lifeboat *James Stevens No. 3* was sent from Gorleston at the request of the local Lloyd's agent, while the Palling No. 1 boat *54th West Norfolk Regiment* took out more beachmen.

With so many men engaged in the salvage operations, which went on for several days, it was deemed necessary to have the Caister lifeboat *Covent Garden* and the *Louisa Heartwell* from Cromer also standing by. It was only after the salvagers had been working for five days that seven Yarmouth tugs, the *United Service, Yare, Meteor, King Edward VII, Gleaner, Tom Perry* and *Express* managed to tow the collier off the sand.

When the second *Margaret* came to the end of her service in 1907 her place was taken by the *Reserve No. 1*, which had previously been stationed at Winterton as the first *Margaret*. In 1909 she was replaced by a new 44ft. 6in. Norfolk and Suffolk built by Thames Iron Works, the *Eleanor Brown*.

Both Winterton stations closed in 1924 following the sending of a motor lifeboat to Cromer. The *Eleanor Brown* went into the reserve fleet, and was sold out of service in 1931. Between them the Winterton lifeboats had saved 438 lives since the RNLI took over in 1858; the number saved by the original boat under the Norfolk Shipwreck Association is not recorded.

As is so often the case with former lifeboats, both the Winterton boats had a considerable life in front of them when they were disposed of by the RNLI. The *Edward Birkbeck*, already almost thirty years old when she was sold out of service, was converted into a yacht and renamed *Mirosa* and the *Eleanor*

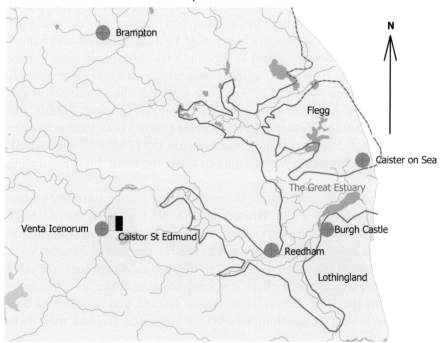

The darker line indicates the suggested coast in the Iron Age, at the time of the Roman occupation. The sandbank on which Great Yarmouth now sits would form in the mouth of the Great Estuary.

Brown became the yacht Mary. Both survived into the twenty-first century.

Commander Thomas Leigh was not the only noteworthy naval man to have lived in Winterton, for later in the nineteenth century the residents included Edward Fawcett, who as a petty officer had taken part in Sir James Ross's Antarctic expedition and also in his first search for the missing Sir John Franklin, who had disappeared while searching for the North-West Passage between the Atlantic and the Pacific. In 1895 Fawcett, describing himself as 'Pensioner, RN', wrote from Winterton to contest a statement that Sir Joseph Hooker, the Halesworth-born botanist, was the last survivor of the Antarctic expedition of 1839-43.[40]

Edward Fawcett, explorer.

'I was on that expedition as captain of the forecastle of the *Erebus*,' he wrote. 'And I was with Sir James on the 1st Franklin search expedition, and accompanied the Commander on his land journeys; was boatswain's mate in the *Investigator*, with Captain McClure, and made the NW passage.'

At the age of eighty-two he claimed to be 'hale and hearty, except a little shaky on my pins'.

Caister

Caister-by-Yarmouth is now almost a suburb of Yarmouth, which has grown outwards so far as to link up with, if not to absorb, its little neighbour to the north. It has a much longer history than Yarmouth, however, for during the Roman occupation a military installation was developed on the north side of the estuary in what is now the parish of Caister. Just to the south was a protected anchorage from which supply ships probably sailed north with provisions for the garrisons on Hadrian's Wall, since there is good reason to believe that this was one of the supply bases linked to the campaign of the Emperor Septimius Severus, who in AD208-211 campaigned in northern Scotland and restored the great wall thrown up by the Emperor Hadrian.

It is likely that the fort was established late in the second century or in the early part of the third. The unusually high numbers of coins dating from AD192 to 222 found on the site is indicative of activity at that period. A connection with the Classis Britannica, the Roman fleet that from the invasion period until some time after AD245 was much involved in operations on both sides of the Mare Saxonicum (the Saxon Sea), is indicated by the discovery at Caister of central Gaulish samian pottery and coarser wares from northern Gaul.

Coal found in Roman deposits at Caister could be evidence of a very early trade in 'sea cole' from the Tyne, the fuel perhaps being a return cargo for ships carrying grain and other provisions to the South Shields supply base. One mentions 'other provisions' because excavation of the Caister fort revealed what might have been a cattle-processing area, possibly preparing meat for shipment.

Indeed, Caister might have been the Roman Gariannonum, though this name was appropriated by antiquarians to the fort at Burgh Castle on the southern shore of the estuary. It is equally possible that Caister might be the site of St. Fursa's early religious settlement of Cnobheresburgh, since the assemblage of Middle Saxon material there lends support to the existence of a monastic site comparable with Butley and Brancaster.

The rectangular, round-cornered walls of the Caister fortress were still visible above ground in the seventeenth century, though they had been quarried and largely forgotten by the nineteenth. Recording that in 1821 the population of Caister was only 772, Pigot's directory of 1830 observed that 'it was at one time a town of some considerable extent and consequence, and had two churches,' the ruins of one of them forming 'a picturesque object in the scenery here'. White's 1845 directory goes further, telling us that the church of Holy Trinity had been 'partly removed for the reparation of the roads,' and that 'the Roman Station' had been 'nearly obliterated by ploughing and other improvements'.

Over the years the beachmen and lifeboatmen of Caister have built up a reputation for lifesaving that is second to none, though that reputation has not been achieved without losses that have hit the village community hard. One has only to walk through the local cemetery to discover the price that the village has paid over the years. There is a stone to Isaiah Haylett, who died in 1889 aged sixty-two, and to two of his sons, William, drowned at sea in 1874 at the age of twenty-two, and Josiah, drowned at sea in 1877, aged sixteen. Another remembers Soloman Brown, lost in the smack *Venus* in 1889, and then there is one to George Brown, beloved son of Mary Ann Pinder, drowned at Grimsby in 1902 at the age of twenty-seven. In every coastal village the gravestones in the churchyard record the names of men and boys who have been lost at sea, but the cemetery at Caister bears testimony to a greater involvement and a heavier loss than is to be discovered in other villages.

Yet Caister's seafaring tradition dates only from the later years of the eighteenth century, for the earlier village was situated inland away from the beach. The first evidence of maritime activity is to be found in the 1790s, when a settlement inhabited by fishermen began to grow up at the end of the road to the beach. It is intriguing that one of the earliest salvaging jobs on record occurred on 11th October 1797 when the Caister men salvaged a section of the bowsprit of Admiral de Winter's flagship which had been brought into Yarmouth Roads after being captured by Admiral Adam Duncan at Camperdown.[42]

The name of the Caister company's yawl *Assistance* appears in the impress registers in 1803, showing that the company was certainly in formal existence

'Skipper' Woodhouse and his brother David were perhaps the last of a long line of Caister beachmen who earned their living from the sea. Here he is at the oars of his beach skiff *Shipmates*.

by then. An entry refers to John Bickers and his crew of eight being granted exemption from impressment by virtue of their 'assisting ships in distress, carrying off pilots and at the Yarmouth Ferry'. In 1816 the company replaced the *Assistance* with a new 44ft. yawl, the *Prince Blucher*, named after the Prussian general who had made so opportune an appearance on the field of Waterloo the previous year.

There was plenty of salvage work to be had in the area and the beach company thrived, its growth aided by the arrival of migrants from Winterton. The first of these to arrive, Robert George, had the Ship Inn built for him at the back of the beach in 1815, and it was no doubt his example that helped persuade other Winterton men to bring their families to live in the new beachmen's settlement in succeeding years. When a meeting was held in the company shed on 24th February 1848 to agree the formal rules of the company sixteen of the thirty-one men who attended were migrants, mainly from Winterton, and the committee elected at that meeting were all men of Winterton origin.[43]

Further migration took place around 1850. 'Skipper' Woodhouse, who was for a long time motor mechanic of the Caister lifeboats, recalled having been told by his elders how some of the new arrivals walked the six miles from Winterton to Caister along the shore, helped on the way by one of their number playing lively tunes on a squeezebox. 'Skipper' was himself descended from those migrants: his maternal great-grandfather was James Haylett, who purchased a share in the beach company in 1852 from Thomas Horth, paying the considerable sum of £35 for it.

Like all the beach companies, that at Caister was governed by a set of rules setting out such matters as the allocation of the earnings for services rendered to shipping. The rules at Caister, first set down in print in 1848, display the influence of the lords of the manor of Caister, members of the Clowes family, who were solicitors in Yarmouth. They took a paternal interest in the affairs of the beach company and often presented the beachmen's case when their salvage claims came before the local admiralty court, held each Tuesday in the old Yarmouth Tolhouse. The beach company's sheds stood on the manor waste, and the lord of the manor was entitled to a share in the earnings of the company in recognition of this fact.[44] The company rules, as amended

Conscious of the Beachmen's heritage, 'Skipper' donated his skiff to the Great Yarmouth Maritime Museum and was assisted by Friends of the Museum in its transfer. The boat is today amongst the collection at the Broads Museum.

Two dramatic drawings by C.J. Staniland, an artist who knew Caister well, illustrating services by the local lifeboats. In the picture opposite the lifeboat has been anchored and is being veered down to the wreck to pick up men who can be seen in the rigging, a technique that was employed in many rescues. When the water on the sands was too shallow for the boat to approach the wreck it was not unknown for members of the lifeboat crew to go overboard and wade to a wreck to save a man who was too exhausted to help himself, as in the picture below.

in 1907, stated that the Caister Company of Beachmen had been formed for the purpose of saving property and rendering assistance to vessels aground, stranded or wrecked on the sands or beach or in any kind of difficulty, distress or disaster at sea. 'The remuneration, earnings, and emoluments arising from any such services shall be divided and apportioned in certain shares for the maintenance of the boats belonging to the Company, and amongst those members of the Company who shall be entitled to share in any such earnings, under and according to the following Rules and Regulations,' states the preamble to the rules.

The first rule, set out with a lawyer's precision, states that 'Every man who shall touch any Coble, Gig, Yawl, or outrigger of the same, or any boat, belonging to or in the use of the Company, as she is going off to any vessel, shall be considered as belonging to that boat, and shall be entitled to an equal share of the earnings and emoluments of the boat, to which he shall thus be considered to belong.' On occasion that rule led to latecomers rushing into the water up to their waists in order to grasp the outrigger of a departing yawl so as to qualify for a share of the earnings. No doubt other members of the shore party saw to it that the latecomer compensated for his tardiness later in the day.[45]

Special provision was made for men injured while on beach company

business and for the widows and children of any who were lost while engaged in beach company work. The widow of a beach company member was also allowed to put a man in to work the dead man's share, provided he was approved by the company members. The 'widow's man' handed over a quarter of his dole to the widow. To some extent the beach companies were co-operatives that looked after the families of members in times of sickness or loss.

In the early days one of the ways in which beachmen found employment was in 'swiping' for lost anchors, which were taken to the Admiralty warehouse in Yarmouth. Before the advent of chain cables it was common for hemp cables to part under the strain imposed by gale-force winds and the seas they brought up, and sometimes a master whose ship was labouring badly at anchor in the roads would order the cable to be slipped so that the vessel could seek refuge in the harbour. In that case it was usual to buoy the end of the cable if at all possible.

If the anchor was swiped from the seabed without there being any indication of its position the salvager received half the value; if the cable had been buoyed the amount received was a third. It goes without saying that the beachmen sometimes destroyed the buoys if they thought they could do so without fear of detection. To find those anchors that were not buoyed the beachmen towed a bight of light rope across the seabed behind two boats. When it caught on

The Caister beach company
shed and tower.

the fluke of a lost anchor the two ends of the line would be brought together and a shackle placed on the doubled line, then allowed to slide down the line until it fastened the bight tightly around the fluke. It was then usually possible to break the anchor out of the ground and hoist it into one of the boats.

One Monday afternoon in June 1847 a Caister yawl with a crew of seven beachmen took an anchor to Yarmouth harbour. After the anchor had been lifted ashore three of the men decided to walk back, leaving the other four to sail the yawl back to Caister. The yawl was running before the wind when it was overturned, throwing the four men into the water. Only one man, Winterton-born John Haylett, managed to swim ashore; the other three, all elderly Caister men, were drowned before other beachmen who put off from Caister beach could reach them.[46]

There were proposals to station a lifeboat on Caister beach in 1841 following the loss of four brigs in the Cockle Gat, and a subscription was raised,[47] but for some reason there seems to have been a delay in implementing those proposals. Nevertheless, early in 1845 the lifeboat from Bacton was transferred to Caister. It has been said that the lord of the manor did not favour the introduction of a lifeboat at Caister because of the share he received from the beach company,[48] but Thomas Clowes, who held this position in the 1840s, was an active member of the general committee of the Norfolk Association for Saving the Lives of Shipwrecked Mariners and took part in the committee's discussion in March 1845 of the effectiveness of the lifeboat then at Caister.[49]

Indeed, it is from a letter written by Clowes to the local newspapers that we learn of the arrival of the former Bacton boat.[50]

Writing in answer to allegations that the Caister men had refused to go to the assistance of a brig on the Scroby and a Yarmouth beachmen's yawl sunk alongside her, he explained:

The Life Boat, at Caister, was brought here on the 6th of January last from Bacton; on the 7th I was informed she was landed on the beach, and requested to allow it with a shed to be built and placed on my land.

This was the first intimation I had a life-boat was to come to Caister, not hearing one word of it before. You may conceive my surprise thereat. I immediately went, and found two country carpenters with the boat and all her materials; and also the materials for a shed on the beach. The men informed me they were come to build the shed, and leave the boat; whereupon I fixed on a place that was considered by the beachmen most proper to erect the shed. The carpenters in a few days built the shed, and went home.

The boat is a small one, about two-thirds the size of the Yarmouth boat, out of repair, and leaky. In landing her at Caister she was damaged, being laden with the materials and stores of the shed, and full of water. I learn that some small repairs have been done to the boat, but so imperfectly, she is not deemed seaworthy in a storm. The beachmen put her off to sea three days before the late gale to try her, and found her so leaky and unfit for the intended service, they would not risk their lives in her.

The Caister lifeboats and a yawl on the beach in 1893. The shorter of the two men standing by the yawl is James Haylett.

If that were the former Bacton boat built in 1822 it was a North Country type, and it was probably that boat which was ordered by the Norfolk Shipwreck Association to be sold after delivery of a new boat for Caister in 1846.[50]

Clowes told the committee that as the sandbanks lay so far from the shore a boat of the kind then stationed at Caister could not reach them, and Captain A.W. Jerningham, the Inspecting Commander of Coast Guard at Yarmouth,

The Caister lifeboat
Beauchamp with her crew,
a photograph probably
taken on the occasion of
her naming ceremony. Among
those standing in the boat is
the Mayor of Yarmouth.

said that without a boat with good sailing qualities the beachmen ran a risk of being blown out to sea when there was a strong north-westerly wind.[52]

The boat at Caister was certainly one that did not meet with the approval of the beachmen who were expected to man it. When the Yarmouth yawl *Phoenix* was lost on 26th January 1845 it was said that three men of the preventive service volunteered to go off in the Caister lifeboat if the beachmen would help to man it, but the beachmen refused, saying the boat was unsafe. Clowes suggested that the three volunteers were inexperienced men who would be incapable of handling the boat in storm conditions. Though they refused to man the lifeboat the Caister beachmen used their yawl *Storm* to save the nine-man crew of the *Elizabeth* of Scarborough, one of six brigs that were wrecked on the Scroby and the Barber during that gale. The six-hour rescue mission was carried out in appalling conditions that taxed the seamanship and courage of the beachmen to the limit. And later that year the Yarmouth beachmen expressed a willingness to go overland to Caister or Winterton if need be to launch and man the lifeboats there, adding a proviso that 'they would hesitate in risking their lives in the life boat at Caister'.[53]

When the general committee met in Norwich in July Captain Jerningham was able to report that he had raised £105 and that the treasurer, J.J. Gurney, and his friends had collected another £60 towards the cost of a new boat that was to be built by Thomas Branford, a Yarmouth shipbuilder of some repute. Designed by William Teasdel on the lines of the larger of the two Yarmouth

A rather less formal picture
of the Caister No.2 lifeboat
Nancy Lucy. The two
men in naval uniform are
Coastguards.

The Caister No.2 lifeboat *Nancy Lucy* which was built by Thames Iron Works in 1903 to take the place of the *Beauchamp* after the 1901 disaster. In the left background is the No.1 boat *James Leath*, transferred from Pakefield in 1919 and ten years later sent to Aldeburgh.

lifeboats built in 1833, it was to be constructed of English oak, copper fastened, under the superintendence of Captain Jerningham and Captain Spencer Smyth, the piermaster at Gorleston.[54]

It took Branford more than six months to build the boat in his yard on the Southtown side of the harbour, from which she was launched on 10th March the following year. If contemporary accounts are accurate he made a very good job of her and lost money on the contract price of £150.[55] Possibly it was foreseeable that he would make a loss, because at a committee meeting the previous year it had been stated that a new boat, with its equipment, would cost £300. Samuel Bradbeer, the sailmaker in Row 100, made the sails for the new boat for the cost of materials only.

After being launched the lifeboat was taken round to the beach and hauled up, both to be fitted out and to be put on show to the public. She must have gone on station at Caister within a short time, for on 21st March she was launched with a crew of thirteen to the assistance of the *Honor* of Blyth, a 154-ton brig built at Yarmouth in 1803, which had gone on the Barber Sand in a gale. The brig's owner, John Dixon, of Cowpen, near Blyth, later sent £13 to be shared among the thirteen beachmen who had manned the lifeboat that night, a quite unusual acknowledgement from a shipowner of the beachmen's daring.

At one stage it was proposed by the committee that the surf lifeboat at Caister, presumably the former Bacton boat, should be taken to Branford's yard and put into storage until a new station could be found for her. The piermaster, Captain Smyth, suggested she might be sent to Gorleston, but the Dean of Norwich protested that she should not be sent out of the county, Gorleston then being in Suffolk. Eventually it was agreed she should be sold, but then it was pointed out that unsuccessful ex-lifeboats were unlikely to prove saleable. What happened to her in the end is unknown.

The Caister men were in action on 4th April 1846 when they saved eight men from the *Henrietta* of Exeter and again on 19th April when they saw a blue light and a rocket from a vessel apparently on the Scroby, but found only a steamer proceeding on her way. Whether they used the new lifeboat or a yawl is not clear from the report.[57] It is quite likely they did use the lifeboat, for the beachmen were said to be delighted with her.

When the *Doncaster* of Stockton was wrecked on the Scroby on 6th December 1847 the lifeboat saved the crew of eight with some considerable

The Caister No.1 lifeboat *Covent Garden* on the right, the yawl *Eclat* and gig *Ubique*, and to the left the No.2 boat *Nancy Lucy* on Caister beach about 1910.

difficulty. The boat was brought as close as possible and a line was successfully thrown to the men on the wreck. It proved impossible to bring the lifeboat alongside, but the eight men were dragged through the water one by one into the boat. The Norfolk Association voted £15 to the crew of the lifeboat for that service.

Both the lifeboat and a yawl put off from Caister when the iron-built schooner *Admiral Blake* struck the Scroby on 2nd February 1848 as she attempted to enter Yarmouth Roads by way of the Cockle Gat. The crew of five climbed into the rigging and wrapped themselves in the furled fore-tops'l after making signals for assistance, and in the darkness the would-be rescuers could see no sign of life aboard the sunken vessel. It was only at daybreak the next morning that the lifeboat wore down to the wreck and took all five men off by hauling them through the breakers into the boat. The *Norwich Mercury* reported that this was 'the second ship's crew which the Caister boat has rescued from this sand in the last two months of this winter'.[58]

No doubt there were other services performed by the lifeboat that year, but the report of the Shipwreck Association quarterly meeting in October 1848 said only that 'There had been several shipwrecks during the quarter, and the beachmen had, with the lifeboats, rescued the crews of the vessels, for which services they were rewarded'.

In the spring of 1849 Benjamin Hodds and other members of the Caister beach company used the lifeboat when they assisted a vessel that had been aground and had lost its rudder because it was said they could not launch a yawl in the prevailing conditions. Aided by a steam tug they saved the ship and its crew and were awarded £150 salvage, of which they had to pay £10 for the tug's services. Each man of the company doled £3 12s. 6d., and two shares, £7 5s., was paid to the Shipwreck Association for the use of the lifeboat.[58] Inevitably the case led to discussion by the central committee of the propriety of allowing the lifeboat to be used for salvage work, and there was a general opinion expressed that the beachmen should be allowed to use the association's lifeboats subject to payment of two shares to the association. Earlier the committee had ruled that the lifeboats were not to be used for salvage work, but strictly only for lifesaving. According to the Northumberland report the Caister boat had saved eighteen lives by 1851, but one suspects that that was an underestimate.

By then the Norfolk Association found itself in serious trouble through lack of funds. It was remarked in 1845 that 'though crews are never wanting, subscriptions frequently are,' and in the 1850s it seemed that the organisation was suffering from a serious malaise. Decisions were all too often deferred until the next quarterly meeting, and by the time of the next meeting members had sometimes changed their minds and so put off a decision even further.

In October 1857 when the brig *Ontario*, of South Shields, was wrecked with the loss of twenty-three lives in the early stages of her voyage to Suez with coal, the Caister lifeboat could not be launched. A boatbuilder had some weeks earlier removed the aircases and otherwise dismantled her in order to do some necessary repairs. He had since neither replaced the aircases nor carried out the repairs, a failure that attracted justified criticism at the inquest on some of those lost from the *Ontario*.

The Caister lifeboat built by Branford in 1845-6 survived the takeover by the Royal National Lifeboat Institution, which did however spend £103 on repairing and altering her. All the other Norfolk Association boats were quickly replaced by self-righting boats of the standard RNLI pattern, and before long it was possible for the Institution to announce that the 'old, heavy, and ill-constructed boats have been replaced by others of the newest and most scientific description,' by which was meant self-righters.[59] Caister never did have a self-righting boat until in 1964 it received an Oakley, one of a new generation of self-righting motor lifeboats.

By an odd coincidence, on 16th October 1864 a new 3,200-ton steamer named *Ontario* went aground on the Haisborough Sand on her maiden voyage from Shields to Alexandria with coal and iron. This time the Caister lifeboat was ready for service and took part in a lengthy salvage operation involving several tugs and a small army of coal heavers from Yarmouth who were employed to jettison the vessel's cargo. Over the course of several days the boat was launched three times to the *Ontario*, but the weather worsened and in the end the steamer had to be abandoned.

The Norfolk Shipwreck Association lifeboat continued to serve until 1865. No count had been kept of lives saved in the years she was operated by the Norfolk Association, but from 1857 onwards she had been launched on twenty-three occasions and had saved 133 lives. Her place was taken by the *James Pearce, Birmingham No. 2*, a 42ft. Norfolk and Suffolk type boat, which became the No. 1 boat when two years later the 32ft. Norfolk and Suffolk type surf boat *The Boys* joined her on Caister beach. Built at Yarmouth by Mills & Blake at a cost of £238, the *James Pearce, Birmingham No. 2* was paid for by the Birmingham Lifeboat Fund, one of a number of local funds established in inland towns to raise money for the lifeboat service.

The decision to open a No. 2 station was made when it became clear that a smaller boat was needed that could reach wrecks in shallow water on the Barber Sand. A gift from *Routledge's Magazine for Boys*, the new surf boat was built by Beeching at Yarmouth at a cost of £152. For the next sixty-two years there were always two lifeboats on Caister beach as well as the boats belonging to the beach company.

The beach company accounts, which still survive, mention several boats operated by the company in the mid-nineteenth century, including the coble *Star* and the yawls *Eclat*, the first of that name, and *Fox*, a large boat with a length of 58ft. The second *Eclat*, built by Jermyn & Mack in 1885, was the last boat owned by the company; launched on service for the last time in 1919, she was sold in 1927 to be converted into a yacht on the Broads.

Yawls as big as the *Fox* required a large crew, sometimes as many as twenty men, and those men had to know what they were about when sailing a yawl in anything above a strong breeze. With a yawl sailing hard the noise of the water striking against the lands of the clinker planking was sufficient to require any conversation on the part of the crew to be carried on in a shout. When the boat went about some of the crew would be throwing the ballast bags from one side of the boat to the other as the big dipping lug was lowered and then hoisted on the other side of the mast. They would also need to spend a good deal of time bailing, for with a yawl sailing hard, perhaps so that the lee gunwale was below the surface, quite a lot of water would come aboard.

In 1875 *The Boys* was lengthened by Beeching to 33ft. 7in. to improve her seakeeping qualities and, renamed *Godsend*, was appropriated to the gift of Lady Bourchier, who lived at Hampton Court. Three years later the No. 1 lifeboat was renamed *Covent Garden*, following a gift from a fund contributed to by tradesmen and others at the London market. It was by no means uncommon at that period for lifeboats to be given new names in order to commemorate contributions from donors to the RNLI.

In her eighteen years at Caister the *Covent Garden*, ex *James Pearce, Birmingham No. 2*, was launched 132 times on service and saved no fewer than 474 lives, an amazing record. Two further boats were provided for the Caister station by the Covent Garden Lifeboat Fund, a 42ft. Norfolk and Suffolk type boat built by Beeching in 1883 at a cost of £300 and a 40ft. boat built by the Thames Iron Works at Millwall in 1899 at a much greater cost of £1,295. The third *Covent Garden* was a great improvement on earlier boats, since she was fitted with water ballast tanks and with two drop keels which gave her much better sailing qualities. Both did excellent work: the first was launched fifty-five times and saved 208 lives, and the second 155 times, rescuing 166.

Launching a boat, be it a yawl or a lifeboat, from an open beach in a storm could never be easy; sometimes it was impossible. About three in the morning of 4th December 1883 a beachman on watch in the Caister lookout saw a flare on board a vessel which he judged must be on the Barber Sand. He lost no time in ringing the bell that hung beneath the lookout tower, and within minutes the whole crew and many others were down at the boat and preparing to launch. Crew and shore party working together soon had the lifeboat at the water's edge, where huge seas brought up by a strong nor'westerly gale were breaking on the beach, throwing spray over the struggling men.

Coxswain Philip George watched for a chance to launch; fourteen men were on the lee side holding the boat steady, and the launching party waited for the coxswain's word. Without warning an immense wave rolled out of the darkness and struck the lifeboat's bow, washing her right off the skeets and several yards up the beach, with the launchers hanging grimly to the lifelines along the boat's side.

Somehow they avoided being washed off and crushed by the heavy boat, but the coxswain was less fortunate. He was carried overboard by the breaking sea, and the undertow dragged him into the surf. Men rushed into the water to his aid, and somehow he was hauled out of the water. Immediately the crew and the launchers began the task of preparing the boat for another attempt at launching, getting her back on to the skeets and making ready the haul-off warp with which they hoped to pull her into deep water.

Seeing his opportunity, Coxswain George gave the word to launch. The launching party threw their weight behind the boat, pushing it down the beach as the crew hauled on the warp. It was all in vain. The heavy seas, like walls of water toppling on to the shelving beach, forced the boat back, thrusting the boat's head aside and casting her up the beach. Time and again the beachmen prepared the heavy boat for launching; again and again she was thrown back.

For four hours the crew and the shore party together fought to get the lifeboat afloat, but at last they had to give up because the anchor on the haul-off warp had come home. Instead of hauling the boat through the breakers, the crew had dragged the anchor to the beach.

The laconic entry in the log 'Caister failed to launch' gives no hint of the long, bitter struggle in which men had pitted themselves against the unrelenting sea, and had striven in vain.

Few salvage services were performed in good weather, but even on a fine night when the wind was no more than a light breeze a routine call could bring tragedy. So it was on 22nd July 1885 when two of the Caister beachmen, Philip George and James Haylett, junior, were on night watch in the company lookout. They were watching a schooner coming down outside the Barber Sand and saw her suddenly swing round with her head to the north-east. They realised at once that she had grounded on the outer edge of the Barber, so Haylett rang the bell to summon the company members.

The yawl *Zephyr* was launched about midnight with a crew of fifteen and set off for the Barber, with old James Haylett at the helm. Some nine years earlier the Caister men had saved the crew of a stone-laden schooner whose mast remained sticking up in the water. As they neared the Barber Jimmy Haylett reminded his crew 'Now, dear boys, keep a lookout for that old stump.'

The words were scarcely out of his mouth when the yawl's port bow struck the broken mast and the boat was ripped open. The crew quickly began to throw out the bags of shingle ballast, while Haylett and another man whipped out their knives and began to cut away the gear. Two or three quietly sat on the gunwale and stripped to their shirts and underpants as the yawl sank beneath them.

John George, who had stripped off his clothes before the boat went down, sang out 'fare ye well, boys, I'm off to the shore' and struck out for the beach a mile away. Old Jimmy Haylett supported himself on two oars, and his son Aaron, William Knowles and Joseph Haylett held on to the foremast, though with some difficulty as it kept on rolling over. Aaron decided to join his father and hang on to the two oars.

By good fortune John George saw a Yarmouth shrimper, the *Brothers*, hailed the crew and was picked up. 'There's fifteen of us in the water about here,' he told the fishermen, who immediately went to the rescue. First to be picked up was Robert Plummer, then Aaron Haylett, Harry Russell, and lastly old James Haylett, who was astride the foremast with an oar under one arm and a sett under the other.

Eight others were drowned, including old James's son and Aaron's brother, Frederick Haylett. Six widows and twenty-nine children were left to mourn

There was a stark reminder of what happened to many a wooden ship in earlier centuries when the barquentine *Luna*, which had left Yarmouth harbour, was cast on to Caister beach by stress of weather. Within hours she had begun to break up, and it was not very long before the beach was strewn with the wreckage of a fine little ship.

their loss. The loss to the community of Caister could not, however, be assessed only in terms of widows and orphans, for it was also an economic calamity from which the village took years to recover. Among those lost were men prominent in the boat-owning community.

The *Godsend* came to the end of her service at Caister in 1892. She had an impressive record over her twenty-five years, launching 126 times and saving 410 lives. Her lifesaving days were not over, however, for she eventually came into the hands of a Lowestoft pleasure boat proprietor, David Cook, who in 1901 moved to the Essex resort of Frinton, where the *Godsend*, renamed *Sailors' Friend*, was used for some years as a volunteer lifeboat.

Her place at Caister was taken by a 36ft. Norfolk and Suffolk type boat built by Henry Critten at his yard in Cobholm, Yarmouth. The gift of Sir Reginald Proctor-Beauchamp, of Langley Park, near Loddon, the new boat was given the name *Beauchamp*, and within a week of arriving on station was launched to stand by a Yarmouth fishing dandy that had grounded on the Barber; the boat refloated with the returning tide.

In nine years the *Beauchamp* was launched eighty-four times and saved 146 lives, but then on 13th November 1901 she herself became a casualty. It was about eleven at night when flares were seen from a vessel apparently on the Barber Sand, and the Cockle lightship, north-west of Caister, fired signals indicating that a vessel was in need of assistance. A nor'easterly gale was sending a heavy sea on to the beach and the night was thick with rain as the beachmen manned the No. 2 boat and prepared to launch.

The first attempt failed. Heavy seas washed the boat off the skeets and flung her back on to the beach. Undaunted, the launching party, working by the fitful light of duck lamps, hauled the *Beauchamp* back up the beach and prepared for another attempt. At last, after two and three-quarter hours of unremitting labour, the boat was got away from the beach and the members of the launching party went home to put on dry clothes, for they were all soaked through.

All went home except seventy-seven-year-old James Haylett, who had several members of his family in the lifeboat. The coxswain, Aaron Haylett, was a son of his, and so was James Haylett, junior, who had been coxswain

The 35ft. 6in. Liverpool type *Jose Neville*, seen here being beached, was the first motor lifeboat to be stationed at Caister. On the opposite page she is being launched by the Case tractor which had replaced the much smaller and less powerful Clayton tractors in RNLI service.

before his brother took over. His son-in-law, James Knight, was in the boat, and so were two of his grandsons. 'Old Jimmy' stayed on the beach, taking shelter in the lifeboat shed.

Once the boat was clear of the breakers the crew hoisted sail and proceeded towards the Barber on the port tack, not knowing that the vessel that had signalled for help had been driven right across the sand and was at anchor inside. As they neared the Barber the coxswain wore the boat round and stood inshore. He put her about again just outside the surf, making another board and then tacking again.

When he tried to put her about once more the boat failed to respond to the helm, and the coxswain gave the order to lower the mizzen and stand by the foresail halyard preparatory to beaching the boat. Before she could be safely beached a huge sea caught the boat on the starboard quarter, and at the same moment the boat grounded. She turned over, the masts broke off and the crew were pinned beneath the upturned boat.

James Haylett's grandson Frederick was making his way back to the lifeboat shed about three in the morning when he heard cries from the water's edge. He called to his grandfather, and together they ran to the spot from which the shouts were coming, no more than fifty yards from where the boat had been launched.

They found the overturned *Beauchamp* lying in the surf. Old James Haylett ran at once into the water and grabbed his son-in-law, Charles Knights, as he struggled to get clear. Frederick Haylett also went into the water and found John Hubbard, hauling him out on to the sand. 'Old Jimmy' then dashed back into the surf and seized his grandson, Walter Haylett, helping him on to the beach.

Those were the only three men to survive. The other nine members of the crew died under the boat; all but two of them were married, and they left six widows, thirty-three dependent children and four other dependent relatives. Again the damage done to the local community could not be measured simply in terms of widows and dependents, for one of those who died was a boatowner and two were masters of steam drifters, men on whom the prosperity of the local community depended.

The Case 1000D tractor pushes *The Royal Thames*, Caister's last RNLI lifeboat, down the beach and into the water; the boat's twin screws are already turning in their tunnels.

The lifeboat is propelled off her almost-submerged carriage and the self-righting tank is filling with water as she makes for deep water.

Members of the crew in oilskins join with the shore party in keeping the boat upright as she is swung round preparatory to being hauled back on to her carriage following her return to the beach.

A meeting was held on 21st December to enrol a new crew, and volunteers came forward without hesitation. And when a few hours later the bell was rung to call the men out 'Old Jimmy' and the three survivors of the *Beauchamp* were there on the beach helping to launch the No. 1 lifeboat *Covent Garden*.

Old James Haylett was awarded the Gold Medal for his gallantry and endurance and his grandson Frederick was voted the thanks of the Institution inscribed on vellum. It was at the inquest on the victims of the disaster that old James made the reply to a juryman's question that has ever since been quoted as 'Caister men never turn back'.

The *Beauchamp* was sold out of service after the accident and was converted into a Broads houseboat. Sixty years later she was acquired with the idea of restoring her as a museum exhibit, but memories die hard; instead she was broken up.

To replace the unlucky *Beauchamp* Thames Iron Works built a 35ft. Norfolk and Suffolk type boat, the *Nancy Lucy*, which served at Caister until 1929. Her replacement was not a Norfolk and Suffolk type boat but a 38ft. Liverpool type, the *Charles Burton*, which had been built by Thames Iron Works in 1904 and had served at Grimsby until transferred to Caister.

The No. 1 station closed in 1929, when the *James Leath*, which had been brought from Pakefield in 1919 to take the place of the third *Covent Garden*, was transferred to Aldeburgh. By the time the *Charles Burton* came to the end of her thirty-seven-year service in 1941 she was the last pulling and sailing lifeboat on the East Anglian coast.

While the *Charles Burton* with her fourteen oars needed a crew of at least sixteen men her replacement, the single-screw Liverpool type motor lifeboat *Jose Neville*, required a crew of only eight. At some stations where motor boats replaced the old pulling and sailing boats the coxswain was handed a poison chalice in having to pick which members of the crew should be retained and which ones should go, but at Caister Coxswain Joe Woodhouse was spared such a dilemma. By 1941 many of the younger members of the crew had joined the Forces and the same problem did not arise.

The problem that did arise was that of finding a crew at all. On one occasion the *Jose Neville* was launched with the seventy-three-year-old coxswain in command of a scratch crew that included three soldiers. Wartime services did not lack variety and saw the boat launched in one instance to the aid of a Supermarine Walrus amphibian; landing on the sea to rescue a fighter pilot who had bailed out of his aircraft, it had got into rough water and been washed ashore. The pilot was picked up by a boat from Scratby and the Walrus was towed into deep water by the lifeboat, which then handed over the tow to an RAF launch from Gorleston.

In 1964 the *Jose Neville* was retired to become a pilot boat at Lowestoft, her place at Caister being taken by an Oakley type boat bearing the name of a well-known yacht club, *The Royal Thames*. Three years later both Cromer and Gorleston received new lifeboats, that at Gorleston being of a new design based on the US Coast Guard's 44ft. lifeboat. With the coming of the new boats the RNLI concluded that there was no longer a need for a lifeboat at Caister, and in 1969 *The Royal Thames* was withdrawn and transferred to Runswick in Yorkshire, despite fierce opposition from the Caister crew and many local people.

Watched by holidaymakers, the volunteer lifeboat *Shirley Jean Adye* is prepared for launching on Caister Boat Day, 1982.

With turbines of the Scroby windfarm in the background, the Caister volunteer lifeboat *Bernard Matthews* shows her speed.

Below: The Dutch-built Valentijn class lifeboat *Bernard Matthews II* at sea. Propelled by water jets, she is capable of a speed of 37 knots, far more than that of her predecessors.

When *The Royal Thames* left in October 1969 the station officially closed, but the closure was not accepted by the Caister men. A 16ft. fibreglass dinghy with an outboard motor belonging to lifeboat mechanic 'Skipper' Woodhouse was immediately taken into service as a temporary lifeboat and a Caister Volunteer Rescue Service was set up to carry on the tradition of lifesaving in the village.

The last service of *The Royal Thames* had brought to 1,814 the number of lives saved since the station had been taken over by the RNLI in 1857, and those concerned with the station were determined that the story should not end there. An inflatable inshore rescue boat was bought by local schoolchildren, and eventually in 1973 a twin-screw Liverpool type lifeboat which had been in use as a fishing vessel at Wells since being sold by the RNLI was acquired. Built by Groves & Guttridge in 1953, she had served at St. Abbs until 1964.

Renamed *Shirley Jean Adye*, she proved as busy as any of her predecessors, saving fifty-seven lives in seventeen years before being replaced by a 38ft. 6in. boat from Lochin Marine at Rye that was fitted out for the Caister Volunteer Rescue Service by Goodchild Marine Services at Burgh Castle. She was named *Bernard Matthews* after the Norfolk turkey producer who made a generous contribution to the cost. In her turn she was replaced in 2004 by an 11m. rigid inflatable lifeboat similar to those employed by the Dutch lifeboat service. Powered by two 450hp Volvo Penta diesel engines and steerable water jets, the *Bernard Matthews II* is capable of 37 knots and is inherently self-righting.

It might seem rather odd that the Caister organisation should go to Holland for its new boat, but the links

'Skipper' Woodhouse in front of the old boathouse with the *Shirley Jean Adye* in the background. The new boathouse bears 'Skipper's' name.

between Caister and the Netherlands go back a long way. The redoubtable lifeboat mechanic 'Skipper' Woodhouse taught himself to speak Dutch so that he could communicate more easily with the Dutch salvage experts with whom the lifeboatmen sometimes worked to refloat ships from the Scroby.

The Valentijn-class boat was named *Bernard Matthews II* by Prince Charles, who with the Duchess of Cornwall boarded the boat before it was launched from its hydraulic carriage, propelled by a Caterpillar Challenger 65C tractor.

The *Bernard Matthews II* is housed in a new boatshed named after 'Skipper' Woodhouse, the old shed having been turned into a heritage centre in which the *Shirley Jean Adye* is on display. Forty years after the RNLI made the decision to close the station the Caister Volunteer Lifeboat Service, as it is now known, is equipped with the very latest and most up-to-date offshore and inshore lifeboats.

The Broadland waterways 8

Behind Yarmouth is a network of rivers that has been used for transport from the earliest days. During the Roman occupation of Britain, when a wide, shallow estuary ran inland to the provincial capital of Venta Icenorum and the site of Yarmouth was nothing more than a sandbank forming in the mouth of that estuary, there was possibly a little fleet of barges carrying goods between Venta and the twin coastal forts on either side of the mouth, at Burgh Castle and Caister – see map on page 186. There was another fort of some kind at Reedham, and it is said that a pharos or lighthouse stood on top of the nearby cliff; if there were one, it would doubtless have been very useful to boatmen using the deeper channels of the estuary.

Since archaeologists have found evidence suggesting that the Caister fort was a supply depot it is very likely that it had shipping links with Arbeia, today's South Shields, at the mouth of the Tyne, which served as a supply base for Hadrian's Wall, and possibly with other east coast forts. Arbeia, whose garrison included a unit of bargemen from the Tigris, at one stage had twenty-three granaries able to hold 3,200 tonnes of food.[1]

Apart from some enigmatic stonework and decayed oak piles excavated at Burgh Castle in the nineteenth century, which might have been the remains of a long-lost harbour below the fort, no relics of Roman maritime installations have been discovered in that part of Norfolk. Even the Great Estuary had largely disappeared by the time of the Norman Conquest; only Breydon Water survives into modern times to remind us of what once was.

Nonetheless, the river channels making their sinuous way towards the sea remained highways of trade for many centuries, enabling maritime trade to extend inland to Norwich, Beccles and many smaller towns and villages. Remembering that Norwich was after London the largest and most prosperous commercial centre in the kingdom during the sixteenth century, it is by no means difficult to imagine small ships bringing a variety of cargoes up the Yare and Wensum to Quayside, and returning downriver with the products of the city's artisans, potters, metalworkers and weavers, as well as the goods exported by the city's merchants. As the city grew in size and wealth, building materials, foodstuffs and agricultural produce, peat dug from the river valleys, and many other commodities were carried by these waterways.

A flourishing trade grew up with the continent which, in later days at least, involved the transhipment of cargoes at Yarmouth, but there was also a more local trade. When the Conqueror's clerks were compiling a record of who owned what land and of what taxes they owed to the Crown, the marshes

Opposite: The mate takes things easy as the wherry *Violet* of Catfield, owned by John Riches, farmer, grain merchant and wherry owner, sails downriver loaded 'to the binns' as the wherrymen put it; but he is ready to seize the quant and give the wherry's head a shove round when they come to the end of the reach and have to tack. In a light wind the bonnet has been laced to the foot of the sail to increase the sail area.

Opposite: The Buck print of
Norwich showing the canal
up to the cathedral.

that had grown up on the former estuary were dry enough to be used for the grazing of flocks of sheep; in the thirteenth century the cathedral priory of Norwich kept a large flock almost year round on Fulholm, between Breydon Water and the Bure. For ten weeks after harvest, however, they were fed and folded on the stubbles at Martham. Entries in the Martham manor account rolls include one concerning 'carrying dung from Fulholm to Martham by water 13s. 6d.', giving us a clear indication that water transport was significant at that period.[2]

Presumably the dung loaded at Fulholm would have been taken up the lower Bure and the Thurne to Martham, which suggests that the connection between the two rivers was in existence by then. The early history of this waterway system is obscure, for while it is obvious from a glance at the map that changes have been made to the river channels over the centuries there is little or no evidence of when those changes were made, or by whom.[3] It is clear enough that a cut was made at some time from below St. Benet's Abbey to link the Bure/Thurne to the lower Bure, yet there is no way of telling when that major alteration was made, incidentally reversing the flow of the Thurne; one can only surmise that the new channel might have been dug by the monks of St. Benet's to alleviate severe flooding in the area near Martham as land levels fell in the post-Conquest period.

The digging of turves for fuel in the river valleys of east Norfolk and Suffolk was a considerable occupation during some four hundred years, and there is evidence in the records of Norwich cathedral priory that peat was supplied to the priory kitchens. In early medieval times East Anglia was the most densely populated area of England, and the eastern part of Norfolk was one of the most prosperous parts of the kingdom, if one is to judge from the tax assessments of 1334; with woodland being relatively scarce in the area there was a ready market for this fuel.[4] Not only are there records of peat being brought to Norwich in considerable quantities both for burning in the priory kitchen and for the use of the citizens, but it is highly probable that a substantial proportion was delivered by river from the turfpits that were to become the broads. At Yarmouth the tolls levied to defray the costs of building and maintaining the town walls included in 1346 one of a penny on every boatload of turves, while at Norwich a similar royal grant of murage in 1297 included a toll of a penny for every boat laden with firewood, turves or other things whatsoever, exceeding 20s.

Stone for the building of the cathedral itself was brought upriver from Yarmouth, to which it had been brought by sea from Normandy; the canal up which it was taken into the cathedral close was still in existence in the mid-eighteenth century.

As the trade of Norwich merchants like Robert Toppes grew in scope in the fourteenth and fifteenth centuries the river played a vital part in facilitating their activities. It was surely no mere chance that Toppes, whose coat of arms included three wooden spinning tops, chose a riverside site in King Street for his magnificent trading hall, built in the mid-1400s, above an existing ground-floor range, for the display and sale of cloth. Now known as Dragon Hall, after the delightful carving of a winged and multi-tailed beast in one of the roof spandrels, this showroom was a visual manifestation of its owner's wealth and social standing – he became Sheriff in 1430 at the age of twenty-five and was four times Mayor of the city and Burgess in Parliament.[5]

Robert Toppes's hall backed on to the river; restored and developed today as a multifunctional centre, it is a splendid example of a Norwich merchant's home and trading warehouse.

Norwich was particularly known for the production of broad-cloth and worsted, but the trade of the city was by no means confined to textiles. When the *Blitheburgesbot* sank in a storm while on its way from Yarmouth to Norwich in 1343 its cargo consisted of sea coal worth 10s., salt worth 12d., three barrels of Swedish iron valued at 13s. 4d., twenty-five boards from Riga and various other goods including herrings, giving an indication of the diversity of imports coming to the city.[6]

Towards the end of the fourteenth century no fewer than seventeen Norwich merchants were trading abroad. Not surprisingly materials required by the textile trade such as dyestuffs, chiefly woad and madder, featured prominently in the list of imports. In 1475-76 the city received sixty-six fullers' kettles, the large lead pans used by fullers and dyers, through Yarmouth. Cloth did not only move downriver, for Iperlyngs, linen cloths from Ypres, and canvas were brought in from the continent to satisfy the local markets.

The port records of Yarmouth have been used by Penelope Dunn to tell something of the shipping operations of Norwich merchants in the late fourteenth century.[7] A group of them hired Ollard Johannson's *Seintemarieschipp of Arnemuth* in 1388 to carry an export cargo of worsted, cheese and rabbit skins. Arriving on 6th December with a mixed cargo belonging mainly to the Norwich merchants, she sailed for a continental port with their export cargo only two days later and was back again on 26th December, having collected a shipment of madder, canvas, soap, oil and wax.

Trading and other links between Norwich and the Low Countries were close and were by no means confined to matters of commerce. While Norwich merchants were quite likely to be met with in Ghent, Ypres or Middelburg, people from the continent were equally likely to be seen in Norwich. John Asger, who became Mayor of Norwich in 1426, was described as a merchant of Bruges.

Norwich was indeed a cosmopolitan community. Professor Peter Trudgill has pointed out how in the twelfth century Norwich contained sizeable groups of speakers of Danish, Dutch and the Jewish form of Spanish known as Ladino, long before Edward III invited Flemish weavers to England and even longer before the arrival from Holland of the Strangers.[8]

During the religious and political upheavals of the seventeenth century links between Norwich and the Netherlands were just as strong as they had been in the fifteenth century, with those whose views brought them into conflict with Bishop Matthew Wren seeking refuge across the North Sea. Of the 923 passengers travelling from Yarmouth to Holland between 1637 and 1639 no fewer than 335 were from the city, some of them intending to settle and others stating that they were visiting for a limited period. Among those who intended to stay were several joining parents, husbands or friends who had already settled there.[9]

Similarly, eighty of the 192 people who sailed from Yarmouth for New England in the *Mary Anne* of Yarmouth in May 1637 were from Norwich, and it has been generally assumed that they were driven out by Bishop Wren's 'rigorous prosecutions and dealings'. Among them were three well-to-do freemen of the city, worsted weavers Nicholas Busbie and Francis Lawes and dornix weaver Michael Metcalfe; with them went their wives and children, and their servants. One of Lawes' two servants, Samuel Lincorne, was an ancestor of Abraham Lincoln.

Robert Toppes's hall is now known as Dragon Hall from the 'dragon' carved in one of the roof spandrels.

James Stark's portrayal of a timber-laden keel on the River Yare at Norwich in about 1830, with one of the two boom towers in the background on the left. When carrying such a cargo hatch covers were not fitted, but earlier keels carrying the products of the city weavers to Yarmouth for export most certainly did cover their hatches to protect so valuable a cargo.

The Norfolk keel

The great majority of cargoes would have been carried upriver in keels, small craft propelled by a single square sail on a mast set more or less amidships that were peculiar to the East Anglian waterways and shared a name, but not their design, with the keels of Yorkshire and those of the Tyne. The name they shared is descended from the Anglo-Saxon *ceol* and the Old Norse *kjoll*, both of which might be translated quite simply into 'boat'.

The likelihood is that the medieval keel was quite similar to the little keels shown on eighteenth-century prints of the city of Norwich such as Thomas Kirkpatrick's of 1733 and that of Samuel and Nathaniel Buck published a few years later, but we have no contemporary pictorial evidence of the appearance of the medieval version. The earliest authentic map of the city of Norwich made by William Cuningham in 1558 shows a number of small vessels berthed in the Wensum along Quayside, and similar craft can be seen on Thomas Cleer's map of 1696, but we have nothing earlier than those. These vessels have a single mast crossing a yard, and appear to be keels not dissimilar from those portrayed by James Stark in the first half of the nineteenth century.

We do, however, have documentary evidence of the men who operated them, men like John Stingate and his apprentice Jonas Whitfield, who was bound to him in 1561. Thanks to the efforts of Shirley Harris we know quite a lot about John Stingate, 'keleman', who lived in South Conesford (the King Street area of Norwich) in the sixteenth century. 'From the time when he became a freeman by purchase in 1545 there is scarcely a set of records dealing with this corner of Norwich and the river down to Yarmouth which does not contain a least a brief reference to John Stingate,' Miss Harris says. 'He seems to have had a finger in every pie.' Both Stingate and young Whitfield his apprentice did very well for themselves, it would seem.[10]

It was normal in former times for workmen to have 'more than one string to their bows,' and Stingate not only ran his keel but operated as a reed merchant and at times as an eel-catcher. Possibly he had more than one keel, for he seems to have employed James Cowell, who was admitted a freeman in 1556. Perhaps Cowell was on his way from Yarmouth to Norwich in 1561 when he and Edmund Hardyng were entertained by Robert Boty, a young fisherman, and his wife Helen at Buckenham Ferry. Over what was probably a convivial meal Hardyng offered to sell Cowell a keel for £60, to be paid in annual instalments of £2, an offer that Cowell promptly accepted; no doubt he saw the acquisition of his own keel as the key to a fortune as great as that of his master. When Hardyng later sought to withdraw the offer Cowell endeavoured to hold him to the deal by an action in the mayor's court; Robert Boty and his wife swore depositions in Cowell's support.

Some of those watermen who operated keels between Norwich and Yarmouth were doubtless attracted by the possibility of making their fortune in the city. The Palling family probably came from the coastal village of that name: Edward Palling, waterman and keelman, son of William Palling, waterman, was admitted to the freedom of the city in 1570. Later generations of the family seem to have spelt their name Pawlin.

The names of twenty-four keelmen are recorded in a list of those who were admitted to the freedom of the city of Norwich between 1548 and 1713.

Others were freemen of the borough of Yarmouth, where the last keelman was admitted in 1795, a dozen years after the admission of Matthew Underwood, the first wherryman to become a freeman of that town.

The importance of the Wensum and Yare to the trade of the city is underlined by the appointment in 1543 of a water bailiff 'to search, see and diligently execute the whole effect of the office of waterbailie aforesaid' in preventing the commission of offences on the waterway.[11] It is illustrated no less by the decision taken in 1663 by the Commissioners of Sewers to widen the river to 'the full breadth of twenty and two yards from the firme bancke on the one side of the river to the firme bancke on the other side of the same river att the turne of the river near Wicklingham Kill' – that is, Whitlingham kiln, presumably a predecessor of the limekiln that still exists on the south side of Whitlingham Reach.[12]

Beer, harlots and felons

The city corporation was naturally anxious to control the use of the river for the transport both of goods and of passengers, and it was not unknown for keelmen to fall foul of mayoral edicts from time to time. One keelman, Nicholas Davy of Norwich, found himself in trouble in 1553 for having 'conveyed eight barrelles of Bere from the Cittie unto Yermuthe contrarye to Mr. Mayour's Commandementes' and was fined for his 'contempt'. In 1570 the Assembly set out to regulate the 'passage boats' and the watermen who operated them, it being enacted that the mayor should license three boats, and that the people running them should obey certain instructions regarding the carriage of people and merchandise,[13] and in 1616 it was ordered that 'no keleman wherryman or other waterman usinge passage upon the said Ryver shall willingly or wittyngly cary or suffer to passe in any their keles wherryes or boates any common Rogue, harlott, ffelon or other person notoriously knowne or suspected to have committed any such cryme . . .'.

It was not only rogues and harlots that travelled surreptitiously by river. When James II was seeking to reinstate Catholicism in England in the 1680s Dr Humphrey Prideaux, prebendary and later Dean of Norwich Cathedral, made use of the river service to disseminate copies of a letter drawn up by the Marquess of Halifax in opposition to James's Declaration of Indulgence. The account of his life, published in 1748, tells how Dr. Prideaux covered up his trail.

> Having made up about a dozen packets with several of these letters enclosed in each of them, he superscribed them in feigned hands, to as many Ministers in the City of Norwich, and sent a person, whome he knew he could trust, to Yarmouth, with directions to disperse them in several Wherries, which came up every night from thence to Norwich: and this being faithfully executed, the letters were delivered the next morning as directed. Now as they were sent from Yarmouth, it was generally believed that they came from Holland . . . .

Keel and wherry

It will be noted that by the beginning of the seventeenth century wherries had joined the keels on the Norfolk rivers. It is not known what these early wherries were like. They might have been large rowing boats like that seen in Corbridge's prospect of Yarmouth or they might have been sailing vessels like the later wherries. In spite of what has been claimed by some writers one must have doubts whether Corbridge's four-oared boat with its cabin and its helmsman standing in a rather elevated position at the stern can have been the ancestor of the sailing wherry, since that craft was present in fully fledged form by 1789.

In that year a horn cup, now in the Castle Museum at Norwich, was engraved with a detailed depiction of the *Happy Return*, a smart little sailing wherry that is basically very similar to the wherries of the nineteenth century; it differs only in size and detail. 'Success to the Happy Return' is inscribed on one side, with 'Robert and Mary Adkins, Irstead, September 12th, 1789' on the other. One wonders what became of the *Happy Return*, for six years later Robert Adkins is recorded as master of another wherry, the *Beeston* of Barton, a village next door to Beeston St Lawrence and not far from Irstead.

For a general description of a keel we can turn to *A Concise History and Directory of the City of Norwich for 1811*, printed by and for C. Berry, jun., in 1810. While it mentions both keels and wherries the description it gives is of a keel.

> The keels and wherries which navigate between Norwich and Yarmouth are acknowledged to be superior to any other small craft in England, for carrying a larger burthen, and being worked at a smaller expense; – their burthen is from fifteen and fifty tons; they have but one mast, which lets down, and carry only one large square sail, are covered close by hatches, and have a cabin superior to many coasting vessels, in which oftentimes the keelman and his family live; they require only two persons to navigate them and sometimes perform their passage (thirty-two miles) in five hours.

Information on individual keels is hard to find, but Peter Allard has provided a copy of a document of 1736 in which two Little Yarmouth (Southtown) shipwrights, John Cabon and Samuel Balls, recorded the sale of 'all that new keelframe or hull lately built by us' to Henry Harwood, a Great Yarmouth keelman. The new keel was 58ft. long and 17ft. in breadth. The price paid by Harwood 'at diverse and several times' for the bare hull was £120, a sum with which Cabon and Balls expressed themselves fully satisfied. The unnamed lawyer who drew up the extremely wordy agreement left no chance of later disagreement, setting down in clear writing that 'the said Henry Harwood Executors Administrators and assigns shall or lawfully may from time to time and at all times for ever hereafter peaceably and quietly have hold possess and enjoy the said new keelframe or hull and every part thereof without any lawful Sell Suit Trouble Denial Interruption or Eviction . . .'.

Five years later Harry Harwood sold a half share of the keel *Christopher & Sarah*, presumably the same vessel, to Richard Porter for £60. The document recording this transaction is a good deal less wordy, and less clear, but it would appear that the day after purchasing that half share Porter sold it on to Thomas Linsey for £90. Thereafter Thomas Linsey, Thomas Linsey junior, James Ives and Thomas Ives appear to have held quarter shares in the same craft.

An Act of 1795 required all inland waterways craft to be registered, and the list subsequently made by the Town Clerk of Yarmouth[14] sheds a sudden, unsustained light on the keels and wherries sailing the waterways of Norfolk and Suffolk. Between July and December 1795 no fewer than 149 vessels were entered into the local register as they berthed at the town's quays; the following year the Town Clerk registered four more, and in 1797 he re-registered just one vessel, the Yarmouth keel *Flora*, since Robert Kett had taken over as master from Roger Page. After that his enthusiasm seems to have flagged, for in 1798 he added just two more vessels; the rest of the register book consists of blank forms.

The first entry, made on July 10th 1795, is formal and not particularly informative, except perhaps that it indicates one of the disadvantages of the keel, that it needed a larger crew than a wherry, which was often worked single-handed and never had more than two hands:

> John Harvey of Great Yarmouth in the County of Norfolk, Keelman, having this Day declared to me, John Spurgeon, Town Clerk . . . that he . . . is at present Master of the Keel called the Edmund of Yarmouth and that the said keel admeasures Ninety Tons, and no more, and is at present worked by the Number of Persons in the several Capacities under-mentioned, viz.
> John Harvey Master
> Joseph Jay Quarterman
> William Riddelsdell Waterman
> Robert Tooley Waterman

The register contains the names of thirty-five keels, twenty of them belonging to Yarmouth and ten to Norwich. Three keels hailed from the North River, the 28-ton *Two Friends* of Coltishall, the 40-ton *Trial* and the 20-ton *Venture*, both of which latter craft belonged to Panxworth, a village that in later days at least had no links to any waterway. Yarmouth not only had the greatest number of keels but also had the largest of these vessels, the 97-ton *Success*. The *Supply* came a close second at 95 tons and the *Recovery* third at 85 tons, with five others of 80 tons. These big keels would have been used in the Norwich trade, taking to the city raw materials such as coal and timber transhipped from seagoing ships in the harbour and bringing back the products of the city, notably textiles for export to Russia, Spain, India or some other far-off place.

Biggest of the Norwich keels was the 80-ton *Susanna*, with the *William & Mary* weighing in at 75 tons and four others at 70 tons. Smallest of the Norwich keels was the *London Lady*, of 35 tons.

It is apparent from this document that the keels had had their day, for alongside the thirty-five keels there were 118 wherries in the register, most of them quite small. By far the largest was the 50-ton *Mayflower*, one of fifteen

At the time the Norwich and Lowestoft Navigation was being engineered Thomas Batley was building seagoing craft at his yard on the river below Norwich. This lithograph of a drawing by Miles Edmund Cotman of the Valley of Thorpe shows what is likely to have been his yard some years after he launched the *Squire*.

wherries belonging to Norwich. Somewhat oddly there were also two other Norwich wherries with this name, one of 40 tons and the other of 20. Largest of the eight wherries belonging to Yarmouth was the 43-ton *Robert & Frances*.

Besides those belonging to the city there were seven wherries from places on the Yare or Norwich River such as Norton, Langley, Cantley and Reedham. Eight came from Aylsham or nearby places on the Aylsham Navigation, a dozen from Coltishall and Horstead, and forty-six from other places on the North River (the Bure and its tributaries), the smallest of all being of only 14 tons. Another twenty-four wherries came from places on the Waveney.

Because of the short period the register covers it provides no more than a snapshot of those keels and wherries trading to and from Yarmouth in the year 1795. No building dates or other details are given. Roy Clarke in his book *Black Sailed Traders* describes a last-ditch fight of the Yarmouth keel owners, telling how they built larger and larger keels in an attempt to defeat the wherries; although he quotes the register as evidence, it does not in any way support his hypothesis.

An advertisement in a local newspaper relating to the sale at Coltishall of the *John and Joseph* in 1779 was specific in referring to her as a 'hatch keel'.[15] The same year the *Norwich Mercury* advertised the sale of 'the keel or vessel called the Hand and Hand, burthen 50 tons, now lying at Norwich',[16] and the following year the same paper carried an advertisement for 'the good Keel, called the JOHN and ELIZABETH, John Clark, Master, of the Burthen of forty Tons or thereabouts, now lying in Yarmouth Haven with Mast, Sail, Rigging, Tackle and Appurtenances thereto belonging'.

While their work was principally carrying cargoes between Norwich and Yarmouth and along the other rivers, keels were sometimes taken out into Yarmouth Roads to lighten seagoing ships which were too deeply laden to negotiate the troublesome bar at the mouth of Yarmouth harbour. In 1782 a keel engaged in taking coals from a collier in the roads suddenly sank 'with upwards of thirty chaldron'; the crew seem to have escaped with a wetting.

The handier wherries with their single fore-and-aft sail had largely taken over from the keels by the 1820s. *A General History of the County of Norfolk*, published in 1829, says that 'the general navigation from Norwich to Yarmouth is performed by keels and wherries; the former are chiefly restricted to the freightage of timber, and are far less numerous than formerly . . .'.

For the carrying of heavy timber it was deemed unnecessary to make use of the hatch covers, leading to the misleading statement so often made that the hold of the keel was open. The description given in *The Norfolk Tour* of 1818 makes it quite clear that until their relegation to the timber trade keels did have hatch covers of much the same form as those of the wherries. It is hardly likely that valuable cargoes such as silken textiles produced in the Norwich silkmills and due to be exported to India and other places would have been loaded into an unprotected hold. Although several of these craft were still in trade, and one was to remain at work for another half-century or more, the predominant type on the waterways of Norfolk and north-east Suffolk was by that time the wherry, with its single mast set right up forward carrying a big loose-footed gaff sail.

In illustration of the importance of the waterborne trade, John Greaves Nall stated in 1866 that 'before the opening of railways, 230,000 quarters of

Wherries unloading at one of the King Street wharves at Norwich about 1830; the one alongside the wharf has a transom stern, which was not uncommon at that period. Above the roof of the warehouse can be seen the cowl of a malting.

Costumed guests travelled on the *Regal Lady* along the New Cut in 1983 to celebrate the 150th anniversary of the opening of that waterway.

wheat, barley and malt, and 150,000 sacks of flour were forwarded by the rivers Wensum, Bure, Yare, and Waveney, from Norwich, North Walsham, Bungay, Beccles, &c., to Yarmouth, to be shipped thence to London, Liverpool, Scotland, Newcastle, &c. The average export of the three years ending 1785 was 270,000 quarters; from 1810 to 1819 it averaged 310,000 quarters; from 1839 to 1843 it exceeded 400,000 quarters yearly; and in 1840 the export of grain from Yarmouth was 480,363 quarters.'

After remarking that the textile exports from Norwich by way of Yarmouth at one time amounted to £1 million a year, Nall added that 'Prior to 1826, two-fifths of the coals and goods imported into Yarmouth were sent up the Yare to Norwich, and more than half the imports and exports to and from Yarmouth belonged to that city.[17]

'Norwich a Port'

The date of 1826 is a significant one, for in that year the Norwich and Lowestoft Navigation Bill was introduced in Parliament in a bid to bring seagoing ships to Norwich by way of a new harbour at Lowestoft and a ship canal across the marshes from Haddiscoe to Reedham. The furious opposition of Yarmouth Corporation ensured that the Bill failed, but when a similar Bill was introduced in 1827 it successfully passed through all its Parliamentary stages and received Royal assent. On 4th September 1827 Alderman Crisp Brown, a prominent Norwich maltster and a leading promoter of the scheme to make 'Norwich a Port', dug the first spadeful of earth at Mutford Bridge, between Oulton Broad and Lake Lothing, soon to become Lowestoft harbour.

The opposition of Yarmouth to proposals to allow seagoing ships up to Norwich, whether through Yarmouth harbour or by any other route, sprang from the fact that for centuries cargoes had been transhipped in the harbour from seagoing vessels into keels and wherries for onward transmission to the city, while the manufactures of Norwich went downriver for export from Yarmouth to many parts of the world.

In 1820 the advertisements of the rival 'old-established Yarmouth & Norwich Shipping Company, from Symond's Wharf, London,' and 'The Norwich and Yarmouth New Shipping Company from Irongate Lower Wharf, St. Catherine's, London' appeared together on the front page of a local newspaper.[18] What neither advertisement made clear was that the regular traders, weekly at first but soon afterwards to become twice weekly, berthed at Yarmouth, so that goods were sent on to Norwich by wherry, with increased risk of damage, loss and pilferage.

This pilfering of cargoes had been one of the reasons for the Norwich merchants to promote the construction of a navigation bringing ships to the city. Crisp Brown told a House of Commons committee on the Norwich and Lowestoft Navigation Bill in 1826 that he estimated his loss by plunder in the preceding year at more than £840. In 1820 a score or more watermen employed by city merchants were committed to Norwich Castle charged with having stolen considerable quantities of coal from wherries belonging to their various employers. Seven of them were accused of stealing coals from the wherry *Accommodation*, belonging to John Morse and William Hall of Norwich; they had unloaded it at Cantley, apparently selling the coal to a

The trading wherry *Albion* and refurbished pleasure wherries assembled on Oulton Broad and then made their way up river for the 1983 celebration.

licensee there. The worst offenders were sentenced to transportation, others to terms of imprisonment.

Yet Crisp Brown told the Parliamentary committee that those court cases had by no means brought the long series of thefts to an end. 'We cannot detect the thieves now,' he said, 'they keep so good a lookout.'

Boatyards at Norwich and in other places on the waterways had given birth to craft such as keels and wherries over the centuries, but with the prospect of Norwich becoming a true port Thomas Batley began building seagoing ships at Carrow, on the Wensum just below Norwich. The second was the *Squire*, a little sloop launched in 1831 and most likely named after a Norwich wharfinger, Matthew Squire, who had premises in King Street.

Some seagoing ships must have been able to get to Norwich before the opening of the Norwich and Lowestoft Navigation, because in May 1828 the 120-ton steam packet *Thames* is reported to have arrived in the city, hailed as the first seaborne vessel to sail from London to Norwich direct. She could only have come upriver from Yarmouth, negotiating the shallow channel over Breydon at high water, since the first vessels to enter the new harbour at Lowestoft did not do so until June 1831.

Indeed, it was not until February 1833 that the little billyboy *Luna*, commanded and no doubt owned by a Captain John Moon, made her way through Lowestoft and down the Waveney and so up to Norwich with a cargo of Yorkshire coal. Captain Moon not only chose an appropriate name for his vessel but had a penchant for pioneering voyages, for in the previous March he had sailed to Beccles with the first cargo of coal to reach that town without having been transhipped into a wherry for the inland part of the voyage.

Customs officials at Yarmouth seem to have raised difficulties which delayed the unloading of the coals in the city, but doubtless these were overcome in due course; meanwhile Captain Moon basked in the glory of being first to reach Norwich by way of Lowestoft, though any kind of official recognition of his achievement was lacking.

Local newspaper editors saw a bright future for the port of Norwich, writing that 'we may hope to see the river at Carrow bristling with masts, spars and cordage. We trust such a spectacle will soon be surrounded with its necessary concomitants – shipbuilders' yards, rope walks, sail-makers' manufactories, and all the signs of maritime trade, a new population, and a brisker general employment.'[19]

Some three months after Captain Moon's first visit to Norwich the directors of the Norwich and Lowestoft Navigation Company gathered on the meadow that lay between Foundry Bridge and Carrow Bridge in Norwich to be shown by the engineer, William Cubitt, and the resident engineer, George Edwards, the site of the five-acre 'floating dock' that was to be excavated to accommodate ships coming up the navigation. Some say that it was to be named the Clarence Harbour after the popular Duke of Clarence, who in 1830 succeeded to the throne as William IV; others aver that that name was to be used for the new harbour at Lowestoft.

'We are afraid it will not be possible to preserve the Devil's Tower, after the water shall be deepened round it for the admission of vessels – and it is besides so much dilapidated that it cannot stand much longer,' reported the *Norwich Mercury*.[20] The fifteenth-century boom tower and its companion on the south side of the river are both still standing; the dock was never constructed.

Nevertheless, the new harbour at Lowestoft came into operation, improvements were made to the river on the approaches to Norwich and the Haddiscoe New Cut came into use. The wherry *Friendship* was the first to pass along the New Cut from the south, on 29th January 1833, and the *Henry*, owned by Norwich merchant Thomas Geldart, was the first wherry to enter it from the Yare. Then, on 30th September 1833, the schooner *City of Norwich* and the little sloop *Squire* officially opened the new port of Norwich when they were towed into the city from Lowestoft, though not without a last-minute delaying action on the part of officials at Yarmouth who declined to open the bridge for the steamer *Jarrow*, which had been engaged to tow the two vessels upriver. Their excuse was that it was a Sunday; the bridge was, they said, never opened on a Sunday.

Captain Wilkinson of the *Jarrow* might have solved his problem by making the twelve-mile sea passage to Lowestoft, but instead he unbolted the funnel and squeezed under the firmly shut bridge. He had, however, lost his tide and had to linger on Breydon waiting for the next flood. As he reached Haddiscoe he met the *City of Norwich* and *Squire* being slowly towed against a nor'westerly wind by the *Susanna*, which was little more than a steam launch with an engine of 7hp. Better progress was made when the *Jarrow* took over the *City of Norwich*, leaving the *Susanna* to tow the smaller vessel.

Then human frailty again took a hand when the little procession had got within some eight miles of the city. Instructions were given that the *Jarrow* and *City of Norwich* should take the lead so as to be the first to enter the city. The crew of the *Susanna* took umbrage at this and cast off the towrope; if they were to be denied the honour of being first, they would not play the game at all. Worse still, a young seaman, the son of Captain Allerton of the *City of Norwich*, fell from his boat and drowned as he carried a towrope from his father's ship to the *Squire*. It must have been a very subdued little flotilla that entered the city that day.

The 74-ton schooner *City of Norwich*, built by John Korff the previous year on a yard at Lowestoft leased from the navigation company, and the 61-ton sloop *Squire* were both owned by the London, Lowestoft, Norwich and Beccles Shipping and Trading Company, which advertised later in 1833 the establishment of a regular weekly service between Griffin's Wharf, in London's Tooley Street, and Norwich.

The company bought the schooner *Sally* from King's Lynn and another schooner, the *Orion*, in 1831, and augmented its fleet in 1834 when the 80-ton schooners *Lowestoft Merchant* and *Norwich Trader* were built at Yarmouth by Thomas Branford. In that same year the company sold the *Orion* to Wells and replaced her by the Wells-built schooner *Sarah*, launched the previous year by John Hammond Parker. It also owned a second *Sarah*, a sloop. In 1838, when it was running two vessels a week from London, one to Norwich and the other to Lowestoft and Beccles, it bought the sloop *Ocean*, built at Wells in 1831. The schooner *Sally* and the sloop *Sarah* were advertised for sale at 'Lowestoft near Yarmouth' in 1840.

The Norwich and Lowestoft Navigation Company failed when it found the income from shipping quite insufficient to pay back the £54,000 it had borrowed from the Public Works Loan Commissioners. Somewhat unsurprisingly, attempts to sell the undertaking proved unsuccessful. Nevertheless, ships continued to sail up to Norwich and a newspaper account of 1846 tells of no fewer than eighteen vessels arriving in the city with cargoes in just one week.

The improvements made to the channel of the Yare between Reedham and Norwich as part of the scheme have not been recorded, but a change made when the Norfolk Railway was constructed between Norwich and Yarmouth in 1844 remains very evident. The old channel at Thorpe St. Andrew ran close beside the Norwich-Yarmouth road and the green, but when the railway line was laid across two fixed bridges a new straight cut was made alongside the line to enable ships to reach the city without having to negotiate the two bridges, which allow little headroom.

The wharfingers

One of the prints by James Stark in his *River Scenery of Norfolk* shows a riverside granary in Norwich with a number of spouts from which grain could be poured into the hold of a wherry. The title of the picture is *Harrison's Wharf.*

James Stark's engraving of a wherry being built on a yard at Carrow in about 1830. Like many others at the time, this wherry has a narrow transom rather than the sharp stern that later became more usual.

The port of Norwich in 1933: the Great Yarmouth Shipping Company's steamer *Norwich Trader* and another vessel lie outside Boulton & Paul's works on the left, and the wherry *Spray* lies on the King Street side of the river, with other vessels almost lost in the mist. The man in the small boat is Billy Royall, owner of the *Spray* and a well-known wherryman.

Opposite: The wherry *Norfolk Hero* unloading at the premises of builders' merchants Lacy & Lincoln just below Duke Street bridge in the heart of Norwich. The crutch block has been hooked on to the spen block to raise the gaff and sail horizontally clear of the hatches and the quants and boat-hook are slung from the gaff. The *Norfolk Hero* is one of the few wherries that had half hatches, with a longitudinal beam to support them; most wherries had hatches that spanned the hold from side to side. Astern of her a smaller wherry has a cargo of deals stacked out on either side; so has another wherry just visible at bottom right.

Situated in King Street, the wharf belonged to Robert Harrison, who in the early years of the nineteenth century was one of five wharfingers operating in Norwich. When he died in 1846 and the wharf was advertised to be let it was said to have 'a most substantial Quay Head and powerful Cranes, an excellent Dwelling House, four Cottages for Workmen' and coal bins, granaries and warehouses.[21]

The wharfingers played an important part in the commercial life of the city, for they organised the carriage of goods by wherry and by other means and in some cases also acted as coal and corn merchants. Some were also wherry owners. While King Street had a number of wharves along its length some of the wharfingers had their premises in the heart of the city, in the parishes of St Margaret and St Swithin.

One prominent business was that operated from Duke's Palace Wharf, close to the site of the Duke of Norfolk's palace, by Boardman and Harmer. Established about 1819 by James Boardman and Daniel Harmer, this firm acted as agents for the Norwich and Yarmouth Shipping Company which operated a weekly service to Iron Gate Lower Wharf in London until moving in 1834 to Fennings' Wharf in Tooley Street. James Boardman lived and worked at Spooner's Wharf in King Street, on a spacious site with a river frontage of 80ft. and a depth from the river to King Street of 110ft; the family house had a first-floor sitting room that 'looked over the river and meadows to the pretty wooded high ground of Thorpe'. Daniel Harmer managed the Duke's Palace Wharf and lived in Chapel Field Road.[22]

Until the Norwich and Lowestoft Navigation came into being the Yarmouth-London traders such as those for which Boardman and Harmer were agents sailed from Yarmouth, items of cargo being carried downriver from Norwich in wherries and loaded into the traders in Yarmouth harbour. Roy Clark in *Black Sailed Traders* lists seven wherries that were owned by Boardman and Harmer, the largest of them being the *Maria* and the *Pilot* at 40 tons burthen. It was not until early in 1834 that the London, Lowestoft and Norwich Shipping Company announced in the *Norwich Mercury* that goods would be carried 'to Norwich via Lowestoft direct in one bottom' and

Wherries being loaded at the 'tips' in Riverside Road, Norwich, a little way below Bishop's Bridge. The nearest wherry has one of the shifting rightups removed and a plank laid across the hold; the hatches are stacked abaft the mast and on the cabin top.

that freight rates would be reduced 'to the full amount that has usually been charged for Wherry Freight by the old Navigation'.

In the same issue of the paper the rival London, Yarmouth and Norwich traders from Symond's Wharf in London disclosed that they had acquired the wherries formerly owned by Jay & Company, one of the Norwich wharfingers, and had taken over that firm's wharves and warehouses in King Street and St Margaret's.[23] It was a time of considerable rivalry between competing shipping companies, and one of them advertised from Harrison's Wharf that 'in future all goods by this conveyance will be delivered at Norwich free of all river freight'.

James Boardman died in 1839, and some time later there came an announcement from Duke's Palace Wharf that the business was being carried on by the surviving partner 'for the mutual benefit of himself, the widow and nine children'. Alterations had been made to the wharf and a new facility 'also under cover' had been erected on the opposite bank in the parish of St Miles. Apparently part of the original wharf had been rented out, because R. & S. Rudrum, another firm of wharfingers and shipping agents, claimed somewhat disengenuously to have 'taken over Duke's Palace Wharf, late in the occupation of Messrs. Boardman and Harmer, where the business will in future be carried on conjointly with their King Street Establishment'.[24] An advertisement was inserted the following week by Boardman and Harmer pointing out that Rudrums' had taken only part of the Duke's Palace Wharf and that the rest of the wharf was still used by them.

When the Norfolk Steam Packet Company put the steamer *Albatross* into service between Yarmouth and Hull Boardman and Harmer became Norwich agents. And when the company had the vessel lengthened, reboiled and re-engined in 1844 it seemed a good opportunity for Boardman and Harmer to publicise the service by inviting 120 of their customers and friends to take a trip in her from Yarmouth to Southwold. Alas, 'a fresh Nor-easter ensured that the trip was not enjoyed by many of the passengers, who were unable to partake of the "sumptuous and enticing" food that had been provided'.[25]

It was undoubtedly a sign of the times when the owners of the sailing vessels working between Fennings' Wharf in London and Yarmouth announced in 1846 that they were discontinuing the service. Boardman and Harmer, who had been agents to those traders for 25 years, invited their customers to 'Alter their consignments to St Katharine's Wharf for the *Ailsa Craig* steamer' operated, like the *Albatross*, by the Norfolk Steam Packet Company.

Daniel Harmer was still operating at Duke's Palace Wharf in 1855, but by 1858 those premises had been taken over by Clarke and Reeve, who were proprietors of the Hull and Newcastle steamers as well as corn and coal merchants and wharfingers. The principals of this firm, Justinian Barrell Clarke and Richard Reeve, were both Norwich men. They had a 'Steam Packet office' on the South Quay at Yarmouth as well as their Norwich premises.

At the beginning of the twentieth century Clarke and Reeve joined with H. Newhouse & Company, which ran the A.B.C. line of steamers. Harry Reeve became managing director of the Yarmouth end of the company. The initials A.B.C. stood for Accelerated Boat Communication; Henry Newhouse's idea was to speed up the carriage of cargoes by water to compete with the railways. To prove its point the company claimed that wheat shipped at Hull at eight in the evening on one day was being manufactured into flour at Carrow Mills at six in the morning of the second day after shipment.[26]

Newhouse set up a second company called the Yare and Waveney Lighter Co. Ltd in 1903 to carry cargoes on the Norfolk and Suffolk rivers. The firm owned five wherries, the *Bell*, *Dora*, *Gertrude*, *Maud* and *Shamrock*, and began building up a fleet of steel lighters, most of them built on the Trent at Gainsborough, together with steam barges and tugs. The first of the fleet, the steam barge *Active*, was very likely a Clyde puffer as she had been built on the Forth & Clyde Canal at Kirkintilloch; the rest of the fleet adopted an alphabetical naming pattern, *Busy*, *Commerce*, *Despatch*, *Expedition*, and so on as far as *Quickness*, *Readiness* and *Speediness*, and a dockyard was constructed at Reedham to service that fleet. It was a spirited attempt on the

Loading the wherry *Caroline* in Riverside Road, Norwich. A large wherry, she has a third beam amidships; most wherries had only two, leaving the hold completely clear. In the background can be seen the training ship *Lord Nelson*, formerly a Lowestoft trawling smack.

Wherries lying near Cow Tower, part of the city defences, at the bend in the Wensum above Bishop's Bridge where it was proposed in 1839 that a lock should be built. On the outside of the bend was William Murrell Petch's boatyard at which the *Caroline* and other wherries were built.

part of coastal shipping interests to compete with the railways, but it came to an abrupt end in 1916 when the lighters were commandeered for war service on the continental canals.

Nevertheless, in the 1920s both J. & J. Colman Ltd, the mustard and starch manufacturers of Carrow Works, and the Great Yarmouth Shipping Company operated fleets of lighters between Yarmouth and Norwich, and there was also increased use of the river by coasting vessels bringing coal, timber, grain and other cargoes to the city. The opening by Norwich Corporation of a large electricity generating station in 1926 boosted the coal trade of the Yare, coasters belonging to F.T. Everard & Sons being able to berth alongside the station to be unloaded by a telpher railway system which carried the coal into the building. Tankers brought cargoes of petrol to a depot at Trowse Eye, where the Yare has its confluence with the Wensum.

The increasing size of ships necessitated better facilities, and in the 1930s a turning basin was formed by dredging out the inside of a bend by St. Ann's Staithe to enable the larger vessels to turn before proceeding downriver. Sailing barges and motor coasters brought grain to R.J. Read's flour mills just above Carrow Bridge and coal to Thomas Moy's coal yard at Cannon Wharf,

This photograph taken about 1880 by Christopher Davies shows a wherry unloading into a small warehouse close to Thomas Smithdale's St. Ann's Iron Works. Smithdale, a millwright and engineer, subsequently moved to Panxworth and then to Acle; the firm was responsible for many of the mills in the area.

while auxiliary sailing vessels and later motorships brought cargoes of Baltic timber to the timberyards further upriver.

The trade of the port was expanded in the 1950s when a Norwich scrap merchant purchased several small vessels and began exporting scrap metal to Belgium, but the day of the small port was passing. The river trade to Norwich declined until ships no longer came upriver to the city, though for a time tankers continued visiting the beet sugar factory at Cantley to take away molasses; even that trade has now gone.

The wherry trade

The largest wherries were those built for the Norwich-Yarmouth trade, some of them coming from yards within the city such as that opposite the Cow Tower, part of the city's medieval fortifications. Operated by William Murrell Petch, this yard saw the birth in 1860 of the *Jessie* and later of the *Caroline*. Like many other Norwich wherries, the *Caroline* was a high-sternsheets wherry in which the helmsman stood on deck rather than in a tiny cockpit as in the smaller craft.

Neither the wherry nor its predecessor was, as has so often been stated, flat bottomed. The lines of the clinker-built wherry were shapely and attractive, with a fine entry and run. There was, too, an attractive sheer, though this flattened out both fore and aft in a way that deceived many an artist who took insufficient note of his subject. The wherry builder did not work from plans nor did he normally use a half-model when determining the design of a new vessel, but was adept at producing a fair shape by eye, using just three moulds to guide his planking up.

Not surprisingly the form of a wherry varied between one builder and another. John Allen, the Coltishall wherry builder, produced craft with rather straighter sides than others, so that the waterside fraternity was able to identify one of his wherries at a glance. The last wherry to come from Allen's yard was the *Ella*, launched in 1912, which was also the last trading wherry to be built.

When carrying cargoes which particularly needed to be kept dry it was usual for the hatches to be covered with a tarpaulin.

With their large hatches and very limited freeboard wherries were by no means seagoing craft, but like the keels before them they did go out into the Yarmouth Roads in fine weather to lighten vessels that were too deep-laden to get over the bar at the harbour entrance. They also made the sea passage from Yarmouth to Lowestoft or from there to Southwold when conditions were sufficiently favourable.

The largest wherry built, the 44 registered ton *Wonder*, launched sideways into the Bure at Yarmouth in 1878 for William 'Dilly' Smith of the Suspension Bridge Tavern, was intended specifically for this work. Built by James Benns and Thomas Cossey, she later passed into the ownership of a Norwich miller and merchant, Thomas Matthews Read, who in due course sold her for conversion to a dredger; she proved difficult to handle in the river, in spite of being given a foresail in addition to the usual wherry mainsail.

While there were many skipper-owners who would carry any cargo that was offered there were also merchants and tradesmen who owned small fleets which they used to transport their own goods, their raw materials and their products. At Sutton, where a branch of the Ant provided a useful channel of

The 'black-snouted' wherry (no white 'eyes' on the bow) *Gertrude* unloading deals at Ranson's timber yard in Norwich.

trade, the miller Thomas Worts ran the eight-storey windmill that still stands beside the road to Hickling and had his own little fleet of wherries to carry his products to his customers. Not only did he grind grain into flour, he also operated a malting beside the mill and ran a brick and tile works not far away; tiles bearing his name can still be seen in the mill.

When the Sutton boatbuilder Richard Southgate took stock of his affairs and decided to emigrate to America Worts gave him the job of building the wherry *Kearsage*, which years later was the last to trade up to Sutton. At nearby Stalham successive members of the Burton family combined milling with a number of other trades and were listed in nineteenth-century directories as 'carriers by water'. Harry Burton had three wherries, the unlucky *Ceres*, the *Cornucopia* and the *Dispatch*, which was later owned by George Rump.

Timber merchant Isaac Wales, of Reedham, had some of the very finest wherries on the rivers, including the *Fawn*, which had the most consistent success of any wherry in the racing at local regattas. Wales took great pride in her achievements, and her skipper, 'Ophir' Powley, used to carry a basket of homing pigeons with him when racing at sea; a pigeon would be sent off at the end of each round with a message for the owner, waiting at home at Reedham.

When picking up felled trees to be taken back to the owner's sawmill the logs were loaded by using the winch and halyard, the latter being taken out of the herring hole (a slot in the masthead containing a sheave over which the halyard was rove) and rove through a block chained to the upper part of the mast. The chain allowed the block to swing in the direction of the load, and a temporary stay was rigged to support the partly lowered mast during such operations.

Both Ransons Ltd. and Jewson & Son, two of the Norwich timber merchants with riverside timberyards, possessed their own wherries, and so did builders' merchants Lacey & Lincoln, of Norwich, who had the *Emily*, *Our Boys* and *Rockland Trader*. Coal merchant William England, whose coal yard was close to Fye Bridge at Norwich, had the *Leveret* and the *Gem* in the early years of the twentieth century, and miller R.J. Read, whose City Flour Mills stood beside the river in Westwick Street, had the *Goodwill* and the *Widgeon*, one of at least two wherries of that name. Robert John Read, born at Wrentham in Suffolk in 1851, acquired the Norwich mills from John Lee Barber in 1896; already he had in 1875 taken over the steam mills in Ingate, Beccles, previously operated by Nathaniel Pells. Some years later Read took over the watermill at Horstead on the Bure, and his firm worked it until its destruction by fire in January 1963.

The next generation, Robert John junior, entered the business about 1901 and played a leading part in developing it. A photograph of the City Flour Mills taken about 1910 shows a large steel lighter being loaded with sacks of flour and four wherries apparently awaiting their turn to unload cargoes of imported wheat.[27] It was about 1930 that Reads built a new power mill in King Street which regularly received cargoes of imported grain brought from the London docks by spritsail barges and motor coasters. Those barges that had not been motorised used to be towed upriver by the Great Yarmouth Shipping Company tugs *Gensteam* and *Cypress*, or in the case of F.T. Everards' barges *Lady Mary*, *Cambria*, *Greenhithe* and *Will Everard* by one of the Greenhithe

While the double-ended form was more usual, some wherries like this one on the Bure near Belaugh were built with transoms. The last transom-sterned wherry was the *Elizabeth*, which was converted to a pleasure wherry and finished her days as a houseboat at Thorpe St. Andrew, on the outskirts of Norwich.

One of the steel wherries built at Yarmouth by Fellows carrying a load of timber cantilevered out on each side. She is passing the rebuilt Red House at Cantley on her way upriver.

firm's motor coasters that brought coal to the city.[28]

Another *Widgeon* was owned by Ling & Co., who ran Buxton mill in succession to Thomas Shreeve. In 1899 they were hiring their wherries *Britannia* and *Bertha*[29] during the summer for holiday cruising,[30] and a few years later the firm had three wherries insured with the Wherry Owners' Insurance Friendly Society, the *Britannia*, *Emily* and *Widgeon*.

There was also another *Bertha*, owned by a North Walsham company founded by members of the Press family. Beevor & Press were corn millers and merchants at Ebridge Mills on the North Walsham and Dilham Canal on the outskirts of North Walsham from the late 1850s, and by 1879 Thomas William Beevor was on his own as a miller in Southtown and Gorleston, and Press Brothers were running both the little watermill at Ebridge and the High Mill in Southtown, Yarmouth. Press Brothers at North Walsham had a fleet of at least seven wherries, the *Bertha*, *Diligent*, *Elizabeth*, *Elsie*, *Ethnie*, *Kate* and *Lucy*, all of which had blue mastheads, with yellow and red bands and with a yellow circle around the herring hole; the hatch covers were stone colour, lined in blue.

As the family firm grew it also extended its interests, diversifying into malting, dealing in corn, coal and seed and even venturing into the manufacture of artificial manure. Edward Press took into partnership a long-term employee who had become his manager, W.W. Pallett, and the firm then became Press & Pallett. About the turn of the century the Yarmouth interests and the North Walsham enterprise appear to have separated, with Press Brothers Ltd. running steam roller mills in Southtown and other mills in Cobholm – possibly the High Mill, the tallest in Britain – and Press & Pallett continuing the North Walsham business.[31] Press Brothers continued to operate the steam mills at Cobholm and Southtown, from 1921 onwards owning the wherry *Lady Violet*.

On the death of Edward Press in 1906 W.W. Pallett became the sole proprietor. He reorganised the North Walsham business, took in as partner another miller, Joseph Barclay, and changed the name of the firm to Pallett,

A wherry on its way up to Bungay seen in Geldeston lock on the Waveney. The bars across the ends of the lock were so placed to ensure that wherrymen lowered their masts and did not sail into the lock, endangering the lock gates. In this case the wherryman has probably raised his mast while in the lock at the photographer's request.

A high sternsheets wherry on the River Yare. In this type of craft the helmsman stood on deck, the tiller being curved upwards to waist level, rather than in a cockpit as in the low sternsheets wherry. High sternsheets wherries were confined to the Norwich River and usually had black snouts (no white 'eyes').

Barclay & Co. Two years later the two partners took over the business of Benjamin Cook at the Dunkirk roller flour mills at Aylsham and set up the firm of Barclay, Pallett & Co., with a head office in North Walsham, to run the Aylsham mills. With Cook's business they acquired the Aylsham wherry *Zulu*, which was caught above Buxton lock at the time of the 1912 flood. Unable to pass through the damaged lock, the wherry had to be hauled out and taken across the road on rollers, to be launched again below the lock.

The other big North Walsham milling firm with a fleet of wherries was Cubitt & Walker, which in the early twentieth century had five wherries, the *Arthur, Cambria, Henry, John Henry* and *Woodman*. Cubitt & Walker's wherries had green mastheads with a yellow band.

On the bank of the North River at Runham Vauxhall, near Yarmouth, was a fertiliser factory that provided many a cargo for the wherries, although the firm, Baly, Sutton & Co., does not seem to have owned any of its own. Around the turn of the century this business was taken over by Prentice Brothers Ltd., of Stowmarket. The trade to the works was unpopular with wherrymen, since the cargo – presumably imported phosphates lightered from steamers in Yarmouth harbour – was an unpleasant one, and the berths alongside the factory dried out, sometimes resulting in a strained and leaking wherry.

Another fertiliser factory that made much use of waterborne transport was constructed at Haddiscoe in the 1870s. Known as the Waveney Valley Chemical Manure Works, this was first operated by Alexander W. Pashley, and when he died in the early 1880s the works was taken over by G. & J. Bagshaw, whose original works was in Norwich near Magdalen Gates; at one time in the mid-nineteenth century the firm had a windmill there that was employed in grinding bones for fertiliser.

The Haddiscoe factory received its supplies of chemicals by water, notably in the *Iron Duke*, a small iron or steel craft that was possibly a Humber keel. According to a note that appeared in successive issues of Kelly's directory, the works carried on 'an extensive home and foreign trade' throughout the first two decades of the twentieth century. About 1920 it was taken over by

Wherry racing produced
keen competition among
the Norfolk watermen. At
Barton Regatta in 1936
the *Hilda* was unfortunate
enough to break her gaff.

Packards & James Fison (Thetford) Ltd., although it continued to be known as Bagshaw's manure works until it closed in the depression of the early 1930s.

Just as Edward Press had purchased the North Walsham and Dilham Canal when building up his North Walsham company, so W.D. & A.E. Walker of Bungay became owners of the Bungay Navigation about 1884. The firm had a long history going back at least to the 1850s, when David Walker was a coal and corn merchant at Bungay Staithe. Possibly he came of a well-to-do family, for a Pearce Walker is listed in an 1855 directory as a gentleman living at Duke's Bridge, on the Bungay to Beccles road, where Billy Brighton built the wherry *Waveney* in 1863. In 1858 David Walker was involved in a court case in which the master of the wherry *Albert* and his son were charged with stealing some of his barley that had been sent down the Waveney to Beccles, where it was to be transhipped into a seagoing vessel to be taken to Newark. Complaints of a shortage in the amount transhipped led to a search which revealed two sacks of barley in the wherryman's bunk.

The firm expanded rapidly after David's son, William David Walker, took into partnership his younger brother Arthur Ernest, and by 1892 W.D. & A.E. Walker were maltsters, corn, coal, cake and lime merchants at Bungay, Ditchingham, Geldeston and Yarmouth. As the firm grew the partners built up their fleet of wherries, some of them built on their own yard at Bungay.

Harry Burton's *Cornucopia*
leaving Barton Broad after
having won the wherry race
in 1928.

The older units of the fleet were the *Enfield*, *Hope*, *Maria* and *Mayflower*. In 1890 the *Eudora* was built for them by John Winter on their yard at Bungay Staithe, and two years later George Davey built the *Iolanthe* for them on the same yard. There is a fine photograph of the latter wherry shortly after her launching, with her new white sail hanging limply in the light wind and her skipper posing on the foredeck holding a quant.[32] With the nineteenth century coming to an end the Walkers decided to have another wherry built, and this time they turned to William Brighton.

Roy Clark says in *Black Sailed Traders* that their intention was that their new wherry should be built of iron, as they felt that an ironpot would stand up better to the lockwork on the Waveney, where the passage of the locks at Geldeston/Shipmeadow, Ellingham and Wainford took its toll of the wooden craft. Brighton, however, would have none of it and suggested that he build them a wooden wherry, of carvel construction. Thus was born the *Albion*, which is today operated by the Norfolk Wherry Trust.

One of the last trading wherries, no longer under sail but still operating under power, seen on the Thurne about 1960.

All the Walker wherries had bright green mast tops, with yellow and blue bands. Individual wherries seem to have been identified by variations in this general design; the *Albion* and *Hope* had a bunch of pears centring on the herring hole while the *Mayflower* had a star in the same position.

When William Butcher, owner of the Bungay Navigation, died in 1884 his executors sold his property, including the navigation, at an auction at the King's Head Hotel at Bungay. Lot one appears in the particulars of sale as 'Commodious Mercantile Premises & Staithe at Bungay and the Bungay and Beccles Navigation'. Walkers were named in the sale particulars as tenants of part of the Bungay property, which included a malting, a double-roofed granary with shoots for loading wherries lying in the boat dyke, a large coal warehouse paved with Yorkshire stone, a limekiln and chalk-house, a timber yard and a wherry slip.[33]

It was probably at that sale in 1884 that W.D. & A.E. Walker acquired ownership of the navigation, which they retained until 1919. It must have made sense for them to become proprietors of the navigation, since they had been paying sixpence a ton on cargoes passing through Shipmeadow lock and a shilling a ton on cargoes passing through Ellingham lock. It might not seem much, but more than £2 on a 30-ton cargo represented a considerable overhead in days when a pint of beer cost only a matter of pence.

In 1908 the firm still had seven wherries, but in that year the *Enfield* was either disposed of or taken out of service. Then in 1914 the *Mayflower* was sold to J.S. Hobrough, who insured her with the Wherry Owners' Insurance Friendly Society until 1920, when she was most likely sunk in some convenient place to protect the river bank. Finally in 1919 the firm sold the malting side of the business, the navigation and the surviving wherries, *Albion*, *Eudora*, *Hope*, *Iolanthe* and *Maria*, to Watney, Combe, Reid & Company.

By 1926 only three of the five wherries survived. They were sold again to the Great Yarmouth Shipping Company, a subsidiary of the General Steam Navigation Company, who in pursuance of their naming policy renamed the *Albion* and *Iolanthe* the *Plane* and the *Elder*. The *Eudora*, however, retained her original name for the rest of her days; she was destroyed by fire during the Second World War air raids on Norwich while lying alongside a timberyard set alight by incendiary bombs.

In spite of the suggestion that an 'ironpot' would be a suitable vessel for the Bungay navigation, all Walkers' wherries were wooden craft. Five 'iron' wherries were built by the Yarmouth shipyard of Henry Fellows & Son, three

The auxiliary barge *Marie May*, built at Maidstone in 1920 and owned by the London & Rochester Trading Company, had not long returned from war service on the Clyde when she brought a cargo of wheat to R.J. Read's flour mills in King Street, Norwich. Ahead of her and already being discharged is the Harwich barge *Vigilant*.

A bill dated 1909 for the repair of the wherry *Leveret*, belonging to Norwich coal merchant William England.

of them for the firm of Woods, Sadd, Moore & Company, agricultural seed merchants, woolstaplers, maltsters, flour millers and oil cake and barley merchants, of Chedgrave and Loddon. The *Uranus* and *Vega* were built in 1895 and the *Sirius* in 1896.

A slightly smaller 'iron' wherry, the *Crystal*, came from the same yard for the Beccles firm of John Crisp & Son, maltsters and corn and coal merchants and shipowners. The builder's specification of the *Crystal* shows that these vessels were built not of iron but of steel; the plating was of 3/16in. steel, and the keel was 6in. deep, of 3/8in. plate, while the deck was of wood. She was 52ft. long, exclusive of the rudder, with a beam of 15ft. and moulded depth of 3ft. 6in. Fellows also built a fifth steel wherry, the *Cygnus*, 'on spec'; she was renamed *Diamond* after being bought by the Great Yarmouth Shipping Company.

Woods, Sadd, Moore was established in 1884 by Arthur Sadd, who took over the business of Walter Vincent Lamb, corn and seed merchant, maltster, woolstapler and farmer and also took over the Loddon watermill from William Chapman & Son in 1886. At that time the Chet was navigable only to Chedgrave staithe and cargoes for Loddon were unloaded there or at Hardley or Langley staithe, but in 1886 Woods, Sadd, Moore and another firm, Case & Steward, corn, coal, salt, cake and seed merchants, importers of oil and nitrate of soda, and wherry owners, financed the digging out of the river so that wherries could reach Loddon, where a turning basin was formed. Besides their riverside premises at Loddon Case & Steward operated at Dukes Palace Wharf in Norwich and in Southgates Road at Yarmouth.

Woods, Sadd, Moore acquired several wooden wherries, the *Benjamin*, *Lowestoft Trader* and *Ursa Minor*, and in 1894 had a new wherry, the *Orion*, built by Allen at Coltishall. With the building of the three 'ironpots' they had one of the larger fleets working on the Broadland rivers, and although they disposed of the *Lowestoft Trader* about 1912 and sold the *Benjamin* in 1917 they continued to operate the other wherries into the 1920s, latterly as dumb barges towed by three little tugs they then owned. In 1922 the *Orion* was sold to George Gedge, of Worstead, who changed her name to *Gleaner*, the same name as the old wherry she was to replace.

Like many another old wherry, the 'ironpots' eventually joined the fleet of James Hobrough & Son, dredging and piling contractors, whose dockyard at Thorpe St Andrew was one of the last places where wherries could be seen at work right into the 1950s, albeit under power rather than sail. The firm is said to have been founded in 1854,[34] but the story goes back well beyond that to Henry Crosskill Hobrough. He had served an apprenticeship to a boatwright in Southtown, subsequently became proprietor of the Queen's Arms and stationmaster at Haddiscoe, sub-contracted to carry out work on a half-mile section of the Haddiscoe New Cut and was concerned with the piling of Mutford Lock during the construction of the Norwich and Lowestoft Navigation. A move was made to Norwich and James Hobrough became licensee of the Bishops Bridge Inn at Norwich, from which base he ran the contracting business.

Remembered for the 'wideawake' hat that he always wore, James Hobrough was a man of considerable stature and great strength; he was known once to have carried a 5cwt. piling bell. Known the length of the rivers as 'Admiral' Hobrough, James died in 1901 and was succeeded in the business by his son,

The spritsail barge *Alderman* of Harwich in the Wensum at Norwich, moored just below the old Carrow Bridge. She was built at East Greenwich in 1905 by Horace Shrubsall for William Groom, her name commemorating William's elevation to the aldermanic bench of Harwich Borough Council.

James Samuel Hobrough. In the early years of the twentieth century the firm had the wherries *John Henry, Mildred, Mystic, Nymph* and *Wensum* insured with the Wherry Owners' Insurance Friendly Society, but it is quite possible that there were others that James Samuel considered not worth the insuring.

Year by year other wherries came into his fleet, the *Caroline* in 1911, the *Gem* and *Jessie* in 1912, *Leveret* in 1913, *Twenty-five* in 1914, *Mayflower* from W.D. & A.E Walker the same year, *Bell, Dora, Maud* and *Shamrock* from the Yare and Waveney Lighter Co. Ltd. in 1918, another *Mildred* in 1923, *Emily* in 1928. As the older craft became too decrepit for further use they were sunk wherever the river bank required protection and buttressing, or else they were moored in dykes at the Thorpe dockyard and allowed to rot away. Among those that mouldered in the dykes at Thorpe were *Macadam* (ex-*Unknown*), *Caroline, Jessie, Emily, John Henry* and *Stalham Trader*. In 1930 a number of old wherries were sunk in a line across Surlingham Broad on either side of the channel dredged across the broad.

Besides carrying out dredging operations all over the rivers Hobrough's used their wherries to carry Norwich refuse from the tips at Fishergate down to Kirby Bedon for disposal on the marshes, carried out piling operations wherever new quay headings were required, worked on the foundations of the beet sugar factory built at Cantley in 1912, and at one time lightered between 1,000 and 1,600 tons of coal a week from Trowse railway sidings to the gas and electricity works in the city of Norwich.

An advertisement of the 1930s[35] offered 'special prices for weed cutting' and the firm was always prepared to accept a challenge such as dealing with the spread of a floating weed that threatened to choke Hickling Broad each summer. J.S. Hobrough converted the *Caroline*, a big Norwich River wherry built by William Murrell Petch on his yard opposite the Cow Tower in Norwich, into a steam-operated suction dredger to combat the Hickling weed.

A steam engine from the old towing launch *Terrible* was installed in the hold to drive a large centrifugal pump with which the weed was to be sucked up through a pipe held by a gantry over the bows and pumped through a floating pipeline on to the marshes. It might well have dealt with the problem, but the equipment does not seem to have been put into operation at Hickling, perhaps because of opposition from local people who were making quite a good living from dydling the weed into reed lighters and taking it ashore that way.

In 1940 J.S. Hobrough retired at the age of seventy-five and the firm was taken over by May, Gurney & Co. Ltd. of Trowse, a firm which has since grown considerably in the field of civil engineering. Around that time the fleet included the wherries *Bell*, *Dispatch*, *Dora*, *Elder* (ex-*Iolanthe*), *Go Forward*, *Malve* (ex-*Olga*), *Maud*, *Primus*, *Secunda* and *Shamrock*, together with the steel wherries *Crystal*, *Diamond* (ex-*Cygnus*), *Uranus* and *Vega*, the last-named being employed to carry tar oil from Norwich gasworks to Riverside, where it was pumped out into the storage depot on the other side of the road. Several of the wooden wherries were fitted with Thornycroft motors and were used mainly to carry mud from the dredger working on the Norwich River to the dykes below the dockyard, where a steam crane fitted with a grab unloaded it on to the marsh.

Eventually there came a time in the spring of 1948 when one of the dykes in which lay the *John Henry* and *Stalham Trader* was filled with mud from the dredger. The intention had been to bury the two sunken hulks, but instead they floated up on top of the liquid mud as it filled the dyke, and in an attempt to dispose of them workmen set fire to them and to an old dredger that had also been sunk there.

In the late 1940s and 1950s the foreman and his men in the big corrugated-iron boatshed were busy rebuilding some of the fleet, including the *Bell*, *Primus*, *Secunda* and *Maud*. Even at that stage a good deal of money and effort was being expended in extending the life of these craft, which were playing a useful if humdrum role in keeping the rivers open to navigation. In spite of that work the wooden craft were all eventually replaced by rather ugly steel lighters that, in a concession to tradition, carried on their bows the white quadrant of the old wherries. One of them was given the name *John Fox* in commemoration of a man, the son of the foreman in the dockyard, who spent his entire working life employed by the firm, and continued to live on the yard until his death.

When her working days were over the *Maud* was sunk in Ranworth Broad and abandoned. Had not Vincent Pargeter, a young millwright from Essex, and his wife Linda salvaged her and spent the best part of twenty years rebuilding her she would have rotted away there. Eventually in 1999 they returned her to the rivers under sail. Just fifty years earlier the Norfolk Wherry Trust had been formed to restore the *Albion* and operate her under sail.

The *Maud* has thus joined the *Albion*; these two graceful old traders are now our most striking and tangible reminder of inland Norfolk's long-standing commercial link with the coast.

The language of the sea

One thing that differentiated the seaman from the landsman was that he spoke a different language. While the farmworker might speak of preparing his horses for the day's work, if a seaman referred to a horse it was likely to be either the footrope on which the hands stood when loosing, furling or reefing the squaresails or doing other work aloft, or the stout timber or iron transverse bar to which the sheet of a fore-and-aft sail was brought. Or it might be a sandbank lying in the middle of a shipping channel.

An emigrant on passage for Canada in the 1840s taking a stroll on deck in good weather might say to his wife that he was going up the front to see where they were going. The seaman, busy about the ship's business, would when he overheard this know that the joskin was going for'd, and that he was likely to get a wet shirt when she put her head into a steep sea.

The author was somewhat mystified when reading an account of a nineteenth-century wreck on the Norfolk coast to find the word *catharpings* used. Although reasonably conversant with nautical terms he found this puzzling, and was not entirely enlightened by Admiral W.H. Smyth's explanation in his *Sailor's Word Book* (1867) that the catharpings were ropes under the tops at the lower end of the futtock-shrouds, serving to brace in the shrouds tighter, and affording room to brace the yards more obliquely when the ship is close-hauled. The futtock-shrouds are 'short pieces of rope or chain which secure the lower dead-eyes and futtock-plates of topmast rigging to a band round a lower mast'.

Captain John Smith in a much earlier book, *A Sea Grammar* (1627), gives a simpler definition of the word. 'Cat harpings are small ropes [which] runne in little blocks from one side of the ship to the other, neere the upper decke, to keepe the shrouds tight, for the more safety of the mast from rowling.' Does that make it quite plain?

Obscure references to the rigging of old-time sailing ships such as this have been avoided in this book, but for the reader who is not entirely conversant with seamen's terms it might be helpful to describe the names of the various rigs employed on the east coast in past centuries. This is the more necessary as the use of some nautical terms has changed over the years. The term *smack* is now commonly used of a fishing boat, and particularly the sailing trawlers that formerly operated from Yarmouth and Lowestoft, but in an earlier period the word was applied primarily to the cutter-rigged craft that carried goods and passengers between one port and another. The smartest and best-known of these were the Leith smacks operating between the port of Edinburgh and London in the eighteenth and nineteenth centuries.

The main sailing ship rigs shown in a page from R.H. Dana's *The Seaman's Manual*, published in 1846. He uses the term hermaphrodite brig for what is usually now called a brigantine.

The main rigs employed during the nineteenth and early twentieth centuries were these:

Ship. Any craft intended for the purposes of navigation; but in a nautical sense a full-rigged ship is a vessel with three (or more) masts, square rigged on all masts.

Barque. A vessel with three or more masts, square rigged on foremast and mainmast but with only fore-and-aft sails on the mizzen. Also spelt bark, from which comes the abbreviation Bk used in the *Mercantile Navy List*.

Barquentine. A vessel with three masts that is square rigged on the foremast and carries fore-and-aft sails on the others.

Brig. A two-masted vessel, square rigged on both masts. A variant is the snow, which has a trysail mast set close abaft the mainmast to carry the spanker.

Brigantine. A two-masted vessel, square rigged on the mainmast and with fore-and-aft sail on the mizzen. In the nineteenth century the term was often used for various other types of craft and a vessel rigged as described was generally called a hermaphrodite brig.

Schooner. A vessel with two or more masts, with fore-and-aft sails on both or all masts; in the case of two-masted schooners the larger sail was that on the second mast, known as the mainmast. Many schooners carried square topsails on the foremast, then being known as tops'l schooners.

Ketch. A two-masted vessel with fore-and-aft sails on both masts; the larger sail was that on the first or mainmast, that on the mizzen being considerably smaller. Ketches also sometimes carried square topsails on the mainmast.

Cutter. A single-masted vessel with fore-and-aft sails, having a running bowsprit which could be run in horizontally on the deck. This was a common rig of fishing craft in the early nineteenth century, and many such boats were lengthened and altered to dandies or ketches. The term cutter was also used of sailing or steam vessels used to run fish from the North Sea fishing fleets to market in London.

Sloop. A single-masted vessel similar to a cutter, but not having the facility of a running bowsprit. In the Royal Navy, however, the word was used for a vessel, usually square rigged, that was classified by its duties or, says Admiral Smyth, according to the rank of the officer in command.

Lugger. A boat having lugsails, fore-and-aft sails that are extended at the head by a yard and are loose footed. This was a popular rig for fishing boats – and for smugglers.

Dandy. A two-masted boat with a boom-sail on the mainmast and a lugsail on a small mizzen.

Wherry. In Norfolk and Suffolk a type of vessel used mainly on the inland waterways having a single mast and a single fore-and-aft sail, without any headsails. The term is also used for a narrow pulling boat used by watermen for carrying passengers, or more generally for various kinds of fishing boat in different part of Great Britain and Ireland; 'numbers of them were notorious smugglers,' says Admiral Smyth.

References

Chapter 1: The Wash

1. C.W. Phillips, ed. *The Fenland in Roman Times*, R.G.S. Research Series no. 5, Royal Geographic Society, 1970; Dorothy Summers, *The Great Ouse: The History of a River Navigation*, David & Charles, 1973.
2. Summers, p. 25, quoting S.H. Miller and S.B.J. Skertchly, *The Fenland Past and Present*, 1878, p. 178.
3. H.C. Darby, *The Medieval Fenland*, David & Charles, 1974, p. 105.
4. Summers, p. 32 and p. 35.
5. Darby, The Medieval Fenland, p. 103.
6. Ibid., p. 96.
7. P. Harrington, *English Civil War Archaeology*, pp. 96-100.
8. *Pigot and Co.'s National Commercial Directory of Bedfordshire, Huntingdonshire, Cambridgeshire, Lincolnshire, Northamptonshire*, 1830, p. 35.
9. H.C. Darby, *The Changing Fenland*, Cambridge University Press, 1983.
10. *North Sea Pilot*, 1905, p. 204.
11. In spite of the name it is traditionally given, this bank is more likely to be of mid or late Saxon date. It is, of course, just possible that the Saxon bank was a rebuilding of an earlier earthwork.
12. *Faden's Map of Norfolk*, with introduction by Chris Barringer, Larks Press Edition, 1989.
13. Ralph Thoresby's diary, vol. 1, p. 12, quoted in Neil Walker & Thomas Craddock, *The History of Wisbech and the Fens*, Wisbech, 1849, p. 29.
14. A.A. Oldham, *A History of Wisbech River*, 1933, pp. 1-2.
15. Neil Walker & Thomas Craddock, *The History of Wisbech and the Fens*, p. 439.
16. *Norwich Mercury*, 13 April 1850.
17. Walker and Craddock, p. 432.
18. *Clayton's Register of Shipping, 1865.*
19. Arthur Oldham, *A History of Wisbech River*, 1933, pp. 27-53.
20. Arthur Oldham, p. 59.
21. *Clayton's Register of Shipping, 1865.*

Chapter 2: King's Lynn

1. Vanessa Parker, *The Making of King's Lynn*, 1971, pp. 4-6.
2. C.M. Fraser, *Newcastle upon Tyne Chamberlains Accounts 1508-1511*, The Society of Antiquaries of Newcastle Upon Tyne, 1987. I am grateful to Peter Northeast for drawing my attention to this source.
3. H.J. Hillen, *History of the Borough of King's Lynn*, King's Lynn, 1907, p. 705.
4. E.M. Carus-Wilson, *Medieval Merchant Venturers*, 1954. Much information on the Iceland trade is to be found in Professor Carus-Wilson's book.
5. E.F. Jacob, *The Oxford History of England: The Fifteenth Century 1399-1485*, Oxford University Press, 1961, p. 363.
6. Professor Carus-Wilson's findings are confirmed by Edward Gillett and Kenneth A. MacMahon, *A History of Hull*, Hull University Press, 1985, p. 80.
7. H.J. Hillen, p. 213.
8. Evan Jones, 'England's Icelandic Fishery in the Early Modern Period,' in D.J. Starkey, C. Reid, and N. Ashcroft, *England's Sea Fisheries*, London, Chatham Publishing, 2000, p. 106.
9. Ibid., p. 107.
10. Ibid., p. 107.
11. *First Report from the Committee Appointed to Enquire into the State of the British Fisheries, and into the Most Effectual Means for Their Improvement and Extension*, 11 May 1685, p. 4.

Opposite: Laid up at King's Lynn in the 1970s in the Purfleet.

12. David Higgins has pointed out, however, that it would have been impossible to see down the original channel from the top (unlike the present view down the Marsh Cut of 1853). In fact these towers seem more likely to have served as status symbols than as effective lookouts.

13. *Norfolk Chronicle*, 7 April 1821.

14. H.J. Hillen, pp. 540-41. He gives details of these extensive cellars, some of which he says dated from the fourteenth century.

15. Pers. comm. David Higgins.

16. H.J. Hillen, p. 542.

17. Norman Scarfe, ed, *A Frenchman's Year in Suffolk, 1784*, Suffolk Records Society, 1988, p. 184.

18. Gordon Jackson, *The British Whaling Trade*, 1978, ch. 3.

19. Basil Lubbock, *The Arctic Whalers*, 1937, p. 9ff.

20. Lubbock, pp. 15-20.

21. H.J. Hillen, p. 788.

22. H.J. Hillen, p. 523.

23. *Norfolk Chronicle*, 11 March 1820.

24. H.J. Hillen, pp. 580-82.

25. *Norwich Mercury*, February 1837.

26. *Norwich Mercury*, 15 July 1837.

27. *Norwich Mercury*, 6 August 1836.

28. *Norwich Mercury*, 27 August 1836.

29. *Norwich Mercury*, 18 April 1835.

30. H.J. Hillen, p. 569.

31. Pers. comm. David Higgins.

32. Frank G.G. Carr, *Sailing Barges*, 3rd edn, Terence Dalton, 1989, p. 305.

33. *Essex Standard*, 21 April 1883, recalling an incident twenty years earlier.

34. David Lyon, *The Sailing Navy List*, Conway Maritime Press, 1993.

35. *Pigot and Co.'s National Commercial Directory*, 1830.

36. For the story of the Rolins' bankruptcy in 1854, see David Higgins, *The Remaking of King's Lynn*, pp. 56-7.

37. *Norwich Mercury*, 21 November 1857.

38. *Norwich Mercury*, 16 February 1850.

39. William White, *History, Gazetteer and Directory of Norfolk*, 1845, p. 561.

40. *Norwich Mercury*, 1 August 1846.

41. *Norwich Mercury*, 28 June 1845.

42. *Norwich Mercury*, 6 September 1845.

43. Armes wrote *The Port of King's Lynn*, published in 1852, and also *Memories of Lynn*, 1864.

44. *Norwich Mercury*, 21 April 1845.

45. A company to construct wet docks 'on an extensive scale' had been proposed twenty years earlier, see *Norwich Mercury*, 8 November 1845.

46. Information from John Leather.

47. Information from Jack Patten, Lynn.

Chapter 3: North-west Norfolk

1. C. Watson, *Seahenge: An Archaeological Conundrum*, English Heritage, 2005.

2. See J. Fairclough, *Boudica to Raedwald*, Malthouse Press, 2010.

3. A. Hassell Smith, ed., *The Papers of Nathaniel Bacon of Stiffkey*, vol. 1, Centre of East Anglian Studies, University of East Anglia, 1979, p. 258.

4. *Norwich Mercury*, 31 July 1824.

5. Theo Stibbons, *The Hunstanton Lifeboats*, Poppyland, 1984.

Chapter 4: North Norfolk

1. W.A. Dutt, *The Norfolk and Suffolk Coast*, Methuen, 1909.

2. *Norfolk Chronicle*, 16 July 1825.

3. William White, *History, Gazetteer, and Directory of Norfolk*, 1845, pp. 662-3.

4. William White, *History, Gazetteer, and Directory of Norfolk*, 1864, p. 1010.

5. William White, *History, Gazetteer, and Directory of Norfolk*, 1864, pp. 1032-3.

6. Information from Peter Elphick.

7. *Lloyd's Register of British and Foreign Shipping*, 1857.

8. *Norfolk Chronicle*, 2 January 1796.

9. *Norwich Mercury*, 28 January 1832.

10. *Norwich Mercury*, 20 April 1832.

11. *Norfolk Chronicle*, 19 May 1821.
12. *Norwich Mercury*, 28 January 1832.
13. *Norwich Mercury*, 23 and 30 January 1830.
14. *Norwich Mercury*, 30 October 1830.
15. A typescript is held by the National Maritime Museum, Greenwich.
16. Crawford was coxswain of the second *Baltic* from 1895 to 1905.
17. J.W. Norie, *New and Extensive Sailing Directions for the Navigation of the North Sea*, 1826.
18. Jonathan Hooton, *The Glaven Ports*, Blakeney History Group, 1996, p. 164.
19. *Norfolk Chronicle*, 26 June 1819.
20. *Norwich Mercury*, 20 January 1849.
21. *Norwich Mercury*, 23 November 1839.
22. Jonathan Hooton, *The Glaven Ports*, pp. 207-210.
23. *Norwich Mercury*, 8 September 1832.
24. *Suffolk Mercury*, 20 April 1872.
25. *Mercantile Navy List*, 1899.
26. Magnus Catling, 'The Bluejacket', in *The Norfolk Sailor* no. 10, 1965.
27. Michael Stammers, *Sailing Barges of the British Isles*, The History Press, 2008, p. 67.

Chapter 5: Sheringham

1. *Norwich Mercury*,
2. The Launch of the Lifeboat 'Henry Ramey Upcher', 1894.
3. Ibid.
4. Ibid.
5. May Ayers, *Shannocks in Wartime*, Larks Press (2001), p. 68.
6. Charles Vince, *Storm on the Waters*, Hodder & Stoughton (1946), pp. 82-4.
7. See Alan Childs & Ashley Sampson, *Time and Tide, the story of Sheringham's fishermen and their families*, Mousehold Press, 2004, pp. 18-21.
8. Magnus Catling and Robert Malster, 'North Norfolk estuary and beach boats,' The Norfolk Sailor 13 (1967).
9. Recorded in the Humber Yawl Club year book.
10. Anne Pope, *Whitstable and the Sea, remembering the 1920s-1950s*. Canterbury Museums & Galleries Service (1988).

Chapter 6: Cromer

1. W. White, *History, Gazetteer, and Directory of Norfolk*, 1845.
2. *Norfolk Chronicle or Norwich Gazette*, 5 June 1779.
3. *Norwich Mercury*, 24 October 1846.
4. *Norwich Mercury*, 3 March, 10 March and 7 April 1832.
5. *Norwich Mercury*, 10 February 1810.
6. *Ipswich Journal*, 25 November 1815.
7. Joseph Wright, *English Dialect Dictionary*.
8. A.C. Savin, *Cromer in the County of Norfolk: A modern history*, 1937.
9. Savin, p. 4.
10. Sir Walter Runciman, *Collier Brigs and their Sailors*, London, T. Fisher Unwin, 1926, p. 83.
11. Neville Long, *Lights of East Anglia*, Lavenham, Terence Dalton, 1983, Ch. 1.
12. *Norwich Mercury*, 7 January 1832.
13. John Whormby, *An Account of the Corporation of Trinity House of Deptford Strond, and of Sea Marks in General*, London, 1861.
14. *Norwich Mercury*, 18 January 1834.
15. *Ipswich Journal*, 10 November 1804.
16. *Norfolk Chronicle*, 29 October 1825.
17. These are the measurements given in the *Life-boat Journal* of April 1858. The Northumberland report gives the dimensions as 31ft. by 9ft. 6in. in beam.
18. *Norwich Mercury*, 9 November 1839.
19. *Norwich Mercury*, 31 January 1857.
20. *Norwich Mercury*, 31 October 1857.
21. *The History of the Cromer Lifeboats and the Brave Deeds of the Lifeboatmen*, Cromer, Rounce & Wortley, 1939, states that it was a boiler explosion, but it seems more likely that the vessel had been mined.
22. In the fog of war and the drama of the day, it seems some of the records made at the time may have been in error. She is referred to here as the *Paddy Hendly*, which is what the RNLI

record and the service boards at the Cromer boathouse say. However, there was no vessel *Paddy Hendly* in the convoy records but there was a *Betty Hindley* that was lost. There was probably confusion as the Hon. Secretary of the lifeboat station attempted to record the events of the day.

23. The convoy number is given here as FS59; it has often been recorded as F559 but as the convoys were either FS or FN, it seems likely that it was then recorded locally with a '5' when it should have been an 'S'.

24. The full story of this rescue is told by Cyril Jolly in *The Loss of the English Trader*, Fakenham, Acorn Editions, 1981.

Chapter 7: East Norfolk

1. British Library, Cotton Nero Dii; the Latin text is published with introduction by H. Ellis in the Rolls Series, 1859.
2. William White, *History, Gazetteer, and Directory of Norfolk*, 1845, p. 768.
3. Francis White, *History, Gazetteer, and Directory of Norfolk*, 1854, p. 488.
4. *On the Means of Assistance in Cases of Shipwreck*, Norwich, 1825.
5. *Norwich Mercury*, 25 February 1832.
6. Presumably Tonnay-Charente, on the Charente river upstream of Rochefort.
7. *Norwich Mercury*, 11 & 18 January 1834.
8. *Norwich Mercury*, 18 November 1845.
9. *Norwich Mercury*, 7 February 1846.
10 *Norwich Mercury*, 2 May 1846.
11. *Norwich Mercury*, 4 August 1849.
12. *The Lifeboat*, 1 July 1869.
13. Walter White, *Eastern England from the Thames to the Humber*, vol. 1, 1865, p. 18.
14. *Norwich Mercury*, 1816; R. Malster, *Saved from the Sea*, 1974, p. 7.
15. *Norwich Mercury*, 16 January 1830.
16. *Norwich Mercury*, 9 November 1833.
17. *Norwich Mercury*, 27 August 1831.
18. *Norwich Mercury*, 27 October 1832.
19. *Norwich Mercury*, 9 March 1850.
20. G.E.S. Cubitt, *Robert Cubitt of Bacton, Norfolk (1713-1790), and his Cubitt Descendents*, 2nd edn, 1963.
21. *Norwich Mercury*, 2 August 1845.
22. D. Higgins, *The Beachmen*, Terence Dalton, 1987, p. 85.
23. *Norwich Mercury*, 5 February 1842.
24. Palmer, *The Perlustration of Great Yarmouth*, vol. 2, p. 267.
25. *Norfolk Chronicle*, 19 & 26 October, 2 & 9 November 1822.
26. *Norfolk Chronicle*, 19 October 1822.
27. *Norfolk Chronicle*, 26 October and 9 November 1822.
28. *Norwich Mercury*, 1 & 8 December 1838.
29. David Higgins, *The Beachmen*, p. 84.
30. E. Ekwall, *The Concise Oxford Dictionary of English Place-names*, 4th ed., 1960, p. 217.
31. Mary H. Trett, *The Tragic Shore*, Happisburgh, nd.
32. Harry Apling, *Norfolk Corn Windmills*, p. 349.
33. *Norwich Mercury*, 6 February 1830.
34. *Norwich Mercury*, 23 March 1833.
35. Higgins, *The Beachmen*, p. 81.
36. See the list of beach company boats in *The Beachmen*, p. 247.
37. *Norwich Mercury*, 4 December 1830.
38. Cobles of a similar design to those found on the Yorkshire and Northumberland coasts were formerly also used on the Norfolk coast.
39. *Norwich Mercury*, 19 February 1831.
40. www.just-plain-folks.co.uk(accessed October 2012)
41. *Norwich Mercury*, 1 January & 19 February 1831.
42. *Eastern Daily Press*, 12 March 1990.
43. David Higgins, *The Beachmen*, p. 70.
44. Ibid., pp. 72-3.
45. Ibid., p. 71.
46. The 1907 rules are reproduced as an appendix in Malster, *Saved from the Sea*, pp. 275-8. For a full discussion of beach company rules, see Higgins, *The Beachmen*, pp. 97ff.

47. *Norwich Mercury*, 19 June 1847.
48. *Suffolk Chronicle*, 25 September 1841.
49. Nicholas Leach, *Never Turn Back, An Illustrated History of Caister Lifeboats*, Tempus, 2001
50. *Norwich Mercury*, 29 March 1845.
51. *Norwich Mercury*, 8 February 1845.
52. *Norwich Mercury*, 1 May 1847.
53. *Norwich Mercury*, 29 March and 5 April 1845.
54. *Norwich Mercury*, 18 November 1845.
55. *Norwich Mercury*, 2 August 1845.
56. Some sources state that the boat cost £250, but this probably included all equipment, sails and rigging.
57. *Norwich Mercury*, 2 May 1846.
58. *Norwich Mercury*, 5 May 1849.
59. *Norwich Mercury*, 5 May 1849.
60. *Suffolk Chronicle*, 22 January 1859.

Chapter 8: The Broadland waterways

1. J. Fairclough, *Boudica to Raedwald*, Malthouse Press, 2010, p. 160.
2. Barbara Cornford, 'Water Levels in the Flegg Area', *Norfolk Research Committee Bulletin* 28, 1982, p. 18.
3. For a more detailed discussion of those changes see R. Malster, *The Norfolk and Suffolk Broads*, Phillimore, 2003, chapter 7.
4. J.M. Lambert and J.N. Jennings, C.T. Smith, Charles Green and J.N. Hutchinson, *The Making of the Broads: A Reconsideration of their Origin in the Light of New Evidence*, Royal Geographical Society Research Series No. 3, 1960.
5. Sarah Knights, *The Story of Dragon Hall*, Norfolk & Norwich Heritage Trust, 1991.
6. W. Hudson & J.C. Tingey, *The Records of the City of Norwich*, Jarrold & Sons, vol. 1, 1906, p. 223.
7. P. Dunn, 'Trade', in C. Rawcliffe & R. Wilson, *Medieval Norwich*, Hambledon & London, 2004.
8. P. Trudgill, *The Dialects of England*, Blackwell, 1990, p. 17.
9. C.B. Jewson, *Transcript of three registers of passengers from Great Yarmouth to Holland and New England 1637-1639*, Norfolk Record Society, 1954.
10. Shirley Harris, *Keels and Kilns: The story of two sixteenth-century citizens of Norwich*, King Street Publications, 1993.
11. W. Hudson & J.C. Tingey, *The Records of the City of Norwich*, Jarrold & Sons, vol. 2, 1910, p. 124.
12. Ibid., vol. 2, p. 395.
13. Ibid., vol. 1, pp. 277-8.
14. NRO, Y/C38/3.
15. *Norfolk Chronicle*, 23 October 1779.
16. *Norwich Mercury*, 27 February 1779.
17. J.G. Nall, *Chapters on the East Anglian Coast*, 1866, p. 415.
18. *Norfolk Chronicle*, 29 April 1820.
19. *Norwich Mercury*, 2 March 1833.
20. *Norwich Mercury*, 1 June 1833.
21. *Norwich Mercury*, 20 June 1846.
22. Article by Humphrey Boardman in *The Quant*, journal of the Norfolk Wherry Trust, Autumn 1989, pp. 9-10.
23. *Norwich Mercury*, 11 January 1834.
24. *Norwich Mercury*, 1 January 1842.
25. *Norwich Mercury*, 1 June 1844.
26. Edward and Wilfred L. Burgess, *Men Who Have Made Norwich*, 1904.
27. *Citizens of No Mean City*, Jarrold & Sons, 1910, p. 102.
28. The *Will Everard* was later fitted with an auxiliary engine and made the passage up the Yare under her own power.
29. It was possibly this *Bertha* which had a transom stern.
30. E. Keble Chatterton, *The Waterways of Norfolk and Suffolk*, 1899, pp. 19-20.
31. Kelly's Norfolk directory, 1904.
32. R. Malster, *Wherries and Waterways*, 1971, p. 148.
33. D. Pluck, *The River Waveney, Its Watermills and Navigation*, 1994, pp. 31-2.
34. Advertisement in Kelly's directory of Cambridgeshire, Norfolk and Suffolk, 1892, p. 33.
35. Kelly's Norfolk, 1933, p. 25.

Bibliography

Ayers, M., *Memoirs of a Shannock*, Larks Press, 1995.

Ayers, M., *Shannocks in Wartime*, Larks Press, 2001.

Bensley, M., *The Sheringham Lifeboats 1838-2000*, Bengunn, 2003.

Brooks, P., *Sheringham - The Story of a Town*, Poppyland Publishing, 1980, reprinted in new editions 1991, 2002

Brooks, P., *Blakeney - Have You Heard about Blakeney*, Poppyland Publishing, 1980, reprinted in new editions 1985, 2001

Brooks, P., *Cley - Living with Memories of Greatness*, Poppyland Publishing, 1984, reprinted in new editions 1988,1998, 2011

Brooks, P., *Weybourne - Peaceful Mirror of a Turbulent Past*, Poppyland Publishing, 1984, reprinted 1996

Carr, F.G.G., *Sailing Barges*, Hodder & Stoughton, 1931; 2nd. edition, Peter Davies, 1951; revised edition, Terence Dalton, 1989.

Castleton, F., *Fisher's End, the story of the ancient fishing quarter of King's Lynn as it was at the beginning of the century*, privately published, 1988.

Childs, A., & Sampson, A., *Time and Tide, the story of Sheringham's fishermen and their families*, Mousehold Press, 2004.

Clark, R., *Black Sailed Traders*, Putnam, 1961.

Cory, R.H., *Fenland Lighters and Horse Knockers*, EARO County Resource and Technology Centre, Ely, 1977.

Cox, P., & Groves, T., *The Fishermen's Lifeboat*, Sheringham Town Council, 1994.

Eden, P., *Waterways of the Fens*, Cambridge University Press, 1972.

Friedland, K., & Richards, P., ed., *Essays in Hanseatic History*, Larks Press, 2005.

Hassell Smith, A., Baker, G.M., & Kenny, R.W., eds., *The Papers of Nathaniel Bacon of Stiffkey*, Centre of East Anglian Studies, University of East Anglia, 3 vols., 1979-1990.

Hassell Smith, A., *A Case of Piracy in the Sixteenth Century*, Centre of East Anglian Studies, 1983.

Higgins, D., *The Beachmen*, Terence Dalton, 1987.

Higgins, D., *The Winterton Story*, Phoenix Publications, 2009.

Higgins, D., *Caister, The Sea Story*, Phoenix Publications, 2010.

Hillen, H.J., *History of the Borough of King's Lynn*, 2 vols., King's Lynn, 1907.

Hooton, J., *The Glaven Ports*, Blakeney History Group, 1996.

Jolly, C., *Henry Blogg of Cromer*, Harrap, 1958; reprinted 1972. Reprinted Poppyland Publishing 2001, 2004, 2008

Jolly, C., *The Loss of the English Trader*, Acorn Editions, 1981.

Larby, E., *Mr Marten's Travels in East Anglia*, Poppyland Publishing, 2012

Leach, N., *Hunstanton Lifeboats*, Tempus, 2008.

Leach, N., *Never Turn Back, An Illustrated History of Caister Lifeboats,* Tempus, 2001.

Leach, N., & Russell, P., *Wells-next-the-Sea Lifeboats*, Tempus, 2006.

Leach, N., & Russell, P., *Cromer Lifeboats, A Pictorial History*, Landmark Publishing, 2008.

Leach, N., & Russell, P., *Sheringham lifeboats*, Landmark Publishing, 2009.

Leather, J., *Gaff Rig*, Adlard Coles, 1970.

Lee, K., *The History of Cromer Lifeboats and Crews, H.F. Bailey 777 1935-1945*, privately published, 1991.

Lewis, C., *Nelson, 'I am myself a Norfolk man'*, Poppyland Publishing, 2005.

Long, N., *Lights of East Anglia*, Terence Dalton, 1983.

Malster, R., *Wherries and Waterways*, Terence Dalton, 1971; revised edition 1986.

Malster, R., *Saved from the Sea*, Terence Dalton, 1974.

Malster, R., *The Sheringham Lifeboats*, Poppyland Publishing, 1981.

Malster, R., & Stibbons, P., *The Cromer Lifeboats*, Poppyland Publishing, 1979. 1981, 1986..

Metters, G.A., *The King's Lynn Port Books 1610-1614*, Norfolk Record Society, 2009.

Nicholls, M., *Norfolk Maritime Heroes and Legends*, Poppyland Publishing, 2008

Pipe, C., *The Story of Cromer Pier*, Poppyland Publishing, 1998.

Pipe, C., *A Dictionary of Cromer and Overstrand History*, Poppyland Publishing, 2010.

Purchas, A.W., *Some History of Wells-next-the-Sea and District*, East Anglian Magazine, 1965.

Softley, M., *The Brancaster Lifeboats 1874-1935*, Norfolk & Suffolk Research Group, 2000.

Stammers, M., *Norfolk Shipping*, Tempus, 2002.

Stammers, M., *Sailing Barges of the British Isles*, Tempus, 2008.

Stibbons, T., *The Hunstanton Lifeboats*, Poppyland Publishing, 1984.

Stibbons, P., Lee, K., Warren,M., *Crabs and Shannocks - The Longshore Fishermen of North Norfolk*, Poppyland Publsihing 1983

Thompson, P., Wailey, T., & Lummis, T., *Living the Fishing*, Routledge & Kegan Paul, 1983.

Tooke, C., *'Skipper' Jack*, Poppyland Publishing, 1988.

Trett, M. and Hoggett, R. *The Book of Happisburgh*, Halsgrove 2011

Vince, C., *Storm on the Waters, The story of the Life-boat Service in the war of 1939-1945*, Hodder & Stoughton, 1946.

Walker, N., & Craddock, T., *The History of Wisbech and the Fens*, Wisbech, 1849.

Walthew, K., *From Rock and Tempest, The Life of Captain George William Manby*, Geoffrey Bles, 1971.

Warren, M., *Cromer - The Chronicle of a Watering Place*, Poppyland Publishing, 1988, reprinted in new editions 1994, 2011, 2012

Whormby, J., *An Account of the Corporation of Trinity House of Deptford Strond and of Sea Marks in General (1746)*, London, 1861.

Wilson, J.K., *Fenland Barge Traffic*, Robert Wilson, 1972.

Woodman, R., *Keepers of the Sea*, Terence Dalton, 1983.

Woods, S., *Out with the Tide - Recollections of Wells-next-the-Sea*, Poppyland Publishing, 1989.

Wren, W.J., *Ports of the Eastern Counties*, Terence Dalton, 1976.

Norfolk Maritime History, catalogue of an exhibition a the Castle Museum, Norwich, Norwich Museums Committee, 1957.

Report of the Committee appointed to examine the Life-Boat Models submitted to compete for the Premium offered by His Grace the Duke of Northumberland, London, 1851.

General index

Note: Page locators in italics indicate illustrations; most entries referring to multiple pages also include illustrations.

Index of named vessels

Notes: This index does not distinguish between different vessels bearing the same name. Sometimes the text identifies them, but in other cases information is lacking to make positive identifications. A page locator in italics indicate that the vessel is pictured on that page.